CW01455808

# PINK FLOYD

# SHINE ON

# PINK FLOYD

THE DEFINITIVE ORAL HISTORY

# SHINE ON

MARK BLAKE

First published in the UK in 2025 by New Modern
An imprint of Putman Publishing
Mermaid House, Puddle Dock, Blackfriars, London, EC4V 3DB

@newmodernbooks
@newmodernbooks

Hardback ISBN: 978-1-917923-05-7
eBook ISBN: 978-1-917923-06-4



A CIP catalogue record for this book is available in the British Library.

Publishing and editorial: Pete Selby and James Lilford
Typesetting: Marie Doherty

3 5 7 9 10 8 6 4 2



New Modern is an imprint of Putman Publishing
www.newmodernbooks.co.uk
www.putmanpublishing.co.uk

Printed and bound in Great Britain by Clays Ltd, Elcograf S.p.A.

'There are three sides to every story: my side,
your side, and the truth. And no one is lying.
Memories shared serve each differently.'

Robert Evans, *The Kid Stays in the Picture*, 2002

# CONTENTS

# CAST OF MAIN CHARACTERS

*By the way, which one's Pink?*

**Roger 'Syd' Barrett:** Pink Floyd's original guitarist and vocalist

**Andy Bown:** musician, 'Surrogate Floyd' band member

**Joe Boyd:** early Floyd champion, produced Floyd's debut single 'Arnold Layne'

**Vivien 'Twig' Brans:** David Gilmour and Syd Barrett's ex-girlfriend

**Rosemary Breen:** Syd Barrett's youngest sister

**Paul Carrack:** musician, Roger Waters' Bleeding Heart Band ex-member

**Libby Chisman:** Syd Barrett's ex-girlfriend

**Glen Colson:** author, lapsed music-biz PR

**Lindsay Corner:** Syd Barrett's ex-girlfriend

**Chris Dennis:** early Pink Floyd Sound/Blues Band vocalist

**Jeff Dexter:** ex-music manager, DJ, Floyd associate

**Bob Ezrin:** Pink Floyd and David Gilmour's producer

**Duggie Fields:** artist, Syd Barrett's flatmate

**Jill Furmanovsky:** music photographer

**David Gale:** Cambridge friend, author, playwright

**Ron Geesin:** musician, co-writer of 'Atom Heart Mother'

**David Gilmour:** guitar player, singer, songwriter

**John Gordon:** Barrett's school friend, guitarist in Gilmour's group Jokers Wild

**Roy Harper:** singer-songwriter, sang Pink Floyd's 'Have A Cigar'

**Dave 'De' Harris:** musician, Rick Wright's musical collaborator

**John 'Hoppy' Hopkins:** photographer, '60s scenester

**Nicky Horne:** radio DJ, presented Capital Radio's *The Pink Floyd Story*

**Brian Humphries:** Pink Floyd's former sound engineer

**Nick Kent:** author, music critic, Barrett aficionado

**Peter Jenner:** Pink Floyd's first co-manager

**Andrew King:** Pink Floyd's other first co-manager

**Rado 'Bob' Klose:** Pink Floyd's ex-guitarist

**Nick Laird-Clowes:** musician, former Floyd lyricist

**John Leckie:** Pink Floyd and Syd Barrett's engineer/producer

**Michael Leonard:** Pink Floyd's ex-landlord, occasional keyboard player

**Nigel and Jenny Lesmoir-Gordon:** Cambridge associates, Barrett's ex-flatmates

**Adrian Maben:** director, *Pink Floyd: Live at Pompeii*

**Phil Manzanera:** Pink Floyd collaborator, sometime David Gilmour guitarist

**Nick Mason:** Pink Floyd drummer, author, raconteur

**Bhaskar Menon:** former Capitol Records chairman; helped sell *The Dark Side of the Moon*

**Clive Metcalfe:** guitarist, Roger Waters and Nick Mason's pre-Floyd college group

**Anthony Moore:** musician, Pink Floyd and Rick Wright collaborator

**Iain 'Emo' Moore:** Cambridge associate, lapsed roadie

**Seamus O'Connell:** Barrett and Waters' old school friend

**Steve O'Rourke:** Pink Floyd's former manager

**Alan Parker:** director, *Pink Floyd – The Wall*

**Alan Parsons:** musician, *The Dark Side of the Moon* engineer

**Aubrey 'Po' Powell:** Hipgnosis co-founder, photographer, Pink Floyd's former creative director

**Guy Pratt:** Pink Floyd and David Gilmour's bassist

**Alun Renshaw:** former Islington Green School teacher (whose pupils sung on 'Another Brick In The Wall, Part 2')

**Tim Renwick:** Roger Waters and Pink Floyd's touring guitarist

**Andy Roberts:** musician, 'Surrogate Floyd' band member

**Mick Rock:** Barrett's friend, music photographer

**Sheila Rock:** Mick's ex-wife, fellow photographer

**Evelyn 'Iggy' Rose:** *The Madcap Laughs* bare-bottomed cover model

**Polly Samson:** author, lyricist, David Gilmour's wife

**Gerald Scarfe:** political cartoonist, *The Wall* cover artist

**Matthew Scurfield:** Cambridge associate, actor

**Nick Sedgwick:** Cambridge associate, author, Roger Waters' ex-golf partner

**Norman Smith:** Early Pink Floyd producer, aka 'Normal' Norman © John Lennon

**Jenny Spires:** Syd Barrett's ex-girlfriend

**Storm Thorgerson:** Hipgnosis co-founder, designer, film-maker, 'Pink Floyd's art department'

**Clare Torry:** session vocalist, sang 'The Great Gig in the Sky'

**Roger Waters:** bass player, singer, songwriter

**John Watkins:** Barrett and Gilmour's ex-college friend

**Clive Welham:** Cambridge friend, drummer in Jokers Wild

**Peter Whitehead:** '60s film-maker, director of *Tonite Let's All Make Love in London*

**John 'Willie' Wilson:** musician, former 'Floyd Surrogate Band' member

**Richard Wright:** keyboard player, singer, songwriter

**Peter Wynne-Willson:** Pink Floyd's early lighting engineer

**Gary Yudman:** comedian, voice actor, MC on *The Wall* tour

# FOREWORD

It's almost summer 2025 and I should have finished writing this book by now. Instead, I'm walking through a gentrified part of London on one of the warmest days of the year. Everybody is overheating and everyone is in a hurry.

Delivery drivers on push bikes jump traffic lights and slalom across the lanes, while pedestrians clutching plastic water bottles race to safety. As I walk past an Edwardian-era cinema and away from the main road, the landscape changes and there's suddenly less people, less clamour.

A couple of minutes later, I arrive at a cobbled street, lined with Victorian-era coach houses – all gleaming white sash windows and pastel-shaded front doors. One of the residents is peering under the bonnet of a vintage sports car so brightly polished that you can see your reflection in it as you pass.

I arrive at my destination, ring the bell and wait. Pink Floyd's guitarist David Gilmour opens the door, defying the tropical temperature in a pitch-black T-shirt and matching Levi's. Up the stairs we go, to a living room devoid of rock-star paraphernalia and dominated by two sumptuous sofas and a Bösendorfer piano.

Gilmour cracks a smile and then, like a conjurer pulling a rabbit from a hat, produces a copy of a book I wrote about his group seventeen years ago. Some of the pages have their corners turned down; on others, I glimpse incriminating squiggles of ink. How is this going to end?

Gilmour puts on his spectacles, kicks off his shoes, wiggles his bare toes and opens the book.

Where to begin, though...

# 1

# 'OH, I'VE JUST BEEN TO DJERBA'

*Sunglasses in winter, 'Anything with a ball', Sylvester's ice cream parlour and 'Très célèbre, hundred-to-one against...'*

❖

It wasn't easy being Roger 'Syd' Barrett's sister. He had two, but he was especially close to the youngest one, Rosemary. As children, they were inseparable and often photographed together. There they are: cross-legged on the sand, squinting into the sun on Hunstanton Beach or dolled up in fancy dress for a primary school fête or catching some rays as teenagers in the back garden at 183 Hills Road.

Rosemary guarded her brother in later life, too: shooing away those disciples who arrived at his house looking for the elusive Syd. Except Syd was gone. Now there was only Roger.

Today, it's a crisp spring afternoon in Cambridgeshire, where a music and mental health charity are due to honour Barrett with a memorial concert at the Corn Exchange (the scene of his last-ever live performance in 1972) and unveil an art installation inspired by Pink Floyd's song 'Bike' – though none of the past or present members of the group will attend.

The memorial is what has prompted Rosemary to agree to an interview. Her chosen venue is the Red Lion, a thirteenth-century coaching inn-turned-gastropub in the village of Whittlesford, seven miles south of Cambridge. Rosemary arrives right on time, and we find a booth at the back of the bar and order a pot of tea.

Rosemary used to be a nurse; one senses she's seen humanity at its worst and doesn't suffer fools gladly. Understandably, she appears a little guarded whenever the conversation touches on her brother's troubled time in Pink Floyd.

Rosemary has heard all the stories and regards Syd's role as a poster boy for '60s psychedelia as both a nonsense and a personal tragedy. It was she, her mother and her siblings who had to put Roger Barrett back together again when he'd stopped being 'Syd'. For years, Rosemary didn't talk about him at all. 'But I decided there is no reason to shut myself away from what is happening,' she says, 'as long as I am in control of it.'

Roger 'Syd' Barrett came into the world on 6 January 1946, with Rosemary following a year and a half later. Their parents were Dr Arthur Max Barrett (known by all as 'Max'), an anatomist and pathologist who once won a medal for rescuing a drowning woman from the River Cam, and Winifred Heeps, whom he'd met at a cub scout meeting and married in September 1934.

Syd was the fourth of their five children. Adored, charismatic and unusual, he was a child star in search of a stage on which to perform. 'We always thought he was going to do something unusual and big in his life,' says his sister, 'but not to this extent.'

The family also presumed it was going to be in art, not music. Rosemary opens a canvas bag and takes out one of her brother's small watercolour paintings. 'It's a lovely bit of sea,' she explains, pointing to the abstract swirl of blues and greens.

Really, the family wished he'd become a painter instead of a pop star. Rosemary never liked her brother's music on those rare occasions when she actually heard it. 'I haven't deliberately *not* listened to it,' she explains carefully. 'I should have, I suppose, but I haven't any interest in it.' She pauses. 'I never liked Pink Floyd, to be honest.'

'The charity is why my family have agreed to do this,' she continues, between sips of tea. 'Because he was my brother, he wasn't that *other* guy. When people came to the house looking for Syd, I turned them away. I was probably over-protective, but he used to say to me, "Don't speak to those people, will you?" and I respected that.'

'Does any of this make sense to you?' she asks.

Yes, it does. Who was Roger 'Syd' Barrett then?

'Oh, he was a child who never grew up.'

✲

*Disc and Music Echo* **(8 April 1967):** 'Born 21 years ago in Cambridge, Syd is the best looking of a rather ordinary bunch. "Freedom is what I'm after," he comments.'

**Rosemary Breen (née Barrett, Syd Barrett's youngest sister):** I will always call him 'Roger' when talking about the young man we knew, and 'Syd' when talking about the damaged person he became. Roger and I had two older brothers, Donald and Alan, our sister, Ruth, and then Roger and me. The two of us were very close and there are no photos of me without him or him without me. He had huge charisma almost from the day he was born. He was very funny, made everybody laugh and always had a twinkle in his eye. As kids, we used to go with our father to Byron's Pool and the woods in Grantchester – any quiet, countryside areas around Cambridge. But he was unusual, even at a young age. His mind and ideas were different from the norm.

**David Gilmour:** Apparently Syd and I first met as children at a Saturday-morning art class in this big semi-attic room at Homerton College on Hills Road. Lots of kids went there. I discovered later that Syd and Roger [Waters] went to the class at the same time for something like three or four years, but I have no recollection of either.

**Roger Waters:** I suppose I was about ten and Syd would have been eight, and we used to make pottery crocodiles. I lived in Rock Road and he was on Hills Road, a few doors away from my aunt. I'm trying to think where he went to primary school, because I went to Morley Memorial [in Blinco Grove] and I don't remember him there.

**Rosemary Breen:** We both went to Morley Memorial and I got fed up with Roger [Syd] getting so much acclaim for his pictures. One day, I took one of his to class and said it was mine – 'Look! I've done this'. But the teacher immediately said, 'No, that's one of Roger's [Syd's].' He was naturally artistic. Roger could just look at something and draw it immediately – still lives, figure drawings, pictures of people in the family...

**Nick Barraclough (musician, broadcaster):** My sister Alison was in Syd's class at primary school. She remembered a very charismatic, beautiful boy. When they were about eleven, the pupils were asked to paint their impressions of a hot day. Most of the children did a beach or a big sun. Roger – as he was still called then – drew a girl lying on a beach in a bikini with an ice lolly dripping over her, which seemed terribly advanced considering his age.

**Rosemary Breen:** My father was a good musician and artist and a brilliant pathologist [at the university]. I don't think Roger ever connected with anyone else in quite the same way. But my father's interests were explored to the nth degree – his music, his art and his pathology. He was very thorough, very enthused, very focused. We'd never heard the word 'autistic' in the '50s and '60s, and I am glad my brother was never diagnosed because they would probably have put him on some awful medication. But we are all *somewhere* on that spectrum and he was way over the other side.

**Nick Barraclough:** My father was a primary school teacher and Roger 'Syd' Barrett and Roger Waters both came to him for coaching before the eleven-plus. They both passed and got into the County [Cambridgeshire High School for Boys], which was a big deal. The County was a grammar school that thought it was a public school.

**Rosemary Breen:** Fantasy was always more interesting to Roger [Syd] than reality. We used to read all the fantasy books. *Alice in Wonderland* was one of his favourites. At his funeral, there were extracts from *The Little Grey Men* [Denys Watkins-Pitchford's 1942 fairy tale], which was also about nature. Roger liked anything with nature or children or the world of make-believe.

**Nick Mason:** You can hear those influences on Syd's songwriting with Pink Floyd. It's all there on *The Piper at the Gates of Dawn*.

**Libby Chisman (née Gausden, Syd Barrett's ex-girlfriend):** I met Syd when he was fifteen at Jesus Green swimming pool [in summer 1961]. I'd gone with some friends, who included Dave Gilmour, and I met him on a seesaw in the playground outside. I'd just been to Germany and had my hair cut very short, and Syd said he liked it. He had a girlfriend at the time who was very pretty and fluffy. But he and I hit it off. We were both unusual-*ish*. On our first date, we took a boat out on the river and he was hopeless at rowing.

We lived about five doors down from each other on Hills Road. Our mothers knew each other. Syd was very witty, always laughing, and he wrote me the most beautiful letters – hundreds of letters. He was my first boyfriend and I thought that's what all boyfriends were like, so it was a bit of a shock later to discover they weren't.

**Rosemary Breen:** Our father was a pianist, so we all had lessons. As children, Roger [Syd] and I did piano duets and won a competition [in 1953 for a performance of 'The Blue Danube'] at the Guildhall in Cambridge. But his first musical instrument was a Jew's harp. From there he went to the ukulele.

**Libby Chisman:** Syd's mum, Win, was ten years older than all our mothers. She'd had Syd's brothers early on. Don was in the RAF and Alan was an academic. They were both bald by thirty, so completely different to Syd. Their father Max was very friendly, but always in his study. We were going out together when his father died [in December 1961]. He had been ill for a long time with cancer. Syd was a great diary writer and usually filled a page of his diary every day. On that day, he just wrote, 'Dear Dad died today' – and that was it.

**Rosemary Breen:** Roger [Syd] was fifteen and I think he was very affected by our father's death. My father understood him. He was an academic, but in touch with his humanity, which a lot of academics aren't. But we all thought Roger was going to become an artist. Art was his first love, much more than music.

**John Gordon (ex-County pupil, later guitarist in David Gilmour's group Jokers Wild):** I met Syd when we were put in the same art class at the County. We had to draw a poster for a post office campaign and everybody else sat down with their HB pencils and came up with the sort of thing any kid would do. But Syd came up with the sort of painting a thirty-year-old would do – full of expression.

**David Gale (Barrett's friend and future playwright and author):** Syd and I lived close to each other, so I would have seen him in the street before I knew who he was. He was quite precocious in the looks and hair department. My house on Luard Road was near the County. One day, I heard a noise behind some shrubbery, and it was Syd and a boy I later discovered was Storm Thorgerson randomly whacking golf balls around the playing field. But I didn't go to the County, I was at the rival, the Perse School for Boys, which was also on Hills Road.

**David Gilmour:** I gave up the art class when I went to the Perse at eleven, because they had classes on a Saturday morning. I got to know Syd properly when we were about fourteen. I didn't sense that there was going to be anything musical about him, but he was already snappily dressed and an all-round attractive human being. You could spot him coming a few hundred yards away because he walked with a bounce – on the front of his feet, with his heels off the ground.

**Storm Thorgerson (future Pink Floyd album sleeve artist):** I was in the same school and Syd was the year below. But Syd and I spent more time together outside of school, lounging around by the River Cam, thinking we were beatniks. But there were a lot of exceptional people in our social group and Syd didn't stand out to me as being any more exceptional than the others.

**David Gale:** During the holidays, my group would hang out down by the Mill Pond, near the weir. Storm was with another group – which might include boys and girls from other schools – near the footbridge and the men's bathing sheds at Sheep's Green. But we would all hire punts from one of the boatyards at the Mill and go up river to Grantchester. Alan Styles, who became a roadie for Pink Floyd [and the 'Alan' of 'Alan's Psychedelic Breakfast' fame] used to work at one of the boatyards.

You saw the same people and everyone knew somebody who knew somebody else. Gradually those groups intermingled and became a core of people who were very enamoured of the beat generation. Kerouac wrote *On the Road* in the late 1940s for fuck's sake – but we all read it as if it had been written yesterday.

**Roger Waters:** We were all pretending to be interested in [the American beat poets] Lawrence Ferlinghetti and Allen Ginsberg and talking about smoking dope but not actually doing it.

**Storm Thorgerson:** Roger Waters was to one side. Roger wasn't really part of the group – not even an annexe – although his mother knew my mother. Although he went to school with me and Syd, he wasn't actually part of this particular group.

**Libby Chisman:** Syd was certainly smoking cannabis – and at a time when you could still get away with smoking it on the top deck of a bus.

**John Watkins (ex-student, Cambridge College of Arts and Technology):** Cambridge was always a bit arty and bohemian. I never saw any evidence of drugs around Syd then, but because of the university and the American airforce bases, Lakenheath and Mildenhall, not far away, the students and GIs were bringing stuff in – blues, benzedrine...

**David Gale:** I had friends who used what we called 'Hoppy's Postal Service'. 'Hoppy' was John Hopkins, who'd graduated from Cambridge University and moved to London. His proper job was a photographer, but, for a price, he used to disguise shipments of cannabis inside photo cannisters.

**Nigel Lesmoir-Gordon (writer, film-maker):** I'd been boarding at Oundle School [in Northamptonshire], where I started a branch of CND, a jazz club *and* joined the Communist Party. But my mother lived in Milton Road in Cambridge, which is how I came to know Storm Thorgerson, David Gale and all that crowd by the Mill Pond during the holidays. I must have met Syd then, too, around 1962. Cambridge was an ideal place. We'd go to a jazz club on the Friday night and then go up the Rex Ballroom on Saturday night and dance to Gene Vincent. After I moved to Cambridge, I started writing poetry and met a couple of undergraduates who invited me to smoke dope with them. Then I heard about 'Hoppy', so I set up my own link.

**Andrew 'Willa' Rawlinson (ex-County pupil, writer, philosopher):** I was at school with Roger Waters and Syd, who was two years younger than us. I was into surrealism, happenings and concrete poetry – as was Syd.

**Tim Renwick (ex-County pupil and future Pink Floyd touring guitarist):** I was a County boy, but Syd and I were also in the same scout group and, believe it or not, Syd was my patrol leader. He was very lively and good spirited.

**Libby Chisman:** After changing into his uniform for a scout meeting, Syd would go home, put on his tight jeans and go to a jazz club. He didn't dress like other boys. He wore a baggy black fisherman's sweater, no laces in his shoes, no socks – he was 'Syd the Beat'.

**Brian 'Fred' Foskett (local drummer and future jazz photographer):** Roger [Syd] wanted to hear some jazz, so I took him along to the YMCA where the Riverside Seven [whose double bass player was named Sid Barrett] were playing. Characteristically for that period, Roger was wearing jeans and wellington boots.

**Rosemary Breen:** I remember walking into Cambridge with Roger [Syd], and he had sunglasses on and it was *winter*. We were laughing about it, but the next week everybody was wearing sunglasses.

**Phil Carlo (Cambridge associate, future Led Zeppelin tour manager):** He wasn't the star then that he's seen as today. 'Oh wow, Syd Barrett!' He was just a young lad who used to lift his heels up in this funny way when he walked. Some people even shook their heads when they saw him.

**Anthony Stern (artist, film-maker):** There was what I called 'licensed eccentricity' in Cambridge. Our headmaster at Kings' College choir school once took us up into the eaves of the chapel, so there were all these kids crawling over the gallery and undercroft, peering down hundreds of feet below. A headmaster would have been arrested if he'd done that today. As kids, you were surrounded by people who, had they been in Barnstaple or Lyme Regis or any other town in England, would probably have been locked up.

**Libby Chisman:** When we grew up, there was a Cambridge eccentric – a woman who used to walk around with a bucket on her head. Syd found it tragic and hilarious at the same time. A visit into town, to the record shop, wasn't complete unless you saw this woman with a bucket on her head. He did laugh about it, but he was also sad and made us all wonder *why* she had a bucket on her head. And, of course, in the end, he sort of ended up like her.

✣

*Syd and Rosemary used a downstairs room at the front of 183 Hills Road as their childhood nursery. After Dr Barrett died and their older siblings moved out, Syd commandeered the space for himself, filling it with paints, an easel, a guitar, his record player and records, a Pollock's toy theatre, and any artistic ephemera that took his fancy. To compound the message that this was now his domain, he even fitted a lock to the door.*

*Meanwhile, Win, like many in Cambridge, took in student lodgers to help pay the bills. At number 183, Muddy Waters' exhortations from the American deep south rang out from behind Syd's locked door as bemused foreign-language students tried to sleep upstairs.*

✣

**Libby Chisman:** Syd loved his art, but played his guitar every opportunity and it went everywhere with him. There were a couple of music shops in Cambridge [Millers and Ken Stevens Music], but they could be really sniffy in there. Unless you showed them you had money, you weren't even allowed to go into the booths and listen to a record, but Ken Stevens would let Syd play guitars for hours – the expensive ones upstairs in the shop too.

**Syd Barrett (speaking in 1971):** 'The first [guitar] was a Hofner acoustic which I kept for a year. Then I joined a local group called Geoff Mott and the Mottoes and splashed out on a Futurama 2. Geoff Mott was a great singer ... Wonder what happened to him...?'

**Clive Welham (Geoff Mott and the Mottoes' drummer):** Geoff Motlow became a nationally well-known headmaster. But the Mottoes mainly played in Syd's mother's front room and, as I was barely out of school, it's quite possible my 'drum kit' was still a biscuit tin with knives. There was me, Geoff, Roger Barrett and another of my friends, 'Nobby' Clarke. Roger Waters used to come round a lot on his motorbike, but he wasn't doing music then. We played our first gig in Cambridge [in March 1962] and I think it was a benefit for CND.

**John Gordon:** Geoff Mott and the Mottoes were an informal band who played at parties. Syd didn't seem to be interested in bands, though. He was just quietly jamming with people, rather than being in a band that got paid for doing dances.

**David Gilmour:** My parents were living in New York and sent me the 1959 Newport Folk Festival albums and Bob Dylan's first album for my sixteenth birthday. It wasn't out in England at the time, so I probably had one of the first copies.

**Libby Chisman:** We went to see Bob Dylan together at the Festival Hall and as soon as he saw the audience, Syd said, 'Oh look, Lib, it's the me and you from every other town.'

**David Gale:** When Bob Dylan emerged, we were all very impressed. I had a Spanish guitar and, in my very amateur way, was trying to learn a few chords. I still have a piece of card on which Syd wrote the chords out to Dylan's 'Oxford Town'. Before that, though, we were listening to Snooks Eaglin, John Lee Hooker, lots of blues.

**John Gordon:** The most common name you hear is Bo Diddley, but Syd was into broader stuff. We were surrounded by American airbases and

Syd had got hold of some rare American imports – real basic Leadbelly-type blues, which as a teenager was quite scary.

**Rosemary Breen:** I liked Adam Faith and Roger [Syd] was *so* rude about him. I remember coming home with an Adam Faith record and being terribly excited. Roger put it on the record player, played a few seconds of the first track, then the first seconds of the second track and the same with the next one – and said, 'No, this is not music'. He wasn't being nasty, but he liked a lot of jazz. When everyone was listening to Cliff Richard and Elvis, he'd be interested in Thelonious Monk. It was the same all through his life. At the end, he had about ten CDs and they were all jazz.

**John Gordon:** My father was a well-known musician in the area and, as part of me not being like him, I shunned piano lessons and took the opportunity to learn guitar with Syd. After school, I'd spend an hour or so over at his place. Syd had an easel and was allowed to slap paint all over the place in his room downstairs at the front of the house. If I took so much as a pen out, never mind paint, my mum worried it would be all over the sofa.

I never really knew where the men in Syd's family got to. He seemed much more worldly and experienced than me. But the way he spoke to his mother embarrassed me sometimes. One minute, they'd be cuddling and the next he'd be telling her to eff off out of the room.

**Stephen Pyle (drummer in Barrett's pre-Floyd band, Those Without):** Syd and I first met at that Saturday-morning art class in 1962, but later on there was a lot of jamming at Syd's house. We all congregated there because his mum had such a liberal attitude.

**Rosemary Breen:** My mother was very free for the time. That was the way the house worked. There was no, 'You mustn't do that'. I went to Germany hitch-hiking with a boyfriend when I was only sixteen and she didn't make any fuss. In those days, there were no mobile phones and I didn't make contact for ages.

**Iain 'Emo' Moore (Pink Floyd familiar, seen on the inside sleeve of *A Nice Pair*):** We met when Syd was sixteen and, before I knew it, I was going round to his and smoking dope all day. His mum used to come in and say, 'What's that smell?'. Syd was always very quiet, never the first one to strike up a conversation, but he'd join in the conversation if you were talking about music or philosophy. He had a great mind, but you weren't aware of it because he didn't have to prove it to anybody. I seemed to drift between Syd's and Storm Thorgerson's house [in Earl Street] because Storm's mum, Vanji, let us hang out there.

**David Gale:** If you think about the Pink Floyd story, there is a pattern – boys and their mothers who let them do as they pleased, mothers who seemed to tolerate all these adolescents coming into their houses any time of the day or night.

✲

*Regardless of these distractions, Barrett pursued his dream of attending art school and followed Saturday mornings at Homerton with life-drawing classes at the Cambridgeshire College of Arts and Technology, aka the Tech, on East Road.*

*His doggedness and talent paid off when he was awarded a scholarship to study an art foundation course at the Tech in autumn 1962. The college hosted several other musically minded students, including his ex-County friend John Gordon, Stephen Pyle, John Watkins and, a term later, David Gilmour.*

*In 1963, pop music in the UK had entered that period where unassuming crooners such as Frank Ifield toughed it out on the chart with Elvis, Cliff Richard and the guitar-wielding Shadows. The new year began with the Beatles' groundbreaking 45, 'Love Me Do', and summer brought the first taste of the Rolling Stones, with their debut single 'Come On'.*

*While still* Roger *Barrett at home, he was often 'Sid' or 'Syd' elsewhere. One school friend insists the nickname was given to him earlier after he'd worn a flat cap to a scout troop meeting – 'Sid' being considered a typical working-class name by these grammar-school boys.*

*Barrett never commented, but his yen for what Rosemary calls 'never doing the same thing twice' was now apparent, as his art pinwheeled between styles and mediums. 'It changed from week to week,' attests John Gordon.*

*Some compared the student Barrett's abstracts to Jackson Pollock's or the American experimentalist Jim Dine, who created pieces with oil paint, fabric and household objects. Others, including the Tech's history of art professor, Jasper Rose, graciously described him a 'born painter ... with a lovely, twirly whirly drawing quality', despite Barrett routinely disrupting his lectures. Syd impressed, challenged and fascinated most who came into contact with him.*

❀

**Rosemary Breen:** Roger's [Syd's] time at art school in Cambridge was happy. It was an exciting time in the world when you could do what you wanted to do and wear what you wanted. He was smoking the odd thing, but this was before he got into too much mischief.

**John Watkins:** The art school was a big deal because Ronald Searle, the cartoonist who drew 'St Trinian's' [comic strip and books] had been there, and the team that later did *Spitting Image* – Peter Fluck and Roger Law. So people took notice.

**John Gordon:** In the first year, you dabbled in everything while you decided which branch of the arts you were going into. Syd knew immediately he wanted to paint, though he probably spent more time painting in his garden then he did at college. He sort of went missing. But on the day you had to bring your work in for an assessment, he'd suddenly show up with a masterpiece and all was forgiven.

**Stephen Pyle:** One of our favourite antics was to sit at the back during History of Art lectures on top of some fitted cupboards, behind which were curtained windows. When the lights were dimmed, we would drop out of the windows and go off for a fag and a coffee, returning just in time for the lecture to finish.

**David Gilmour:** After I left school, I went to the Tech in September 1963 to do A-levels in modern languages. Syd was already there, at the art school, and we used to meet up most lunchtimes in the canteen to play guitar. I remember learning 'Come On' by the Rolling Stones when that first came out. There was a lot of Beatles and Stones and Bo Diddley stuff – lunchtime jamming and discussing how these songs had been put together.

**Warren Dosanjh (ex-Cambridge County pupil and manager/roadie of Those Without):** On the corner of East Road by the Tech was an ice cream parlour called Sylvester's. Students would go there and have a float – Pepsi Cola or dandelion and burdock with a scoop of ice cream on top. Apparently, that's where Steve Pyle came up with the name 'Pink Floyd' one lunchtime.

**Stephen Pyle:** A regular pastime of Syd and myself was inventing band names. We were listening to a blues compilation and the sleevenotes mentioned other bluesmen not on the album, including Pink Anderson and Floyd Council. When I re-introduced myself to David Gilmour at Clive Welham's funeral [in 2012], he told me Syd had told him that I had come up with the name 'Pink Floyd'.

**Libby Chisman:** Around this time, Syd and I went to see the Rolling Stones, and it must have been something they were contracted to do before they got big. I think it was in some village hall just outside Cambridge.

After the show, Mick Jagger came to talk to us. I was wearing something unusual and he commented on that and what I'd done with my hair, and then he started talking to Syd. He talked about the fact Syd looked a bit like a young Bill Wyman – very dark and thin. I remember Mick had the most *awful* voice – worse than it is now – because in Cambridge we all spoke properly. But it was extraordinary that he just came over to us. Mary Quant was the same later on. She decided to chat to Syd. He was always picked out, however many people were there.

**Rosemary Breen:** You don't think about it when you grow up with it, but I did notice when we went out together to Woolworths on a Saturday, how quickly we got served, because he was so good-looking. Girls adored him from early on. All my mother's girlfriends seemed to be in love with him.

**Libby Chisman:** I don't know how much older Mary Quant was than us, but it was inevitable she'd talk to Syd. There were other grown women at parties he'd give his number to. They used to ring him up and the two of us would sit and listen to what they said. We used to laugh at this – and he'd arrange to meet them and then never turn up. We were such innocents, really. We broke up and got back together again I don't know how many times.

**Nigel Lesmoir-Gordon:** We were all *rebelling* – or trying to. I was the same age as Roger Waters and, through him, I'd get on my Vespa and go to some of those Sunday afternoon sessions at Syd's house. I'd also see him and his girlfriend Libby in the El Patio where I worked the espresso machine. I wasn't musical, but we were still interested in him because of his extraordinary looks and because he seemed to be going somewhere.

**Libby Chisman:** Nigel's crowd were older and they had to sort of stoop down to our teenybopper crowd, because they all liked Syd. The age difference wasn't an issue, though, but I think Syd worshipped Nigel and Dave Gale. But Syd could also be in a crowd and then just disappear. As soon as he bought his car, we were off looking at rivers and hills. There were other wonderful things to do or places we'd been invited to – and he'd just want to sit in the Gog Magog Hills with nobody else there.

**John Gordon:** Because of my home life I moved out of home when I went to the art school. I had a flat in a house in Clarendon Street that was a crash pad, where people would just drop by in the middle of the night. The place was always full of girls and smoke.

**Aubrey 'Po' Powell (co-founder of album sleeve designers Hipgnosis and Pink Floyd's future creative director):** When I got kicked out of the King's School in Ely, I found a room at 27 Clarendon Street. My father was in the RAF, so he and my mother were stationed in the Middle East and didn't have a clue.

I was sixteen years old with no money, but it was the beginning of a huge adventure. Peter Cook's sister Sarah lived in the basement, but there was a whole bunch of people who frequented that building and number 25 next door. Emo and his friend [Ian] 'Pip' Carter, who later became a roadie for Pink Floyd, were in and out of the place all the time.

We had a mutual friend, a townie dope dealer called Norman 'Nod' Brown, and it was 'Nod' who introduced me to Storm, David Gale, Nigel Gordon and all that crowd, including Syd Barrett. One minute I was at boarding school sharing a dormitory with [future BBC1/BBC2 controller] Alan Yentob, and the next I'm mixing with all these beatniks. They'd all read Kerouac, and watched foreign films, and drank in the Criterion, and had hitch-hiked to Morocco and Ibiza...

**Phil Carlo:** All that lot wore reefer jackets and desert boots or plimsolls, walked around with jazz albums under their arms, and smoked those horrible Gauloises or Gitanes cigarettes. The girls were lovely but looked the same, except they'd sometimes have those knitted bags over their shoulder that meant they'd been to Greece or Elba or Formentera. I only knew people who'd been to Costa Brava.

**John Gordon:** Syd and I had access to a projector and paint and ink from the college and microscopic slides because his father worked at the university. So we started messing around with a projector and experimenting with slide shows. So some of what became part of the early Pink Floyd show started with Syd in my front room.

**Rosemary Breen:** Roger [Syd] experienced what we later discovered was called 'synesthesia'. Even as a child, when he talked about how he felt, he would call it a colour. Sound was colour – and colour was sound to him. A loud noise was 'black' and I sometimes wonder if that psychedelic thing, with the thump of the music and the lights at the same time, was part of that.

**Libby Chisman:** Syd got us tickets for the Beatles [at Cambridge's Regal Cinema], but it was the day of his interview for Camberwell art school [November 1963] and he had to be in London. He was terribly disappointed to miss the Beatles.

**Peter Whitehead (artist, early Floyd film-maker, director of 1967's *Tonite Let's All Make Love in London* documentary):** I'd been studying at Cambridge and was taking six months off to concentrate on painting. I moved into a Georgian house at 60 Grange Road, belonging to a family called the Mitchells – Syd was having an affair with the daughter of the house, Juliet.

His band used to rehearse there, very loudly, right next to my studio. They sounded awful. So I put on my Bartók and Janáček even louder. They were just a bunch of guys playing rock 'n' roll and I have no idea if it was the Pink Floyd then.

Syd discovered I was a painter and he was a painter, so while the others in his group were fiddling around, we would chat. He was already experimenting with the guitar and I told him I didn't like pop music and preferred classical and the Modern Jazz Quartet. I played him a few things, so I'm sure I influenced him in that crucial moment to do those long, meandering, semi-classical pieces. So, of course, I will modestly claim to have invented the Pink Floyd sound.

**Anthony Stern:** Syd and I decided to host an exhibition of our paintings. Whitehead had done one before so we decided to follow him. We launched our painting careers with an exhibition at the Lion and Lamb, a pub in Milton [in May 1964]. The exhibition was not a resounding success and we didn't sell a thing. But it was a turning point. My paintings were feeble attempts at psychotic surrealism and Syd's were still lives with oil on canvas – much better.

***Cambridge Evening News* (30 May 1964):** 'Barrett's prints, monotypes and drawings are student exercises. But in two still lives, a landscape and two convincing portraits, he is already showing himself a sensitive handler of oil paints.'

**Stephen Pyle:** At that time, Syd was singing and playing bass in our group [which evolved from the Hollerin' Blues into Those Without], but he was a good lead guitarist as well. We played Bo Diddley and Jimmy Reed numbers – all the stuff Manfred Mann and the Yardbirds were doing. But the group sort of fell apart when he buggered off to art college in London.

**Warren Dosanjh:** The band [Pyle, Barrett, guitarists Alan Sizer and Robert 'Smudge' Smith] was called Those Without after a novel by the French author Françoise Sagan called *Those Without Shadows*. We threw out the 'Shadows', but we used to get the mick taken out of us – 'Oh, those without talent, those who can't sing...' and all that.

Syd only played with us during the holidays from his course at Camberwell. In August, he arrived for a band practice at the Ancient Druids pub in Fitzroy Street, excited about a new release from the Kinks called 'You Really Got Me'. He kept playing it over and over again.

Then it went to number one in Miller's Music shop charts and, that night, we held a farewell party for Syd who was heading back to London. It was at Steve Pyle's parents' home at Cheshunt College Lodge. The invitation, drawn by Steve, welcomed people to 'Bo Siddley's Perverted Bleach Party' [a spoof of the LP, *Bo Diddley's Beach Party*] and, as a memento, the band gave Syd a copy of an album called *Jimmy Reed Plays 12-String Guitar Blues*.

**Storm Thorgerson:** Syd was already writing his own songs because he played them at parties – things like 'Effervescing Elephant', which was whimsical and nursery rhyme-like. His efforts were nice enough, but showed little indication of the greatness to come. But it's amazing what you don't notice because it's sat right next to you.

**Rosemary Breen:** Roger [Syd] went to Camberwell in summer 1964 at the same time I went to St George's Hospital [in Tooting, south London] to study nursing.

**Libby Chisman:** Syd was disappointed not to get into Chelsea art school, until he realised Camberwell was even better. But I still thought art was something to do while he was waiting to do his music.

❋

*It's a disconcerting sound. In the Azure Suite at London's May Fair Hotel, with its umber carpet and powder-blue furnishings, Roger Waters leans forward, elbows planted on his knees, summoning a globule of phlegm. A lock of iron-grey hair falls across his forehead as the mucus ascends his throat. Then it stops, a second before he delivers a perfect but mercifully dry imitation of somebody spitting.*

*Waters is re-enacting the time he spat on a would-be stage invader at a Pink Floyd show in Montreal. It wasn't just the intrusion that prompted this reaction; apparently, he was also screaming for an old Floyd song called 'Careful With That Axe, Eugene'. A spittable offence, then.*

*Today's conversation centres around Waters' latest album,* Is This The Life We Really Want?. *George Roger Waters' life began on 6 September 1943, the second son of schoolteacher turned soldier, Eric Fletcher Waters, and schoolteacher Mary Whyte. Eric was from a coal mining family in County Durham; Mary from Golders Green, north London. Both were devoutly left wing.*

*After war was declared, the Waters family moved to Cambridge from the Surrey village of Great Bookham, believing they were less likely to be bombed. But the pivotal early moment in Waters' life was the death of his father. Second Lieutenant Eric Waters was part of the Royal Fusiliers' Company Z and killed in the battle for the Anzio bridgehead on Italy's Lazio coast.*

*Waters wrote Pink Floyd's 'When the Tigers Broke Free' about this and the time he discovered a commemorative scroll from the office of King George V hidden in a drawer in the family home; a scene recreated by director Alan Parker in his movie,* Pink Floyd – The Wall.

*Really, though, Waters had been writing about the futility of war long before then and many times since. Decades later, the politically opiniated and trenchant Waters is still spitting fire or poison, depending on one's point of view.*

*'How do we allow things like Donald Trump to happen?' he asks, before moving on to the subjects of impending ecological disaster and organised*

*religion. 'We live on a tiny, insignificant planet that a bunch of god-botherers think is the centre of the universe, and there's a god who cares about us all and he made it.*

*'Is there any wine?' asks Waters.*

*'There is,' replies his PA, 'but we can't find the corkscrew.'*

*Waters closes his eyes and sighs.*

❦

***Disc and Music Echo* (8 April 1967):** 'Roger Waters, 22, and the bass player, says "I lie and am rather aggressive" – and attempts to act the part by shooting down questions if he can.'

**Roger Waters:** When my father was called up for military service at the start of the war, he went before the tribunal as a conscientious objector, saying he was a Christian and wasn't prepared to kill people. So he drove an ambulance through the Blitz, but he met lots of Communists, his political ideas developed and he decided he'd made a mistake and that Hitler had to be fought. He went back and said, 'I've changed my mind'. He went to officer training school, was commissioned for the Royal Fusiliers, went off to Italy after the landings and was killed a couple of weeks later.

**War Diary of Intelligence Summary (17–18 February 1944):** 'Z Coy [Company] reported an attack on the left forward platoon. The bosch [slang for Germans] called on them to surrender but were answered with all available SA [Semi-Automatic] fire. Casualties were inflicted, situation well in hand, enemy decided to withdraw... Further attack on Z Coy, this time in greater strength than previous attack. Enemy in close contact. Unable to send assistance. Z Coy reporting enemy all round their positions. Very stiff fighting going on. Lieut Walters [sic] killed and Lieut Hill wounded. Situation now critical.'

**Roger Waters:** My father did see me, but I was only a couple of months old and I don't remember him. When the men in uniform came to collect their children, that's when I realised I didn't have a father anymore. But instead of an ordinary person, I've had to live with a father who wasn't an ordinary person but a dead hero.

**Rosemary Breen:** Roger Waters behaved differently, because he was older than the rest of us and a bit dismissive. But if you knew his mother, you'd understand why. She was a teacher and taught us at Morley Memorial.

**Roger Waters:** My big brother John and I went to Morley Memorial, where our mother started teaching [in 1951]. I liked primary school. My problems came later with grammar school. I even wrote a song, 'When We Were Young,' about the boys' playground at Morley Memorial. There was a bog there – an open-air area with a gutter – on a wall painted with black pitch. The song is about being ten years old and trying to piss vertically up that bog wall.

**Warren Dosanjh:** Mary Waters was the secretary of the East Anglian wing of the CND. I'd grown up in a working-class, left-wing family and joined the Young Socialists. Mary lived at 42 Rock Road, which is where I later went for meetings to talk about canvassing, leafleting and the support of local candidates and visiting Labour MPs.

**Roger Waters:** My mother was nothing like the one in *The Wall*. But she lived in the service of others. She had done her teacher training in Bradford, in the north of England. It was a real eye-opener. The first winter came along – really cold, snow on the ground – and she noticed that half the kids in her class were walking to school with no shoes. This would have been in 1935, 1936 – so she started to look into social conditions and understood that there were inequalities in the context of the society that she lived in that she felt a personal need to do something about.

In the evening, my mother used to take John and I to British China Friendship Association meetings, where we'd watch old black-and-white films of Chinese blokes in kapoks fighting Chiang Kai-Shek or the Japanese imperialist invaders or whatever it might be. We nearly always went to the Friends Meeting House [on Jesus Lane], which was owned by the Quakers in Cambridge. I'll never forget my mother saying, 'As you know, I am an atheist and don't believe in their religious beliefs and politics but these are very very good people, very humane' – much more humane than the Roman Catholic church, for instance.

So there was this attachment to the idea that, because you believed in God, you didn't have to be awful. You could be good people, who were charitable and wanted to help people less worse off. My mother thought Communism was all about helping other people.

She left the Party in 1956 after the Russians invaded Hungary, along with almost everyone else who could no longer close their eyes to the authoritarian nature of Uncle Joe [Stalin] and his archipelagos. She became a member of the Labour Party and I completely took it on – lock, stock and barrel.

✤

*In summer 1954, Waters enrolled at 'the County', which had just transitioned from the stewardship of headmaster 'Brin' Newton-John, a wartime code-breaker whose daughter, Olivia, would become a pop star, to A.W. Eagling, a classics scholar unafraid to dispense six of the best.*

*Over time, Waters' opinion of the County has wavered from complete loathing ('A battery farm, I hated it') to 'I hated it, apart from games, which I loved'. Waters was both a fly half for the County's rugby XV and a wicket keeper in the cricket first XI. 'Anything with a ball,' recalled one of his old team mates.*

*There wasn't much music around 42 Rock Road, though, with Waters claiming Mary 'could just as easily have been listening to a washing machine'. But her son acquired a 78rpm of Gilbert and Sullivan's* The Mikado, *a 45 of Frankie Lane's 'Champion, The Wonder Horse' and was thrilled to catch a West End performance of* Salad Days *during a Communist Party jolly to London. He also sang in the combined school choir (completed by pupils from the Cambridgeshire High School for Girls) until puberty intervened and his voice broke.*

*Waters displayed the same contrary mix of broiling rage and empathy later found in his songwriting. He was 'moved to tears' by the Italian drama*

The Bicycle Thief, *but so annoyed his fellow boy sailors in the navel cadets that they physically beat him. But he was still* really *good at games.*

❀

**Storm Thorgerson:** Roger and I played on the same rugby team at school. This thought crossed my mind many times during the years when he wasn't talking to me because of an argument we'd had about the artwork for [Pink Floyd's] *Animals*. I'd think, 'I used to pass the ball to you'. Roger was annoyingly good at anything involving a ball.

**Roger Waters:** I liked watching the boat races at Cambridge, but I liked it when weird things happened at the races. You'd sit on the bank and see these blokes cycling down the towpath shouting at the teams, waving Webley service revolvers and firing blanks. Then, at the end of the road, the cox of the winning boat had to jump in the river. I found that a very exciting piece of sport – just like when the flying pig escaped over Battersea Power Station for *Animals*.

**David Gale:** Of course, Roger being good at sport ran counter to all the ideas about what beatniks and bohemians were supposed to be like. None of the musicians in what became Pink Floyd were bohemian, but they managed to maintain this vast bohemian image and following.

**Roger Waters:** I had several great friends at school, including 'Willa' [Andrew Rawlinson] and Seamus [O'Connell], and I spent most nights as a teenager listening to blues and jazz at Seamus's house [on Cherry Hinton Road]. His mother Ella and his father Michael were separated. Michael was an Australian artist and lived next door to [the sculptor] Henry Moore, and Ella was a wonderful, bohemian woman who'd stay up all night cooking sausages for these fifteen-year-olds.

**Seamus O'Connell (ex-Cambridge County pupil):** Roger was the year above me. The relationship was a bit fraught. He could sometimes be not all that pleasant to me, but we still counted each other as friends. There was also an overlapping social circle with Syd Barrett, who used to have these Sunday afternoon gatherings. I went along once or twice as, like a lot of middle-class white boys, we were all deeply enamoured of black music.

**Roger Waters:** We had some good teachers, but we had a fair number who were serving their time and were extremely bitter and would treat the kids abominably. It was T.E. House who told me I was a complete fucking idiot. He was an English teacher and my form master when I was thirteen. He said I would never become anything and might as well give up and shoot myself.

**Warren Dosanjh:** There was quite an arsenal at the County, containing old Bren guns and dismantled .303 rifles. If you think back to 1956, '57, most of the masters at that school had been at the tail end of the war, maybe not in a combat situation, so they revelled in it.

When you were fourteen, you went into the CCF [Combined Cadet Force]. You could be excused on the grounds that you were a pacifist, but you had to have a letter to that effect from your parents. Then you were sent off to do gardening and weeding in full view of the cadets, so there was cat calls and bullying. If you were in the army cadets, you put on an itchy khaki uniform and a blanco belt, and square-bashed every Wednesday afternoon.

**Roger Waters:** I couldn't bear the itching of the army uniform. So I became a [naval cadet] leading seaman. I spent my weekends on HMS *Ganges*, a boat for training boy sailors. But I was hated by most of the people involved. You weren't allowed to leave. So I just handed my uniform in and said I wasn't going anymore. My final school report said, 'Waters never fulfilled his considerable potential and was dishonourably discharged from the cadet force'.

**Tim Renwick:** The story around school was that Roger refused to do Combined Cadet Force training anymore because he was a conscientious objector or something. It caused quite a fuss.

**Roger Waters:** If you look at my behaviour at school, it may be that there was an element of not having a male authority figure in my home life and therefore resisting the idea of anyone else taking on that role.

**Warren Dosanjh:** One day I was being disruptive with three other boys in an art class and we were told to go to the bottom of the school field next to the railway line, where there was an orchard. We were told to come back after drawing an apple – it was just to keep us out of the way. So we all drew a circle with a stalk coming out of it – and that was the end of it.

**Roger Waters:** One night, about ten of us went out because we'd decided that the man in charge of gardening needed a lesson. He had one particular apple tree that was his pride and joy. We went into the orchard with stepladders and ate every single apple on the tree without removing any. We were terribly tired the next day but filled with a real sense of achievement.

Years later, they found the school's punishment book. I was only beaten a couple of times. One of my entries reads '1959 – six strokes for fighting', of which I am inordinately proud. I don't know why I am, because it's so archaic now – the idea of hitting people with a stick to make them do things.

I stayed on for a third year in the sixth form, because I'd failed one of my A-levels and I was the only boy in the school who'd stayed on for a third year in the sixth form without being made a prefect.

✤

*At this point, drawing posters for gigs by Geoff Mott and the Mottoes and watching Syd Barrett play guitar was the sum total of Waters' involvement in music, and he struggled to engage with art lessons 'because the teacher was so ineffectual'.*

*In 1961, he and Barrett went down to London to watch Gene Vincent at the Gaumont State Cinema in Kilburn: 'And on the train home I clearly remember sitting with Syd making a drawing of all the equipment we thought we'd need if we ever had a group – and it consisted of two Vox AC30s.'*

*Despite prime minister Harold Macmillan telling the British people that they'd 'never had it so good', the fear of nuclear Armageddon still loomed.*

*Waters joined the Aldermaston March to Trafalgar Square and listened to the philosopher Bertrand Russell and CND chairman Canon John Collins preach against the need for a nuclear deterrent. This experience later inspired Pink Floyd's 'Two Suns in the Sunset' – 'a warning about how we might wake up one morning and the Third World War had started'.*

*Waters also piloted a Norton motorcycle and his mother's Austin, sometimes recklessly, around Cambridge and further afield on trips through Europe. But his peer group were breaking up. As Waters muddled through his extra year at the County, Andrew 'Willa' Rawlinson took up a place at Cambridge's Pembroke College and Seamus O'Connell and his bohemian mother prepared to move to London.*

✤

**Roger Waters:** I always remember, one night, very drunk, having a race with a friend, who owned a car. There was a roundabout about ten miles out of Cambridge. We gave this guy a big start and then Syd [Barrett] and I climbed on. I had an old Norton motorcycle and I drove with Syd on the pillion as fast as I could to this roundabout and back. As we drove into the front drive of his mother's house, the back tyre went 'Bang!'. So it was only by a hair's breadth that Pink Floyd existed at all because Syd and I could so easily have been killed on that motorcycle doing a stupid childish thing.

**Libby Chisman:** We all behaved if Roger Waters was there. It was like somebody coming in to the room and teaching us. Roger had a motorbike before any of us had driving licences – and a leather jacket and a lovely girlfriend called Judy Trim.

**Storm Thorgerson:** Roger, 'Willa' and I were all chasing Judy who was, literally, the girl next door [on Rock Road]. But Roger got the girl and eventually ended up marrying her.

**Roger Waters:** You saw these guys on the Aldermaston marches with their guitars, singing Woody Guthrie songs, with long-haired girls swanning around. I started hitch-hiking around England when I was fourteen and, as soon as I could drive, I went to Europe and visited Anzio where my father had died.

**Andrew 'Willa' Rawlinson:** Because we were best mates at school, Roger and I went to Paris together when we were sixteen.

**Roger Waters:** It was 1959 and I saw them fishing bodies of Algerians out of the Seine every morning. That whole OAS [Organisation Armée Secrète, a French paramilitary group opposed to Algerian independence] thing was going on there at the time. It was the end of French colonialism in north Africa. These were tumultuous times.

**Andrew 'Willa' Rawlinson:** Two years later, we took his mum's Austin and drove to Istanbul, via France, Italy and Greece, which took about three months.

**Roger Waters:** 'Willa' was my best mate and suddenly he was gone, off to Pembroke College. Willa had an interesting relationship with whisky, until he gave all that up. One night, he jumped off Mill Road railway bridge and came round in the shunting yards at Ely. But he got rusticated [temporarily suspended from the university] after he knocked another student through the plate-glass window of the department store Eaden Lilley after a night in the Criterion, which was the pub we used to frequent.

**David Gale:** Seamus O'Connell and Roger Waters were never big drug heads. But Rawlinson was a wilder figure – a brilliant student, quite a maverick – lots of long hair. Rawlinson was a very impressive, articulate guy who picked up the zeitgeist and told us what was coming.

**Roger Waters:** When I left school, I was all set to go to Manchester University to study mechanical engineering, but the thought of another three years of sixth form was more than I could stand, so I took a year off. My career choice was made by the National Institute of Industrial Psychology. They told me I could do well at architecture [Waters enrolled at Regent Street Polytechnic to study architecture in summer 1962].

**Andrew 'Willa' Rawlinson:** [In 1962] Roger joined me and three friends from the university on a trip to the Middle East in an ambulance called 'Brutus'. We knew nothing about engines, put no water in it and it blew up in Beirut.

**Roger Waters:** 'Willa' and I had three undergraduates with us, and the five of us decided to go our separate ways, and I hitch-hiked back to England. It was an extraordinary experience. The first night of that journey I was taken in by a Lebanese Arab family. They insisted I slept in the only bed in the place and they slept on the floor behind a curtain. My first ride out of Beirut was in a taxi. I had no money, but the passengers allowed me to travel for free. This was all very much part of being in Cambridge at that time – the idea of going east in search of adventure. So I wrote a song about it later, [2004's] 'Leaving Beirut'.

When I first got a guitar, it was a classical Spanish thing. I took a few lessons from a woman in Cambridge who used to keep her guitar in bed as if it was a sexual thing.

But I remember sitting around and playing acoustic guitars with Syd in Cambridge before I left. We always had this notion that when we hit London – because it was clear he was going to come up to London as well, because London was the mecca and that was where one had to be – that we would start a band together.

**Libby Chisman:** Syd didn't take *himself* seriously, but Roger Waters took Syd seriously – and I think that ended up making a big difference.

✲

*As a young teenager, David Gilmour's room in the family home had the dimensions of a linen cupboard. That's because it had been a linen cupboard before somebody managed to squeeze a single bed inside.*

*Apparently, Gilmour would lie in this claustrophobic cubbyhole contemplating his mortality – a morbid pastime for a thirteen-year-old, but one that later fed into his music. You only have to look at his song titles: 'Near the End', 'I Can't Breathe Anymore'... 'And "Childhood's End",' he says, 'from [the Pink Floyd soundtrack album]* Obscured By Clouds.*'*

*David Jon Gilmour CBE has a complicated relationship with all this. He doesn't know why he writes about death (or, rather, he's reluctant to say) and he doesn't believe in an afterlife. 'I'm afraid mortality is one of the topics I go back to time and again and, at my incredibly advanced age, it still is a topic,' he offers today.*

*Gilmour, two years shy of his eightieth birthday at the time of writing, is in the control room of his floating studio,* Astoria, *a charming Edwardian-era houseboat with a mahogany deck large enough to accommodate a ninety-piece orchestra.*

*The guitarist is wearing blue suede shoes (really) and one of his regulation black T-shirts. Gilmour has made several Pink Floyd and solo records on this boat. There's something peaceful and womb-like about the place. Unhurried, too, rather like its owner.*

*A conversation with David Gilmour tends to move at a glacial pace. Think the verbal equivalent of those long suspended notes at the beginning of 'Shine On You Crazy Diamond, Part I'. He's not disengaged so much as reserved, and any enthusiasm is often tempered by a note of caution.*

*With his bald dome and chilly blue eyes, Gilmour also comes across, in the words of his wife and lyricist, Polly Samson, as 'invulnerable'. Gilmour was born on 6 March 1946. So is it a post-war thing? Or because he was billeted in boarding school as an infant and then left behind when his parents emigrated to the United States? A psychologist would probably know – although Gilmour's last attempt at therapy ended poorly because both he and his analyst sat there not saying very much.*

*If he could find a way to communicate directly via the guitar, he probably would. But he's not as bad with words as he sometimes makes out. Especially when it comes to Pink Floyd. 'You want a story,' he once told me. 'You have to get a story, and I understand that. But then it becomes like an episode of* EastEnders, *where you're concentrating all the bad moments that happen into a small space and squeezing out all the good moments.'*

*But what a story – good and bad.*

❦

**David Gilmour:** I was born in the village of Trumpington and then my family moved to a house on Huntingdon Road, the main road into Cambridge, then a little village called Cottenham. After that, from age ten onwards, I was in Grantchester Meadows. There's Grantchester, then a couple of miles of fields, the meadows, the River Cam and the beginning of Cambridge.

**Roger Waters:** I spent many, many happy hours fishing for roach with a bamboo rod and a piece of bread in that bit of the River Cam. I have powerful memories of the warmth of summer mud oozing up between my toes.

**David Gilmour:** My father [Doug] was a lecturer in zoology and genetics at Cambridge and my mother [Sylvia] had been to teacher training college but never really went into teaching. Later, she worked for the BBC as a film editor on *Junior Points of View*. They were both left-of-centre, *Manchester Guardian* readers and many of their friends went on the Aldermaston marches.

In summer 1951, my father was offered a six-month sabbatical to perform research at the University of Wisconsin–Madison. My mother went with him and left my sister [Catherine], brother [Peter] and I in a boarding school in Steeple Claydon in Buckinghamshire. I thought it was when I was seven or eight, but I read some papers my mother gave me later and it turned out I was five years old and my brother was four. They came back at Christmas, but continued living the high life for the next two terms and left us in school. I think that makes one quite resilient, and certainly instilled independence in myself and my brother and sister.

After that, I was at Chesterton Prep School until eleven and then into the Perse. My parents loved each other and enjoyed each other's company, but I think they found us rather inconvenient, to be honest. We holidayed together when we were very little, but as soon as we got to the age where we could be bounced off into something else, like the boy scouts, we never went on holiday together again.

**Rado 'Bob' Klose (Pink Floyd's ex-guitarist):** David and I have known each other almost since we were born, as our fathers knew each other. I'm not sure if he actually took guitar lessons from me, but we both played.

**David Gilmour:** Bill Haley's 'Rock Around The Clock' had come out when I was ten years old, followed closely by [Elvis's] 'Heartbreak Hotel', which I still think is one of the best records ever made. When I was thirteen or so, I borrowed a guitar from our next-door neighbour's son. He had no interest in it and so eventually I never gave it back. The first guitar I bought had the neck broken off and I said to the bloke in the shop [Ken Stevens Music], 'What's happening to that guitar?'. He said, 'It's in for repair', and I got it for thirty quid.

**Rado 'Bob' Klose:** I remember when the Ventures' single 'Walk Don't Run' came out, David was one of the first guys that picked up how to play it while it took the rest of us a lot longer.

**David Gilmour:** I had a four-mile cycle ride home from the Perse school and some of it was through the fenland. There was a short cut over the Cam and a millstream called The Cut. Next to the swimming area was a verge of grass and, on my ride home, I started noticing people gathering there. I just muscled my way in and got to know this group of boys and girls, of which Storm Thorgerson was the leader and the loud one, and at school with Syd Barrett.

**Storm Thorgerson:** David, rather like Syd, tended to have a lot of girls following him around – which could be rather dispiriting for the rest of us.

**Vivien Brans (Barrett and Gilmour's ex-girlfriend, aka 'Twig', name-checked in Barrett's solo song 'Dark Globe'):** I was sixteen at the Cambridge Grammar School for Girls and I used to do a paper round. I'd cycle over to Newnham at six in the morning and when I came back, there was often a paperboy in the street who used to say hello to me. One day he was stood there with David Gilmour, whom he'd told about me, so it wasn't an accidental meeting. The next time I saw him was at a youth club. I remember dancing with him – and then we started going out.

**David Gilmour:** My parents had gone to America again [taking Gilmour's seven-year-old brother Mark], as my father was offered a post at Columbia University in Manhattan. So the rest of us went to live with different families in the area.

**Vivien Brans:** David had to look after himself. He was very practical. I think he was living with a family called the Martindales over in Chesterton. He took me there one day and he had this horrible dark little room. He tried to teach me to play the theme music to *Steptoe and Son* on the guitar. Of course, I couldn't play a thing but I remember thinking, *This place is* so *miserable*.

**David Gilmour:** I wasn't expelled from the Perse, strangely enough. But I stayed on for one term in the sixth form and then gave it up and moved to the Tech. I'd like to say it was because I was so dedicated to my music and practising guitar fifteen hours a day, but that would be stretching the truth. I just wasn't overly motivated towards achieving in school.

**John Gordon:** At the end of school, I joined a band called the Ramblers, where Clive Welham was the drummer. I think I first met David when he came to watch us, and played a few gigs, and then he turned up at the Tech. He was a shy guy but he was aware of his own talents and knew what he was all about.

**David Gilmour:** I wasn't in the Ramblers, but I played about two gigs after their great guitarist, 'Albie' Prior, left. The first band I was really in were called the Newcomers when I was seventeen. I doubt if I played any gigs for money before then. When you're young, you think these things last so much longer than they do, but the Newcomers were only for a few months.

**Clive Welham:** When David joined the Newcomers, he'd come on a hell of a lot. I had seen him play a year or so before and he wasn't really there. He must have put in a lot of work. Then we came together with David and John Gordon to do a new group, Jokers Wild [completed by bassist Tony Sainty and vocalist Dave Altham, in February 1964]. Because we could all sing and do five-part harmonies, that made it easy to do anything in the chart.

❦

*Jokers Wild made their debut at the Old English Gentleman pub on Fitzroy Street in February 1964. Gilmour had learned every song on the Beatles' debut LP* Please Please Me *and everyone in the band was required to sing harmonies on the likes of 'The Shoop Shoop Song (It's In His Kiss')', 'Why Do Fools Fall In Love?' and 'Big Girls Don't Cry'.*

*This winning combination led to a stint at Cambridge's Blue Horizon, regular nights at the Dorothy Ballroom (aka 'The Dot') and a residency at Les Jeux Interdits in the Victoria Ballroom.*

*The last was popular with students from the Bell School of Languages, including Pablo Picasso's son, Claude, who befriended them all, including Syd's girlfriend Libby. 'Muddy Waters was a bit boring,' she says. 'Jokers Wild played songs we could all dance to.'*

❦

**Warren Dosanjh:** Syd Barrett and Those Without had a residency at the Blue Horizon. One night, a lot of the audience had been smoking weed and the band played 'Hey! Bo Diddley' and our friends from The Mill pub all jumped on stage and did more verses, so it just went on and on and on. The song never ended – it was anarchic. After that, we were told our contract was no longer valid, and we were replaced by Jokers Wild.

**Jenny Spires (Syd Barrett's ex-girlfriend):** I first saw David Gilmour in Grantchester Meadows. I used to work at the tea rooms – a wooden shed with a hatch at the front mostly selling ice creams. Whenever I saw him, he was with some amazingly beautiful French or Swedish girl. Then I went to a club at Brewer's Yard to dance and Jokers Wild were playing.

**David Gilmour:** Jokers Wild became very popular because we were the band everyone wanted for their parties. But I had completely not done my A-levels. I just didn't sit all the exams. I dropped out in the middle of doing them, so going on to a career that was considered a normal option by my parents was out of the question. I think they more or less thought I should just get on with whatever I wanted to do at that point. They would come to the gigs and help out sometimes. I even remember them helping to lug a bit of gear around.

We had some interest from London and I did audition for Brian Epstein, though he never offered me anything specific, and I also met the Kinks' manager Robert Wace, and Lionel Bart. 'How do I put this?' I was a fresh-faced lad and these people were gay and I wasn't. So I don't think my perceptions of what was going on were entirely accurate in terms of what was *really* going on. I also auditioned for the Stones guy, [their first manager] Andrew Loog Oldham. I did do something and two of the musicians I worked with on one of those auditions were Jon Povey and Wally Waller, whom I later knew in the Pretty Things.

**'Willie' Wilson (future Jokers Wild and Pink Floyd's *The Wall* surrogate band drummer):** Dave did a couple of things with Lionel Bart and Andrew Oldham. They put up some money and told him, 'We are going to make you a star.' I think they saw a pretty boy. He told me they wanted to sign him, but not the rest of Jokers Wild, so he told them to stuff it.

**David Gilmour:** I was very happy with the protection of my little unit around me, doing cover songs, and I really wouldn't have known where to start with anything else at that stage.

**Vivien Brans:** His life was that guitar, and I used to wash his clothes and buy him these sweaters from a posh shop on King's Parade. My mother used to say, 'You don't give him money, do you?'. But I did feel sorry for him when his parents left, so I suppose I did mother him a bit.

**David Gilmour:** Most gigs you'd start at eight and finish at ten-thirty, with fifteen minutes off in the middle. But there were a lot of parties and college balls that were longer, where you were expected to do every song you knew three times. There was a lot of pill-popping going on

– dexedrines and 'blues' were commonest in those days. You could keep yourself awake and enthusiastic with those things.

During the slacker periods when we were maybe doing only two gigs a week, I did day jobs as well. I was a soft drinks delivery boy, I did furniture removals, worked loading sheet metal… Lots of different jobs so I could update and improve our PA and equipment.

**Vivien Brans:** When David's parents emigrated to America [after Doug Gilmour was offered a permanent university post in 1965], his younger brother Mark went with them, but the others stayed here. Peter and David moved into this thatched cottage at Fen Ditton, owned by [a young university academic] Dr Richard Morton – Dick Morton – who was supposed to be looking after them. But it was like an open house. We'd have parties there – boyfriends and girlfriends – and Dick was worse than any of us. That cottage in Fen Ditton became *the* place to go. It was raucous and riotous, and my mother never knew a thing about it.

**Phil Carlo:** I knew a girl called Maureen Howe, who fascinated me because when I first met her, she said, 'Oh, I've just been to Djerba'. I'd never heard of Djerba. David Gilmour rolled me my first joint in Maureen's little terraced house. There were some traffic lights outside. I got in my car and just sat there. The lights changed about four times before I moved. Gilmour and Maureen thought it was hilarious, and I thought I'd gone mad.

**David Gilmour:** That whole period in Cambridge was a good musical education. Jokers Wild wanted to play the dances and we wanted to earn our money. But after a couple of years of that, I thought, *This pond isn't quite big enough and I'd rather move on*.

**Vivien Brans:** He always knew he was going to make it. When the Everly Brothers played the Regal Cinema, we went to the backstage door because I had my autograph book for them to sign. David offered to sign it while we were waiting for them to come out and he wrote, 'David Jon Gilmour, 109 Grantchester Meadows. In case, one day, I become très célèbre, hundred-to-one against.'

# 2

# 'SHALL WE GO PURPLE TONIGHT?'

*Kippers up the walls, 'twistravegrooveyhipblockedtwistravegrooveyroo...', a lot of 'Oh wow, man!' and Syd's wisdom tooth comes out...*

❖

It's February 2020 and we've not yet gone into lockdown and Pink Floyd's drummer Nick Mason is discussing his newfound love of travelling by tour bus. It's a novelty, because Pink Floyd didn't take the bus even in their early days. Now the late-seventy-something drummer and his group, Nick Mason's Saucerful of Secrets (a redux celebration of Floyd's early hits and non-hits), are doing just that.

'Chuck your bags in, get on board, find your bunk,' Mason grins. 'Everybody is so enthusiastic so it feels like a school outing. I'm not saying touring with Pink Floyd was miserable, because it wasn't. But...'

After Waters' exit from the group in 1985, Mason threw in his lot with David Gilmour. But he and Waters had a shared history that wasn't easily abandoned.

When Waters joined Saucerful of Secrets on stage one night in New York in 2019, he tickled his old friend under the armpits, like they were still students horsing around at Regent Street Polytechnic. Not that this has stopped them slagging each other off.

'Roger made Stalin look like an old muddle-head,' suggested Mason.

'Nick likes the attention and he likes the money,' claimed Waters. And so on...

Nicholas Berkeley Mason CBE was born on 27 January 1944 to Ailsa Kershaw and film-maker Bill Mason. His maternal grandfather played in an Edwardian-era banjo ensemble whose song 'The Grand State March' became a sheet-music hit, while Bill's father was once the lord mayor of Birmingham.

Bill was an ex-Communist Party member turned shop steward in the cinematographic technicians' union when he moved his family to north London's exclusive Hampstead Garden Suburb. Nick attended Frensham Heights near Farnham in Surrey, a school which seems to have been as liberal as 'the County' was authoritarian and where he played in his first group, the Hotrods.

Mason is the only member of Pink Floyd to have appeared on every one of their studio albums. He left his mark on early songs such as 'Set the Controls for the Heart of the Sun' and today has great fun performing its trademark busy drum fills with his own band.

Really, Mason has led a charmed life. Being in Pink Floyd has enabled him to race sports cars, fly aeroplanes and acquire a collection of vintage vehicles which he used to hire out to film and TV companies. He also owns Queen Camilla's pre-royal family home, Middlewick House, in Corsham in Wiltshire, where he and his second wife Nettie throw an annual garden party.

In the absence of many songwriting credits, Mason assumed the secondary role of Pink Floyd's ambassador/cheerleader with a ready supply of self-deprecating quips: 'I'm not Henry Kissinger – I'm more Neville Chamberlain,' 'I'm the closest this band has to an Enid Blyton character'... and so on.

Today, in his designer overcoat and Paul Smith scarf, Nick Mason resembles the (retired) architect he would have probably been were it not for Roger Waters and Syd Barrett.

'What advice would I give my younger self?' he ponders. 'Look out, you're in it for the long haul.'

❀

***Disc and Music Echo* (8 April 1967)**: 'Nick Mason, the 22-year-old drummer describes himself as a "very mediocre, ordinary youth" and thinks his arrival in the Pink Floyd was possibly connected to his grandfather once penning a "fine, regal march" entitled "The Grand State March".'

**Nick Mason:** Growing up, we had an eclectic mix of records at home – classical music, 'The Teddy Bears Picnic', 'The Laughing Policeman'. My mum was musical and could play piano, my dad not at all. But he was very interested in music and, being a film-maker, he worked with a lot of composers including, later, Ron Geesin, who worked with Pink Floyd on *Atom Heart Mother*.

The first live concert I ever saw was Tommy Steele, playing the Hackney Empire with several novelty acts. I actually went there from school wearing short trousers and carrying a satchel. After that, I went with school friends to see the Spencer Davis Group, and their singer Stevie Winwood looked even younger than us. I was terribly impressed.

**Libby Chisman:** I can remember going in the Pink Floyd's van to Nick's parents' house and being gobsmacked. We thought we were beatniks because we wore black clothes and had shaggy hair, but we were made to feel welcome by parents who we wouldn't have thought would have made us feel welcome at all.

**Peter Jenner (Pink Floyd's first co-manager):** I recall being incredibly impressed that Nick Mason's parents had a swimming pool in their back garden.

**Nick Mason:** I think my father acquired some African drums during one of his work trips and then somebody gave me a pair of wire brushes. I really wasn't serious about it. But I ended up playing drums as one of my friends at school wanted to form a band called the Hotrods. He already had a guitar and I thought, *I'm buggered if I'm going to be the bass player*. So I went to Foote's, the drum shop in Denman Street [in Soho], and bought a basic kit for about a tenner – probably equivalent to a hundred quid now. Years later, I ended up owning the shop. Really, I fell into studying architecture, but I didn't have any great ambition.

**Clive Metcalfe (guitarist in Mason and Waters' Regent St Poly groups):** Another student, Keith Noble, and I had a job in the evenings singing and playing guitar in a bistro in Albermarle Street [in Mayfair]. Keith put something on the student union noticeboard – 'If anyone wants to start a group...'. The other people that turned up were Keith's sister, Sheilagh, a guitarist called Vernon, Roger Waters and Nick Mason. Roger wasn't really playing an instrument then. He was still learning the guitar.

**Nick Mason:** I always borrow one of our college friends' quotes when asked about my first impressions of Roger Waters, but it's so true – 'Roger was a tall, menacing figure stood at the back of the classroom.' We were all in the same class: me, Roger and Rick [Wright] – DA1, Design Arch. 1. But Rick's position in the band was a bit tenuous because he didn't have a keyboard. So he would only play if the pub had a piano.

**Clive Metcalfe:** Rick Wright, who was a lovely, talented guy, was not really part of the set-up. We didn't have a name to start with. Then it became Sigma 6. We would just get together and play. I had a repertoire of songs from playing in the bistro – everything from Peter, Paul and Mary to the Beatles – but with the group we never seemed to get beyond an endless twelve-bar blues and [the Coasters'] 'Poison Ivy'.

We were called the Abdabs and the Screaming Abdabs, although we didn't do a lot of screaming [also the Meggadeaths, after the topical phrase for a million deaths by nuclear explosion]. Rick Wright's girlfriend Juliette [Gale, who was studying modern languages at the poly] would get up and sing 'Summertime' from *Porgy and Bess*.

I remember us all nearly getting electrocuted when we played a party at some student's flat. We also auditioned for EMI, but Roger spent too long tuning his guitar so they walked out. None of it was terribly serious.

**Roger Waters:** Encouragement to play my guitar came from the head of my first year. He encouraged me to bring the guitar into the classroom. If I wanted to sit in the classroom and play guitar during periods that were set aside for design work and architecture, he thought it was perfectly alright.

**Nick Mason:** Juliette and Rick both left the poly, and Rick, who was the most talented musically, went to music college instead. We stayed in touch with him, but this sort of left Roger and I in charge. Big mistake.

**Clive Metcalfe:** Nick's and Roger's education was very different from mine. I grew up in the country and had a fairly sheltered background at secondary school. Nick was easy going, but I struggled with Roger. He was acerbic and challenging, and I was an easy target. He could make a fool of me and I found that rather difficult.

Keith and I were also writing songs together and one of ours, 'A Summer Song', did nothing in the UK but became a US hit for a duo called Chad and Jeremy. I didn't get on well with Roger, so it seemed like a waste of time to carry on with them, so I left [in summer 1964]. I never met Syd Barrett, but Bob Klose was hanging around as he'd come to the poly to study architecture. He was a brilliant guitarist, but I thought he was a bit over-clever.

**Roger Waters:** With the advent of Bob Klose [in September '64], we actually had someone who could play an instrument. I was demoted from lead guitar to rhythm guitar and finally bass.

**Clive Metcalfe:** Really, the embryonic Pink Floyd came together once Keith and I withdrew. I joke that Pink Floyd owe all their money to me because if I hadn't left, they wouldn't have become so successful. It really didn't start to happen, though, until they met that guy who became their landlord.

✣

*'I'm sorry I didn't reply to your letter before,' says Mike Leonard over the phone. It's been several months since I wrote to him requesting an interview. But it feels impolite to mention that the project I wanted to interview him for has passed. No more is said and we agree to meet anyway.*

*For three years, from the end of 1963, all of what became Pink Floyd lodged at Leonard's three-storey house at 39 Stanhope Gardens, Highgate.*

*Leonard was an architect who lectured part-time at Regent Street Polytechnic and Hornsey School of Art.*

*He was around fifteen years older than his tenants, but lived alongside them with his bountiful collection of 78rpm blues records, a grand piano, a Balinese xylophone, Indian tablas, electronic echo chambers and two cats, who accessed the property via a permanently open letterbox.*

*In autumn 1964, just after he began studying at Camberwell, Syd Barrett joined Rado 'Bob' Klose in Waters and Mason's group. The Spectrum 5 or Leonard's Lodgers (the names changed repeatedly) sometimes rehearsed on Leonard's roof terrace, until they tired of hauling the drum kit up the stairs and chose to make an ungodly racket in the front room instead.*

*Leonard joined the group on keyboards at a private party in Oxshott and at pub gigs around Crouch End, alongside lead vocalist Chris Dennis, as neither Waters nor Barrett fancied singing.*

*Number 39 was something of a salon, then, with Barrett, Waters, Mason, Wright, Klose and various Floyd familiars passing through. Crucially, Leonard was also involved with Hornsey Art College's Light and Sound Workshop. He and his colleagues built light machines, using coloured glass, oil slides and metal pinwheels, which could project images in time to music. Leonard, his light machines and the sound of a noodling Pink Floyd later featured in a 1967 episode of the BBC science show,* Tomorrow's World.

*Long before then, the band provided the music for some of the Workshop's experiments and performed at least one gig, at Camberwell Art College, while Leonard's light show flashed images to accompany the band's rudimentary blues.*

*'The place hasn't changed much since the Floyd lived here,' said Leonard, when we finally met. There was something of Miss Havisham's wedding feast about the teetering piles of books and sheet music scattered about the place. When Leonard died in 2012 and the house was put up for auction, the attic was found to contain a Binson Echorec, an electronic delay unit of the type used by the early Floyd, preserved like some dusty relic in a pharaoh's tomb.*

*'A lot happened here,' Leonard told me. 'This is where they turned into what became the Pink Floyd.'*

❀

**Chris Dennis (Pink Floyd Blues Band/Pink Floyd Sound ex-vocalist):** I was a technician for the RAF at the airbase in Uxbridge, but I knew Bob Klose from Cambridge and bumped into him in a guitar shop in Soho. I wanted to play rhythm 'n' blues after seeing the Stones at the Rex Ballroom – and Bob told me they wanted to be a strict blues band. The band didn't even have a name then.

**Nick Mason:** Bob Klose was a great player, but Roger had this sense that if Syd joined the band, we could become a very different thing. We were told Syd was a Cambridge star. But when he finally arrived, he was terrific and very friendly. Some people at that time could be so very cool, but Syd wasn't like that. He was very open.

**Mike Leonard:** The neighbours were always complaining about the noise and even set up a petition. But Syd was charming, jolly and funny.

**Nick Mason:** Mike had two cats, Tunji [named after a John Coltrane song] and McGhee [after blues/folk musician Brownie McGhee]. The walls of his house were covered in hessian and he used to trail a kipper across it. Then he'd signal to the cats that it was mealtime by blowing a motor horn. The cats would fly up the walls until they found this kipper nailed to the ceiling.

**Roger Waters:** Mike liked to think that the cats needed to be entertained. He'd lock them in a room somewhere and then he'd take a piece of chicken, go all the way around the house, rubbing it on the hessian, and then hide it behind a curtain, before letting them out.

**Peter Dockley (ex-Hornsey Art College student and Floyd collaborator):** I moved into Stanhope Gardens later on, when Roger and Rick Wright had that front room, which I recall they shared with a very large pile of fish and chip papers.

**Nick Mason:** Rick wasn't in the band yet. But Mike Leonard played the piano and we persuaded him to buy a Farfisa organ and become our keyboard player.

**Mike Leonard:** I didn't know half the tunes they played, so I just joined in on the twelve-bar ones. I was more into boogie woogie – people like Pinetop Smith and Ferdinand Morton.

**Chris Dennis:** We used to rehearse at their landlord's – orange-painted walls, coconut matting and suits of armour around the place. We played private parties, college gigs.

**Nick Mason:** Syd's arrival was the biggest change, because he could write songs. We still played covers, but we now had some original material.

**Chris Dennis:** You get bands where there's usually one member that's there because he's a friend of somebody. I thought Syd was surplus to requirements and I didn't think he had the presence to be a frontman. Then he came down to the hall one night and said, 'We've got a name now – Pink Floyd.' The others all seemed to like it. I didn't. I got used to it but I didn't think it rang true at the time [the band performed as The Pink Floyd, the Pink Floyd Blues Band, the Pink Floyd Sound and the Tea Set in the coming months].

**Nick Mason:** Chris didn't really fit in with us. He used to do this thing on stage where he'd put a harmonica under his nose like Hitler's moustache and make up names for some of the songs, like 'Looking Through the Knotholes in Granny's Wooden Leg'.

**Chris Dennis:** I didn't think I *didn't* fit in. But I did make song titles up and Roger, who was the leader, would say, 'We shouldn't do that. We should tell them exactly what the song is called.' We were playing black blues that people didn't know anyway – Lightnin' Hopkins, Slim Harpo, Howlin' Wolf – so I said, 'It doesn't matter what we call the songs.' And that didn't go down too well either. They just didn't have any sense of humour. I must have been with the group for about six months, but it wasn't really my thing. I certainly had no indication of what they were going to become.

**Libby Chisman:** I used to stay at Stanhope Gardens. Who knows what was going on there. Mike was much older and their landlord but it was rather strange because he couldn't keep away from them. I think he saw the group's potential and wanted a foot in the door.

**Nick Mason:** Mike thought of himself as one of the group. We didn't, so I'm afraid we started leaving the house to play gigs without telling him – and then Rick joined.

*

*One of the enduring anecdotes from 39 Stanhope Gardens is the one about Rick Wright allegedly fitting a padlock to his food cupboard. Waters jokily blamed it as the source of all their future disagreements: 'He used to lock his fucking cornflakes up! How could there not be tension?'*

*This set in motion an intra-band joke in which Wright was cast as overly frugal with money. 'The cornflakes story' was later usurped by the 'Tokyo restaurant story', in which Wright refused to split the bill equally because his fellow diners had ordered an extra helping of prawns.*

*Both tales re-surfaced after Wright died in September 2008. 'I'm afraid,' admitted Mason, 'we also gave him this character and were quite happy to work on the same joke for forty-odd years, because it never gets boring especially when the person in question finds it irritating. The joke never changed. We never grew up, we just grew older.'*

*However, Mason conceded that Wright's natural diffidence meant his contribution to the group could be unfairly overlooked; 'the George Harrison of Pink Floyd', if you will.*

*The last time I met Rick Wright was backstage at the Olympia Theatre in Paris, where he was playing in David Gilmour's band. He was smoking a pre-gig cigarette, but looked a bit harried, which, in fairness, was his default setting. 'I'm getting a cold,' he announced wearily.*

*Exuberant European audiences had taken to chanting his name – 'Reeeechard!'– whenever he played the opening note to Pink Floyd's 'Echoes'. They adored him and Gilmour told interviewers how much he liked having him in the group. But one had the impression Wright was still unsure of his talents, even after all this time.*

*In Pink Floyd's winter 1974 tour programme, Richard William Wright was humorously described as a 'man with no history'. But he was the oldest member of the group, born in Hatch End, a suburb of Harrow, north-west London, on 28 July 1943, to biochemist Robert and his wife, Daisy. Educated at the local grammar school Haberdashers' Aske's, Wright was the one who taught his school bandmates how to master the songs on that first Buddy Holly LP.*

✲

***Disc and Music Echo* (8 April 1967):** 'Rick Wright plays organ. He is also 21, rather quiet, very easy going and exceedingly absent-minded, which explains why he locked the group's car and left the keys inside.'

**Paul Bailey (drummer in Wright's school group):** Our parents played bridge together – Rick's father was a bridge fanatic – and we lived around the corner from each other. Rick and I were both part of this middle-class gang and out of that came our little group who used to play at the youth club next to St Anselm's Church in Hatch End.

We were Rick Wright and the Rebels – not bad for four public schoolboys in white shirts and ties. Most of our gigs were at youth clubs, and it was all based on meeting girls, really. We played a couple of originals that were absolutely awful and a lot of covers. Rick played the guitar but was also having piano lessons and was the one arranging the songs. When Buddy Holly's first LP came out, we took it to Rick's and dissected it, because I was having trouble with the drum parts in 'Peggy Sue'.

**Richard Wright:** The first music I ever heard was classical because I was growing up in the days before rock 'n' roll. But then I was exposed to jazz and started listening to Humphrey Lyttelton and Kenny Ball, and then Miles Davis, John Coltrane...

**Paul Bailey:** Other than music, we did all the things teenagers usually do. After he left school, Rick got a job at the Kodak factory [near Harrow & Wealdstone station]. The band drifted apart when we all went off to college. I ended up playing in a big band and disappeared into obscurity. I didn't have any idea Rick was in Pink Floyd, until our old bass player, Mickey, phoned me up and told me to go to a record shop and have a look at this LP called *The Piper at the Gates of Dawn* – and there was Rick on the cover. Before then, I didn't have a clue.

**Richard Wright:** When I was at architecture school, the first thing they said was, 'Out of all of you, one of you might become an architect, and the half of you will be designing toilet systems in housing systems for London County Council, and the other half won't make the grade.'

**Nick Mason:** I don't think Rick was into architecture at all, and he quite rightly packed it in and went off to music college [the Royal College of Music]. Rick was the only one of us with any proper training, but the best things he did were the opposite of his classical training, and I'm glad they didn't knock that out of him.

Mike Leonard owned a keyboard and Rick didn't, so if there wasn't a piano at the venue, Rick would play guitar or trombone or sit out the gig. He was into trad jazz and he'd even worn the bowler hat, like Acker Bilk.

**Richard Wright:** I was fascinated by the piano. I'd just hit notes and work out the chords myself. Nobody told me where to put the fingers. Of course, my technique is completely wrong. I still can't play a scale in the way that you're meant to play it.

**Nick Mason:** When Rick was at music college, he wrote a proper pop song and sold it ['You're The Reason Why', recorded by a Liverpudlian trio, Adam, Mike and Tim, in 1964] – and that was before the rest of us were even operational. It was through a friend of Rick's that we managed to get some free time in a studio in West Hampstead.

❀

*The Pink Floyd began their first recording session in December 1964 at a studio in West Hampstead, via a recording engineer friend of Wright's named Paul Clay. This was the nascent Pink Floyd/the Tea Set, decked out in Cecil Gee ties and houndstooth jackets.*

*With Barrett singing lead vocals, the demo straddled blues, R&B and what the music press called 'beat pop'. There was a cover of Slim Harpo's 'I'm A King Bee', but also several Barrett originals: 'Lucy Leave', 'Double O Bo', 'Remember Me' and 'Butterfly', a slow jogging blues with Syd threatening to catch 'all you girlies' in his 'butterfly net'.*

*Also recorded was Waters' song 'Walk With Me Sydney' (a spoof of Hank Ballard and the Midnighters' 'Work With Me, Henry'), where Barrett shared lead vocals with Juliette Gale. Yet he was still unsure about being the group's lead vocalist, and, presciently, told Libby Chisman he wished Gilmour (whose nickname was 'Fred') was in the band with him.*

❀

**Jenny Spires:** It was Boxing Day 1964 and my brother Rod asked me if I wanted to go to a party at the Union Cellars. Rod was friends with Steve Pyle, and Syd was back in Cambridge playing bass in Steve's band. I had no idea they were called Those Without and I wasn't interested because I couldn't dance to them.

In the break, I was leaning against the bar drinking orange juice and Syd introduced himself: 'Hi, I'm Rog but people call me Syd … I'm at art school in London and in a band called Pink Floyd…' He was very bright and animated and told me, 'We've been doing some recording in London which we're going to finish when I get back.' I thought 'Pink Floyd' was a strange name, but I had some Mary Quant clothes with her flower logo on them and somehow I linked it to this.

I was still at the Cambridgeshire Grammar School for Girls, very shy and three years younger than Syd, but he had no airs or attitude. So when he suggested we meet up at the Guild coffee shop in the week, I agreed.

After the holidays, he started writing to me. The first one was a pink tissue letter written in black ink over a sketch of me standing at the bar in the Union Cellars.

**Chris Dennis:** I'd gone by then. They all wanted me gone, but I wasn't really into the music they were doing and the RAF posted me to Bahrain anyway. So that was that.

**Syd Barrett (letter to Jenny Spires, 10 January 1965):** 'Now we have got rid of Chris – Bob phoned him on Monday and yesterday he collected all his gear. Also, yesterday we went to the centre of London, and bought about £230 stuff to replace Chris's! Funny to think I, with my voice, will be singing through all that money. Now all we need is an electric piano for Rick and we're set ... Last night we had a huge Indian meal in Hampstead to celebrate.

'Very soon at school we are having an assessment of our work and then say whether they might throw you out in the summer. I think I'll be OK provided I can do two more good, large paintings. I'm thinking very hard...

'Last year I did a self-portrait which was an old shirt stuck to a board which they raved about, so I want to do something similarly kinky...

'Incidentally, a policeman came round to give us a writ, which said 'BE QUIET' in effect. If we don't [we] pay £5. We'll just have to pay up, I suppose, 'cos we can't possibly stop playing now. C'est la vie (I think).'

**Jenny Spires:** I visited Syd at Stanhope Gardens the day they were going into the studio to finish the demo. He was sharing a room with Roger Waters – and it was the first time I'd met Roger. Syd wanted me to stay and I didn't, so it was a bit awkward.

**Syd Barrett (letter to Jenny Spires, 17 January 1965):** 'I'll tell you everything that happened at the recording. We took all the gear into the studio, which was lit by horrid white lights and covered with wires and microphones. Rog had his amp behind the screen and Nick was also screened off and after a little bit of chat we tested everything for balance and then recorded five numbers more or less straight off but only the guitars and drums. We're going to add all the singing and piano etc. next Wednesday. The tracks sound terrific so far, especially 'King Bee'.

'When I sing, I have to stand in the middle of the studio with earphones on and everyone else watches from the other room, and I can't see them at all but they can all see me. Also I can only just hear what I am singing.'

'I hope you got home alright Jen, and that you had a good time. You wouldn't have been able to come into the recording and anyway it went on till after midnight and would have been a whopping drag for you … I am a bit fed up with everything today. And I want to be in Cambridge or Greece, but not in London, where all I do is spend money and travel.'

**Jenny Spires:** Stanhope Gardens was no place to be at the weekends either, and it seemed like everyone else was going home. Nick and Rick both had relationships with girls and were probably taking their washing home to their parents anyway.

Syd was always going back to Cambridge at weekends. I still had ballet classes on Saturday mornings and afterwards he'd meet me, and we'd walk into town before heading back to his mum's.

**Syd Barrett (letter to Jenny Spires, 24 January 1965):** 'As I'm very ill this week, I'm writing to you in bed. My wisdom tooth is pushing up and cutting the gum like MAD and fuck it hurts. So I'm not about and twisting, but I am groovy groovey to Radio London … Yesterday the lovely blond Paul Clay came round with our records! Hooray, they're not very good and we're going to put some more singing and sax and trombone and clapping on them next week.'

**Syd Barrett (letter to Libby Chisman, circa January 1965):** 'Emo says why don't I give up as I sound horrible, and he's right, and I would, but I can't get "Fred" [David Gilmour] to join as he's got a group … So I still have to sing.'

**Nick Mason:** It was great to have our own rehearsal space, but it made it impossible to study. So I'd moved back to my parents' house and Bob

Klose had taken my place in the room. Then Syd moved into the room with Roger, then Rick...

**Syd Barrett (letter to Jenny Spires, 28 January 1965):** 'Now I am in school Wednesday. And I'm writing this in the lunch hour in the library. I've just bought this pen, and it cost me a shilling. The bloke said do you want a pen to keep or throw away? And I said I could only afford a cheap one. So he gave me one to throw away, but I kept it so I could write a letter to you.

'My tooth came out with great ease. And I was out in about 3 minutes. Didn't hurt at all! Now at last I can close my mouth and eat ... Also I don't have to have any pills, but he said I should probably have to have another wisdom tooth out soon.

'Today I have tried to do some pottery. I wanted to make a mug but I can't even manage to do that yet and used up tons of clay and I got fed up and came up here....

'I have just been looking at the notice board here and there are several rooms advertised but without any price. I think I'll find them in a minute. Just for interest, Bob [Klose] was saying yesterday that he was considering leaving the flat because he never gets any work done, so it looks as though something a bit drastic could happen. I should like a room to myself anyway. You can have too much of Roger, even though he's a good mate.'

**Nick Mason:** We sent out the demo tape and went to lots of auditions, including for [the ITV music show] *Ready Steady Go!*, but everybody turned us down. Then, in spring 1965, we managed to get a residency at a little club off Kensington High Street called the Countdown.

**Syd Barrett (letter to Jenny Spires, 28 January 1965):** 'On Thursday we're going to finish off those recordings, I hope, and that'll be that. We haven't heard from the Countdown yet, but it should arrive before long. It's rather nerve-racking waiting, because we had a similar audition at Beat City in Oxford Street, and they said forget it. But we didn't!

'By the way Jen, don't forget my sister's [Ruth] wedding on Saturday, if you'd like to come. I'm going to be an usher. They're using my room for the reception, and I've got to take down all the pornography! But after that I can do what I like in there, including putting paint on the walls. Beatniks...

'Twistravegrooveyhipblockedtwistravegrooveyroo... Now I shall go and do another pot if I can.'

**Jenny Spires:** His room at 183 was sparse – a single bed, quite low, like a divan. No headboard. Above the bed, a small oil painting, a still life of a green glass bottle. There was rush matting on the floor, a small amp, an electric guitar against the wall, an acoustic guitar against the wall at the foot of the bed. A tall, paint-spattered easel in the middle of the floor and, in the alcove of the chimney breast to the left, stacks of canvases, and there was that lovely smell of turps or linseed.

**Syd Barrett (letter to Jenny Spires, 26 February 1965):** 'Tonight I went to the 100 Club in Oxford Street – twisteavegrooveygroove – and saw the best group in the world except for the Stones and the Beatles. They are called the Tridents and their lead guitarist [Jeff Beck] looks a bit like Mick Jagger and the drummer is very pretty...

'Dear Jen, your letters always sound like you don't care a bugger and when I'm in Cambridge you act like you don't care a bugger. Perhaps you don't give a bugger! Oh well, come to think of it I never asked you whether you wanted to go out with me or not; so perhaps you don't really; your [sic] just too kind to say anything (pause while I slip into a large puddle of self pity on the floor)...

'I have written a song about Bob Dylan. Yeh! Yeh! Soul God etc. "I got the Bob Dylan blues and the Bob Dylan shoes and my hair an' my clothes in a mess, but you know I just couldn't care less." In fact a bit satirical and humorous...'

**Vivien Brans:** David and I had a break and I went out with Syd for a while. It was when he was back from Camberwell. Syd drew a picture of my young nephew, Philip, which I still have.

Syd and I had fun together. We used to dye our clothes if we were going out for an evening – 'Shall we go purple tonight?'. But if I was going out with somebody, I wanted to be with them and I don't want all these other people around. You'd go to Syd's and his mum would wheel in a trolley of food and tea – 'Here you are, Rog' – and all these other people would start to arrive, and I'd think 'Oh dear, no'.

I saw Syd in London and he took me to the Planetarium and then to the Countdown where he was playing with Pink Floyd. They were just starting out and I didn't like it at all. It was a dingy little place. Rick was very sweet and Roger didn't even look at me.

**Roger Waters:** We were still doing things like Rufus Thomas's 'Walking The Dog', Wilson Pickett and a lot of Bo Diddley. We had quite a wide repertoire of other people's stuff.

**Nick Mason:** We'd play from nine o'clock at night until two in the morning – anything in the hit parade, including the Stones and Beatles. Then, after three weeks, the Countdown had a noise injunction served on them. So we persuaded them to let us play acoustically – with Rick on the upright piano – doing things like 'Long Tall Texan'. We were *that* desperate.

**Vivien Brans:** One night, Syd turned up at my house in Cambridge and knocked on the door – 'I've come to see you, Twig.' 'Oh,' I said, 'OK.' Then he told me he'd walked all the way from London. I don't know if I believed him, but I'd gone off him a bit by then.

**Syd Barrett (letter to Jenny Spires, 15 May 1965):** 'I'm longing to see you again on Friday. We shall come to Cambridge during the day [to play the Homerton Summer Dance on 22 May] and arrive at about five ... Apparently it's a ball, so you'd better wear a dress or something, Jenny...'

**Jenny Spires:** I went with Syd to see them play the Homerton Summer Dance – or the May Ball as we called it. We picked up Roger Waters as they were going to rehearse first at their old school, the County. Judy Trim arrived and Roger rolled down the window and said, 'Here she is, my beautiful girl, all dressed in pink.' And she was. She had on this little pink mini and a pink top with boots.

Syd had suggested I wear a dress, so I'd bought one in Wallis but had no shoes with heels, so I wore an old pair of ballet shoes I'd bought from Galeries Lafayette. I also met Juliette [Gale] and Lindy [Rutter, Mason's future wife], and I was in awe of them both. They were amazing women, and Lindy had been a ballet dancer in New York.

All the gear was set up in the common room and they started doing 'Louie Louie' with Syd singing. Bob Klose had left the band by then, but I remember him being there too.

**Richard Wright:** I think Bob had some exam problems and felt he ought to apply himself to work, whereas the rest of us weren't so conscientious.

**Rado 'Bob' Klose:** I left the Pink Floyd because I felt it was time to change direction. I felt adrift. The question everybody asks is, 'Would I have left had I known what was going to happen with the Floyd?'. And, probably, I wouldn't, but I still should have.

I have good memories of being in the Floyd. But I never thought, *This is something I could make a living out of*. It was a very college-y thing, a bit arty. Back then, most people probably thought you couldn't make a career out of it. But the music we were playing before was influenced by the fact that I was such a facile guitar player – always whizzing around. Syd's writing gave them the push to stop doing R&B covers and go off in a more original direction. Syd had begun to write his own songs and I could already see he was going to become an irresistible force in this band.

I became a photographer and I wouldn't have picked up on that had I stayed in Pink Floyd – and that would have been a huge mistake in my life. But, looking back, if you were to have asked me, 'What would Dave Gilmour have become?', I would always have said, 'a musician'. But with Syd, I always thought he was going to become a painter.

**Syd Barrett (letter to Jenny Spires, 15 May 1965):** 'This week the group has split up, as I thought it would and we're not playing together again after Cambridge, but that will probably make it more fun when we do play.'

**Jenny Spires:** He was sad when he thought the band was over in the summer of '65. He loved playing and he'd been writing little songs with his guitar long before I met him, so he was in limbo. The others had all finished their courses at the poly, but he was three years younger. He also complained that travelling from north London to Camberwell was getting him down.

**Seamus O'Connell:** I'd done well at the County and they had me down as heading for Cambridge University. Then I went a bit off my nut, due to a disturbed family background. So my mother, Ella, decided to go to London and I decided to go with her to retake my A-levels. My mother wanted to live in Tottenham Street because it had a W1 post-code, but [number 12] was a rundown transient place, really scruffy and quite unpleasant, with a greasy spoon café underneath it. Others from Cambridge ended up renting rooms there and David Gale and Syd moved in for a bit.

**David Gale:** That flat was in a street opposite the department store Heals, and Syd and I had a scummy little room there for a few months. I was taking a year off before starting my film school course at the Royal College of Art and working at Better Books [the beat literature bookshop on Charing Cross Road]. I remember Syd and I going to London Zoo and seeing a baboon picking shit out of its arse and eating it. Syd drew a picture of this and pinned it on the wall of our awful room. I think Ella O'Connell introduced him to the *I Ching*, too. Ella was very interested in such things.

**Seamus O'Connell:** She would do palm readings and tarot readings, but only if asked. Not many people's mothers did that in those days. She and Syd always got on well. On the day of my wedding, years later, they sloped off to the pub together.

**Roger Waters:** Syd's interest in the *I Ching* produced 'Chapter 24' [on *The Piper at the Gates of Dawn*]. To start playing around with those kind of ideas was radical. You could also say his attachment to Kenneth Grahame and Hilaire Belloc and those kind of influences was radical too, because you didn't expect that kind of literary middle-class stuff to surface in rock 'n' roll.

**Rosemary Breen:** Something like being able to walk through a wardrobe into another world, like in [CS Lewis's] *The Lion, the Witch and the Wardrobe* appealed to his brain – the idea that you could make something magically happen.

**Syd Barrett (letter to Jenny Spires, August 1965):** 'Dear Jenny, I was in Cambridge last weekend, but I didn't see you. I thought I would. It was sunny on Sunday (rhyme). But never mind, the group is nearly not anymore, but it doesn't matter. I'm sorry if all this is difficult to understand. I will just draw, I can't write. I hope you are alright and the [Cambridge] Tech [where Jenny was now studying] is okay ... When I was at the Tech last it seemed a bit of a shambles with little kids puffing at the herb in every dusty corner. Bye bye for now, love Roger.'

**Jenny Spires:** After my birthday in July, he'd asked me if I'd like to go to *Ready Steady Go!* with him. The tickets were the consolation prize for not winning the band competition. He was sad that the band wasn't playing anymore, but it was the summer holidays and that's when Syd went off to France with David Gilmour.

**David Gilmour:** Syd and I were friends by this time and I met up with him in the south of France [in August 1965 to stay at Claude Picasso's mother Françoise's house in Vallauris]. He had gone with another friend of ours in a Land Rover and I'd hitch-hiked on my own earlier.

We camped together and then we got arrested for busking in Saint-Tropez. Then we came back to Paris and went round the stalls by the Seine and bought books that were illegal in England – *Story of O* and *The Naked Lunch* – and went back to our campsite, read them by torchlight and got nervous on the ferry back to England because we were worried we would get busted for ownership of illegal books.

Syd was delightful company. He had a natural poetic gift for words. If you were with him, he'd be punning – 'I've got aches in Aix-en-Provence! I've stayed too long in Toulon!'

**Syd Barrett (letter to Jenny Spires, September 1965):** 'Dear Jenny, it's very wet here today, Tuesday. Sort of yellowing grey. But it is funny to see everybody rushing around with scowls on their faces, as if water could do them any harm. But it will be nice when summer comes, and it's all beautiful blue in the evenings with the windows open. I spent most of yesterday cleaning up my room and now I am cooking some food. It makes everything smell for days but I tried to counteract it with hundreds of joss sticks. It would be nice to see you in the holidays, Jenny. And nice to talk to you. Love Roger, please write if you feel like it.'

✣

*Summer 1965, then, and Pink Floyd had effectively split up. Waters took a job in an architect's office (designing bank vaults); Mason moved into his girlfriend's parents' house near Guildford and began working for his future father-in-law, architect Frank Rutter; and Wright and Juliette Gale disappeared to Greece.*

*In the meantime, Doug and Sylvia Gilmour were now living in Manhattan while their son's group, Jokers Wild, had become the darlings of the Cambridge club scene.*

*Pink Floyd (possibly now calling themselves the Tea Set – memories are conflicted) didn't get back together again until 30 October, when they and Jokers Wild were booked to play the same social function. Storm Thorgerson's girlfriend, Libby January, and her twin sister Rosie were celebrating their 21st birthday at the family home, Milton House, in Great Shelford. Their father, Douglas, was a well-known local estate agent and the house's sweeping lawn and French windows later appeared on the cover of Pink Floyd's* Ummagumma *LP.*

*The guests broadly fell into two camps: sensible young couples at one end of the garden's marquee, and the 'ragged band' (to quote the Floyd song 'High Hopes') of 'Pip', 'Emo' etc at the other.*

*Paul Simon, an up-and-coming American folk singer spending the summer in Cambridge, roamed the house and the marquee playing his acoustic guitar. Then the Pink Floyd/Tea Set in matching white shirts, blue jackets and blue Levi's (aside from Barrett who'd gone rogue with white jeans) offered their ramshackle take on Chuck Berry, while Jokers Wild performed their slick repertoire of Beatles and Beach Boys hits. Then everyone trooped off into the garden to watch the fireworks.*

*Douglas January later offered film student Thorgerson a blank cheque in exchange for never seeing his daughter again. Storm refused.*

✿

**David Gilmour:** I felt pretty superior, I have to say. Syd was very talented and Rick was a good musician, but Nick and Roger were fairly pedestrian at that time. The Pink Floyd were possibly more original than what we were doing, but we could do all sorts of wonderful harmonies.

Paul Simon got up and jammed with us on 'Johnny B. Goode', which I told him about years later – and he was quite surprised. I'm sure he did [Simon & Garfunkel's future hit] 'The Sound of Silence' in his own set. The folk singing bard! He wasn't bad.

**Aubrey 'Po' Powell:** There was an obvious divide, which is why Douglas January made Storm an offer: 'I'd rather you didn't go out with my daughter, so what do you want? What will it take?' I think he regarded us all as a bunch of reprobates.

**Rosemary Breen:** I don't know if he [Syd] was happy at Camberwell, but he seemed to get into a lot of other stuff, including drugs, terribly quickly.

**David Gale:** We'd all heard about [American psychologist and LSD advocate] Timothy Leary and we'd all read Aldous Huxley's *The Doors of Perception* and wondered how to get hold of this wonder drug. We managed it without very much effort, as people simply brought it down from London on blotting paper. Each blot had 500 microgrammes – no mucking about.

**Iain 'Emo' Moore:** Summer 1965 was the first acid summer in Cambridge. But Syd and I took Morning Glory seeds together first. You could buy them legally from a florist in Cambridge. You had to take 500 seeds, but once you made it past the retching pain in the guts, you started flying and seeing fairies. Syd and I turned up at Dave Gale's house after taking it.

**David Gale:** Oh yes, the famous afternoon at my parents' house... They'd gone to Australia for the summer, leaving me in the house alone, and various people, including Emo, sort of moved in. That afternoon, Syd had supposedly taken something and he went into my parents' kitchen and came back with a plum, an orange and a matchbox, and became utterly engrossed in them, as one does on psychedelics.

**Storm Thorgerson:** Syd seemed to be fascinated by those items. This is why years later Hipgnosis put a photo of a plum, an orange and a matchbox on the cover of Syd's album [1974's *Barrett* reissue]. It was a coded message for those of us who'd been there that afternoon.

**Nigel Lesmoir-Gordon:** I took it with Syd twice and he definitely became stranger and more distant. Quite immediately, I noticed a profound change. One weekend in Cambridge, myself, my wife Jenny, David Gale, Andrew Rawlinson, his girlfriend Lucy Pryor, Syd Barrett and another friend of ours, Russell Page, went out to the chalkpits in the Gog Magog Hills.

I was studying at the London School of Film Technique and borrowed an 8mm camera from a mate, took it back home and filmed Syd and the others in this quarry. Jenny's the one wearing a Mary Quant mac and talking to a tree. Syd was perfectly happy to be filmed – it wasn't planned, it was entirely unself-conscious.

But I never called the film *Syd's First Trip* and I'm not convinced it was his first trip either. The film was bootlegged and ended up on the internet, so [Pink Floyd's later manager] Steve O'Rourke bought it off me. I suppose David Gilmour and Nick Mason own it now. But it's still on the internet.

**David Gale:** It's just a film of a group of young people messing around – nothing more than that.

**Vivien Brans:** Libby and I never touched a drug, ever. We knew it was going on, but it was never pushed on us. No one said 'Oh go on…' They respected us. I remember seeing Pip Carter climbing the walls after taking a sugar cube with LSD, and being at a house in Mill Road and people began to take drugs and I think it was Storm who said, 'Would you rather not be here, Twig?'.

There was also an incident when Syd and I went to a party at Dr Alice Roughton's [later a CND campaigner and psychiatrist] house. We were sitting on the grass, chatting, and then suddenly he went – didn't say a word, disappeared. Then I saw him over the other side of the garden and he didn't come back, so I decided to go home.

I started walking and he drove up beside me in his rickety old blue car and told me to get in. But I refused. I think he'd taken something and that's why he disappeared. In the morning, my dad passed me a letter that had come through the door and it was from Syd saying, 'I'm sorry'.

**Rosemary Breen:** The other problem with my brother was he was always looking for the next thing – and that applied to drugs: 'Oh, if I take one of these and feel like this, what will I feel like when I take two?' We all have a bit of that in us, but most people know when to stop. He didn't.

**David Gale:** By this time, though, we were also seeing a split in our social group. One of our friends, Paul Charrier, had been with him at my parents' house that afternoon when Syd was tripping. Paul, an energetic, bombastic but loveable fellow, went to the toilet, while on acid, and found a book called *Yoga and Bible* [*Yoga and the Bible: The Yoga of the Divine World* about the Indian mystic Huzur Maharaj Charan Singh Ji] and, while having a shit, had this revelation that *this* was where it was at.

Paul came out of the toilet a changed man and announced that he was now going to India to see this guru. It was the acid talking, but in his case it transformed his life.

Within a few weeks, he was off to India [to an ashram in Beas] and came back after six weeks having been initiated into the master's path of teaching [known as 'Sant Mat'] and given a series of spiritual tasks. Paul became a follower – called 'satsangi'– and cut off his hair, bought a suit, became depressingly ordinary looking, got a job and began proselytising like mad – no drugs, no alcohol, just meditation.

At which point, Andrew Rawlinson and other key figures fucked off to Delhi and converted. Then they *all* came back, proselytising again, and converted a whole load more people, while the other half of us were going, 'This is bollocks!'. But Syd would have read the books and have been forced to do so by Paul and Paul was insufferably full of it – 'This guru is God, what are we waiting for.' So Syd was very interested in following the path.

The master used to come to London to meet his British followers, some of whom were quite ancient and came from the back end of the Raj era. He would check into a Bloomsbury hotel and give an audience – this very pleasant bloke in his sixties with a big beard wearing a turban. Syd went along, met the master to see if he could be initiated and the master told him he wasn't ready.

**Storm Thorgerson:** The master told Syd he should complete his studies. To some extent, I think that was a problem. But, in hindsight, you think all sorts of things about people's fragile personalities. I went to see the master too and thought he was very good. He told me two things: don't eat meat and use your intellect. He had a strong presence, but then gurus do because of the people giving them a lot of attention.

**Nigel Lesmoir-Gordon:** Syd turned up at our place after meeting the master and told me he wasn't smoking dope anymore. But I handed him a joint and he still took it.

✲

*'What about 1pm next Monday? Walk N from the Angel on W side of the road about 50 yards. There are 2 noodle bars separated by a fast pizza firm. I prefer the one next to Abbey Bank (the Thai noodle bar). We can sit at the back its fairly quiet (I wear floral hats & a pony tail) OK? Hop.'*

*Despite John 'Hoppy' Hopkins' simple emailed instructions, on the day I went to the wrong noodle bar and presumed he was running fashionably late. When I did call him, 'Hoppy', who'd returned to his flat, launched into a schoolmasterly tirade about wasting his time. He was quite right and I could only apologise.*

*John 'Hoppy' Hopkins' back story was fascinating. After studying natural sciences at Cambridge, he became a nuclear physicist at the Harwell Atomic Energy Research Establishment. Then, in 1958, he and a group of bohemian friends travelled to Moscow in a repurposed hearse, adorned with a CND symbol.*

*The* Daily Mirror *reported on the Moscow trip and MI5 offered Hopkins a job. Unwilling to become a spy and disillusioned with Harwell, he joined CND and tried his luck as a photographer.*

*Hopkins was present at the birth of London's counterculture, centred around the alternative bookshop Better Books, the Indica Gallery (where Yoko Ono staged her first UK exhibition) and his flat in Westbourne Terrace, where he put up visiting American poets and jazz musicians, and was later busted for marijuana.*

*'Hoppy' was always big on what he called 'the democratisation of information' and compiled a list of the names and numbers of 'London's movers and shakers' – musicians, poets, activists, actors, artists and Pink Floyd's future managers Peter Jenner and Andrew King.*

*In March 1966, he, Jenner, King and an American record company scout Joe Boyd were among the founders of the London Free School, a community hub in then rundown Notting Hill. 'The work of patronising middle-class intellectuals,' commented one critic. Hoppy began a Free School newsletter,* The Grove, *which became a springboard for the UK's first underground newspaper,* International Times.

*Hoppy's tirade was a reminder then that there was more to him than the grinning stoner portrayed in some accounts of the '60s. I let the dust settle and emailed him a week later, asking if we could try again. 'Sure, no problem, never was,' he replied.*

*'Hoppy' showed up at the restaurant, with his floral hat and ponytail, and told me he was just back from Goa. Unbeknown to me then, he'd recently been diagnosed with Parkinson's Disease.*

*When he sat down, he placed a sheaf of papers on the table, each one covered in his meticulous script. It was then I realised good timekeeping and neat handwriting were prerequisites for a lapsed nuclear physicist trying to corral a bunch of beat poets and nascent hippies.*

*'You need to speak to Steve Stollman,' he said, passing me his phone number…*

✿

**Steve Stollman (organiser of the 'Spontaneous Underground' happenings at London's Marquee, 1966):** My brother Bernard had started ESP Records in New York which was putting out weird records by people like Albert Ayler, Sun Ra and the Fugs. I'd done a little bit of work for them, but I was interested in getting out of the United States. I wasn't happy with the world and the way things were – like most people of twenty-one years old. So I went to London and was told to go to Better Books, which is where I was introduced to Miles and 'Hoppy' and all these amazing people.

**Barry Miles (author, manager of Better Books and co-founder of *International Times*):** We stocked a lot of underground magazines and visiting Americans came to visit. I arranged for Allen Ginsberg to do a poetry reading that was so popular we had to keep the shop door open so people could listen from the street.

**Steve Stollman:** Barry Miles was funnelling politically inspired, culturally daring information through underground newspapers or poetry or whatever he thought would shake things up, and I wanted to help my brother get some visibility for his label. Frankly, I don't know who came up with the idea to put on an event. But I went to the Marquee and spoke to a woman with a very English surname and her husband [club owners Barbara and Harold Pendleton] and arranged to rent the place on a Sunday when nobody else wanted it.

The whole thing was arranged as a benefit for [the therapist] RD Laing's Kingsley Hall [a social experiment where therapists and patients lived together in a communal house in east London]. There was a lot of interest in this idea, a lot of admiration for Laing and we raised a few bucks.

**Nigel Lesmoir-Gordon:** I met Steve Stollman and arranged for what was then called the Tea Set – they'd not yet reverted to the Pink Floyd – to play the Marquee. It was a jamming session and nobody else wanted the Marquee on a Sunday afternoon. I'm not musical, but me and Russell Page jumped up on stage with them, dancing and playing the tambourine.

**Jeff Dexter (future record producer and club DJ):** These sort of 'happenings' started in 1966. People were creating alternative scenes around town. Jay Landesman had the Electric Garden in Covent Garden, and Keith Albarn, father of Blur's Damon Albarn, had 26 Kingly Street, which was a gallery with art installations, lights, sounds, foam, smoke and mirrors – very original stuff. Then you had Cream going 'Bomp bomp bomp bomp bomp / I feel free'. I went to the Spontaneous Underground at the Marquee and I didn't really get it at the time.

**Barry Miles:** Donovan arrived, wearing thick black kohl and henna eye make-up, each eye drawn with an Egyptian eye of Horus. The next day, he had no memory of ever being there.

**Steve Stollman:** I didn't know the Pink Floyd from the Green Floyd. But they played a few of these Sunday afternoon happenings for us [most likely beginning on 13 March]. They played for a long time. I swear it was three hours but nobody wanted to stop them, as it was very much in the spirit of the times.

**Roger Waters:** Bob Klose leaving had a lot to do with us stopping playing blues. When he left, we hadn't anyone who had any blues knowledge, so we had to start doing something else. So we started making strange noises instead of the blues. I found if you turned the bass up loud, used a plectrum to bang it hard, it made strange noises, clicking noises.

**Seamus O'Connell:** I was into jazz and blues and was a bit snotty about the Floyd when they started. I even turned down an invitation to see them in a pub in Crouch End – 'No, no, no, *far* too noisy.'

**Nick Mason:** We were used to playing parties and suddenly we were being encouraged to develop the extended solos that we'd only really put into the songs to pad them out during our Countdown Club residency.

**John 'Hoppy' Hopkins:** Pop music was opening up – the Byrds had made *Mr Tambourine Man* and the Beatles had made *Rubber Soul*. There was this tremendous cross-fertilisation between jazz and blues and soul and white music. We were getting everything from John Cage on the one hand to Georgie Fame on the other and everything that lay between.

My context for listening to the Pink Floyd was what the Velvet Underground were doing with their wall of sound. My girlfriend brought back tapes of the Velvet Underground playing live in New York. So the Floyd fitted into that. The first thing I noticed at the Marquee was their sound and the coloured lights.

**Mike Leonard:** I asked the group if they wanted to come to the workshop in Hornsey and play music while I projected my images. We did it a few times. They were still playing stuff like 'Green Onions', but I encouraged them to get away from that standard 4/4 thing into more free rhythms.

**Roger Waters:** The idea of us playing to a light show came when we did a gig at Essex University [on 11 and 12 March] and someone showed a film on the wall next to us while we were playing. Then we discovered how to do it with bubbles and oils.

**Peter Jenner (Pink Floyd's co-manager, 1966–68):** I went to one of those Spontaneous Underground events [in June '66]. I was lecturing at the London School of Economics, but was a bit of an avant-garde music nut and I knew Steve Stollman, because I'd founded [the independent label] DNA Records with 'Hoppy'. It was similar to what Bernard Stollman was doing with ESP, except we only put out one record.

It was a Sunday afternoon, I was bored of marking exam papers, so I went down to the Marquee. The Pink Floyd were doing one of these standard bluesy songs like 'Dust My Broom' or 'Louie Louie', and Syd would take a solo but instead of the usual howling, wailing guitar, there'd be this strange noise.

I didn't listen to much pop music – I got into black R&B, a bit of Bob Dylan and the Byrds – but I didn't think white men could sing the blues. Pink Floyd didn't sound like anything else I'd heard, and I rather liked that. I suppose I was naive. They were very avant-garde and I thought I was too, and it was all going to be very beautiful, man. Let's have another hit on the joint and all that.

After the show, I asked if they wanted to be on our record label and Roger told us what they really needed was a manager. They were still fooling around, but quite serious in a sort of semi-pro way. Some of them were still living out in Highgate with Mike Leonard and I went to see Roger there. He told me everyone was going on holiday and we could talk again in September.

**Nick Mason:** By then, I was already in America, looking at great buildings as part of my architectural studies. My girlfriend Lindy was there working as a ballet dancer and we had a $99 Greyhound bus ticket. I remember seeing Thelonious Monk but also the Fugs in New York, whom I suppose were like the beginnings of psychedelia. In New York, we came across a counterculture paper [*East Village Other*] and there was an article in there [written by Barry Miles] which mentioned 'the up-and-coming Pink Floyd Sound'. It made me realise that the band had some potential.

**Nigel Lesmoir-Gordon:** That summer, Jenny and I went to the Greek island of Patmos, with other people from Cambridge, including Roger Waters and his girlfriend Judy, but also Rick Wright. Roger had a Chrysler-Plymouth which he'd had sprayed pink and we drove it across Europe, until it broke down in Germany.

**Jenny Lesmoir-Gordon:** Rick Wright was driving and we woke up in the middle of the night to find that it would only go backwards – and we were on the autobahn. Rick reversed it off the road to a garage, where the mechanic told us it had gone kaput. So we made our way to Greece by train. But Roger was always putting Rick down. It was like he was using him as his punchbag.

**Richard Wright:** There was friction between Roger and I when we were still students at Regent Street Polytechnic. There was this thing between us. We would not choose to be friends, even at this time.

**Jenny Lesmoir-Gordon:** When we reached Patmos, we stayed in this old house and Roger and Judy – she called him 'Roge' and he called her 'Ju Ju' – insisted on having the best room. I think Roger and Rick had their first acid trip there. Poor Rick stayed out in the sun too long and ended horribly sunburnt and Roger stood in the corner looking out the window for ages.

**Roger Waters:** It wasn't what you'd get on bits of blotting paper or sugar cubes. This was off a dropper out of a bottle and it was pure lysergic. It was an extraordinary experience and it lasted about forty-eight hours. I took some more a couple of years later in New York City. And I thought, *No, I don't want to ever do this again*.

**Peter Jenner:** DNA Records had received some money via an American we'd met called Joe Boyd, who was living in London and working for Elektra Records. We had a very avant-garde, improvisational group called AMM, who played the Spontaneous Underground and made a record for us [*AMMMusic*], and I think were an influence on Syd.

AMM later played on the same bill as the Floyd and Syd watched their guitarist, Keith Rowe, who used to use a cigarette lighter and ball bearings on the strings. But we still needed a pop group, even an avant-garde pop group. So, after the holidays, I asked my friend, Andrew King, if he was interested in doing something with the Pink Floyd.

**Andrew King (Pink Floyd's early co-manager):** Originally, Peter and Joe Boyd were going to run DNA Records and I was going to manage the band. I had a job in public relations at British European Airways – I knew nothing about managing groups.

**John 'Hoppy' Hopkins:** We were all quite networked. I remember taking an acid trip with Andrew King and I must have met Peter Jenner through him. My name was on the *Grove* as secretary, so I was paying for the production of the newsletter. Although I'd been doing rather well in Fleet Street as a photographer in the early '60s, by this time I was getting poorer and poorer, and I realised I couldn't afford to go on paying for this, so we decided to hold a benefit which turned into a series of benefits, involving the Pink Floyd.

**Roger Waters:** Jenner and King were good, middle-class vicars' sons with degrees from good universities.

**Peter Jenner:** We did what nice middle-class vicars' sons do and we held a fundraiser in a church – the All Saints Hall [in Powis Gardens] – and we asked Pink Floyd to play.

**Joe Boyd (Pink Floyd's first producer):** I was opening the London office of Elektra Records and, around the summer of '66, Peter and Andrew said, 'There's this group that we want you to hear, and here's a tape.' Then they played at the church at a benefit to raise funds for the London Free School. And I heard them there and I thought they were terrific.

**Roger Waters:** What was the Free School all about? What was it meant to do? I never gathered what it was.

**John 'Hoppy' Hopkins:** The Free School was in the basement of 26 Powis Terrace. It was owned by a guy called John Michelle, an upper-class eccentric who wrote about flying saucers and ley lines. [The civil rights activist] Michael De Freitas [aka Michael X] was instrumental in getting the loan of the building and arranged for us to use it. The Free School was an open-ended idea rubbing shoulders with other things that were happening. The Notting Hill Carnival didn't actually start there, but it enabled people to claim that's where it started.

**Emily Young (née Kennet, sculptor):** I used to go there because I was a troubled teenager and really bored at Holland Park School. I was a bit of a raver, as we used to say. The Free School was like an open university and you could just turn up there. There were tramps, or vagabonds, you might say now. There were junkies, artists, poets, scientists, visionaries. The idea was lots of people could come together and discuss the new ways of thinking.

I was a good beatnik, but very young. So my ears were flapping and I couldn't believe what I was hearing and seeing. It was magical for me – a real education, but quite heavy in some ways because there were a lot of drug opportunities. So there was a certain amount of sitting around, smoking joints. I met Syd Barrett, though I don't remember any mind-shattering conversations with him.

**Andrew King:** I saw Pink Floyd at All Saints Church Hall [30 September 1966, on a bill with Soft Machine]. They were doing 'Candy and a Currant Bun' [still called 'Let's Roll Another One'], which ended up as the B-side of 'Arnold Layne'. But I really remember 'Louie Louie' and thinking it sounded weird, but Syd exuded the magnetism of a true performer.

**Emily Young:** I was there dancing with my friend from school, Angelica Huston. Angelica was staggeringly beautiful and I no doubt had my charms at that time. Syd apparently said, 'Who are those two girls?'. And someone said, 'Oh, one of them, her father's a lord, and he's in the government [Wayland Young, 2nd Baron Kennet], and the other one is the famous film director John Huston's daughter.'

**Andrew King:** After the gig I said to the band, 'We'd like to be your managers', and I clearly remember Nick Mason saying, 'Well, no one else wants to be, so you might as well'. And that was it.

**Peter Jenner:** Andrew and I formed a company called Blackhill Enterprises with the Floyd. We named it 'Blackhill' after a Welsh cottage that Andrew's family owned. Andrew also had a small inheritance from an aunt who'd died. The Floyd needed some equipment, so we bought them some, they put it in a van and it got stolen that night.

**Roger Waters:** There were about twenty people [at the All Saints Hall] when we first played, the second week 100. And, after that, many couldn't get in.

**John Leckie (future Floyd engineer and producer):** I grew up around Ladbroke Grove and saw them at those London Free School gigs. You'd be watching the light show and someone would jump up and start doing that 'idiot dancing', as we called it. But this was in a space sometimes used as a school hall, so there'd be all these little kids' table and chairs. Incongruous.

**Joe Boyd:** I brought Chris Blackwell [Island Records founder] down to see them too at the All Saints Hall and he didn't like them.

**Nick Mason:** When it came to psychedelia – or what people were calling 'the underground' – I still think Pink Floyd were in the right place at the right time. Syd was part of it, but the rest of us were just college kids along for the ride. We weren't deep into it, the way 'Hoppy' or maybe even Syd was. We just turned up and played the gig.

❀

*Barrett and the Cambridge crowd were now billeted across London. David Gale, Seamus O'Connell and, later, Syd, were at 2 Earlham Street, a spindly Dickensian tower overlooking Cambridge Circus.*

*The Lesmoir-Gordons had a flat (where Nigel kept phials of LSD in the refrigerator) at 101 Cromwell Road, a Regency terrace in London SW7 which attracted a shifting coterie of students, artists, teenage runaways and common or garden drug fiends.*

*Waters lodged there for a time and invited the Pink Floyd to rehearse in the kitchen with their primitive light show set up among the filthy crockery. 'I ended up doing the washing up,' recalls Jenny Spires.*

*Down the road, Storm Thorgerson and Aubrey 'Po' Powell had taken over Flat 1, Egerton Court, a stucco townhouse opposite South Kensington tube station. Thorgerson was studying film at the Royal College Art, and Po was a TV set designer.*

*There would be a steady traffic of friends and familiars between all three properties. Barrett moved into Earlham Street in spring 1966, followed by 101 Cromwell Road, and then Egerton Court.*

✢

**Duggie Fields (pop artist, 101 Cromwell Road resident):** While the Pink Floyd were rehearsing at Cromwell Road, I was trying to paint. It was a lot of noise because they didn't know where they were going yet. Some of it I liked, some of it I didn't. I was working in a record shop and was into James Brown and American R&B, so I'd put on one of my records as loud as I could. They had no sense of rhythm or subtlety. But I'd go and see them performing and there was something special there some of the time. So I had very mixed emotions.

**Jenny Spires:** I'd moved to London in summer 1966 to attend the Lucie Clayton School of Modelling. I'd split up with Syd, but we were still friends, and he was now with Lindsay Corner. She'd been at Ely High School and I knew her from a distance at Little Shelford Youth Club and village hall dances – small world Cambridge.

**Lindsay Corner (Barrett's ex-girlfriend):** I came to London to go to Lucie Clayton too and moved in with Syd at Earlham Street. It had a bright purple door and there was a fish and winkle stall outside.

We shared it with Peter Wynne-Willson, who did lights for Pink Floyd, and his girlfriend Susie [Gawler-Wright, later nicknamed 'the psychedelic debutante' and an *International Times* cover model]. Those days were good fun before poor Syd went a bit bonkers.

**Andrew King:** It was like a typical studenty digs with paintings around and a record player with the Rolling Stones' *Between the Buttons* normally playing. The room below Syd and Lindsay's was like a workshop for Peter Wynne-Willson and the lighting guys.

**Peter Wynne-Willson (Pink Floyd's early lighting engineer):** The furniture was mostly out of crates that I'd got from Covent Garden – hardly domestic. When times were really hard, we would go out late at night and scavenge for fruit and veg.

There were some colourful people through Earlham Street. Pip and Emo were frequent visitors, and Pip's junkie hangers on. I didn't feel very easy about that. Pip wasn't always very seemly.

**David Gale:** It was Peter who had the idea of taking a pair of welding goggles, replacing the dark glass with clear glass and Aralditing two glass prisms onto the front and making what I called 'cosmonocles'.

**Jenny Spires:** I have a photo of me wearing those prism glasses. I don't know why, but they always reminded me of those awful wartime gas masks. I later gave mine to the Salvation Army.

**Peter Jenner:** We encouraged Syd to write songs at Earlham Street. The Beatles, the Stones and the Who wrote their own songs and so did Hendrix, so we better start doing it. It was as uninteresting as that. They were all encouraged to write, but Syd was the one who came out with the great songs. It was just so obvious.

**John 'Hoppy' Hopkins:** At the Free School gigs, a visiting American couple called Toni and Joel Brown brought their slide projector and put on a light show. When they went back to New York, a lot of other talented people became involved with the lights. There was Mark Boyle, who later did the lights at UFO, and there was Jack Bracelin, who also owned a nudist club out near Watford.

**Peter Jenner:** My wife Sumi and I did Pink Floyd's lights for a time. We bought timber shelving, some spot fittings from Woolworths, and ran some light-duty cable from them to a domestic light switch, which was switched on and off by hand. God, so amateur! Peter Wynne-Willson got it much more together, with oil slides and projectors and mirrors.

**Peter Wynne-Willson:** I was a lighting engineer in the New Theatre on the first run of *Oliver!*. When the theatre threw bits of stuff out, I'd take them home and renovate them. I saw the Pink Floyd at All Saints Hall and started off shifting gear with Russell Page. A young guy called Joe Gannon was doing the lights, but he went back to America. Then I started roadie-ing *and* doing the lights. I didn't have a driving licence, but that wasn't a problem as Rick drove the van.

**Peter Jenner:** We had the sheet for light projections pretty early on too. So the audience were getting these moving shadows. It was very effective, but it also made the group invisible, so the audiences often ended up looking at the shadows instead.

**John 'Hoppy' Hopkins:** We set up *International Times* in October 1966 to write about all the things straight society didn't want to write about – art, poetry, pop music, street politics, experimental theatre, sex, the price of drugs...

***International Times* launch party flyer:** 'All-Night Rave to launch new underground newspaper International Times. The Soft Machine. The Pink Floyd. Trip. Trips, Happenings. Movies. Pop. Op. Costume. Masque. Drag Ball... Bring your own poison, bring flowers and gass [sic] filled balloons. The Round House. Opp. Chalk Farm underground. Saturday 15th of Oct, 11 PM onwards.'

**Aubrey 'Po' Powell:** I was designing sets for *Z-Cars* and *Dr Finlay's Casebook*, but was woefully under-qualified, so one day they said, 'You're fucking useless. The only thing you know how to do is paint.' The weekend after I was fired, Peter Wynne-Willson said, 'You've got a mini-van, do you want a job, Po?'. All Pink Floyd had was a Commer van to carry their equipment and they needed something to put the lights in. The first gig I did was at the Roundhouse.

**Jenny Spires:** On the afternoon, we were all in the upstairs room at Earlham Street. I'd smoked dope with Syd, but hadn't done anything else in Cambridge. Nigel was there and he gave me a cube of sugar [impregnated with acid] and I left with him in a taxi to go to the gig.

It was a vast, dilapidated train terminus. Arnold Wesker, the playwright, had been transforming it into a community performance space and now the railway sleepers had been cleared. It was a spectacular night. Looking around, it seemed to me that I knew everyone there.

**Aubrey 'Po' Powell:** The Pink Floyd played on one of those old horse-drawn flatbed carts left over from the distillery days – like something out of *Steptoe and Son* – and I recall hanging up a big sheet behind it on which they projected their lights. God only knows how any of this would look today. So amateur, I guess.

**Barry Miles:** People arrived in head dresses and face paint. Paul McCartney came dressed as an Arab and Marianne Faithfull in an extremely abbreviated nun's habit that didn't quite cover her bottom.

Gerry Fitzgerald [of the communal art group Exploding Galaxy] made a huge jelly using a bathtub as a mould, but Syd Barrett and the Pink Floyd's roadie Pip accidentally destroyed it by removing a key piece of wood that was holding it in place.

**Jeff Dexter:** I remember that huge jelly. I didn't think much of the musical show, but the people show was fantastic. I was intrigued by Floyd's little entourage and all these girls around Syd – Lindsay, maybe Jenny. I spoke more to Rick at that time. He was quiet, but Juliette got him out of his shell. But there wasn't that much conversation because there was an awful lot of, 'Oh, wow man' in those days.

**Peter Jenner:** *International Times*, the Free School… it all made sense because Andrew and I tended to go for an upmarket arty vibe. Because of that we were big on causes. So Pink Floyd played benefits for Oxfam [*You're Joking!* with Peter Cook & Dudley Moore and others at the Albert Hall, and an anti-apartheid thing [*Psychodelphia Versus Ian Smith*, both in December '66] at the Roundhouse.

**Nick Mason:** We were bottom of the bill at the Oxfam benefit. Alan Price [of the Alan Price Set] got a laugh at our expense by hammering the reverb on his Hammond organ and announcing that this was 'psychedelic music'.

**Peter Jenner:** The Floyd fitted into that whole, cutting edge, middle-class, arty thing – a bit like Tracey Emin and Damien Hirst years later.

**Roger Waters:** You'll never get me to take this stuff seriously. However hard you try, it's not gonna happen, okay? We were just young guys getting together, wanting to be rich and get laid.

# 3

# 'THE OLD TIGERS ARE SCARED, BABY!'

*Sucking the pocket, 'I ran out of potatoes to throw at the gong', Jenny's lovely bells and 'Now I* don't *know about the Mandrax'...*

✲

There's no longer a Number 31, Tottenham Court Road, London W1, as urban re-development has wreaked havoc with the numbering system. There's a Number 30, occupied by Costa Coffee, but next door is the Japanese eatery YoumeSushi! at 37.

In winter 1966, somewhere in between was the Berkeley Cinema, above an Irish dancehall bar known as the Blarney Club. In December 1966, John 'Hoppy' Hopkins and Joe Boyd asked the club's manager, Mr Gannon, if they could rent the space after the Friday night cèilidh.

Gannon seized the opportunity to charge these 'freaks' – the preferred descriptor before 'hippie' – £15 a week, but couldn't understand why they didn't want a bar. Aside from licensing restrictions, LSD and booze didn't mix. So Gannon insisted on a further cut by running the soft drinks concession.

Flyers – showing Pete Townshend's future wife, the designer Karen Astley, with a painted face – were distributed for the launch night, in Portobello Road market and the boutiques, Granny Takes A Trip and I Was Lord Kitchener's Valet.

The Pink Floyd played the inaugural 'UFO Presents Night Tripper' on Friday 23 December 1966, after which the clans began to gather every Friday at 'UFO' (an acronym of 'Underground Freak Out', but pronounced 'Ewe-Fo'), just as the surrounding pubs kicked out.

Fashionably dressed and often chemically enhanced, UFO's clientele descended the red-carpeted staircase, past the garish, Day-Glo walls and into the womb-like space. Had someone broken the spell and put the overhead lights on, they'd have seen a traditional ballroom with a sprung dancefloor and a glitzy mirror ball.

What transformed it was the sensory overload: the soundtrack provided by the Pink Floyd and their friendly rivals, the Soft Machine; the theatre groups and performance artists; the free jazz ensembles (with names such as Hydrogen Jukebox and Giant Sun Trolley); the silent art movies flickering on the walls; and the liquid light shows, where paint, oil, saliva and, occasionally, blood and semen merged to cast amoebic blobs over the group and its audience.

Come 6 a.m., Tottenham Court Road started to fill with disoriented people trying to find their way home. 'UFO was the original all-night rave,' says regular visitor Jeff Dexter.

✣

**John 'Hoppy' Hopkins:** It was the momentum of what was happening at the Free School that propelled us towards starting UFO. UFO was Joe Boyd and I. He did the music, I did the visuals and the organisation.

**Joe Boyd:** UFO embodied what was happening by the end of '66 and the start of '67. Britain was changing. A lot of the assumptions people had worked with were jarred loose and this led to a questioning of society. Drugs played a role, but it was more than the right to smoke dope or take acid. There was a personal revolution going on. People were ditching their day jobs to do something more exciting. There was a sense we could do anything.

**Jeff Dexter:** Joe Boyd invited me to UFO and I went there with my friend [songwriter] Ian 'Sammy' Samwell and arranged to meet Denny Laine from the Moody Blues. At the time I was the DJ at Tiles on Oxford Street. Tiles was a mod club, but I'd already discovered the sacrament, as we called LSD, so I was flowered up by the time UFO came long.

In summer '66, I'd gone to Deià in Mallorca where the Soft Machine and some friends were hanging out. I went with a test-tube full of Sandoz acid which was still legal at the time. Unfortunately, the air pressure in the plane popped the cork in the tube and it all came out in my pocket. So I pulled out the lining of my jacket and sucked on it. So that was my arrival in Mallorca. UFO felt to me like an extension of what was already happening.

I've heard these stories about how there was someone at the top of the stairs at UFO offering you LSD as you came in. But I wasn't aware of that and we had our own.

**Barry Miles:** There was a German acid dealer called Manfred who gave away as many as 400 trips but sold a lot more.

**Robert Wyatt (drummer, Soft Machine):** UFO was very dreamlike. There were pillars and columns like you'd get in catacombs. They had a stage there, but the wall went on and on beyond the stage. It wasn't just contained. Then there was another place with films and people sitting around, hanging out, being stoned.

**Jeff Dexter:** There were lots of people there I recognised, like Nigel Waymouth from Granny Takes a Trip and later Hapshash [Hapshash and the Coloured Coat, UFO poster designers] and a lot of the Chelsea freaks. Mr Gannon kept an eye on things, but I don't think he knew what else was going on. It was all 'pie and mash' – cash – to him.

**John Leckie:** There was a competition between the Floyd and the Soft Machine between my friends as to who was most stretching the boundaries. Soft Machine could play better, but they didn't have Syd Barrett. Floyd were more abstract but Roger Waters was scary on stage. He was tough, he could scream.

**Libby Chisman:** Sadly, this was the moving-on period. We Cambridge people were thinking, *Oh, this music's a bit crap*, but London was embracing it. That's what Pink Floyd always wanted to do, but the psychedelic stuff was not easy to dance to. It used to amaze me that all these people came to watch them and you couldn't do anything except *writhe* to it.

**Jeff Dexter:** UFO's house bands were part of the furniture rather than being the main attraction. It was all part of the same people show. On one of my early visits there, I saw a poet called Michael Chapman, a huge guy who'd do concrete poems, as he called them. He was six-foot-four, but he'd stand on a chair and then leap off shouting 'G-r-e-e-e-e-n… bombs!'

There were no records played as such. The DJ, Jack Henry Moore, told me the dancefloor made the tone arm skip, so he worked with a reel-to-reel tape machine, on which he'd recorded songs and sounds, and a cine projector with bits of film. He did eventually install a turntable – along with several hods of bricks to stop records jumping – in May when John Lennon brought in a white-label test pressing of *Sgt Pepper's Lonely Hearts Club Band*.

In the meantime, I'd bring him my soul records and Jack would tape them. So you'd hear the Mar-Keys in with the Mothers of Invention and the Grateful Dead. You could dance properly to the soul records and then idiot dance, which was just waving your arms and not really dancing at all, to the Floyd.

The lighting guys worked next to Jack or Mark Boyle on another set of rickety scaffolding. The club ceilings weren't that high, so he'd lie down and make the oil slides. You had these two odd places where the light and sound was coming from and it all melted into one.

**David Gale:** I always remember, at one of these early Floyd shows, Peter Wynne-Willson stretched a condom over a wire frame and dropped oil paint on to it. Then he tapped it while shining a strong light through it to get that oil slide effect.

**Joe Boyd:** Pete Townshend came down one evening and spent the whole night at the right-hand corner of the stage, tripping on something. When I came by, he pointed at Roger Waters' open mouth and told me it was going to swallow him.

**Anthony Stern:** When you went down to UFO, you'd be surrounded by groups of people sitting on the floor and it was like I'd imagine going to an American Indian camp at an old creek and seeing lots of tipis and campfires. You could go from one campfire to the next and sit in on other people's conversations and smoke their smoke and inhale their incense.

**Jeff Dexter:** Stuff was happening elsewhere by the start of the new year ['67]. [Promoter] Dave Housen put on 'Freak Out Ethel' at the Seymour Hall, which the Pink Floyd also played. That was another early gathering of the tribes running parallel to things in California, like the Human Be-In [at San Francisco's Golden Gate Park in January '67].

**Nick Mason:** We had no idea until we went there ourselves what was happening in America, never mind California. We heard these names like Country Joe and the Fish, whom we assumed were at the sharp end of psychedelia, but were more like a country and western band. Jefferson Airplane we did come across eventually, but I don't think we heard them until we went to the States.

**Mick Farren (musician, writer, UFO doorman):** The crowd at UFO was building, so I suggested to Hoppy that I look after the door, make sure Paul McCartney or Brian Jones could get in, but also dealing with the tripped-out psychos, threatening skinheads and undercover drugs squad in Carnaby Street sunglasses.

**Jeff Dexter:** I'd worked at what you'd call street-level clubs like the Flamingo and the Roaring Twenties. You did get confronted by 'Oi, you long-haired prick!' and 'Are you a geezer or a bird?'. There'd always been aggro from one source or another. But Joe and Hoppy came from the literary side of music rather than the street level, so perhaps they hadn't encountered it before.

**Peter Jenner:** By now, *Melody Maker* had given us a centrespread, saying that this was what was going to be happening next year, *Queen* magazine did a feature and there was an interview in the *Sunday Times*. Somehow or another, we had hit that middle-class, post-young graduate audience.

✲

*In October 1966, the Pink Floyd had recorded what Jenner calls 'another primitive demo' at a studio in Hemel Hempstead. It included the instrumental 'Interstellar Overdrive' and 'Let's Roll Another One' (later given the family-friendly title 'Candy and a Currant Bun').*

*The demo reflected pop music's evolution. Over the past two years alone, the Who's 'Anywhere Anyhow Anyway', the Yardbirds' 'Shapes Of Things' and most of the Beatles'* Revolver *and* Rubber Soul *albums, to name just a few, all showed that pop music didn't have to be bound by convention. LSD loosened the shackles further.*

*'Interstellar Overdrive' was like the soundtrack to a trip; photos from the time showed a spidery-moustached Barrett with hooded eyelids and/or a thousand-yard stare. In December, a group of Earlham Street's psychic adventurers dropped a tab before hearing a performance of Handel's* Messiah *at the Royal Albert Hall.*

*Everybody marvelled at the spiritual music and ornamented surroundings, and then Syd went home for Christmas and wrote his first hit single.*

✿

**Jenny Spires:** By then, Lindsay wanted to move out of Earlham Street and asked me to go with her. She'd found a flat in Maida Vale and I agreed. I later found out she and Syd had split up, and he was seeing Kari-Ann Moller. But he and Lindsay were soon back together.

**Mick Rock (rock photographer):** That Christmas was when I first met Syd. I was studying at Cambridge University… LSD mostly, but my parents thought it was modern languages and literature. I met Syd when the Floyd played at the art college party. A friend of mine, the Peek Freans biscuit heir, had already introduced me to Pip and Emo. So it was a head thing – those that imbibed and smoked.

Afterwards there was a little party in Syd's room at his mum's house. We spliffed away – tobacco and hashish, a disgusting habit, but that was the way it was in England – and we talked about Arthur C Clarke's

*Childhood's End* and the scene at the end when these kids dance themselves into oblivion. Syd was very cheerful and very communicative, and we became good friends.

**Jenny Spires:** On Boxing Day, the phone rang at my parents' house. It was Syd. He wanted to play me what was going to be their new single. He arrived in his mum's car, and he had Rover with him. Rover – full name Rover Angelica – was Syd and Lindsay's cat and he said he wanted me to have her. Later, it was decided she should stay with my parents. We got to 183 and I sat on the bed while he played me an acoustic 'Arnold Layne'. It was catchy. I could hear that.

**Syd Barrett (speaking in July 1967):** 'I was at Cambridge at the time I started to write the song. I pinched the line about 'moonshine washing line' from Rog our bass guitarist – because he has an enormous washing line in the back garden of his house. Then I thought, *Arnold must have a hobby*, and it went on from there. Arnold Layne just happens to dig dressing up in women's clothing.'

**Joe Boyd:** Both Syd and Roger's mums used to rent rooms to students, so both often found lingerie drying on backyard clothes lines. There was also a local Cambridge panty-theft case at some point in Syd's teen years.

**Andrew King:** Syd said it took him a fortnight to write the lyrics to 'Arnold Layne'. Everyone thinks he got up around lunchtime, took some acid, then wrote a genius song, but he worked very hard and took it seriously.

**Jenny Spires:** Syd told me how different it was to write a single. I thought he had the hang of it anyway. At one point later, his mum knocked on the door: 'Rog, you must keep the noise down.' We hadn't realised it was so late and we must've kept her awake. She saw me sitting there and looked surprised. 'Oh, Jenny. Hello... Happy Christmas...'

✲

*Meanwhile, Blackhill Enterprises were expanding their operation from their Paddington office/communal house and hired Marc Bolan's future wife, June Child, as their secretary. At the beginning of the year, Blackhill struck a deal with the Bryan Morrison Agency, who put the Pink Floyd on a band wage of £400 a week.*

*'They went from twenty shows a year to 250,' said Morrison, an East End-born entrepreneur who later played polo with the future King Charles.*

*Morrison's junior agents, Tony Howard and Steve O'Rourke, would also play crucial roles in Pink Floyd's story. '"Sammy" [Ian Samwell] worked for Morry's agency,' explains Jeff Dexter. 'And he and I had already bought them down to UFO.'*

*Meanwhile, Joe Boyd was pitching Floyd's demo to Elektra Records. 'Interstellar Overdrive' quickly became a UFO anthem, but its roots were more prosaic. Pete Jenner said it was inspired by 'My Little Red Book', a Bacharach & David song covered by the US underground group Love, while Roger Waters claimed it was a mangled version of Ron Grainger's theme to* Steptoe and Son.

*'There is much more truth to the rumour that it came from 'My Little Red Book'* and *the theme tune from* Steptoe and Son,*' suggests David Gilmour, who'd be playing it regularly within a year.*

*Either way, the song fascinated two aspiring young film-makers.*

✣

**Anthony Stern:** I know this sounds like some apocryphal story but I assure you it's true. I ran into Peter Jenner, whom I barely knew, in a shop called Drum City on Shaftesbury Avenue. He said to me, 'Syd's falling behind. Do you want to be the second guitar player in Pink Floyd, because you know some of them from Cambridge?' My guitar playing was not great, I'd never been in a band, and I spontaneously said, 'Oh no, I'm a film director.'

Following that conversation, Jenner gave me a tape of the first recording of 'Interstellar Overdrive' and said, 'Use this in your film, do what you want.' The song was abstract, but with lots of pulse, and absolutely right for a film I wanted to make.

I was this young curly-haired ingenue, who'd been offered £500 by two wealthy ladies at a party in California to make a film called *San Francisco*. Then Peter Whitehead heard the track...

**Peter Whitehead:** I'd made *Wholly Communion* and the Rolling Stones film *Charlie Is My Darling*, and Anthony Stern was my assistant. I was making another film about what was happening in London and Anthony reminded me about Syd Barrett. 'Do you remember him? He's got a group in London now.'

**Jenny Spires:** I'd met Peter in the King's Road, when he was filming at Granny Takes A Trip. Peter told me he was making a documentary about Swinging London [*Tonite Let's All Make Love in London*] and I went back to his flat to see the footage.

He was living in Carlisle Street, in a fourth-floor mansion with a fairy-tale turret. He explained that he might have to compose the soundtrack himself because he couldn't get permission to use anything he'd recorded. I asked who, and he mentioned the Stones.

I watched the pulsating, smudge-and-blur cuts and the mishmash of mini-skirts and dancing girls, and was reminded of the light shows I'd seen at gigs. I suggested that he should use an up-and-coming band, like Pink Floyd. To my surprise, he said he knew who I meant, as he'd met Syd in Cambridge. Ant Stern, whom I didn't know then, was also a friend of Syd's and now Peter's assistant – a strange coincidence. The next time I heard from Peter he was coming to see the Floyd play at UFO.

**Peter Whitehead:** I went to see them at the Royal College of Art and then again at UFO with Jenny Spires, with whom I was smitten. I thought, *What are all these globules floating around on the screen behind them?* The music was dark and semi-classical, and I thought, *This is really rather good*, because I didn't want another bloody Rolling Stones. I went backstage and spoke to Jenner about having them play 'Interstellar Overdrive' for my film. All thanks to Jenny.

**Anthony Stern:** Jenny slipped into my flat in Norfolk Mansions in Battersea for a while as others were drifting out. For me, she was the first girl who totally encapsulated the vibe of UFO – she was the spirit of a new age. One night, I heard a door opening and closing, and then this lovely sound of bells jingling, like a reindeer.

Jenny had these bells on her ankles – and it was a most wonderful vision. I didn't hear that sound again until 1972 when I went to Afghanistan and a town called Herak, where the horses had the exact same bells – and I suddenly had a slap-bang vision of Jenny Spires coming to Afghanistan.

**Jenny Spires:** They were dancing bells that strapped to your ankles and I bought them at an Indian music shop on the corner of Oxford Street and Marble Arch. I came across them in the loft years ago and gave them to the Salvation Army. I had no idea the effect they had on Ant, though...

**Anthony Stern:** Peter decided he was going to have 'Interstellar Overdrive' for *Tonite Let's All Make Love in London* and would film the Pink Floyd recording a new version in the studio. I had the original for my film. I'd recorded thousands of images of America from New York to San Francisco – abstract images that tried to replicate the Pink Floyd's light experience. I got a small grant from the BFI [British Film Institute] to finish the film. It won prizes and promptly got forgotten about.

**Peter Whitehead:** I paid £85 for two hours in Sound Technique Studio with the specific intention of them doing 'Interstellar Overdrive'. There was still an hour left and the band said they'd improvise if I wanted something longer. They jammed 'Nick's Boogie' for another fifteen minutes, so I had that in the can as well.

**Andrew King:** If you look at the Whitehead film, it's almost like Syd is playing 'Interstellar Overdrive' for himself. He's absolutely absorbed in it, and the band seems to be watching him and wondering where he's going to go next. He's clearly in control.

**Peter Whitehead:** I shot them at UFO a couple of days later. Syd looks fantastic with his arms outstretched and the lights [performing 'Pow R. Toc H']. That film was kept in a barn with 500 other cans of film until I found it again about fifteen years later – and it was pristine. If you look at it, *that's* the Pink Floyd.

**Peter Jenner:** As I recall, Joe's deal with Elektra was agreed and all it needed was the approval of his boss Jac Holzman, who flew in from the States to hear the band. He didn't like them. It might have been a different thing if he'd seen them at UFO, but he saw the Floyd in a cold rehearsal room and he passed. That rather blotted Joe's copybook in our eyes.

**Joe Boyd:** That was part of a series of events which led to a 'You can't fire me I quit' conversation. It wasn't the issue which triggered my leaving Elektra, but part of a pattern. Jac wanted me to focus on promoting [US singer-songwriters] Judy Collins and Phil Ochs, and I wanted to be scouting out English bands and signing them.

**Peter Jenner:** So Joe went to Polydor and they were very interested, and we decided to do Syd's song 'Arnold Layne' as a single with Joe producing.

✲

*The Pink Floyd recorded 'Arnold Layne'/'Candy and a Currant Bun' at Sound Technique over January and February 1967. But was there a knicker-stealing Arnold in real life?*

*Theories abound: David Gale recalls a Cambridge postman nicknamed 'Rigor Mortis' who was forever gawping at women's underwear hanging on washing lines. But 'Arnold Layne doesn't exist at all,' said Waters at the time. 'He's purely fictitious.'*

*Joe Boyd produced the single, which made a feature of its composer's deadpan English vocals and Rick Wright's wobbly Farfisa melody. In the vernacular of the day, it sounded like a kinkier Kinks. The group, looking impossibly young and jolly, later made a video for the song, goofing around on West Wittering beach in Sussex with face masks and a tailor's dummy.*

*However, during rehearsals, Morrison and his Chelsea-booted, silk-scarved foot soldiers Howard and O'Rourke marched into the studio to check on their investment. 'Joe would have been intimidated by Morry, Steve and Tony because they were a force to be reckoned with,' admits Jeff Dexter.*

*Morrison told the group that he'd found Polydor's contract wanting. He offered to fund the recording of 'Arnold Layne' (for a chunk of the publishing) and convinced them EMI would make a better offer.*

*Morrison was proved right. Within weeks, the Pink Floyd had signed with EMI and been allocated their in-house producer, Beatles engineer Norman Smith (nicknamed 'Normal' by John Lennon on account of being in his early forties and unswinging).*

*The Pink Floyd and Smith were soon recording their debut album,* The Piper at the Gates of Dawn, *at EMI's Abbey Road Studios, while the Beatles created* Sgt Pepper's Lonely Hearts Club Band *down the corridor. But it was the beginning of the end for Joe Boyd.*

✲

**Peter Jenner:** Bryan [Morrison] told us you go to the biggest company with the most money and that saves you thinking – and that was EMI. There was no indie sector then, so there was no choice. It was Decca or EMI, who were considered much hipper because they had the Beatles and Abbey Road.

We tried to get Joe in, but there was a corporate structure at EMI. The A&R guy [Sidney] Beecher-Stevens helped talk us into it and was a very smooth operator. So we signed to EMI for a £5,000 advance. The lawyer we used specialised in conveyancing and not the music business, but we still ended up with the first-ever deal where EMI agreed to release an album regardless of whether the band had any hit singles. The problem for Joe was, EMI didn't like using outside studios or outside producers.

**Nick Mason:** Peter had the unenviable task of breaking the news to Joe, who'd formed his own company [Witchseason Productions] and thought he would be working with us. But in those days, you didn't bring your own producer into EMI. So we were given Norman Smith, who'd worked with the Beatles and who was hoping we'd go the Beatles route and produce a pop album.

**Joe Boyd:** Naively, I guess, I presumed that if we made a great single, they wouldn't want to break up a winning team. But I was wrong.

**Peter Jenner:** There was always a bit of needle between Joe and us after that because he felt he had been done over, which, it has to be said, he had. But Joe helped us make the first record, 'Arnold Layne', which convinced EMI we could make records that would sell.

**Norman Smith (EMI producer):** I knew absolutely nothing about psychedelia and wasn't that interested. Bryan Morrison took me to the UFO club. The music did absolutely nothing for me, but on the strength of what I could see, I figured we could sell some records. But the initial meeting at EMI was difficult. Roger and Nick did all the talking, and Syd hardly said anything.

**Jeff Dexter:** Norman didn't really want the job, but it was an opportunity for him to have more power at EMI. I think he would have preferred to be doing the Bee Gees.

**Nick Mason:** Once we'd signed to the Morrison Agency, we started playing more shows and much further afield. I couldn't combine the band and studying architecture anymore. I went to my year master and told him, 'I don't know what to do here', because there was no point in me continually getting my friends to sign me in and say I was attending lectures.

To his credit, he said, 'Take a year off and we'll hold a place for you.' So he actually invented the gap year. Thank you, Mr Mayo! Years later, I had lunch with his daughter at Goodwood [Racecourse] and she told me her father thought I would have made a good architect.

Quite quickly from when we went professional, we started getting press, which suggested we were different from what else was around. There was interest from newspapers and colour supplements, and I think that sat comfortably with my parents.

**Jill Furmanovsky (music photographer):** When I was eighteen, my dad would tell me about a draughtsman in his office who played in a band. He described him as gloomy but perversely inclined to wear psychedelic shirts and ties. He was Roger Waters.

**Roger Waters:** If music hadn't worked out, I might have gone into smuggling or property development, something more rewarding than architecture, anyway.

**Rado 'Bob' Klose:** I remember they played at the Regent Street Polytechnic and I'd not seen them for a while. They'd just turned professional and Rick's girlfriend, Juliette, told me that it was the most horrendous wrench for Syd to commit himself – to say, 'I'm not going to be a painter.'

**Rosemary Breen:** When Roger [Syd] left Camberwell, he'd said 'I'm just taking a break and will be back.' He'd wanted a year out because he thought it would be fun doing the group with Roger Waters. I'm sure he did intend to go back and that would have been wonderful.

**Andrew King:** I was driving them back from a gig once and someone said, 'Fuck art, show me the money, right!'. Syd said, 'I've been studying art for seven years and I think it's really important and you shouldn't say things like that.' People took art seriously in those days.

**Jenny Spires:** I think signing himself away to EMI was against his principles. He wasn't into the notion of big corporations or being a pop star and saw the music industry as a bit of a sausage factory. But he loved the little bit of income he was getting. When he was a student, he was always complaining about being broke.

**Norman Smith:** We were in Number 3 studio waiting to do the first session for *The Piper at the Gates of Dawn*, when the door opened and who should walk in but Paul McCartney. He introduced himself to Pink Floyd, then tapped me on the shoulder as he left and said, 'You won't go wrong with this chappie'. I think they were impressed.

**Nick Mason:** In my memory, we were taken into Studio 2 where the Beatles were recording 'Lovely Rita'. We sat quietly at the back before being ushered out again. I'd like to tell you there was more to it than that.

**Richard Wright:** The first thing that came into Syd's head were the lyrics. He'd come up with a melody later, but never paid much attention to time signatures. Syd's songs were great, but the tempos were always changing.

**Roger Waters:** Syd also soaked up musical ideas from other people. He was a great copycat in terms of music. He would listen to the more avant-garde end of American popular music at the time, things like the early Doors.

**Peter Jenner:** Norman's job was to discourage what I called 'the live ramble'. There was 'Interstellar Overdrive', which was a licensed ramble to show that we hadn't forgotten what we did live, but we knew we couldn't just do what we did live in the studio.

**Nick Mason:** We tried to re-record 'Arnold Layne' and it didn't work, so we went back to the version we'd made with Joe and that became our first hit single [a UK Top 20 hit in March 1967].

**Andrew King:** We spent a couple of hundred quid trying to buy it into the charts. The management did that, I should add, not EMI.

**Peter Jenner:** Radio London objected to the subject, though – a chap stealing women's underwear from washing lines – and wouldn't play it. But we had a bigger problem when the newspapers started writing about the hallucinatory effects of psychedelic music.

**Roger Waters (in the *Sunday Times*, 30 October 1966):** '[Our music] is a complete realisation of the aims of psychedelia. But if you take LSD what you experience depends entirely on who you are. Our music may give you the screaming horrors or throw you into screaming ecstasy.'

***News of the World* (29 January 1967):** 'The Pink Floyd group specialise in psychedelic music, which is meant to illustrate LSD experiences.'

**EMI disclaimer (February 1967):** 'The Pink Floyd does not know what people mean by psychedelic pop and are not trying to cause hallucinatory effects on their audience.'

**Roger Waters:** I was obviously being tongue-in-cheek. The idea that psychedelia had aims is ridiculous. There was never any feeling that we were aligned to someone like Timothy Leary who thought the world could be saved by dropping acid.

**Richard Wright:** Hippies used to be a large part of our audience, but I don't think even Syd or I were hippies. None of us believed in the hippie philosophy. We were part of a wider movement that was all about freedom. And freedom for me meant 'Wow, we can actually go on stage and make these weird sounds, and people are going to pay you for it.'

**Norman Smith:** Syd Barrett was the most important member of the group. But it was like talking to a brick wall. Syd would do a take, come back into the control room and have a listen. I'd make some suggestions, Syd would just nod, go back into the studio and do another take and it would be exactly the same as the one before.

**Andrew King:** I don't know what Norman was whingeing about. He spent his whole time looking at lists of suburban properties he was able to buy with all the overtime he was getting. I remember Syd being very on the case, operating the faders on this funny little desk for the final mix of 'Chapter 24'. He knew what he wanted.

**Peter Jenner:** In retrospect, his songwriting was becoming very strange – like the lyrics for 'Astronomy Domine' which was the names for all the stars – 'Titan' and 'Oberon' – which Syd had me narrating in the studio from a book about astronomy. That's my voice on the record.

**Jeff Dexter:** By now, UFO had attracted the weekend hippies. They put on beads and bells, and wanted to be part of it. A lot of our friends resented it, but a club can't survive with just a small clique. By then, too, other musicians were following Pete Townshend and coming down to UFO as well. Everyone was getting in on it.

The Speakeasy had also opened on Margaret Street and while that was a club for music biz people to buy bottles of champagne and show off, there was also this underbelly of freaks that would travel backwards and forwards between the Speak and UFO, bringing new people with them.

**Aubrey 'Po' Powell:** At UFO, there was a corridor by the side of the stage. I was sitting there smoking a joint one night when the Floyd had played and Paul McCartney came in. Paul was a very affable guy and we passed the joint around.

Roger Waters didn't normally smoke, but he took a hit on it because Roger knew when to play the game. But Syd was a bit over-awed. When McCartney had gone, he said, 'Wow, that was Paul McCartney and he's come to see Pink Floyd.' I said, 'Hey, Sydney, you are pretty cool too.' I think it was the first time I had an inkling Syd might not be able to handle fame and success.

*

*The Pink Floyd played two events in April and May, marking the end of one chapter and the beginning of another. On the night of 29–30 April, they headlined above the Soft Machine and other UFO regulars Tomorrow and The Crazy World of Arthur Brown at The 14-Hour Technicolor Dream, inside north London's Alexandra Palace.*

*Some 10,000 people gathered to watch bands and dance troupes performing on two stages, to stare at the light show projected on to sheets draped from a skyscraping scaffolding tower, and to rediscover their inner child on a fairground helter-skelter.*

*A BBC camera crew captured the people show, including the Exploding Galaxy dance troupe performing a new piece called 'Fuzz Death Ballet', Yoko Ono having her clothes chopped off with a pair of amplified scissors and a tripping John Lennon mooching around in Granny glasses and an Afghan waistcoat.*

*The Pink Floyd began 'Astronomy Domine' just as the sun was coming up, but this was the last hurrah for the band and the underground. They were moving too fast for Hoppy, UFO and* IT...

✲

**John 'Hoppy' Hopkins:** UFO was now generating a certain amount of income. Then *IT* got busted [in March 1967, on obscenity charges] and the money was needed to help fund that. One of the things we did after the raid was a benefit concert, The 14-Hour Technicolor Dream. I was the one that parlayed the rent of the hall – and the owners were still looking for me years later.

**Jenny Spires:** I went with our friends Jock and Sue [future actor Alistair Findlay and his partner, model Susan Kingsford]. Peter Whitehead filmed Sue that night with a daffodil in her mouth. She was wearing a muskrat coat and I had on a little velvet jacket Jimi Hendrix gave me – beautifully braided but not very warm – as we trudged up that endless hill to the palace.

It was a vast, echoey, draughty space, but things were beginning to happen. I watched the people on the helter-skelter, sitting around in small groups smoking, some looking shattered and crashed out against the walls.

**John 'Hoppy' Hopkins:** Ten thousand people must have gone through those doors at some point in the night, but there were several entrances to the building and Michael X and his people were covering some of them. Unfortunately, not all the money found its way back to central control.

**Jenny Spires:** The variety of bands playing was reflected in the mix of the crowd ... There were freaks and hippies, long-haired students and young blokes who looked as though they'd just tumbled out of the pubs at last orders. They all seemed to be waiting for the Floyd to play. I didn't see the band arrive, but I could see Syd looking pretty exhausted or spaced out.

**Aubrey 'Po' Powell:** By now, Syd was falling apart a bit. Sometimes he would travel in the mini-van with me to gigs instead of with the band.

Not on that occasion, but sometimes the other guys said, 'You take him Po'. On one drive home, he spent the whole time giggling. I found him a bit odd.

**Nick Mason:** The significance of the Technicolor Dream was that we'd played in Holland the same night and we didn't get to Alexandra Palace until three in the morning. The significance was it was bloody hard work.

**Peter Jenner:** I have a strong recollection of sitting on the banks of a canal in Amsterdam with the Kinks and Pink Floyd because we'd all done the same TV show. On the night of the Technicolor Dream, on the last lap of the journey, I was tripping while I was driving the van. I popped it early as I really wanted to appreciate the gig. I never did that again.

**Aubrey 'Po' Powell:** We'd been to Amsterdam and we must have all been up for thirty hours. Unfortunately, Roger Waters had started to become a bit of a pop star – 'Where's this? Where's that?...' It was interesting to see. Syd wasn't like that at all – not lovely, beautiful Sydney. But Roger Waters was. I talked to Peter Wynne-Willson about it and Pete was laughing – 'Oh fucking hell m-a-a-n, we are all supposed to be in this together.' But, of course, we were not all in this together, because Roger – God love him and good luck – was on a mission to become a pop star.

**Peter Wynne-Willson:** I didn't enjoy the Technicolor Dream. There were a lot of drugs around and Roger Waters was in a state about something.

**Aubrey 'Po' Powell:** We got to Ally Pally and suddenly Roger said, 'Where's my fucking whisky, Po?'. 'What whisky?' I replied. 'I always have a bottle by the side of the stage,' he said. I told him, 'I'm sorry, Rog. I don't know. I am just here to drive and carry the lights.' But then he said, 'Well, fucking find me one!'

To be fair, he was tired too, but I said, 'No, goodbye', got in my van and left. That was the last Pink Floyd gig I did. It was fun while it lasted, but I wasn't going to be talked down to. I went home to bed – and left them to it.

**Jenny Spires:** The Floyd did rise to the occasion though. The atmosphere changed to mellow and, as they began, the dawn light gradually filtered on down from the tall windows. I left before the very end and have no memory of the journey home. The next time I saw them was at Games For May...

**Games For May (promotional flyer, Queen Elizabeth Hall, London, 12 May):** 'Space age relaxation for the climax of spring – electronic composition, colour and image projection, girls, and the Pink Floyd...'

**Peter Jenner:** Games For May was down to my wife, Sumi, who had worked with Christopher Hunt, the classical promoter. Beforehand, we visited the BBC Radiophonic workshop where Syd met Delia Derbyshire [who'd arranged the *Doctor Who* theme tune] and the band made tapes which they used during the show. Rick now had a device we called the 'Azimuth Co-ordinator', which we'd had made and which had two joysticks that allowed him to pan the sound in any direction around the venue. The whole thing was more like performance art.

**Roger Waters:** I spent hours in a cold, ghastly basement off of the Harrow Road, making quadrophonic tapes for Games For May. I made bird noises recorded at half-speed to be played in the theatre's foyer as the audience was coming in.

***Financial Times* (review, 13 May 1967):** 'Flowers were thrown at the audience, followed by darkness, hysterical laughter... At times, the band members wandered the stage, playing with friction cars and blowing bubbles.'

**Roger Waters:** In those days, you could get away with stuff like chasing clockwork toy cars around the stage with a microphone. Everyone in the group was into doing something different. I ran out of potatoes to throw at the gong and thought if I kept moving, nobody would take any notice.

**Peter Jenner:** The whole ethos was, 'there is no barrier between the stars and the audience'. So the band blew bubbles and threw daffodils into the stalls to make them feel involved. But we got into trouble with the management, who claimed the bubbles smeared liquid on the floor and the daffodils stained their new leather seats.

**Roger Waters:** Now, my feeling is that pushing a toy car across a stage and following it with a microphone is a joke and has absolutely nothing to do with music. But I was always interested in the possibilities of rock 'n' roll, how to fill the space between the audience and the idea with more than just guitars and vocals.

**Nick Mason:** Games For May was one of the most significant shows we have ever performed, since the concert contained elements that became part of our performances for the following thirty years.

**Norman Smith:** What I was trying to do with Pink Floyd was develop more melody and lean away from psychedelia. When they came to do the second single, 'See Emily Play', I thought, *At last,* this *is the one.*

**Nick Mason:** We did 'See Emily Play' back in Sound Technique – where we'd done 'Arnold Layne' – because Norman felt we should go somewhere more relaxed. Abbey Road was fairly formal at the time. 'Emily...' shows the level of Syd's writing.

**David Gilmour:** I was in Paris playing with my group [by now called Flowers]. We'd had our microphones stolen and it was cheaper to take the train to London and buy some second-hand ones. So I came back and went to the 'See Emily Play' session and at that point Syd had definitely turned a corner into madness. Quite how far he had turned is debatable. Some people think he hadn't really gone round that corner, but maybe some of the people close to him were too close to see the changes.

**Syd Barrett (speaking in October 1967):** 'I was asleep in a wood after a gig in the north of England when I dreamed of a girl coming through the trees – shouting and dancing. That was Emily.'

**Emily Young:** The day of Games For May, I was wandering around the South Bank wearing a long white dress with flowers, as we did in those days. I thought about going backstage and saying hi but didn't.

Years later, a friend of mine, a novelist called David Flusfeder, rang me and said, 'I'm reading this biography of Syd Barrett and it mentions someone called Emily Kennet. Did you know that you were [the inspiration for 'See Emily Play']?' I'd always thought, 'Well, maybe'.

I think it's a beautiful song. 'Float on a river forever and ever...' – what a lovely line. But 'Emily tries but misunderstands...' – I'm not sure what it is I was misunderstanding. But, then, I don't think it was actually about me.

**Jenny Spires:** 'Emily' was the name Syd wanted to call his first daughter. He loved the name, and both Libby and Lindsay would probably tell you the same.

**Peter Jenner:** Roy Featherstone at EMI came up with the immortal slogan 'Straight To Heaven in '67' for 'See Emily Play'. Very naff perhaps, but very appropriate, because soon we were on our way to having a hit [eventually number five] and being asked to play *Top of the Pops*.

**Norman Smith:** I went along with the band to the BBC. In the dressing room, I told them what would happen. 'You won't be playing live, you'll be miming, but they'll do your hair and make-up...'

**Nick Mason:** My main memory is finding the road crew having their hair done. Nobody knew who anyone was, so as long as you had long hair and wandered in, someone would wash it for you.

**Norman Smith:** Syd looked terrific. Then he went straight to the mirror, messed up all his hair and grabbed a load of tissues to wipe off his make-up. So that demonstrated the kind of character I had to deal with. I had a go at him and told him he was going to destroy our recording career if he carried on like this.

**Jenny Spires:** The first *Top of the Pops* was great and Syd loved it. The second one, I think he had been tripping and turned up at Jock and Sue's in the afternoon when he should have been at the BBC.

**Susan Kingsford (Cambridge friend and ex-model):** Syd came round to our flat in Beaufort Street – 'Bang bang bang!' on the door. He had no shoes on, his feet were bleeding and he looked completely out of his head. He came in, grunted, we gave him some Sugar Puffs and a cup of coffee. But he just sat there.

About an hour after he arrived, 'Bang bang bang!' on the door again. I think it was Pete Jenner. 'Is Syd here?' 'Yes, he's in the kitchen but he's not very well.' 'I don't give a fuck.' Later that evening, I discovered they'd dragged him off to do *Top of the Pops*. The reason he was sitting on a cushion during the show is he couldn't stand up.

**Andrew King:** Getting him down to *Top of the Pops* for the third week running for 'See Emily Play', we couldn't find him. This is the BBC – 'Erm, sorry, we can't find the lead singer.' It was unheard of. You can chart his decline through those three performances. The first one he looks lovely, the last one he looks rough.

**Nick Mason:** Syd's argument was 'John Lennon doesn't have to do *Top of the Pops*, so why should I?'

**Norman Smith:** After *Top of the Pops*, they were due to go on a radio programme called *Saturday Club* [on 28 July]. I warned them there'd be a lot of sitting around, waiting. When they eventually called us to go on, nobody could find Syd. The doorman told me he'd seen him go out the door. Roger Waters and I went out and, sure enough, we could see him just about to turn the first corner into the street, and that was that...

**Peter Jenner:** I think it was around then Syd started living in 101 Cromwell Road. There were lots of people wanting to be his best friend, there were lots of messianic acid freaks. We heard stories of people spiking drinks.

**Jenny Spires:** It started to go wrong in summer 1967. I'd seen some signs of nervous exhaustion before this though as he was clearly under pressure to produce/write singles and more material for them. Syd's heart wasn't in it. I think he moved into 101 to get away from it all at first. He took over Jock and Sue's room when they moved to an upstairs flat in Beaufort Street.

**Lindsay Corner:** Syd and I went into 101 after Earlham Street. It's been pulled down now, but it was the most beautiful building, with a wonderful sweeping staircase, that became the stairway to hell. Everybody was completely out of their heads. Not Duggie Fields – Duggie was fine. But it was an insane time. One day, I went home to Cambridge for the weekend and locked my door as I was the only one with a television set. I came back and found everyone in my room, watching TV, having broken in. That was the sort of existence it was.

**Nigel Lesmoir-Gordon:** Jenny and I had a flat there. Ginsberg stayed over and Mick Jagger and Marianne Faithfull used to visit. Vince Taylor the pop star turned up one night, out of his mind on LSD. He'd created this grand cosmology where different rock stars represented Greek gods. He talked about it for hours.

**Iain 'Emo' Moore:** I'd moved to London and got to know people in the movie world through UFO, so I'd end up in these strange, unscripted films. Some Italian directors made a film in Nigel and Jenny's flat. The crew couldn't speak English, but gave us £10 each, a bottle of wine, a pizza and a big piece of silver foil filled with grass, and then one of the girls took her clothes off...

**Mick Rock:** I stayed there one summer and it was wild. But you also have to remember how young everyone was. There was a film out called *Wild in the Streets* [tagline: 'The Old Tigers Are Scared, Baby!'], in which everyone over twenty-five was like poison. Twenty-five was the cut-off point. Who knows what we were up to.

**Joe Boyd:** By now, people were getting arrested. Mick Jagger and Keith Richards got busted [and briefly jailed for drug possession in June]. The Beatles and the Stones were like deities. But they were a threat to the order of society and so there was the inevitable crackdown.

**Jeff Dexter:** I thought we were going to win – to persuade everyone that we weren't the enemy. The enemy were our leaders, not us. We were going to show the world a better time and not have any more wars. Of course, it didn't quite work out that way.

The producer Guy Stevens was the first to go out of the UFO gang. He had a little bit of dope and got sent to jail, which seemed so unfair. He was about to have the hit of the summer with Procol Harum's 'A Whiter Shade of Pale', which was played for the first time ever at UFO. Then Hoppy was sent down...

**John 'Hoppy' Hopkins:** I was sent to Wormwood Scrubs [for cannabis possession] in June for six months and two days, which became six months and three days for not emptying my piss pot on the first morning, because I didn't know the rules.

Allen Ginsberg came to see me and started chanting and tinkling his finger bells in the visitor's room. I don't think the screws understood, but I guess it was his spiritual release. The second week I was inside, *Sgt Pepper...* was released – and that saw me through some of those worst times.

**Anthony Stern:** On the day *Sgt Pepper...* came out, I went over to Earlham Street. Someone had given us some opium and we listened to the album twice with Syd and Peter Wynne-Willson – a moment of pure joy. The opium had actually been stolen from the Botanical Museum in Kew Gardens.

**Jeff Dexter:** Pink Floyd had a hit and that changed the whole complexion of what was going on at UFO. Steve O'Rourke and Tony Howard were pretty fair, but they weren't going to let Pink Floyd play for the same price as before and that put some noses out of joint. UFO could have increased their prices a little, but Joe didn't want to do that.

We tried hard to get them on at Tiles. But the booker was [blues vocalist] Chris Farlowe's wife and she couldn't see it, didn't think they were right. After the first trickle of radio plays for 'Arnold Layne', she realised she was wrong and we had them in June. I've read stories that Syd was gone by then, but he was fantastic on the night.

**Mick Farren:** I remember the words 'Pink Finks' being painted on the wall of the UFO toilet. But what bothered me more was that they seemed to back off in major haste from the drug culture in which they'd made their name when the shit started going down. That seemed like a cop out.

**Joe Boyd:** There was a story in the *News of the World* [headlined 'Hippie Vice Den'] and the police told Mr Gannon they were going to raid UFO. So we moved it to the Roundhouse. But we couldn't make enough money in the long term and it closed for good in October.

**Nick Mason:** In all honesty, psychedelia had been a good launch pad, but we didn't entirely understand it. What we did understand is you couldn't go on complaining about the 'suits, man' for too long. That's hardly surprising when you've got a record company desperate for you to do something and a public who aren't that interested in poetry readings.

**Peter Jenner:** Bryan Morrison booked the Floyd into London discos – places like Blaises and the Speakeasy – and blues clubs in pubs. They played a place in Ealing called the Feathers and someone threw a big old penny at Roger Waters because they weren't playing proper blues music.

**Roger Waters:** It made a bloody great cut in my forehead and bled quite a lot.

**Richard Wright:** The only time I'd get annoyed with Roger on stage was when he'd be playing out of tune. We'd be in D and he'd still be banging away in E because he couldn't hear it. I had to tune his bass on stage – he'd stick the head of the bass over the keyboards and I'd tune it.

**Nick Mason:** That *did* happen. I watched it occurring, but I would like to make it clear that Roger is capable of tuning his guitar... though it might take a while. But there was an element of, 'What *are* they doing?' because of our far-out music. It was fine at UFO, but not if we were out of town doing a Top Rank ballroom. We might be topping the bill as we'd been on *Top of the Pops*, but chances are we'd get blown off stage by Marmalade or the Move, who were proper pop groups. Other bands seemed so professional, because they'd been doing it solidly for two or three years – and we hadn't. We always felt like dilettantes.

**Peter Jenner:** People would get upset because they weren't getting a nice set of songs that sounded like 'Arnold Layne' or 'See Emily Play'. I think it was in Dunstable when someone in the balcony poured a pint of beer over Roger in protest. Somehow, it was always Roger who ended up as the target.

**Rosemary Breen:** I didn't understand Pink Floyd's music. Perhaps I wasn't clever enough. I'm sure it was very different and exciting, but only to a minority who did understand it or pretended to understand it. I went to see them at the Roundhouse that summer and it wasn't nice. Roger [Syd] was away with the fairies.

**Andrew King (press release, August 1967):** 'It is not true that Syd has left the group. He is tired and exhausted and has been advised to rest. We have decided the whole group will holiday for the next fortnight...'

**Dr Sam Hutt (future singer-songwriter Hank Wangford):** Pete Jenner and I were mates from Cambridge University and I was about to become a doctor, so the idea was to send Syd to the good doctor who knows about drugs and isn't going to freak out. So there was a therapeutic side to it which unfortunately didn't work.

We went to Formentera with Syd, Lindsay, Rick, Juliette, Roger and Judy. In the summer you'd get these fantastic electrical storms in the Mediterranean. During one, Syd was completely out of his head. You get sheet lightning behind the clouds and the sky lights up fluorescent – and it could affect you even if you weren't taking anything. Add acid to the equation and Syd was literally trying to climb the wall, trying to get himself off the floor.

**Jeff Dexter:** I remember hearing about that trip to Formentera. Sam and Rick's girlfriend, Juliette, both said Syd was not in a good place.

**Peter Jenner:** Syd's behaviour was avant-garde and I thought avant-garde was good. Of course, in hindsight, we should have taken a break, but none of us knew what we were doing and we had an album out.

✣

*Shortly after Games For May, the musician Hans Keller had interviewed Barrett and Waters on the BBC arts show* The Look of the Week. *Keller was baffled ('Why has it all got to be so terribly loud?'), but offered a pearl of wisdom and said their music reminded him of 'a regression to childhood'.*

*This certainly applied to* The Piper at the Gates of Dawn, *released in August. 'Matilda Mother', 'Bike' and 'The Gnome' evoked the Gog Magog hills, the River Cam, dons cycling down Silver Lane and Syd's childhood library containing* The Wind in the Willows, The Little Grey Men *and* Nursery Rhymes Of England.

*Also present, though, was grown-up stoned Syd poring over the* I Ching *('Chapter 24'), Sir James George Frazer's* The Golden Bough *('The Scarecrow') and Marvel comics ('Astronomy Domine') or serenading his beloved cat and 'Jennifer Gentle', presumably Jenny Spires, in 'Lucifer Sam'.*

*Musically, Barrett was cherry-picking too, borrowing the dissonant intro from AMM's 'Later During a Flaming Riviera Sunset' for 'Flaming', while the whole band raided the studio for bells, gongs, clocks and oscillators with which to decorate the songs.*

'The Piper at the Gates of Dawn *is pop but very free and full of improvisation,' said Waters at the time.*

*'Exploratory and freeform?' he blustered forty years later. 'Apart from "Interstellar Overdrive", everything else on it was ordinary.'*

❀

**Vic Singh (*The Piper at the Gates of Dawn* cover photographer):** Pete Jenner asked me how much I charged and I told him 300 quid. I listened to the album and had never heard anything like it. I didn't want to do a straight portrait picture, but I couldn't work out what to do instead. If I'm honest, I thought, *Christ, they've gone so far out with this music, it's unlikely to be successful.*

Anyway, they turned up for the session at my studio in Bourdon Place and I had a prism lens George Harrison had given me that could split each image up into four or five. So that was the idea – and it worked.

Of course, I invoiced them and never got paid because they didn't have 300 quid to give me.

**Nick Mason:** To start with, all of us, even Syd, were happy to head down to Carnaby Street and get kitted out with satin shirts and have those rather bouffant hairstyles.

**David Gilmour:** After summer 1966, I was gone from Cambridge for nearly a year and a half, so I never saw Pink Floyd in their psychedelic heyday. But I heard their album and thought they sounded terrific. I was sick with jealousy. Great songs, different but fantastic.

**Andrew King:** Syd and Lindsay moved into my flat in Richmond Hill. Rick and Juliette were already there, so our logic was it would be a better environment for him. Of course, after 'See Emily Play', there was that traditional music-biz pressure – Where's the next single? – which was one of the factors in driving Syd to desperation. Syd was the most likely person to come up with a hit single, so it was Syd we were pushing, more than Roger or Rick.

**Nick Mason:** We'd started recording again already. We had 'Set the Controls for the Heart of the Sun', which Roger had written on his own and which I think really signposted the way we should have been going but didn't for a while. But I still think 'Bike', 'Scarecrow' and 'Chapter 24' have a charm and have lasted pretty well.

**Andrew King:** At the start, it did feel like Syd plus the other three. By the time the first album came out, Roger was doing his best to crack that – or at least to make people feel that he had a stronger role.

**Peter Jenner:** Syd was at my house just before he had to go and record, and because a song was needed, he just wrote a description of what he was wearing at the time and a chorus that went, 'Vegetable man, where are you?'.

Things like 'Vegetable Man', 'Jugband Blues' and 'Scream Thy Last Scream' which was also from those sessions were ... interesting, different. But EMI were hardly going to accept these songs as a follow-up to 'See Emily Play'.

**Andrew King:** The last single with Syd wasn't very good, but at the time, I probably thought, *Oh dear, this is the best he can come up with*. In fairness, 'Apples and Oranges' wasn't *that* bad.

**Syd Barrett (talking about 'Apples and Oranges' in November 1967):** 'It's a happy song and it's got a touch of Christmas ... It's about a girl I saw just walking around town, in Richmond.'

**Peter Jenner:** For me, it was all still fine – everything was fine – but then Andrew took them to America. And when he came back, he was shell-shocked.

✣

*Pink Floyd's debut US tour began in November, more than a week later than scheduled, at San Francisco's Winterland Auditorium. This was the moment British psychedelia ran up against its American counterpart. Like freeways, shopping malls and food portions, the US version was bigger.*

Rolling Stone *photographer Baron Wolman shot the visiting Brits at Sausalito's Casa Madrona hotel, where Syd balanced sugar cubes on his tongue presumably as a sign of solidarity with other LSD users.*

*In between live dates, they mimed on* The Pat Boone Show *and Dick Clark's* American Bandstand, *where Rick Wright, rather than a vague-looking Barrett, answered most of the host's inane questions. Then things went downhill from there.*

✣

**Andrew King:** Everything went wrong from day one. I went out to San Francisco before the tour was to begin and sat in the promoter Bill Graham's office. The record company was an absolute waste of space, the visas hadn't come through and I felt like a complete prick. Bill ended up getting the American ambassador in London out of bed in the middle of the fucking night and the visas were on the plane the next day.

Pink Floyd missed the first show and Bill found a replacement, the Ike and Tina Turner Revue, which had been playing in the Bay Area. That was the first time a black act played the Fillmore – another little comment on American hippie culture, which was as racist as redneck country and western, as none of these kids had heard black music before.

**Peter Wynne-Willson:** Just before that trip, Syd, myself, possibly four of us in all, went to Vidal Sassoon's and had our hair permed. I always wonder if Syd had an adverse reaction to the perm because it seemed to be coincident. I remember the horror look that came into his eyes afterwards and it wasn't long before the American adventure.

Once we were there, he started to do some strange stuff with the front of his hair. He would straighten two bits down here and there and completely ignore what was happening at the back – and a slept-on perm without a bit of fluffing was not a good look.

**Andrew King:** Pink Floyd arrived and we brought our own light show which was absolutely useless. The Joshua Light Show [used at the Winterland] had the same sort of effects, but they were doing it on an industrial scale, and we were doing it on a primary-school play scale.

**Richard Wright:** Big Brother and the Holding Company with Janis Joplin performed well. Then the audience had this weird, English psychedelic band going on stage and not playing anything they recognised.

**Peter Wynne-Willson:** I remember Roger – and Nick, to a lesser extent – getting very interested in drinking a bottle of Southern Comfort with Janis at the Winterland. There was a lot of it and I'm sure Syd had some too. But what also happened was two young women took Syd and I off to some hillside ... I wouldn't call it a retreat ... just a phenomenally beautiful house.

While we were there, they plied us with a prodigious amount of dope. It may be smoking grass in the States took it up that extra notch. Afterwards, that was the first time I saw Syd standing on stage unable to play the guitar.

**Roger Waters:** We did *The Pat Boone Show* and, on the run-throughs, Syd would be miming away, but when they went 'Action!', he's just stand there, still. 'Cut! Cut!' Then he'd do it again, and again, until finally we had to say, 'Listen, he's a bit weird. I'll mime it.'

**Nick Mason:** We played the Cheetah Club in LA and Syd decided his permed hair was too curly. He sent someone out for a tub of hair gel, which he then applied in copious amounts.

**Richard Wright:** Someone came into the dressing room and said, 'You've got to see what Syd's doing.' And he'd crushed up all this [legal sedative] Mandrax and mixed it up with Brylcreem, and rubbed it in his hair. Then he came on stage and it all started melting.

**Andrew King:** Now I *don't* know about the Mandrax. That's just one of those stories. But he had lots of Brylcreem in his hair. It was like he was saying, 'Look, I'm really strange, what are you going to do?'. He performed in a minimalist way. It was bass and drums and Rick doing endless solos on the Farfisa to keep it going. Alice Cooper was there with his band, the Nazz, and rescued us. They invited Syd round, just to unwind a bit.

**Alice Cooper:** The Floyd ended up staying with us for a couple of nights at our place on Beethoven Street in Venice. I remember getting up one morning and there was Syd staring at a box of cornflakes the way you or I would watch television.

**Roger Waters:** Syd was no longer with us in any real sense. There's a bit in the movie [1982's *Pink Floyd – The Wall*] where the cigarette burns down between [the character] Pink's fingers. I went into Syd's hotel room in LA and saw that. He was in a very sorry state. By this point, I was saying to Peter and Andrew, 'Look, we can't go on like this.'

**Nick Mason:** We wanted to be pop stars and Syd didn't, and it polarised us. We all thought that's where we were heading, and suddenly someone is going, 'Is this what I want to do?'. But it wasn't even verbalised as clearly as that.

**Libby Chisman:** Syd came to see me at work after the American tour. Everybody else in the group was being sensible, but he'd spent every penny he earned – and he didn't know where any of it was, except he'd bought a pink car and was having it shipped home. I can see him now to this day, doubled up with laughter. He thought music was for spending money and having fun.

I was working as a translator at a university and about to get married. My boss saw Syd and said to me, 'Don't get tempted by that one. He's *very* peculiar?' Did he ever get the car shipped over? I don't know, but he certainly paid for it.

**Peter Jenner:** Andrew and I were trying to hold it together. But, after America, the trouble continued on the Hendrix tour when Syd started not turning up to some of the gigs.

**Nick Mason:** I think the first time I ever signed an autograph was on that tour. We were fourth on the bill to Amen Corner or someone [alongside the Nice, the Move and the Jimi Hendrix Experience, November 1967], travelling around Britain on a coach. There were even screaming girls, though that had limited appeal.

**Davy O'List (guitarist, the Nice):** The rest of us were on the coach, but Hendrix could afford a car – he had a limousine. I used to watch the Floyd and picked up on what Syd was doing. But I noticed he used to go off for long walks and not arrive until two minutes before he was due on, and one night he didn't turn up until after the show. He'd missed two gigs, including a matinee. That's when the rest of the band asked if I could stand in for him. It may have been at the Liverpool Empire, but it was definitely up north.

I told them I knew 'Interstellar Overdrive' and that it started in B. That's when they produced Syd's hat and said, 'You better wear this.' I decided to play with my back to the audience and girls started screaming, thinking it was Syd. Roger Waters was smiling away, thinking they'd got away with it – which was the point at which I turned around and the screaming stopped. We only did one show and, as soon as Syd found out, he came back. He never looked me in the eye on the coach after that.

**Jeff Dexter:** At 'Christmas on Earth Continued' [at the Olympia] in December, Syd didn't really play, he just flaked around. I was probably having as good a time as him, and many of my friends were too. But Syd became unwell. The trouble is, everyone falls in love with people that are on the edge because it all seems so romantic. We had it first with the pre-Raphaelites and it's never changed.

**Susan Kingsford:** Late in 1967, I was at Cromwell Road one night, everyone stoned, and nobody had said anything for a couple of hours. Then Syd suddenly said to me, 'Are you going home to Cambridge?'. I said, 'Yes, I'm going home at the weekend.' And he said, 'Do you know what? That's *all* I want to do. I just want to go home.'

*Syd Barrett's 1967 ended on New Year's Eve at the King family's cottage in the Welsh Black Mountains. He was joined by a gaggle of thrill-seekers, including the Lesmoir-Gordons bearing a generous supply of LSD.*

*One of the party, the Rolling Stones' playmate, 'Prince' Stash De Rola, son of the French-Polish artist Balthus, had to be dissuaded from sitting on a log fire, convinced that 'the love' would stop him getting burnt. Stash later claimed that he saw Barrett's torso 'replaced by the body of a giant teddy bear', with just his head remaining. A policeman called at the house, looking for an escaped convict but, incredibly, didn't arrest the lot of them.*

*Meanwhile, Barrett, while under the influence, spent most of one night holding a ceiling beam and balancing on a wine bottle, before challenging his friends' liberal sensibilities by leaving a shit on the doorstep. It was certainly an 'Oh wow, man!' moment.*

*A few days later, everybody put themselves back together enough for the long drive home. 'But I never really spent any time with Syd after that,' admitted Nigel Lesmoir-Gordon. 'Although we thought we were so switched on, reading Kafka and Beckett and Miller, the truth is we couldn't deal with a mad person.'*

# 4

# 'YOU HOLD THE LEG, AND I'LL BANG THE NAIL IN'

*'You can't do twenty minutes of this ridiculous noise', inside the mythical linen cupboard, 'Now everybody knows my bottom' and the £28,500 floorboards...*

✲

David Gilmour squints into the morning sun before walking barefoot from the front door of his Sussex farmhouse to his home studio. As we climb the stairs, a groundsman steers a motorised mower along a stretch of lawn and a horse pokes an inquisitive head over a stable door. Not a bad life, then...

Gilmour is talking about the summers of 1966 and 1967. By then, Jokers Wild had recorded a mini-LP and a cover of soul duo Sam and Dave's 'You Don't Know Like I Know' as a single. 'We pressed fifty copies of both and gave some to our friends,' he says. But record companies weren't racing to sign them up.

Music wasn't paying enough, but £50-a-day modelling jobs for Cambridge University's *Varsity* magazine didn't appeal as an alternative career. 'Dave is caught in these exotic multi-coloured trousers ... and gives the photographer a nonchalant glance' runs a blurb from *Varsity*'s June 1966 issue, alongside a picture of a shirtless Gilmour in floral legwear.

However, Gilmour had attracted the attention of blues pioneer and talent scout Alexis Korner. One of Korner's associates, Jean Paul Salvatori, whose management credentials largely hinged on his sister being married to the Move's manager, offered Jokers Wild a six-week residency at a hotel in Marbella. Only Gilmour, keyboard player/

saxophonist Dave Altham and drummer John 'Willie' Wilson were willing to make the move, so recruited their friend Rick Wills to play bass.

In July, the new group undertook an epic ferry and rail journey from London to Malaga, fraught with missed connections and lost luggage. Gilmour and co were sharing a carriage with donkeys and chickens somewhere in Spain when their fellow passengers congratulated them on England's victory over Germany in the World Cup final. The band didn't care: they were too busy working out how to retrieve their equipment, which had been left behind on a platform at Gard du Nord.

When they arrived in Marbella, they discovered Hotel Los Monteros was still under construction and their billet was essentially a disused bomb shelter. Fortunately, a neighbouring golf resort, popular with holidaying celebrities, needed a house band for the next few weeks. Italian actress Monica Vitti was among those peering at the young Brits playing Wilson Pickett's 'In the Midnight Hour' night after night.

The name Jokers Wild didn't work in Spanish, so Salvatori christened them Bullitt (although the Steve McQueen movie of the same name wouldn't come out until the summer of 1968). Dave Altham left soon after, before a residency in Saint-Étienne. 'And then two or three months at a club called Le Bilboquet in Paris and another six or seven months, gigging all over France,' explains Gilmour.

Soon after, Salvatori suggested changing the name to Flowers to sound more in tune with the times. Gilmour, who was fluent in French, was asked to squire Jimi Hendrix around Paris for the night and was hired to sing on the soundtrack for Brigitte Bardot's new romantic drama, *Two Weeks in September*, while all three played on a demo for French pop royalty Johnny Hallyday.

Any glamour, though, was offset by penury. By late summer, the gigs were drying up and they were surviving on the cheapest meals they could find at the Wimpy bar on Saint-Germain, and stolen bread and milk.

'In the end, I had to go to hospital,' says Gilmour, in his usual casually understated way. 'I think it was malnutrition. A promoter owed us a lot of money and I just thought, *I've had enough of this*.'

The group's Ford Thames van, which they'd accidentally filled with diesel, gave up just as their ferry docked in Dover. It was a symbolic moment. Wilson and Wills found their way back to Cambridge, but Gilmour didn't really have a home to go to.

He pulls one leg across the other, bare foot dangling: 'And going home anyway would have felt too much like giving up.'

✤

**David Gilmour:** The first time I saw Pink Floyd again was after I came back from France, and on the Hendrix tour at the Albert Hall. They did seventeen minutes – just about time for Syd to get tuned up. I had a day job, working as a van driver for Ossie Clark, from his shop, Quorum, in Chelsea. So I was doing that in the daytime and trying to formulate my next band move.

I think the next time was at the Royal College of Art in December and Syd was a bit on the gone side by then. That's when Nick Mason said to me, 'So... what would you say if we thought about asking you to join?' He sort of broached the subject.

**Davy O'List:** All of Pink Floyd, apart from Syd, turned up when the Nice played at the Marquee and the ICA at the beginning of the new year. They were standing by the side of the stage and I was hoping they'd say something because I knew they were looking for a new guitarist. But [the Nice's drummer] 'Blinky' Davison whisked me away into the dressing room – probably protecting his business interests.

**David Gilmour:** It was Nigel Gordon who rang me in January on Pink Floyd's behalf and said, 'You better get down there and meet up.' I suppose I was the only other person they knew who could sing and play guitar. But I think the other person they had in mind was Jeff Beck. That would have been interesting.

**Nick Mason:** We didn't have the courage to actually phone Jeff Beck and ask him.

**Peter Jenner:** There was a sort of audition at Abbey Road in Studio 2 and Dave Gilmour did this amazing impression of Jimi Hendrix. We thought, *Wow, he can do it*. I'd never met him before then.

**David Gilmour:** I'd first seen Hendrix at Blaises in South Kensington and our little group in France played a lot of songs from that first album, *Are You Experienced*.

**Andrew King:** The idea was David would be out on the road and Syd would stay home, writing great songs. Syd was quietly enthusiastic, if only for a week. Gilmour did what he had to do in the most graceful way he could.

**Rick Wills (bassist in Bullitt, Flowers and, later, Foreigner):** I was disappointed that the band fell apart in France, but it was logical for Dave to make the next step. The way he fitted into Pink Floyd was so perfect – it was as if it was written in a book. He was one of the few people Syd Barrett trusted and Roger, being the shrewd bugger he was, knew what needed to be done.

**Iain 'Emo' Moore:** I was helping the road crew on £15 a week and saw two gigs with Syd and Dave in the band. Syd would sit there strumming or not doing anything coherent, or he'd get the songs muddled and leave a verse out. At one gig, he was standing face to face with Dave. Then he started walking around him, almost checking he was a three-dimensional object, as if to say, 'Is this real? Am I dreaming this?'

**David Gilmour:** We only did a few gigs with the five of us and I don't have any memories of being on stage with Syd. But Nick's got a piece of film shot on a 8mm camera in a dressing room somewhere, probably Weston-super-Mare. Syd, Roger and Rick are standing in a line, I think, tap dancing in the dressing room – having a laugh.

So there were moments which felt almost normal and there were moments, like one of the first rehearsals we did at a place in Brondesbury Park, that didn't – like when Syd tried to teach us his new song. That was the have-you-got-it-yet? moment.

**Roger Waters:** He'd play us the song and say, 'It goes like this, right'. We'd all start playing together and then he'd do it again, slightly different, and say, 'Have you got it yet?'. And then he'd change it again – 'Have you got it yet?'. After the sixth time, I said, 'Yes, I've got it' and put the guitar down.

**Peter Wynne-Willson:** I know it's illogical, but I thought they ganged up on Syd. I remember a very difficult meeting at Blackhill's office on Edbrooke Road. Roger was saying, 'We can't deal with it anymore' and I couldn't believe he was saying such a thing. But, of course, they couldn't go on like that.

**Roger Waters:** In the end, I said to Peter and Andrew, 'Syd obviously can't perform live. Perhaps he could keep writing the songs and turn up at recording sessions?' They said, 'No, Syd wants two girl saxophone players in the group ... or something like that.' I went, 'Forget it.' And that's how our ways parted.

**David Gilmour:** We were playing a gig in Southampton [25 January] and were driving up Ladbroke Grove. Someone said, 'Shall we go and pick up Syd?' and someone else, probably Roger, said, 'No, let's not.' So we didn't. We drove down to Southampton and that was it.

I think the desire for survival outweighed other considerations. We all thought he was impossible to work with and therefore shouldn't continue to do so. Obviously we were wracked with guilt about it later on, but I don't think it was immediate.

**Nick Mason:** The weirdest thing is that it didn't feel strange. We were just so relieved to go back to how it had been before, which was really enjoying what we were doing. That was it then – we just stopped picking him up.

**David Gilmour:** I had to very quickly adapt to them and play stuff that I hadn't got a clue what I was doing. It was also excruciatingly embarrassing to the extent that I used to play with my back to the audience. I was very anxious to try and play these songs the way Syd and the band had been playing them for some time. But I was conscious that I needed at some point to try and make it more my own.

I remember when we played [the underground club] Middle Earth in Covent Garden [in March '68] and Syd came and stood in front of the stage and looked up at me – whether it was a look of anger, hatred or annoyance, it's hard to judge. But from my paranoid position being up there as the person who had taken his place, it wasn't all good vibes. There have been reports that he came to lots of gigs and followed us around the country in his Mini, but that's bullshit.

**Peter Wynne-Willson:** I left during the Hendrix tour because I didn't think they were taking the lighting seriously enough. There, you've found the chip on my shoulder... I left Susie [Gawler-Wright] to do the lights, which she did when it suited her. Then they got in John Marsh, who was a lodger at Edbrooke Road, and very good. I was hugely frustrated about the whole situation, though, and probably felt part of Syd's embattlement.

**Peter Jenner:** In hindsight, we put Syd under an awful lot of pressure. What we didn't realise at the time was what a short period this took place in. From the time I first heard Pink Floyd to when they left was just under two years, and the real juice of the story was from September 1966 to January or February 1968. So Syd went from being a carefree student living on his grant and having a bit of a smoke now and again to having all these people wanting to be his best friend and wanting to know the meaning of life and relying on him to bring in the money.

The idea that Roger Waters was going to become the main songwriter in the Floyd didn't cross my mind. But I did think that Rick could come into his own. I remember him sorting out the harmonies and middle-eights, and telling people what to sing on that first album. He also used to tune Roger's bass guitar. I'd like to know more about the way Rick and Syd worked, as I suspect there is a lot more to their working relationship than history allows.

**Richard Wright:** Peter and Andrew thought Syd and I were the musical brains of the group and we should break away. Believe me, I would have left with him, if I thought Syd could do it.

**Peter Wynne-Willson:** Peter and Andrew adored Syd. Both those guys had much softer centres than one might have imagined and I'm tempted to think now that maybe Roger had the same feelings for Syd.

**Peter Jenner:** By now, Blackhill were heading into tax issues, so we thought we'd better get an accountant. An accountant came along and asked to see our books, and we said, 'Books?'. He said, 'Have you paid national insurance?'. 'National insurance?' 'Have you saved up any money to pay your tax?' 'Tax?'

The Floyd were no longer such an easy sell. 'Apples and Oranges' wasn't a hit and it was difficult to get gigs because of Syd. The Bryan Morrison Agency were probably wondering whether they'd all turn up.

**Bryan Morrison (Pink Floyd's agent and future manager):** Jenner and King decided that they wanted to stay with Syd, which left Pink Floyd without a manager. The band approached me about fulfilling this function and it was agreed that I would become their manager.

**Peter Jenner:** I always wondered whether Bryan dried up the work deliberately. As soon as the Floyd transferred to him, the work started up again. Bryan is the man who told us, 'If any musician ever asks you for any money, say "yes", provided you sign a publishing contract.'

Nevertheless, Tony Howard was a fantastic agent and a great fan. I think partly because Tony was there, I had the confidence he would book them well. But, of course, by sticking with Syd rather than Pink Floyd, we backed the wrong horse.

**Richard Wright:** Syd was the songwriter and then we came in and had to take over the songwriting and it was a lot of responsibility. We could never write like Syd. We never had the imagination to come out with the kind of lyrics he did.

**Nick Mason:** It was an awful record [April 1968's first post-Barrett single 'It Would Be So Nice']. In that period, we had no direction. We were being hustled to make hit singles.

**David Gilmour:** Being in a covers band like Jokers Wild, what we were really good at doing was getting an audience dancing. We weren't something that you sat and listened to. I think I started trying to write a couple of songs when I was in France. I've got one memory of a song I wrote that I'm not going to divulge. Rather embarrassing.

When I joined Pink Floyd, I was twenty-one and the others were twenty-four – a big difference then. You have to fight your way to equality. In some ways, even all these years later, I still feel a little bit like that. Isn't that tragic?

At one point in the first few days, I left over musical differences, but went back again. I can't remember what it was about. Probably to do with Roger's teasing. He was being so unbearable, in a way that I'd later get used to.

**Roger Waters:** I took responsibility for the writing after Syd, largely because no one else seemed to want to do it and that is graphically illustrated by the fact that I started to write most of the material from then on.

**David Gilmour:** I don't think Syd ever came to the studio for the sessions I was involved in, though. 'Jugband Blues' had been completed and Syd's contributions recorded before then. One of the first ones was 'Set the Controls for the Heart of the Sun'. Then we did things like 'Corporal Clegg', and then moved on to 'A Saucerful of Secrets' through the early months of 1968.

**Norman Smith:** Once Dave Gilmour got on the scene, it was a different story altogether – so much easier. I wasn't that knowledgeable about the music they were playing, but I was able to get them to think more melodically.

**Richard Wright:** Norman Smith gave up on the second album. He said, 'You can't do twenty minutes of this ridiculous noise.'

**David Gilmour:** I remember, Nick and Roger sitting in the control room and drawing out something on a piece of paper and not really understanding it, but being happy to go along with it. I think the title track, 'A Saucerful of Secrets', is fantastic. I wouldn't want to play it these days, but I think it was a fascinating way of looking at music from a different angle.

I think they explained it to me in terms of mood and power, and we all thought it was about a war. The first part was the omen – and the feelings before it started. The second section was the actual war – very violent – and finally there was a requiem for the dead.

**Nick Mason:** We didn't read music, so we scored the whole thing on a piece of paper, using our own hieroglyphics. I'm very self-conscious maintaining anything we've ever done was art, but, if pressed, I think 'A Saucerful of Secrets' was naive art.

**Richard Wright:** I cringe at some of my songs, such as 'Remember a Day'. We were pretty amateurish at the time, but I don't think it was just my stuff that doesn't sound so good now. Something like 'Corporal Clegg', which was one of Roger's, is just as bad.

**Roger Waters:** 'Corporal Clegg' is about my father and his sacrifice in World War II. It's somewhat sarcastic – the idea of the wooden leg being something you won in the war, like a trophy.

**Nick Mason:** 'Set the Controls for the Heart of the Sun' was a high point. This was Roger moving on from 'Take Up Thy Stethoscope and Walk' [from *The Piper at the Gates of Dawn*], which is, in my opinion, not his greatest song, to 'Set the Controls…', which is one of them.

Roger sang lead vocals and it had this great rhythm that gave me the opportunity to play like one of my heroes, Chico Hamilton, whom I'd seen in [concert film] *Jazz on a Summer's Day*. That got me into using timpani mallets – although I looked at the film again, years later, and Chico didn't seem to have any mallets. So I don't know where I got that idea from.

**Peter Jenner:** 'Jugband Blues' is a really sad song – a portrait of a nervous breakdown.

**Nick Mason:** 'Jugband Blues' was the most wonderful poignant farewell, with the Salvation Army Band. So mournful. But it was a difficult session. At the same time, we'd recorded 'Scream Thy Last Scream' and

'Vegetable Man'. It was felt that those two songs weren't right for *A Saucerful of Secrets*. We didn't want to put any more of Syd on there than we had to.

**Phil Manzanera (future Roxy Music and David Gilmour band guitarist):** *A Saucerful of Secrets* is a nostalgic album for me. Our school band could play the little riff to 'Set the Controls…' very easily and just jam on it for half an hour, which was incredibly useful.

My brother was at Cambridge University, met David Gilmour and arranged for us to have lunch together. I was seventeen and David had just joined Pink Floyd. I met him in a restaurant on Brompton Road. He said, 'keep practising the scales or keep taking the tablets'.

**David Gilmour:** I was a bit lost and lonely in London when I first came back from France, and Storm and Po's flat in Egerton Court was one of the places I spent time hanging out. You used to go up one floor in this rickety old iron lift, and Nigel and Jenny Gordon had the nicest room overlooking Dino's, the Italian restaurant.

**Jenny Lesmoir-Gordon:** Nigel and I had moved out of Cromwell Road and into Egerton Court. Dave Gilmour used to come round to the flat a lot. He and Po would come into our room and just muck about – getting very stoned, pretending to be Frenchmen and things like that.

**Aubrey 'Po' Powell:** Roman Polanski shot some of his film *Repulsion*, with Catherine Deneuve, in the corridor at Egerton Court. After they were finished, the crew left their lights on the stairs, which then found their way back to Storm's room.

There was a lot of dope smoking and deep conversation in that flat. Storm was in his final year at the Royal College of Art. I'd nearly been sent to prison for my part in a bank fraud – so stupid! – and Peter Jenner had stood my bail. By now, Storm had taught me how to take photographs, and he and I had shot some book covers – pulp westerns, with our friends dressed up as cowboys in Richmond Park – and some things for Bryan Morrison's clients.

**David Gilmour:** I continued to hang out at Egerton Court when I wasn't working on *A Saucerful of Secrets*. One day, Storm said, 'Hey, can't you get them to book us to do the album cover?'. And I thought, *Hey, not a bad idea*. So I approached the others and the management, and that swung it.

**Aubrey 'Po' Powell:** When Storm and I saw what the artist Peter Blake had done with *Sgt Pepper...*, it changed our thinking overnight. We realised record sleeves didn't just have to have a boring photograph of a band.

So Storm and I created a collage of all the things we thought were associated with the Pink Floyd: Marvel comics – Doctor Strange is in there – astrology, alchemy, outer space. We also wanted it to be reminiscent of one of the band's light shows. EMI insisted there was a photo of the group, so we shot them on Hampstead Heath and ran it as small as we could get away with.

Then we used the dark room in the RCA's film school to develop the film. Totally illegally, I hasten to add, as Storm shouldn't have been in there and I wasn't even a student at the RCA. Really, this was the beginning of [Storm and Po's art house] Hipgnosis. We called the company Hipgnosis after Syd Barrett wrote the word in Biro on our front door at Egerton Court. At first, we were angry that we'd have to repaint the door. But we liked the word – 'hip' for fashionable and chic, and 'gnostic' for wise.

**Nigel Lesmoir-Gordon:** It wasn't Syd Barrett who wrote 'Hipgnosis' on the door. It was another friend of ours, the poet Adrian Haggard. Definitely not Syd, although I suppose that's a better story.

**Storm Thorgerson:** At first, designing record covers was a lot of fun. We were kids, it was exciting and Pink Floyd were just emerging. The main thing would be we were all part of a movement which was trying to wrest control from the record companies.

EMI hated our cover for *A Saucerful of Secrets* because they had their own art department and were being presented with this *thing* by a couple of unknown amateurs – and it didn't even have a big picture of the band on the front. But the band liked it, or at least I think they partially liked it.

**Nick Mason:** A lot of this was to do with the Beatles proving to EMI the artist knew better than the company in terms of dealing with the music and the graphics and the rest of it. After *Sgt Pepper...*, it was like, 'Great! Let's do our own album cover.' For a group that had just lost its lead singer and chief songwriter, we were incredibly confident. Or foolish.

✣

A Saucerful of Secrets *was released in June and reached the UK Top 10 without having a hit single. Instead, the album was defined by its marathon title track and 'Set the Controls for the Heart of the Sun'. Elsewhere, World War II and Cambridge were represented by 'Let There Be More Light' (about roadie 'Pip' Carter's father supposedly spotting a flying saucer over the Fens), and 'Corporal Clegg', the first of Waters' many songs addressing the futility of war.*

*Despite their composer's antipathy, Wright's 'Remember a Day' and 'See-Saw' came closest to mimicking Barrett's gentle whimsy. Syd's guitar was supposedly somewhere in the mix on 'Remember a Day' and 'Set the Controls...', but the faltering metre and self-questioning lyrics on 'Jugband Blues' was his true swansong.*

*In 2017, the song's original video, showing Barrett staring into the camera lens, was screened during a press conference for the upcoming Pink Floyd exhibition, 'Their Mortal Remains'. Aubrey 'Po' Powell was on stage with Mason and Waters, but didn't turn his chair to watch 'because I found it too upsetting'.*

*Summer '68 was a happier time, at least for the band, who launched the album by playing alongside their underground rock peers (including Marc Bolan's new group Tyrannosaurus Rex) at 'The Midsummer High Weekend', a free concert in Hyde Park.*

✣

**David Gilmour:** Peter Jenner and Andrew King were nice middle-class boys who used their connections to swing a free concert in Hyde Park, which had never been done before – certainly not with pop groups. It was in a place called the Cockpit, which was down by the Serpentine in a natural amphitheatre. The Stones did the next one – Mick Jagger in his frock, releasing butterflies for Brian Jones – but that was much bigger.

**Andrew King:** We put Pink Floyd on because we never actually fell out with them – there were no rows. Somebody on the inside once told me, 'Roger Waters doesn't dislike you as much as he dislikes everyone else.' I'll take that as a compliment.

**Peter Jenner:** We'd taken on Marc Bolan's group Tyrannosaurus Rex. Marc was a huge Syd Barrett fan, if rather difficult to manage.

**David Gilmour:** Marc used to hang around in our office and sit on the floor, strumming his guitar, flirting with our secretary, June Child, whom I think he later married. He was quite fun, probably a big pain in the arse too, of course, because he was very full of himself. He always liked being called the 'Bolan Child'. People thought it was some magical, mystical name, but it was what was written on the doorbell of his flat in Ladbroke Grove. It had his surname, 'Bolan', and our secretary's surname, 'Child'.

**Nick Mason:** Hyde Park in '68 was more of a picnic in the park than a mini-Woodstock. It also reminded us that we were part of this thing which was now a commercial venture, but gave us some credibility. It showed the better side of the business.

UFO was over. We couldn't get onto the Top Rank ballroom circuit anymore because we hadn't had a hit since 'See Emily Play'. But the college circuit, the red-brick universities, and the blues clubs had opened up to us. You now had students who weren't into the hit parade, but into albums, had long hair and long coats and sat cross-legged on the floor listening.

**Peter Jenner:** If you played clubs or pubs, you might be on £50 a night. But social secretaries at universities had bigger budgets and a captive audience. If they could get a thousand people in for a Friday-night gig, you could get £1,000.

**David Gilmour:** In those early days, there was still a bit of a divide in the band. We used to drive this vintage Bentley to gigs – a terrible heap. Roger would drive with Nick in the front passenger seat and they would always stop at the first off-licence and buy a bottle of whisky and a bottle of Stone's ginger wine, which they would mix into mugs and sip on the way.

It was terribly *un*politically correct and not something I would advise anyone to do. But Rick and myself would sit on the back seat, which had little tables that folded out from the seat in front like in an aeroplane, where we would skin up joints.

So Roger and Nick were the 'straights', with their alcohol, and Rick and I were the more fuzzy brained ones with our weed. I think Syd would have been in the backseat camp, and definitely felt, as many people did then, that if you were a 'head', you were in some ways morally superior.

**Nick Mason:** There were also these psychedelically painted hippie venues on the continent – places like the Paradiso in Amsterdam – that modelled themselves on the Fillmore West in California that welcomed us. They kept us going and their audience saw us as a form of intellectual rock 'n' roll. We were still doing rather more curious music than the norm.

**Roger Waters:** Those gigs in Holland were because of one guy, Cyril van den Hemel, a very young, ambitious promoter. But we would do gigs in the afternoon without telling the management. These would be mainly in primary schools where Cyril would say, 'You only need to bring the drum kit and one amp,' and he'd wheel us into the school auditorium in front of a load of eight-year-olds.

We'd play for about fifteen minutes to these poor kids sitting cross-legged and wondering what the hell was going on. Then Cyril would say the same thing: 'We got the money, we go now', and we would get the £20 or £30 or whatever it was, say 'Thank you very much' and leave.

**Rick Wills:** I remember Gilmour coming back to Cambridge after he played in Holland and he had about £80 in cash on him. He went straight to Ken Stevens Music shop to buy some headphones you could plug straight into the guitar while practising. He also had a Fender Strat by then, the long hair, the velvet jacket, the black sailor pants and these boots that we all had made at Gohil's in Camden Town. He was really looking the part.

**Vivien Brans:** I went to America to work as a nanny in 1966 and met up with David when Pink Floyd came to New York. Roger wouldn't have any truck with me – maybe I wasn't strident enough for him? – but I didn't mind. We all ended up sharing a cab back to Grand Central Station and I remember thinking, *Wow, David. You've come a very long way from the Victoria Ballroom.*

✲

*Pink Floyd's second US tour had begun in July 1968 as chaotically as their first, with delayed visas and stolen guitars. In New York, Waters braved his second and final LSD trip, and was overcome by fear in the middle of Eighth Avenue. 'I ended up stood there, frozen and unable to move.'*

*The American press weren't fully sold on Pink Floyd, and* Rolling Stone *magazine denounced* A Saucerful of Secrets *as 'psychedelic muzak'. However, the patrons at hipper clubs, such as New York's Scene or Chicago's Kinetic Playground, were like those at Middle Earth or UFO. Better still, most of them didn't know who Syd Barrett was.*

*At the Scene, Waters hurled a glass at the gong during 'A Saucerful of Secrets' and lacerated his hand – all in the name of art. He was simply trying to show off and put on a show. Earlier, Blackhill Enterprises had applied to the Arts Council for a £5,000 grant to fund Floyd's earlier scheme: an ambitious live production 'like a fairy tale, with the Floyd providing the music,' said Waters at the time, before admitting it was a desperate ploy to stop the company going bankrupt.*

*The council turned their request down, shortly before Pink Floyd's next single, 'Point Me at the Sky', failed to chart.*

✲

**David Gilmour:** 'Point Me at the Sky' was probably the first thing I wrote with Roger, round at his flat in Goldhawk Road. One of the problems in those early days was there was no medium to record things on. So when you made up a tune, if you didn't have access to a recording studio, you couldn't remember it because I couldn't read or write music. So I had no way of hanging onto things.

**Nick Mason:** We became an albums band – a deliberate policy devised by the great British public that wouldn't buy our singles – for the next eleven years until 'Another Brick in the Wall [Part 2]'. EMI were happy to let us carry on, as long as we sold albums, and we were now playing larger venues. We couldn't write hit songs, but were selling tickets. I suppose you could still describe some of what we were doing as performance art.

**Aubrey 'Po' Powell:** Hipgnosis designed the poster for what was called 'The Massed Gadgets of Auximenies [More Furious Madness From the Pink Floyd]' concert at the Royal Festival Hall [on 14 April 1969]. It was a crude artwork in the style of the surrealists in the 1930s – the way Man Ray would have created his artworks in a dark room by sticking photos over other photos. So ours was a layered collage of images including ears – possibly Storm's – and clocks and flowers, of which I felt extremely proud.

***Melody Maker*** **(review of 'The Massed Gadgets of Auximenies…', 19 April 1969):** 'Pink Floyd performed two pieces of music, "The Man" and "The Journey". Bird sounds signified daybreak, followed by band members hammering and sawing amplified logs, which signified work…'

**Roger Waters:** 'The Man' and 'The Journey' was the story of a day in the life of 'Everyman'. Sleep, work, play, start again…

**Nick Mason:** So much of this stuff is just lost, because we never thought to film it at the time. It was great fun, but some of it was absolute nonsense – the rhythm of the sawing wood and whistling kettles. The table building thing we did with the four of us – 'You hold the leg and I'll bang the nail in'. Who was the best carpenter? I don't think any of us were particularly good.

**Aubrey 'Po' Powell:** They spent twenty minutes building a table and I think there were roadies making tea. It was incredibly avant-garde, but the longer it went on, I started to feel embarrassed. I'm not sure they felt totally comfortable either, especially David Gilmour. In retrospect, it was the beginning of what Roger Waters has since described as 'electric theatre'.

**Roger Waters:** Some might say it was experimental – sitting on stage making cups of tea – but I have to say, looking back it was pretty embarrassing. But, to be honest, we probably did all this improvisation because we hadn't yet come up with constructive songs to perform.

**Tim Renwick:** It was very odd – a bit art school, but quite light-hearted. It wasn't terribly heavy. They had a bloke dressed up as a gorilla, I think, running around scaring people. They always seemed to do something to make it more than just a rock show.

**Nick Mason:** One of our art school friends, Peter Dockley, created a monster costume involving a gas mask and some genitalia rigged up with a reservoir to enable him to urinate on the front row of the audience.

**Peter Dockley:** I was doing sculpture at Hornsey College of Art, but was interested in performance art and started making costumes to wear. Pink Floyd paid me £10 a night to dress up as what we called 'The Tar Monster'.

My performance accompanied a piece which included the sound of water dripping in a cave. I'd quietly make my way through the stalls, sniffing those in the aisle seats. Once people got over the shock, they were fine – though a girl in the front row one night screamed and rushed out of the building.

I ended up skipping around like a lively orc from *The Lord of the Rings* before spraying people with fake urine. The phallus was the largest washing-up liquid bottle I could find. Once, I threatened to spray the band as well. It could have been the greatest rock 'n' roll story – 'Tar Monster Electrocutes Pink Floyd On Stage' – but I thought better of it. I did the whole tour and several venues with them, including the Albert Hall.

**Nick Mason:** Rick played the Albert Hall organ and Norman Smith conducted the choir and we let off cannons and a smoke bomb. The powers that be weren't terribly impressed.

❦

*The term 'multimedia' wasn't in common use yet, but definitely applied to some of Pink Floyd's ventures around this time. In the summer of '67, there'd been vague talk of a* Magical Mystery Tour*-style TV movie,* The Life Story of Percy the Ratcatcher*, and, in December, they'd unsuccessfully submitted a sparse soundtrack of clicking bass and dissonant guitar for conceptual artist John Latham's animated movie,* Speak.

*In April '68, Pink Floyd created something marginally more tuneful for director Peter Sykes' film noir,* The Committee. *Then came an offer from Swiss-born arthouse film-maker Barbet Schroeder to compose the soundtrack to his latest movie* More. *The story tapped into the post-summer of love: a German hitch-hiker is bewitched by an American heroin addict, before casual nudity and drug abuse ensues on the Spanish island of Ibiza.*

*During recording, parts of the soundtrack songs 'Cymbaline' and 'Quicksilver' were incorporated into live performances of 'The Man' and 'The Journey'. Similarly, some of the live suites were recycled for the studio tracks on Pink Floyd's next album, the half-live/half-studio double set,* Ummagumma.

More *and* Ummagumma *arrived in June and November respectively. The first was a charming mix of cod-jazz, psychedelic pop and loud rock. But* Ummagumma*'s studio half disappeared up its own fundament, with laboured sound effects ('Several Species of Small Furry Animals Gathered Together and Grooving With a Pict') and a clattering Stockhausen-inspired piano concerto, 'Sysyphus Parts 1–4'.*

*'There was,' cautions David Gilmour, 'an awful lot of floundering around.'*

❦

**Barbet Schroeder (film director):** I had Pink Floyd's first two albums and I thought their music was the most extraordinary thing I had ever heard. I went to London and took them a print of the *More* movie and they said, 'Yes'. It was as simple as that.

The band liked the film and they liked that it was making a difference between heroin and grass and psychedelic drugs. That point was important for them, because at that time, all drugs seemed to be mixed into one. But I also think they learned a lesson about making music in two weeks rather than spending months on it.

**Nick Mason:** A lot of things were offered to us at that time – film music, especially – and we rarely turned work down. We would have loved to have done [Stanley Kubrick's 1968 sci-fi epic] *2001: A Space Odyssey*. I know we pushed for it, but I suspect the deal broke down because the money was so poor. We took on *More*, but because it was an outside project, we weren't allowed to use Abbey Road Studios.

**Roger Waters:** We booked some time in Pye Studios, which is where we first met the engineer Brian Humphries. I was sitting at the side of the studio writing lyrics while the others were putting down the backing tracks.

**Brian Humphries (studio engineer):** They wanted a studio where they could work from midnight until first thing in the morning. Some of the other engineers at Pye were married. But I said I'd do it because I was available and had nothing to go home for – and that's how we first met. Of course, it was already two versus two even then. Roger and Nick on one side, Dave and Rick on the other... Me as piggy in the middle.

**Barbet Schroeder:** It was a very intense two weeks. The sound engineer couldn't believe the speed and creativity of the enterprise. I didn't believe in 'film music'. It was not meant to be music made by the minute for the movie and recorded with the image on the big screen. I wanted to believe that this was the music that the characters were listening to. So, during the party scene in the film, the music came out of a loudspeaker in the room. Their music was beautiful and fantastic.

**Nick Mason:** We liked Barbet, but later that year we worked with [director] Michelangelo Antonioni for his film, [the student drama] *Zabriskie Point*. We flew to Italy and had to use his studio from midnight onwards and it was terribly hard work. Antonioni didn't like anything we did. He rejected one of Rick's pieces ['The Violent Sequence'] saying it was 'too sad' and we ended up using it years later on *The Dark Side of the Moon*.

**Brian Humphries:** They asked me to go to Rome and be their engineer on *Zabriskie Point*. I didn't want to lose the gig, so when Steve O'Rourke asked me how much I wanted as a fee, I told them 300 quid. Steve agreed immediately and then said, 'Oh, you could have asked for much more on that, Brian. We're not the ones paying you.' I found out I could have added another nought on there.

**Richard Wright:** Antonioni was in the studio with us every night for two weeks until eight in the morning… every night for two weeks, just to get twenty minutes of music.

**David Gilmour:** Doing film music was a path we thought we could follow in the future. It wasn't that we wanted to stop being a rock 'n' roll group. It was more of an exercise. I don't think we knew what we were doing, except we knew what we were doing best at the time was playing live.

So we recorded two gigs – at Mothers in Erdington and Manchester College of Commerce. Mothers was a great club, but the recording of that night doesn't really do it justice, so I think most of the live album ['Astronomy Domine', 'Careful With That Axe, Eugene', 'Set the Controls for the Heart of the Sun', 'A Saucerful of Secrets' on sides one and two of *Ummagumma*] came from Manchester.

Then someone – probably Roger – suggested we should make a double and all do a solo ten minutes on the other album. So we all went in to try and do our things, whatever they were.

**Peter Mew (Abbey Road studio engineer):** By the end of the '60s, the producers were no longer in control. The bands were. But the challenge was trying to translate what they heard in their heads.

My recollection of *Ummagumma* is that everybody assembled in the studio on the first day and the producer, Norman Smith, asked, 'Have you got any songs?', to which they replied, 'No' – after which it was decided, after some discussion, that they would have a quarter of the album each. There was no grand plan, as I remember it. Norman did try to direct what was going on, and he definitely directed.

Those songs all ended up to their full potential, shall we say. If you start from the point of view that you don't know what you're doing and you're making it up as you go along, it's difficult to know where it's going to end up.

**Roger Waters:** We did those [songs] in total isolation. We played everything ourselves, with minor exceptions. We never even heard what the other three did.

**Nick Mason:** It was like being back at school and told to write an essay. There are some bits on *Ummagumma* I like. But I'm not tempted to bring 'The Grand Vizier's Garden Party' out again. That's best left where it is. I still don't like drum solos. I see them as an opportunity to go and get a drink.

**David Gilmour:** I have never listened to my song, 'The Narrow Way', since then. I experienced a feeling of alarm when Roger suggested we do a bit each – 'Hey, you've got a ten-minute slot to yourself.' We were at a loose end and didn't know what the fuck else to do. I was aiming for melody. I was always keen on that because I saw myself first and foremost as a musician and that was the dominating force in what I wanted to do. But I ended up ringing Roger and asking him to write some lyrics for me and he said, 'No, do it yourself' and put the phone down.

**Tim Renwick:** I was coming down to London from Cambridge by now – trying to be an aspiring musician and not really knowing how to go about doing it. I'd bumped into Syd on Charing Cross Road and was very impressed by what Pink Floyd were doing at the UFO. But listening to those early records with David – I thought he was kind of underused, really, because his voice and his guitar playing were wonderful.

**Roger Waters:** The individual studio things we did were just scratching around. My songs ['Grantchester Meadows' and 'Several Species of Small Furry Animals Gathered Together and Grooving With a Pict'] had a little bit of humour in them at least.

**Peter Mew:** 'Grantchester Meadows' ends with the sound of a fly being swotted – so it's all rather tongue in cheek. They were exploring the boundaries of technology on that album. So there are a lot of cute little effects – double speed, reverb stuff – bearing in mind the state of the technology at the time. But it was spread over a long period. There were a few sessions in January and then again later in the year, so *Ummagumma* wasn't a coherent work.

**Iain 'Emo' Moore:** I could barely read or write when I left school. 'Pip' Carter was a fen boy and you couldn't understand what he said, until I taught him normal English. So it was like we had our own language. 'Ummagumma' was one of my sayings. 'Ummagumma' is like 'I'm-a-gonna...' as in, 'Ummagumma... go home and, er, shag my girlfriend...'

**Storm Thorgerson:** Ironically, *Ummagumma* had a picture of the band on the cover. We actually gave EMI what they wanted! It was my partner Libby January's idea to photograph them at her parents' house, where Jokers Wild and the Floyd had both played that famous birthday party.

**Aubrey 'Po' Powell:** The band were unknown and enigmatic, and usually covered up by their light shows, so I think they finally thought *Let's be on the front*. But we didn't want to photograph them in the normal way. Storm came up with the idea of picture within a picture, which we called 'The Droste Effect', because we'd seen it on the packaging for a Dutch cocoa called Droste. The woman pictured on the packet is holding the same packet on a tray and so on.

We stuck the record sleeve for [the soundtrack of the 1958 musical] *Gigi* against the wall simply because we needed something to fill the space. There was no hidden meaning, despite what anyone might think.

**David Gilmour:** *Gigi* was only there because Storm needed a shadow on the wall. I think on the American version of *Ummagumma* they blanked it out because the record wasn't on EMI in the States.

**Aubrey 'Po' Powell:** *Ummagumma* came out on Harvest, EMI's little imprint label for what was called underground or progressive music. This was a gift to Hipgnosis, because *Ummagumma* became a hit [UK number five] and we were asked to design covers for other groups on Harvest – people like the Edgar Broughton Band, Quatermass and Syd Barrett. Between Harvest and the Bryan Morrison Agency, we were getting a lot of clients.

**Bryan Morrison:** At the end of the Royal Albert Hall concert ['The Final Lunacy'], I walked into the dressing room and Roger Waters asked me to step outside as he wanted to talk to me about something urgent: 'Bryan, you're fired.' The pity of it is I was within months of passing my management of the band on to Steve O'Rourke anyway.

**Aubrey 'Po' Powell:** I liked Bryan. He was an old-time music biz guy – always smoked a big cigar, wore an immaculate suit and a lot of aftershave. I got to be friendly with him later and went to see him, after he had a burst ulcer, in the south of France. He said, 'None of those other fuckers came to visit, Po.' In fact, I just happened to be in the area, around the corner from the hospital, but anyway... Steve O'Rourke was great for Pink Floyd. Roger might disagree, but I don't think David would.

**Andrew King:** I was a bit jealous, but they couldn't have had a better manager than Steve. He sorted out some big mistakes we'd made in our contractual relationship with EMI. He had an eye for the main chance and used it to the band's advantage. He was the archetypal modern manager, whereas Peter and I were the first of the middle-class Oxbridge guys. The old-school manager would have had his finger in many pies. But Steve had one client – the band – and nothing compromised him in what he would do for the band. He was untouchable.

✲

*The end of the '60s seemed to spell the end of the Cambridge contingent's long, tortuous psychic journey. The drugs hadn't worked and, despite the Beatles proclaiming otherwise, you needed more than love. Now some were looking for answers elsewhere: in religion, psychiatry, meditation and the ancient Indian discipline of yoga.*

*In the summer of 1968, Syd Barrett and Lindsay Corner moved into the Lesmoir-Gordons' old room at Egerton Court. In a surprising volte-face, Nigel and Jenny had gone to India to be initiated into the Sant Mat spiritual movement. The couple renounced the hedonism of the previous years to follow an abstemious path: no drugs, meat or alcohol; just copious meditation.*

*'Nigel and Jenny were the first to go,' says Peter Wynne-Willson, 'and then Susie and I and Russell Page followed in 1969.' Another Cantabrigian and Egerton Court resident, John 'Ponji' Robinson, also made the trip east. His half-brother, the future actor Matthew Scurfield, stayed on at the flat and experienced Barrett's curious behaviour first hand.*

*Stories of Syd taking LSD on a daily basis are rife, but completely unsubstantiated and most likely exaggerated. On paper, his move into Egerton Court made sense, then. Jenner and King thought his chance of writing songs again would be improved by being around old friends. The reality was rather different.*

❊

**Aubrey 'Po' Powell:** When Syd and Lindsay arrived, it was falling apart at Egerton Court. Psychiatry had become very fashionable and you had the Tavistock Institute which was started by the radical psychiatrist R.D. Laing. Dave Gale was going to see one of Laing's colleagues and Storm and I were seeing therapists too. Suddenly, after years of just having fun, the reality of life was kicking in.

In my case, I was freaked out after my court case [for bank fraud] and by taking LSD. I never had a bad trip, but if I smoked a joint, I started to get the fear. So I stopped smoking dope and started taking Valium, or whatever the equivalent was back then. Seeing Syd go over the edge at Egerton Court increased the fear of it happening to me.

**Matthew Scurfield (actor, Barrett's ex-flatmate):** I remember seeing Syd experimenting with a clock and putting it in a bath tub full of water at Egerton Court and trying to record the sound it made. I'd met him at the Criterion in Cambridge a couple of years earlier and we became friends. He used to take me to London to see my brother 'Ponji' in his old, clapped-out Morris. He was a sweet guy. But, later on, he frightened me because he was so unpredictable.

**David Gale:** Syd started to behave very strangely at Egerton Court. In that period, he was very turbulent indeed. He'd have groupie girls coming round who specialised in making exotic shirts for rock stars and then shagging them.

Lindsay was very upset by all this. I had the tiny room next to his and Lindsay's, and I'd hear thumping noises and screams. Syd would tickle her and then it would quite quickly get darker. She would beg him to stop and he would start banging her head on the floor.

**Peter Jenner:** Syd's relationship with women is something I don't want to get into. There was a dark side to it, which I think was to do with the communication issue.

**Jonathan Meades (future author, broadcaster):** I knew Po and Dave Gale, but I was very peripheral, always an outsider, in that scene. I was at RADA [Royal Academy of Dramatic Arts] and that Cambridge lot were much more reckless and gung-ho than I was. I remember visiting Egerton Court and hearing this noise, like heating pipes shaking, and someone – I think, Po – told me, 'Oh that's Syd having a bad trip, so we put him in the linen cupboard.'

Po has said retrospectively that I was being fed a line. But I saw Syd a few times after that and I think he could be quite selfish and demanding, and couldn't see beyond his own preoccupations, which is why they probably locked him in a cupboard.

**Aubrey 'Po' Powell:** There wasn't a linen cupboard at Egerton Court. I made a flippant comment to 'Jonty' Meades and was mortified to read it repeated in a newspaper years later. What happened was Syd locked himself in the lavatory – he was probably stoned and disorientated – and he couldn't work out how to undo the lock. I think we spent twenty minutes outside, talking him down.

**David Gale:** Because I'd been having psychoanalysis with R.D. Laing's colleague, David Cooper, I was able to ring up Laing and tell him I was a friend of Syd Barrett's and I thought he would benefit from psychotherapy. Laing said he wasn't going to see anybody who didn't come of their own accord. I said, 'Leave it to us. If you give us an appointment, we'll persuade him', and he agreed. We didn't mention it to Syd, until the very last minute. But when the taxi arrived, he refused to get in.

**Roger Waters:** Oh, how history develops. Who took Syd to see R.D. Laing? *I* took him in *my* car and he wouldn't get out of the car. This was around the same time I contacted his brother Alan. I spoke to him on the telephone and I persuaded Alan, against his wishes I might add, to come to London and see Syd, which he did. Then Alan wrote to me and said, 'Roger [Syd] has had some problems, but he's fine now, so don't worry anymore...' But I can see Syd pulling the wool over his big brother's eyes and pretending to be normal.

**Jenny Lesmoir-Gordon:** When Nigel and I came back from India, we visited Egerton Court. Syd and Lindsay had gone by then and we found one of Syd's drawings discarded under the bed. It was of a human skull with a train entering one side and coming out the other, and above it were the words 'That's weird'. It would probably be worth some money now...

**Duggie Fields:** In 1968, I went to America with a friend who worked at Ossie Clark and Alice Pollock's shop, Quorum, where Dave Gilmour was the van driver that all the girls fancied. When I came back, I needed somewhere to live, as did Syd, who'd left Egerton Court and had split up with Lindsay.

An estate agent told us about a place [Flat 29, Wetherby Mansions] in Earls Court, which was an area in decline, but it was all we could afford. David Gilmour was living on Earls Court Square too, in Richmond Mansions, and from our kitchen window, we could see into his flat. We used to go round there quite often and Syd's two solo albums wouldn't have happened without Gilmour.

**Peter Jenner:** I'd produced some sessions with Syd [in spring 1968] because Andrew and I both wanted him making music again. This was me being an amateur psychiatrist because of my academic background – 'Don't treat him like a looney. Maybe Syd's the sane one and we're all mad...' Of course it didn't work. Then Malcolm Jones, the head of Harvest Records, heard some of Syd's new songs and offered to produce him. Personally, I can't distinguish between the two albums, *The Madcap Laughs* and *Barrett* [both released in 1970] because they were all a mess.

**'Willie' Wilson:** Syd asked me to play on the album [*The Madcap Laughs*] and our friend [Humble Pie drummer] Jerry Shirley came along too. Jerry played some bass. But the songs were never the same twice. Syd started off okay and then he'd be strange, then he was fine for a day, and then two days a bit strange again...

**Peter Mew:** Malcolm Jones was a nice young chap. He wasn't a standard Abbey Road producer, so I don't know how he got involved. I think a lot of producers would have been scared of working with Syd.

The first session was a test session. In those days, you'd do two or three takes of each song – ten minutes each – because people used to do their preparation in rehearsal rooms or at gigs. I did the first session with Syd and he'd start a song and tail off halfway through. Then he'd walk around a bit and try something else. It may go all the way through, it might not. I did the session [in May 1969] when he brought in Soft Machine, and ended up listening to the same thing over and over again, people making mistakes.

**Robert Wyatt:** I was surprised when I got the call. So we trooped along to Abbey Road, the three of us in Soft Machine [Wyatt, bassist Hugh

Hopper and keyboard player Mike Ratledge]. The songs would stop, start and falter like you'd get with an old blues singer. I enjoyed that, though. But you had to do a bit of mental arithmetic, because Syd's songs were random and unpredictable.

**David Gilmour:** I don't know the exact timings and when Syd was with Peter Jenner and Malcolm Jones. I only know that they had stopped working with him and EMI were going to dump his album [*The Madcap Laughs*] because they had spent so much money getting to that point where they only had half a dozen tracks.

Syd asked if Roger and I could help him and I negotiated with EMI to get a few more days to finish *The Madcap Laughs* [in July]. But it was terribly disjointed because we were having to go into Abbey Road to do stuff for *Ummagumma* and then get a train to Wales to play a gig on the same day.

**Roger Waters:** In spite of the fact that he was clearly out of control, some of the work is staggeringly evocative. Dave and I worked with him on the first one [*The Madcap Laughs*]. There was a backlog of material he'd written before he flipped. It's the humanity of it all that is so impressive. It's about deeply felt values and beliefs and feelings. Maybe that's what *The Dark Side of the Moon* was aspiring to. A similar feeling.

**David Gilmour:** Our task was to record a few new tracks – just get Syd to sing into a microphone – and add a bit of backing stuff on afterwards. I even played drums on some of it.

Syd would have all these anarchic changes in metre, things I'd never be brave enough to do. I loved that line [in 'Octopus'] – 'Little minute gong coughs/Clears his throat'. I could play it perfectly well because I knew that when the words finish, the chord changes. I followed it on the drums in an unlearned way.

But there were times when it was murder trying to get him to do anything. He'd have taken Mandrax and would sit on a stool and then fall off it. You could practically hear him falling asleep on some of the takes.

**John Leckie:** I was the tape op on the second Syd album. Later, there was an album called *Opel*, which is a compilation of Syd Barrett songs, and inside they've got a picture of a tape box – 17th of July 1970, which credits 'PB', which is Peter Brown, the engineer, and 'JL', which is me. We did the song 'Effervescing Elephant', but I can't spell 'effervescing', so if you look at the picture of the tape box, there are two or three attempts by me.

**Aubrey 'Po' Powell:** Storm and I had found a studio in Denmark Street because we couldn't carry on developing prints in my girlfriend's bathroom, next to her drying underwear. We needed an assistant and had hired Mick Rock, who was learning to be a photographer and was a friend of Syd's. Mick practised yoga, so he'd stand on his head in the corner of the studio when clients came to visit, which broke the ice.

**Mick Rock:** I moved into Egerton Court after Po left. I have a bit of silent footage of Syd in that flat laughing. It was shot on a Bolex. Storm was still there and he made two appointments to photograph Syd at Duggie's for the cover of *The Madcap Laughs*, but they were both cancelled. Eventually, on the third time, we went round to Wetherby Mansions and a naked girl everyone called 'Iggy The Eskimo' let us in.

**Duggie Fields:** Syd had painted the floorboards in his room blue and orange. He hadn't swept the floor first, though. So there were cigarette ends and fluff stuck in the paint. He'd also started painting in the doorway and worked his way backwards, so he had, literally, painted himself into a corner – which seemed rather symbolic.

**Mick Rock:** I don't know who Iggy was or if she was even Syd's girlfriend – or an Eskimo. Iggy wasn't an official girlfriend like Lindsay was. She was passing through. But she got into the picture on the back cover, and then I took photos of her and Syd with his car on Earls Court Square. Syd had [Tyrannosaurus Rex's percussionist] Mickey Finn's Pontiac Parisienne Convertible, which he'd swapped his Mini for. But I don't think Syd ever drove it. There was a tyre missing and the police stuck a notice on the windscreen, warning it was going to be towed away.

**Jenny Spires:** I'd met Iggy in Kensington High Street when she admired a dress I was wearing and invited me to a party being thrown by Dusty

Springfield. She was older than us, a great dancer, and had been around the club scene, but she never seemed to have anywhere to live. I'd been staying at Wetherby Mansions and before I left to go to America in February '69, I took Iggy round there.

**Mick Rock:** Whatever happened to Iggy? Fuck knows. The story was she married some rich guy…

❀

*It's October 2010 and I see Iggy as soon as my train pulls into the station. She's hard to miss: braving the autumnal chill in a flimsy leopard-print dress and with her coal-black hair matched by swathes of Cleopatra-style eye make-up. After a nervous greeting, she takes my arm and totters down the steps towards the car park where her husband Andrew, a painter and decorator, is waiting in his van.*

*This is a strange scenario. Until recently, Andrew didn't know his wife had been part of what Jeff Dexter calls 'a group of wonderful '60s girls', dancing at clubs such as UFO and the Cromwellian. Nor that it was his wife's bare backside on the back cover of* The Madcap Laughs.

*Iggy herself didn't realise she was on the sleeve until a journalist from the* Croydon Guardian *tracked her down and told her. Now the genie was out of the bottle, Iggy went online for the first time.*

*A neighbour typed the words 'Iggy The Eskimo' into her computer and, in the parlance of the '60s, Iggy's mind was 'blown'. Then, after discovering I'd written a magazine article speculating on her whereabouts, she made contact.*

*There followed several phone calls, during which she revealed that 'the Eskimo thing was a joke'; her birth name was Evelyn Joyce and her father had been a British army officer who'd met her mother, a member of the Mizo community, while stationed in north-east India.*

*Iggy grew up in Brighton before flitting between flats, floors and sofas in London – a permanent presence in the clubs as the soundtrack shifted from Tamla Motown to beat pop to psychedelia.*

*Eventually, I offered to take her to lunch, which is how we ended up chauffeured by Andrew to a gastro pub near their West Sussex home. Here, Iggy regaled me with stories of her friendship with Barrett, but also Eric Clapton, Rod Stewart, Jimi Hendrix, Ronnie Wood and Brian Jones; some tales couldn't be published without fear of legal action.*

*Apparently, her marriage in 1978 was a turning point. Instead of more late nights at Tramps nightclubs, she worked by day as a cook at a racing stables and, later, at her local Somerfield supermarket.*

*Every now and again, the past came back to haunt her. A Pink Floyd fan and student shelf stacker once asked if she was the 'Iggy' from the Syd Barrett album. Iggy denied it. She did the same when another spotted her naked in a late-night screening of director Stephen Dwoskin's art movie,* Central Bazaar. *Then Iggy was fired by the manager – for yelling at the customers, she told me – and, as far as I know, never worked again.*

*After we met, late-night documentaries about the '60s often prompted her to call. One morning, she rang up after spotting her younger self in a programme about music festivals, and she told me seeing footage of Pink Floyd performing 'Pow R. Toc H' at UFO was like experiencing an acid flashback.*

*In March 2011, Iggy attended an exhibition of Syd Barrett's art in London's Brick Lane, where the comedian and future* Great British Bake-Off *host Noel Fielding made a fuss of her.*

*It was Jeff Dexter who phoned in December 2017 to tell me she'd died, half an hour before she turned seventy. I often wondered if she regretted being outed, but as Iggy once said, despite the lack of financial renumeration, 'now everybody knows my bottom'.*

✻

**Evelyn 'Iggy' Joyce (*The Madcaps Laughs* cover model):** I didn't know Syd was a pop star. It was the same when I met Eric Clapton at the Cromwellian. I didn't recognise him. Syd was beautiful-looking and someone who had presence, but I had no connection between him and the person I had seen at UFO.

He used to play the guitar and sing, and I thought, *Oh God, there's no tune to it*. But the way he moved and played, I just melted. He said, 'Do you think I look good?'. I said, 'You look amazing, like a Greek god.' All those people mention his dark side and his madness, but we had a wonderful giggly time.

One day, Syd said, 'Would you listen to this?' and he brought out a big reel-to-reel tape recorder. 'Tell me what you think.' He played me this song that went, 'I really love you... dad-a-dad-a-dada...' [most likely 'Terrapin']. I said, 'That's catchy Syd', and, of course, he wasn't really into catchy. It was a long tape and, at the end, he said, 'Do you like it and would you like to be a rock star's girlfriend?'

**Duggie Fields:** Iggy was just around. She didn't officially live here. I remember being at the 31 bus stop once and seeing her coming down the stairs in this elegant gold lamé 1940s dress that had bell sleeves buttoned to a train, but *no* underwear – completely exposed and with not a care in the world.

**Evelyn 'Iggy' Joyce:** On the day of the photos, we jumped off the mattress onto the painted floor. Syd said, 'Quick, grab a paint brush!' He did one stripey bit and I did another. It was all spur of the moment. When Storm and Mick arrived, I said, 'I'll go and put something on' and Syd said, 'No, don't.' That was his wicked sense of humour. He was as sharp as anything – the manipulator – and he was in charge. I was the one who put the kohl around his eyes and tussled up his hair. 'Come on Syd, give us a smile – moody moody moody.'

**Storm Thorgerson:** I was more interested in the floor than I was in Syd. Photographs of pop stars don't interest me much. Part of Syd's character was in the floor, which is why we made a feature of it.

**Evelyn 'Iggy' Joyce:** One day, I thought Syd was seeing another woman and I got a bit jealous, a bit pouty. Duggie knew where Syd had gone but wouldn't tell me. So I plastered my face with make-up and painted my lips black so I looked like Medusa – like a banshee.

Duggie took me round to Dave Gilmour's place. His flat was nicer than Syd and Duggie's – it was warmer for a start. I saw Syd sat there and went in, shouting, 'Okay, where is she?', thinking there was a woman in one of the rooms. But, of course, the meeting had been with Dave about the album they were making together. Syd left, and I was rather the worse for wear and knocked the needle on Dave's record player scratching his copy of the new Pink Floyd album. So he threw me out...

**David Gilmour:** As soon as he had left Pink Floyd, Syd became surrounded by this coterie of hangers-on. There were a lot of people who wanted to be imbued with the magic and the charisma Syd had – and thought that, by providing him with drugs, they would become his friends – and that seemed to be what was happening when he lived in Earls Court Square.

**Evelyn 'Iggy' Joyce:** One evening, we persuaded Syd to go to the Speakeasy, but it was full of posers and someone asked the DJ to put on 'See Emily Play', which was a stupid thing to do. I got up and started dancing, but Syd ran off. He was obviously very sensitive about it all.

One day, I was naked and he painted two big eyes on my breasts with tears coming down towards my belly button and an arrow, and underneath a picture of me with a big belly. He said, 'There's life in there. I could give you my life.' That wasn't what I wanted. I panicked and scrubbed it off.

I don't know how long I stayed at Wetherby Mansions, but I left and when I went back to the flat later, Duggie wasn't so friendly. He said, 'Syd's not here and don't bother trying to get hold of him.' I think he'd gone back to Cambridge.

**Susan Kingsford:** I remember watching the Moon landings with Syd when he was over at Duggie's [on 20 July 1969]. We all thought it was a 'conspiracy, man' by the Americans. But Syd just sat there, getting quieter and quieter.

**David Gilmour:** We performed in the BBC studio [during televised coverage of the first manned Moon landing]. There was a panel of scientists on one side of the studio, with Pink Floyd on the other. It was a jam. Every now and again, I'll hear one of these old things being used in a documentary.

**Iain 'Emo' Moore:** Some of us went to Ibiza and Formentera that summer [August 1969] and Syd followed. I saw him in the square in San Fernando and he was wearing the same clothes we'd last seen him wearing in London – his velvet trousers and his satin shirt – and he had a bag stuffed with dirty clothes and cash. He could be very funny but then he'd suddenly change, walking up and down the beach telling people he was a pop star and getting horribly sunburnt.

**Duggie Fields:** Syd was happier after he left the band. But, over time, he became more lost and sad because he didn't know what he should be doing. He didn't have the need to do anything because he had money coming in from the Floyd – not a lot, but it removed the pressure to get up in the morning and go to work.

I never had a conversation with Syd about him being a pop star until he wasn't one. Then it was a significant conversation. He'd say, 'I'm a failed pop star but who are you? You're twenty-three and you've never been famous...' Then he'd say, 'I have to get another band together', but he couldn't do it as he didn't have the drive.

I don't know if Syd's drug use was as big as implied either. There was never any acid in the flat, but there was marijuana and Mandrax. I had a perfectly legal prescription for Mandrax. But in the world we lived in, madness was also considered socially acceptable. There was almost a romance about mental disturbance, the same way there was about drugs.

**David Gilmour:** My flatmate at this time, an Italian chap called Francesco, was a great admirer of Syd's and thought because Syd was mad and a genius, that madness equated to genius, and if he could drive himself mad, he would therefore become a genius.

One night, Francesco wanted to get into my room at Richmond Mansions, which was locked, because I had my hi-fi in there and he was probably ruining my records. So he climbed out of his window into my window while blind drunk and fell off the second-floor balcony. Somehow he managed to miss the iron railings with spikes on top and land on the earth. He slept for two-and-a half days and was fine when he woke up.

Francesco tried his very best, with the aid of the same things as Syd, to make himself go mad and succeeded in partially making himself go mad, but with no trace of genius.

**Aubrey 'Po' Powell:** I went back to Wetherby Mansions to take some publicity photos of Syd for *The Madcap Laughs* that year. Duggie let me in – and there was no sign of Iggy. The curtains in Syd's room were drawn and the vibe was dark and oppressive. Syd had his shirt off and did some yoga poses. But he didn't say a word to me – not one word.

**Robert Wyatt:** I got a copy of *The Madcap Laughs* [released in January 1970] and was relieved our names weren't on it. But then I listened and thought, *No, it's alright*. I'm a big fan of English comedy writers, people like Carroll and Lear, and it reminded me of that era. Syd's songs stopped and started almost like speech patterns. They had a rhythm, but not a pulse.

**David Gilmour:** I don't remember much about Syd's concert at the Olympia [The Extravaganza '70s, Music & Fashion Festival, on 6 June 1970]. I was playing the bass, Syd was playing guitar and singing, and Jerry [Shirley] was playing drums. We played in the front foyer in the daytime and we were behind those big glass-fronted doors. We did a few songs, then Syd just put his guitar down and we all left.

Roger didn't want to do the second album [*Barrett*, released in November 1970], so I asked Rick to help. We had more time to do it and it was more polished, but we still had the same problems we'd had on the first one.

**Jeff Dexter:** The last time I saw Syd was when he was recording at Abbey Road. I didn't go for it myself. The songs were a bit child-like – whimsical, if that's the right word. I didn't think Syd was very well either. I felt awkward about it too because I was worried that sort of thing could happen to me.

**David Gilmour:** I actually think 'Dominoes' is a perfect portrait of Syd at the time. We'd recorded several normal, forward guitars on the song, and they were all rubbish. We were tearing our hair out and Syd said, 'I want to do a backwards one.' We said, 'Oh Christ no, you must be fucking mad' – and he was fucking mad. But Syd played the guitar solo through once and we turned the tape over and it was perfect. How he could do that I still have no idea.

**Andrew King:** I know people love Syd's solo albums, but I think of them as unfinished. It's like seeing the preparatory work for Michelangelo's drawings. There are dabs of genius, but it's all a bit of a mess.

**David Gilmour:** When we finished the album, I gave Syd a lift back to Earls Court and went up to his flat with him in a lift, with one of those iron gates you draw across. Syd turned to me, looked me in the eye and said 'Thank you' – and that's the only moment I can pin down where he made his feelings clear. It was quite shocking – that one moment of lucidity.

**Duggie Fields:** After Iggy, Syd's girlfriend Gala Pinion moved into Wetherby Mansions – with her dog, a little Highland terrier that shat everywhere. There were lots of domestic explosions, lots of arguments. One minute it would be lovely and then there'd be fights that I'd have to get involved in.

**Gala Pinion:** I'd been at school with Lindsay and I knew Po from Cambridge. I was nineteen and had been working as an au pair in Switzerland and it turned out to be a big mistake, so I came home.

Po told there was a room going in a lovely house in Kensington, where he was living with his girlfriend. That's how I came to London, got a job as a waitress at the Chelsea Drugstore and shared the room with a posh girl called Edwina, who went back to her parents' country house most weekends.

Then Syd turned up to see Po and said there was a spare room at Wetherby Mansions with him and Duggie. I suppose I also liked the idea of a rock-star boyfriend, but not long after that, Syd announced that he wasn't going to be a musician. He wanted to be a painter.

**Duggie Fields:** Syd tried shifting from music to art, but I was never impressed with his paintings because he couldn't finish anything. He had this wistful yearning to do something, rather than actually getting on with anything. He'd lie in bed all day with the curtains drawn. Then he pinned a layer of hessian over the curtains, so the room started to smell.

I found the whole thing with Syd and Gala so stressful. There were other people, hangers-on, coming and going and knocking on the door at all times of the night. I tried to move out and lived with a friend, Alice Pollock, in her flat in Cromwell Road. But she was even madder than Syd. So I had to go back.

Then Gala went home to Cambridge and Syd let her room to a bunch of people who were complete strangers. After a while, Syd followed Gala to Cambridge and the two of them started living at his mother's house – and then she rang to tell me they were engaged.

**Libby Chisman:** My son was born in 1970 and I took the baby round to Syd's mum's house. By that time, he wasn't in great shape, but he had this beautiful girlfriend, Gala, and he actually thought my son was *his*. I remember Gala's face as if to say, 'Oh God...'

**Syd Barrett (speaking in March 1971):** 'I've been at home in Cambridge with my mother. I've got lots of, well, children in a sense. I've been getting used to a family existence. I work in a cellar, down in a cellar...'

✿

*Syd and Gala moved into the cellar at 183 Hills Road as Win Barrett had rented the other rooms to lodgers. Syd filled this new space with unfinished canvases and told everyone he was a painter.*

*The couple bought a ring and announced their engagement in October 1970. Then, during a celebratory lunch, Barrett's mood flipped and he tossed a bowl of tomato soup over his fiancée and fled to the bathroom. Bizarrely, the rest of the family ignored what had happened, before Syd re-appeared, having hacked several inches off his hair. No explanation was given.*

*Gala went to live with her parents in Ely, and received a letter telling her the engagement was over, signed 'Yours sincerely, RK Barrett'. Two days later, she received another: 'Ignore the letter you received ... I think we should get married ... Lots of love, Syd.'*

*The couple bought a second ring, before Barrett accused Gala of cheating on him and the engagement was off for good. The 'rock-star boyfriend' thing hadn't worked out.*

*Back in London, Gala worked as a fashion photographer's assistant and a magazine and record cover model (she's the glowering redhead on the sleeve of AC/DC's* Dirty Deeds Done Dirt Cheap*) before moving to Germany.*

*Duggie Fields became a successful artist and remained at Wetherby Mansions until his death in March 2021, after which Flat 1's new owners tore up the carpet in Barrett's old room and auctioned the seventy painted oakwood boards – complete with Syd's cigarette ends – to an anonymous buyer for £28,500.*

# 5

# 'GRAFTING A TOMATO ONTO THE BACK OF A HAIRBRUSH'

*Marcel Duchamp's dirty cow, 'The Madonna had worked another miracle!', a lethal Jack-in-the-box and 'That bloody phantom song!'...*

✲

A writer in the 1970s once described Ron Geesin as resembling a cross between Elton John and Aleksandr Solzhenitsyn, but 'with the crazed energy of Spike Milligan'.

From some angles, it's possible Geesin has a touch of the Soviet dissident about him – maybe it's the facial hair – but his energy certainly helped get Pink Floyd's fifth album, *Atom Heart Mother*, over the finishing line.

Ayrshire-born Ron played in a revivalist jazz group in the early '60s before becoming a sort of improvisational one-man-band. The BBC Radiophonic Workshop, concrete poetry, jazz, film soundtracks and classical symphonies inspired what Geesin calls his 'electro-melodic sound painting' and what critics, including this one, usually described as 'avant-garde music'.

'I was never in the "avant-garde",' Geesin tells me. 'The easiest place to hide is in the "avant-garde".' Still, Geesin operated on the fringes of the mainstream and found a receptive audience at Middle Earth and The 14-Hour Technicolor Dream, where he was probably one of the few attendees whose brain wasn't scrambled by chemicals. 'I was always a pint-of-beer man,' he insists.

By the late ’60s, Geesin had become part of Pink Floyd’s milieu: Bayswater dinner parties with Rick Wright, sailing trips round the south coast with Nick Mason, rounds of golf with Roger Waters...

‘Ron was experimenting with tape delays long before anyone else,’ recalled Waters. ‘He invented the technique of pulling the tape out between the record and playback heads on a tape recorder ... and looping around a mic stand and back into the machine.’

The sound effects on Geesin’s 1967 album, *A Raise of the Eyebrows*, certainly influenced Waters’ contributions (including a manic fake Scottish accent) to *Ummagumma*. Later, the two composed a soundtrack for an arty documentary called *The Body*, which upset the BBC with its nudity.

It was only a matter of time, then, before Geesin worked with Pink Floyd. In the summer of 1970, he began composing an orchestral score for a twenty-minute-plus instrumental nicknamed ‘Epic’ (and sometimes introduced on stage as ‘The Amazing Pudding’ and ‘Consequently’).

Recent albums, such as Deep Purple’s *Concerto for Group and Orchestra*, explored the trend for velvet-trousered rock groups to make so-called ‘serious music’ with classical players, a coupling that the taste-making DJ John Peel once compared to ‘grafting a tomato onto the back of a hairbrush’.

Pink Floyd didn’t want *Atom Heart Mother* to sound, as Nick Mason put it, like ‘the London Philharmonia plays Pink Floyd’, and Ron Geesin envisaged explosive-sounding trumpets of the kind heard on a Duke Ellington LP. In the end, both parties would be a little disappointed.

In 1973, Geesin’s album *As He Stands* included a sound collage which spliced together a gusting wind, a crackling bonfire and his spoken-word commentary. It’s title: ‘To Roger Waters Wherever You Are’...

✣

**Ron Geesin:** I’d like to stand up and say, ‘Look here, world! I’ve done 2,000 pieces of work, some of which I think are much better than *Atom Heart Mother*!’ But no one has heard them.

**David Gilmour:** The main theme part of *Atom Heart Mother* was something of mine, probably left over from one of our soundtrack things.

**Nick Mason:** We'd finished working in Rome with Antonioni and instead of taking a break, we just carried on. We created this very long but unfocused piece which we'd started to play live [in January 1970]. We'd add bits and take bits out, but it needed something more.

**Roger Waters:** We all thought the same thing, which was that [Gilmour's riff] sounded like the theme to some awful western – almost like a pastiche – which is why we thought it would be a good idea to cover it with horns and strings and voices.

**Ron Geesin:** The Rolling Stones' tour manager Sam Jonas Cutler was a mutual friend and introduced me to Nick Mason. Pink Floyd were all, essentially, very nice boys – sensitive, well-educated and considerate – who subsequently plunged themselves into the impossible task of handling fame.

I'd barely heard their music before then and, when I did, I called it 'astral wandering'. My stuff is black jazz and the great classical composers. I think it's significant that I took all of them, except for Roger Waters, to see Wagner's *Parsifal* at Covent Garden and they all fell asleep.

I became especially close friends with Roger and he asked if I would do something with a tape they'd compiled at Abbey Road Studios. None of the group could read or write music in the conventional sense, but they wanted something big and epic.

All I had was a rough mix of what they'd put down and edited together. But one of the problems was the speeds didn't always match up. It would accelerate and you'd expect the next section to be at that accelerated speed, but then it would go slightly slower – and this was a problem when we came to the final score.

**Nick Mason:** Roger and I had played the track straight in one take and, I'm afraid to say, our timekeeping left a lot to be desired.

**Ron Geesin:** I recall Rick Wright coming round to my home studio and we went through a few phrases. It wasn't whole phrases – probably just him playing chords on the piano and saying, 'I think it would be nice to have long notes here and short notes there.' Rick was not a great technician. But then neither was anyone else, including me, because my keyboard fingering's all over the place. I still only use nine fingers out of ten.

I didn't have much to do with Dave Gilmour, though. He was a quiet fellow with a loud guitar and would probably have been the most suspicious because he knew the least about me. But I still have the scraps of paper from those meetings and I have one from Dave on which I jotted down his suggestions for the theme – a kind of arpeggio – and, on the other side, the theme I came up with.

It was hot that summer and I had no air conditioning in my top-floor flat at 208 Ladbroke Grove. The band went off to play in the States and I sat there in my underpants, slaving away at this score.

**Nick Mason:** We were now selling out shows in America, but this was not being reflected in record sales. Our American record company [Capitol Records' offshoot Tower] didn't have a clue what they were doing. There was a story about Steve O'Rourke trying to get to speak to one of them and it was so difficult. He had to find out where this executive got his shoes shined and went and sat there until this guy pitched up.

**Roger Waters:** What I remember most from those days is that we spent interminable amounts of time at the Mohawk Motor Inn on the outskirts of Detroit, where you could get a room for $8 a night. Hour after hour was spent sitting by some crappy swimming pool with no money to go anywhere.

**Ron Geesin:** The first time the group heard what I'd done was when they came back from the States and we all went to Abbey Road for a session. But the EMI players [the EMI Pops Orchestra] had been hired by Norman Smith. They were not my choice.

**Norman Smith:** The last thing I did with Pink Floyd was *Atom Heart Mother* and they put me down as 'executive producer'. I told them they should do the production themselves, but I did say, 'If you get stuck, call me.' I only received one phone call, so it was clear they could look after themselves.

**Ron Geesin:** I was not a conductor and I made the mistake of giving EMI's brass players more credit for thinking than they deserved. I'd ask them, 'What do you think of this bit here?' and they'd reply, 'Well, *you* tell *us*.' And then it got worse. 'What do you want? ... Tell us what you want...'

The reason I asked their opinion is because I'd been working with the New Philharmonia Orchestra on TV commercials. They'd make suggestions: 'What about this? What about that?' The EMI players weren't like that.

For a more experienced director, it would have been a normal display of nerves and status-jostling, and would have been swiftly put in its place. But when I reached the stage of almost hitting one of the horn players – who was being particularly mouthy – I was removed from the studio.

**Alan Parsons (EMI engineer):** It was a big moment for me to land a mixing job on *Atom Heart Mother*. But I seem to remember the intro section to 'Atom Heart Mother' [side one's six-part track] was difficult to achieve and had to be abandoned. It was virtually unplayable.

**Ron Geesin:** At the time, I was distraught, thinking, *Fucking hell, I've wrecked myself doing this work*. The melodies were good and deserved to be projected properly, and then I'd got this arse being obstructive. That's the reason I left and they got [choirmaster and conductor] John Aldiss in...

**Nick Mason:** I think the orchestral players thought Ron was some interloper from the world of rock 'n' roll – which was just not true – and so they gave him a hard time.

**Ron Geesin:** John Aldiss did a fine job with the brass and the choir, but my influence was jazz and I don't think John had a clue about that. My writing was percussive: it had a more articulated delivery with the trumpets, like you'd hear with Mingus or Ellington. So I thought the delivery on the final piece was a bit wet. But the Floyd always needed what I'd call a 'pastel wash' on their music. The end result was reasonable but it was a compromise.

I didn't have anything to do with the songs on the second side of the album. Although I remember Roger's song, 'If', which I always felt was about a relationship – about being close but also very far away.

**Alan Parsons:** Pink Floyd had a general aversion to record company people, which is often the case with bands when an A&R guy shows up at the studio. On one occasion, Roger and Ron Geesin offered to play this guy a bit of the new album. But they had a turntable and 78rpm record under the desk which we played. He looked completely confused, but we were unable to keep straight faces.

**David Gilmour:** I was still finding it difficult, as Roger was beginning to develop as a lyricist. So my paranoia about my abilities and my laziness, combined with his ascendence, created a dynamic where most of the time I'd write music and Roger would write the words. So I still think of 'Fat Old Sun' as the first song I ever wrote, the first time I really heard *my* voice.

**Nick Mason:** 'Alan's Psychedelic Breakfast' started with the sound of a match lighting a gas ring and then our roadie, Alan Styles, frying bacon, boiling a kettle and buttering toast. Great fun, but I am not entirely sure it worked on the record. Alan was with us for years – that's him on the back cover of *Ummagumma* with our other road manager, Pete Watts. But eventually we had to let him go.

**Jeanette Holland (Alan Styles' sister):** Alan got dumped on. I think they voted him out. After he left Pink Floyd in the mid-'70s, he stayed in San Francisco, hand-built a boat and lived on the water for years until he had a stroke [Styles died in December 2011]. Alan loved Roger Waters and later told me he thought he got a bum deal from David Gilmour.

**Jeff Griffin (BBC engineer and producer):** Steve [O'Rourke] said that Pink Floyd were working on this new project and we pencilled in something for the middle of the year. So I went to see them perform at Bath [Bath Festival of Blues & Progressive Music '70 at Shepton Mallet] in June.

***Disc and Music Echo* (review of Bath Festival, June 1970):** 'We were into the early hours of Sunday morning before Pink Floyd made it on stage ... The spectacular close to their set woke everyone up ... They were joined by a choir, a brass section and went into a twenty-minute thing, which will be one side of their new album.'

**Jeff Griffin:** Pink Floyd were due to play Hyde Park [Blackhill's Garden Party on 18 July]. Two days before, they'd agreed to do an in-concert session for the BBC. Steve O'Rourke told me it would serve two purposes: we'd get a recording and they'd get a rehearsal. Only then did he tell me they needed the twelve-piece Philip Jones Brass Ensemble and a twenty-piece choir. I nearly fell over. But we wanted Pink Floyd, so I thought, *I'll have to find the money from somewhere*.

John Peel was compering the performance [at the Paris Cinema on 16 July] and he said to the band beforehand, 'Come on guys, I can't go out there and say, "This is the Pink Floyd with their new piece of music that doesn't have a title."' Then he wandered out to get an evening paper.

**John Peel (DJ, speaking in 1988):** 'I strode to Piccadilly Circus, bought an *Evening Standard* and returned to the Paris. Having rejected the traditional "Footballer in Tug of Love Shock", the attention of the Floyd was drawn to a story about a woman who had been equipped with some sort of nuclear pacemaker.'

**Jeff Griffin:** Peely said, 'Oh, look!'. And there was a picture of a lady who'd had this heart operation to put in a pacemaker and above it was the headline 'Atom Heart Mother'. And Roger said, 'Well, let's call it that.' As far as any of us could work out, the title had nothing whatsoever to do with any of the music.

**Ron Geesin:** There was a newspaper on the table and *I* said to Roger Waters, 'You'll find your title in there...'

***Evening Standard* (16 July 1970):** 'The Atom Heart Mother Is Named: Britain's first atomic-powered mum is 56-year-old widow Mrs Constance Ladell of Hadley Wood, Barnet. So successful was the operation which gave her a radioactive plutonium 238 pacemaker, that she was expecting her first visitors just 24 hours later...'

**Jeff Griffin:** On the night, the Philip Jones Brass Ensemble were very impressed by Pink Floyd. In those days, those sort of musicians didn't like any form of rock music. But I remember one of them looking at the band and saying to me, 'How do they know what to play? They haven't got any sheet music.' I replied, 'No, it's not written down. It's all in their heads.' 'Oh, very good...'

**Ron Geesin:** I went to the Hyde Park show two days later [Blackhill's Garden Party, 18 July] and left in tears. The performance of the brass was disgraceful.

***Disc and Music Echo* (review of Hyde Park, July 1970):** 'A middle-aged father who had lost his son in the crowd was handing in a message when he suddenly grabbed the microphone from [compere] Jeff Dexter. The bewildered man shouted, "I just wanna tell you kids – because that's all you are – that I think this bloody music of yours is a load of rubbish!"'

**Storm Thorgerson:** Personally, I always thought the sleeve for *Atom Heart Mother* was better than the music, but don't tell the band that. It was a conscious attempt to do something very un-psychedelic – almost a non-cover. The cow was named Lulubelle III and we found her in a field near Potters Bar. We had to airbrush some of the dirt off her backside, though.

**Aubrey 'Po' Powell:** I think the idea to photograph a cow originally came from [the French painter] Marcel Duchamp, who took the most everyday objects and turned them into a piece of art. How much more everyday can you get than a cow?

But walking into EMI and saying, 'Here's the cover', we were met with 'Where's the band's name? Where's the album title?' – neither of which we'd included. 'This is what the band want and if you don't like it, call Steve O'Rourke.' Of course, EMI *hated* us for it. But we enjoyed bucking the system. People were burning cars in Paris and rioting against the Vietnam War. It was a time of youthful upheaval. Anything was possible.

**David Gilmour:** Of course, the thing is now the cow itself has become iconic, so it's not a non-cover anymore.

**Ron Geesin:** I then had a call from Steve O'Rourke saying they needed some section titles for [the track] 'Atom Heart Mother' to increase the American royalties because, at that moment, it was down as just one long single piece of music.

Steve was a heavy, heavy man whom I knew, strangely enough, before he was anything to do with the Floyd. It was when he worked for Bryan Morrison and looked after some jazz bands.

So the sections that were settled on for 'Atom Heart Mother' [which included Geesin's suggestion 'Father's Shout', after jazz pianist Earl 'Fatha' Hines, and 'Breast Milky', inspired by Lulubelle III] were entirely artificial and derived from a necessity to maximise income.

**Nick Mason:** After *Atom Heart Mother* went to number one [in winter 1970], our royalties covered us. For years previously, all our royalties and everything else were just being used to pay our running costs.

**David Gilmour:** We were in debt when I joined and, nine months afterwards, I remember when we gave ourselves £30 a week, and for the first time we were earning more than the roadies.

**Roger Waters (speaking in December 1970):** 'I had my E-Type Jaguar for two months and I've just got a Mini now. There's a great danger in getting into that sports car bit ... and we had great arguments in the band about it, because I proclaim vaguely socialist principles.'

**Ron Geesin:** Should I have had a co-credit on the album? Certainly. But it was never discussed. I was glad enough to be registered as a joint copyright owner and eligible for royalties. Later, I considered the missing credit to be a typical example of the great mincing machine and the little piece of meat.

❦

*Pink Floyd would have a complicated relationship with* Atom Heart Mother. *In 2001, Gilmour described it as 'shit ... possibly our lowest point artistically'; Waters suggested it 'should be thrown in the dustbin and never listened to again'.*

*At the time, though, the band compared the suite's theme to Elmer Bernstein's score for* The Magnificent Seven. *Listening now, each part fitted a different imaginary movie: 'Father's Shout' for a spaghetti western, 'Breast Milky' (a '60s spy thriller) 'Funky Dung' (maybe a low-budget porn flick) and so on...*

*Despite his misgivings, Gilmour performed 'Atom Heart Mother' with Ron Geesin and a brass and string ensemble at Chelsea's Cadogan Hall in 2008. 'Ron persuaded me,' he said. 'I did enjoy it on the night but I think it's a pretty flawed track and I don't diverge from that view.'*

*However, Gilmour has played 'Fat Old Sun' on several solo tours, while Nick Mason's Saucerful of Secrets have performed some of the title track and even Waters' 'If' live.*

*Wright's 'Summer '68' is the LP's forgotten gem, with its composer mourning a fleeting encounter with a groupie. 'In the summer of '68, there were groupies everywhere,' Wright divulged. 'They'd come and look after you like a personal maid – do your washing, sleep with you and leave with a dose of the clap.' A tougher call, perhaps, for Wright's girlfriend Juliette Gale, whom he married in 1969.*

*At this time, though, the worlds of film and TV were still on Floyd's radar. Stanley Kubrick requested to use 'Atom Heart Mother' in his dystopian chiller* A Clockwork Orange. *But he wanted to chop it up to fit the film, and the band refused, though Hipgnosis's cow appears briefly in the movie's record shop scene.*

*Other ideas came and went, including a soundtrack for* Rollo, *a sci-fi TV show with animations by the Beatles' illustrator Alan Aldridge, and French choreographer Roland Petit's offer for Pink Floyd to score a ballet based on French novelist Marcel Proust's twenty-volume* À La Recherche Du Temps Perdu.

*'Roland thinks there's some good gear in there,' said Waters in 1970, 'so I'm madly reading all Proust.' The band members all gave up by volume three and the collaboration took two more years to reach fruition, minus Proust.*

*It's 'Alan's Psychedelic Breakfast' that sums up this time, though, as a rare artefact of the fusion of music and found sounds Pink Floyd were exploring on stage. Alan Styles making breakfast and muttering in his soft East Anglian burr, while the group busked away, embodied what David Gilmour later described as 'our weird shit'.*

❃

**David Gilmour:** At the time, we felt that *Ummagumma* and *Atom Heart Mother* were a step towards something or other. Now I think they were both just blundering about in the dark.

**Richard Wright:** Like a lot of bands, we got interested in the concept album. At the time, I thought we were making the most incredible music in the world. But looking back, it wasn't so good.

**Ron Geesin:** My impression when I started working with them was that Pink Floyd were exhausted, because they were really being pushed by EMI and Steve O'Rourke.

What isn't usually discussed, though, is that while we were working together, Roger frequently expressed dissatisfaction at the group's suitability as a tool/machine/mouthpiece for his ideas. In my opinion, this was a normal statement from any creative individual – it's the dilemma of the 'individual' against the 'group'. I just said, 'Leave!', but the cogs of the machine had entrapped every member.

Roger left Pink Floyd when he could afford to and there was no apparent risk then. He didn't want to bite the hand that feeds.

**John Leckie:** Most of the underground acts, whether it was Pink Floyd, Roy Harper, Kevin Ayers or Third Ear Band, were on Harvest. They were the sessions to get on because they were much more creative and looser. They were the people I wanted to be with.

**David Gilmour:** For *Meddle*, we did loads of bits of demos which we then pieced together – and for the first time it worked.

**John Leckie:** I started with Pink Floyd at Abbey Road [in January 1971] and there were all these little bits – guitar things, effects pedals, pianos, various jiggery-pokery – which the band called 'Nothings'.

I was the one with the tape box and whenever there was a good take, I would ask, 'What's it called?' and someone would say, 'Oh, call it "Nothing"'. So I wrote down 'Nothing' and I think we got up to 'Nothing Number 24'.

George Martin had sixteen tracks at AIR Studios in Oxford Street and Abbey Road was only eight. So we filled up the eight tracks with 'Nothings' and then took them to AIR. I was so enthusiastic that [engineer] Pete Brown left me to get on with it.

**Nick Mason:** We spent a long time starting that record. We worked through what we called the 'Sounds of Household Objects' project, which we went back to later but never finished.

**Roger Waters (speaking in 1973):** 'I've always felt that the differentiation between a sound effect and music is a load of shit. Whether you make a sound on a guitar or a water tap is irrelevant ... We started on a piece a while ago where we don't use any recognisable instruments at all – bottles, knives, felling axes and stuff like that – which we will complete at some juncture.'

**John Leckie:** This was when they started messing around with household objects – tearing newspapers to get a rhythm, squirting an aerosol can to get the sound of a hi-hat cymbal.

**Nick Mason:** There was a lot of fun being had, but we never actually got any further than that. We'd sort of built ourselves a Victorian musical instrument, but we hadn't actually got any songs to play on it.

**John Leckie:** Pink Floyd didn't suffer fools gladly. They wanted everything to be done properly. Roger and David were the leaders and the ones who took over the talkback.

**David Gilmour:** When we were in the recording studio, I would put in my twopenneth. My method was to be more loud and bolshie than I would normally be – in order to prove to myself and others that I was there and taking part.

**John Leckie:** Rick Wright would sit at the back and not say anything for days, but his piano playing was always a highlight – and that's where 'Echoes' came from.

**Richard Wright:** I was playing around on the piano, but it was actually Roger who said, 'Would it be possible to put that note through a microphone and then through the Leslie [cabinet]?' That's what started it.

**Nick Mason:** The idea was to create a continuous piece of music that went through various moods and this was the album that established that. The most useful 'Nothing' was a single note on the piano played through a Leslie speaker, which had a rotating horn and amplified the sound. Rick's note sounded like a submarine sonar – ping!

**Chris Adamson (Pink Floyd's ex-production manager):** One day, I wired David Gilmour's wah-wah pedal the wrong way round. So when you switched it on, you got this high-pitched scream. They loved it, so I built a switch. When it was in one position, it worked as it should, and in the other position, you got the scream.

I'd forgotten all about this until I went to the Pink Floyd exhibition at the Victoria & Albert Museum and saw that pedal board in a glass case – and the memories came back.

**John Leckie:** The band went away and rehearsed and arranged all these pieces of 'Nothing' into one piece, which was something like twenty-five minutes long. It wasn't called 'Echoes' then. It was called 'Return of the Son of Nothing', which they started to play live [for the first time at Norwich Lads' Club on 22 April 1971 and again at the Crystal Palace Garden Party on 15 May].

**Roger Waters:** I don't remember whose idea it was, but we made a giant octopus, sunk it in the lake and then pumped air into it in the middle of the gig at Crystal Palace. So it rose up out of the lake, with its tentacles which, I'm sure, looked amazing.

**Peter Dockley:** I was making inflatables with a company called Event Structure Research Group [ESRG] and we put the octopus in the pond in front of the stage. It was meant to inflate during the show, but it was a hot day and some of the audience cooled off in the pond, trod on the deflated octopus and filled it with water. So one of the guys from ESRG waded in and had to shake the limbs out to get it to rise up, while I was there, heaving dry ice into the water to create smoke.

**Aubrey 'Po' Powell:** Things like the inflatable octopus at Crystal Palace followed on from building tables on stage at the Festival Hall and led to what eventually became *The Wall*.

**John Leckie:** While they were doing *Meddle*, the [compilation of early singles and tracks] album *Relics* came out in May. I think it was contractual and if Pink Floyd didn't choose the songs, then EMI would.

**Nick Mason:** At the time, there was a budget set by EMI of £25 for doing album covers and it seemed like a good idea do the cover of *Relics* ourselves. I don't remember any discussion about it. I just know I ended up doing the drawing as a sort of tribute to [the English cartoonist] Heath Robinson. It's the only evidence of my time studying to be an architect, though I don't recall getting my £25.

**John Leckie:** I think they were lost at that point. Even then, people wanted radio-play singles. Steve O'Rourke was always kicking them, saying 'Come on, lads. You'll get dropped from EMI.'

**David Gilmour:** It was a genuine attempt to find something beyond the three-minute pop single. 'Echoes' was very much the father and mother of *The Dark Side of the Moon*, in that it had a lot of similar techniques.

**John Leckie:** What you heard on *Meddle* is the band playing 'Echoes' straight through. We did this thing with two tape recorders – run the tape through one machine, thread it through the other, and record on the first one and play back on the other. So there's this delay. The end of 'Echoes', where David and Rick's voices swell up, is a snippet of that technique.

**Roger Waters:** The lyrics in 'Echoes' are about two strangers meeting. How does it go? 'By chance, two separate glances meet / And I am you and what I see is me / And do I take you by the hand...'. All that stuff about making connections with other people became essentially the meaning in my work from then on.

**Ron Geesin:** I'll never forget Roger getting all this fan mail and I asked him what he did with it. He said, 'I bin it.' I said, 'That's a bit cruel, isn't it? People write to you because they want to know things.' And he said, 'Oh no, the moment you do that, you let the buggers in and they'll be bothering you all the time.'

**John Leckie:** Of the other songs on *Meddle*, 'Fearless' [with a sample of Liverpool FC's supporters singing 'You'll Never Walk Alone'] was the classic one.

**Nick Mason:** That idea of using the Kop Choir was interesting because it was the sound the Kop Choir make. But Roger was an Arsenal supporter – still is. We were north London guys, so it felt like sacrilege to use the opposition's chanting, but it's very powerful.

**John Leckie:** 'One of These Days', which we did from scratch at AIR Studios, was a freak-out jam session that had Nick Mason's voice [reciting the line 'One of these days I'm going to cut you into little pieces'] sped up and slowed down. I was always disappointed it got edited and cut down.

**David Gilmour:** It just sounded very violent... It's an old thing for us, 'I'm Going To Cut You Into Little Pieces' and 'Careful With That Axe, Eugene', they're similar sort of things.

**Nick Mason:** 'San Tropez' was one of Roger's and inspired by the Floyd's trip to the south of France the previous summer and a house we'd rented. The title 'Pillow of Winds' came from a scoring combination in the tile game Mahjong, which Roger and I used to play with our wives at the time.

**John Leckie:** Then there was 'Seamus'. Dave Gilmour turned up one morning with a collie dog [belonging to the Small Faces' Steve Marriott] that howled when you started playing the harmonica and we recorded it. I was surprised when that ended up on the album.

**David Gilmour:** 'Seamus' was fun, but I don't know whether we ought to have done it the way we did, because it wasn't really as funny to anybody else as it was to us.

**Nick Mason:** We all bought video cameras when we first went to Japan [in August 1971], but they were silent. So there's loads of silent footage of Pink Floyd running around like Benny Hill at double speed. After three weeks of doing this, everyone got bored and left the cameras at home.

On the way to Australia, we stopped over in Hong Kong and Roger rang Storm in London to talk about the cover for *Meddle* and told him we wanted an ear underwater.

**Storm Thorgerson:** It was a very bad telephone line, but I *think* that's what Roger said. Unlike *Atom Heart Mother*, I think the music on *Meddle* was much better than our cover.

**Aubrey 'Po' Powell:** Pink Floyd's music was fluid and watery, and we'd heard 'Echoes', so that was our thinking. But the cover of *Meddle* was a disaster. The thing is you have to have a particularly beautiful ear for it to be an attractive thing.

For the inside sleeve photo, we had another brief from Roger Waters: 'We don't want any of your fancy trickery, Po. We just want a straight photograph of us all sitting in a row.' Very conservative. But we had to shoot them in pairs and then splice them together, because we couldn't get the four of them in the studio together at the same time.

**Jill Furmanovsky:** I was a Pink Floyd fan before I became a photographer, and I used to stare at the photograph in the middle of *Meddle*, mesmerised by it.

**David Gilmour:** Roger's got this fabulous dimple in his chin [in the photo] that only shows under stress.

***Melody Maker* (review of *Meddle*, November 1971):** 'The vocals verge on the drippy and the instrumental workouts ... are decidedly old hat.'

**Michael Watts (*Melody Maker* writer and *Meddle* reviewer):** After that review appeared I was sent a carefully wrapped parcel that turned out to be a bag of offal. We all gathered around in the office and everybody had a bit of a laugh at my expense. There must have been some message inside because I was able to identify it as being from Pink Floyd.

Then sometime after that I received a posh-looking package, wrapped in nice paper and everyone gathered around again as I unwrapped a big red box. We all looked at it for a while until somebody said, 'It could be a jack-in-the-box. Why don't you press it?' So I did, the lid flew back and out sprang this boxing glove. Thankfully, I wasn't leaning over, otherwise it would have taken my fucking head off.

**Nick Mason:** Making the box was not difficult. But I had to order the springs to get the right size to take a boxing glove on the end of it. It was designed to have the maximum effect. I certainly made more than one of them. One went to the *Melody Maker*, but I've still got one even now in my office just in case, so be warned.

✲

Melody Maker*'s antipathy didn't prevent* Meddle *reaching number three in the UK in November, though the US was tougher to crack, despite Steve O'Rourke's persistence.*

*As good as it was ('Seamus' aside),* Meddle *was defined by 'Echoes'' suspenseful guitar solos and Gilmour and Wright's hippie choirboy vocals. Gilmour later cited* Meddle *as the album on which Pink Floyd found their true calling, with 'Echoes' his personal highlight.*

*Waters shared his bandmate's affection for the work, but later believed that the musical theatre impresario Andrew Lloyd Webber had borrowed a chord sequence for the theme to his West End hit* The Phantom of the Opera.

*'The beginning of that bloody phantom song is from "Echoes",' he told* Q *magazine in 1992. 'It's the same structure and the same notes and everything' – although, as Pablo Picasso is meant to have said, 'All art is theft', and Waters' lyrics for 'Echoes' had been inspired by the poem 'Two Planets' by the Islamist philosopher Sir Muhammad Iqbal.*

*Waters responded with a solo song, 'It's a Miracle', in which he denounced 'Lloyd Webber's awful stuff' and hoped 'the piano lid comes down and breaks his fucking fingers'. Nick Mason later divulged that 'Echoes' was referred to as 'The Phantom' by his Saucerful of Secrets bandmates.*

*Back in summer 1971, while* Meddle *was still being made, a twenty-seven-year-old French film-maker named Adrian Maben visited Pompeii. The Neapolitan city had once been buried under volcanic ash following the eruption of Mount Vesuvius in 79 AD and was now a popular tourist destination. Maben and his girlfriend visited the local amphitheatre and ate lunch on the same stone cavea where Pompeiians once watched gladiators fighting to the death.*

*Maben lived in Paris, had studied in Rome and now directed music films for Belgian TV. Earlier that year, he'd visited Steve O'Rourke and David Gilmour in London to pitch an idea.*

*'When I listened to Pink Floyd's records, I remember asking myself, "How on earth did they do that?" Or, "Where did those sounds come from?",' he says. 'In a way, you could draw a parallel between their music and the [European art movement] Nouveaux Réalistes – Tinguely, Arman and César – who used ordinary objects to make their paintings or collages.'*

*Maben told Gilmour and O'Rourke he wanted to present Pink Floyd's music to a tableaux of artworks. 'The atmosphere in the office cooled,' he recalls. 'Then David replied, ever so politely, "Well, thank you. We'll think about it and ring you back, au revoir."*

*'I returned to Paris feeling depressed, but decided to wait in case the telephone did ring. After six months, I realised nothing was going to happen. So I plucked up the courage to ring Steve for the second time.*

*'He remembered who I was and his reply was immediate. "No, we don't want to do anything like that. But if you could find somewhere interesting to film a concert, then we might reconsider..."'*

*That evening in Pompeii, Maben realised he'd lost his passport and retraced his steps back to the closed amphitheatre. It was 8 p.m. when he persuaded the security guards to let him inside. Maben couldn't find his passport, but discovered an arena bathed in shadows with the silence broken only by the buzz of insects and bats flitting between the walls: 'And it was then, I had an idea...'*

✣

**Nick Mason:** *Pink Floyd: Live at Pompeii* is a great example of where we were at that time. It's got the good feel of a live music performance but without the attendant problems of an audience.

**David Gilmour:** I don't think any of us thought it would be as well-received and last in people's minds for as long as it did. All credit to Maben. It's his idea and it was great.

**Adrian Maben (director, *Pink Floyd: Live at Pompeii*):** After visiting the arena at dusk, I went back to the hotel and wrote a letter to Steve O'Rourke suggesting Pompeii had everything for a concert film.

I had the idea that concert films with audiences jumping around were becoming something of a cliché. It's always the same idea over and over again. [The film] *Woodstock* was the best or the worst example depending on your point of view. If rock music had started a revolution, then it needed a new visual approach, a new idea.

*Pink Floyd: Live at Pompeii* was conceived as an anti-Woodstock film where there would be zero audience, except for a few French and Italian cameramen, their assistants and a script girl. They would be part of the film just as the 150 metres of tracking, all of the lamps, the parasols and the 35mm cameras would be. The film would make visible everything that is normally kept hidden and it would hide any spectators with their distracting applause, but also with Pompeii's amphitheatre, the streets, the ruined temples and mosaics as part of the film.

Pink Floyd agreed, but the first problem was getting permission from the official authorities, La Soprintenza Alle Antichite Delle Province di Napoli. Classical music concerts had been filmed there, but rock was associated with hooligans and noise.

As luck would have it, I contacted Professor Ugo Carputi, who taught history at Naples University. He was a friend of the head of the Soprintenza and keen on Pink Floyd. He explained that their music was different, that it would be good publicity and that, since we didn't need an audience, there would be no risk of damage to the monuments.

Steve O'Rourke had said to me on the phone, 'Oh and by the way, where's the money coming from?'. A production company in Paris persuaded [French TV station] ORTF and others to invest enough to get the film started. Then Reiner Moritz, the executive producer, searched for finance in America and Canada...

**Roger Waters:** Maben had got some money to finance the film from some shyster and we, stupidly, were still wet enough behind the ears to do a fifty/fifty deal that left control to the producer. After that, we never let anything get out of our control.

**Adrian Maben:** Steve needed £2,000 to get the trucks and Pink Floyd to Pompeii. The executive producer Reiner Moritz said that he couldn't find the cash immediately. My mother, who had died a few years earlier, had left me £2,000 in her will.

I gave it to Steve thinking that this film had better get started immediately before everybody changed their mind. In retrospect, I think that it was the right thing to do. It meant that there could be no turning back.

**Nick Mason:** Performing in Pompeii was all down to Adrian and Steve O'Rourke. We were wise long after the event, but we'd not given very much thought to what we were going to do or how it was all going to work. I do know we had to ditch a couple of gigs in England which had been booked – something we were loathe to do as we needed the money.

They were a couple of university gigs, probably worth about 500 quid a night. But by the time we'd re-scheduled them, it was after *The Dark*

*Side of the Moon* and our price had gone up and we were on a couple of thousand.

**Adrian Maben:** The authorities agreed to let us have the amphitheatre for six days. On day one came the first disaster. We couldn't get the electricity to work. Or it would come on for a minute or two and then go dead. On day two, the same thing happened again, in spite of help from the Italian electricity board who sent reinforcements from Pompeii and Naples. It just fizzled out after five minutes and we had to stop filming again. I couldn't make a film with shots of the band playing frisbee while they waited for the current to come on.

**Roger Waters (speaking in 1972):** 'There's some rather *Top of the Pops*-ish shots of us walking around the top of Vesuvius and things like that. But I think Pink Floyd freaks would enjoy it.'

**Adrian Maben:** Since we couldn't film anything in the amphitheatre, I decided that we might as well go to Pozzuoli and nearby Solfatara, which is connected underground to Vesuvius, to film the Floyd walking round the pools of bubbling mud and fumaroli. It's also the place where, according to legend, the Romans conceived the idea of the gates to hell.

Alas, this was the first Sunday in October, the day of the procession of the Madonna, the Blessed Virgin of the Rosary, between the cathedral in Pompeii and the Piazza Garibaldi in Naples. The procession lasts three days and thousands of pilgrims block the streets. So Pink Floyd and the camera crew just sat in their car and waited and waited. I began to despair.

We finally arrived at Solfatara and managed to get some images, and after returning to the amphitheatre in the evening, we heard some good news: the electricity was working. A cable had been connected from the town hall to the amphitheatre, which was quite a distance. But then we had to get someone to watch over it. The Madonna had worked another miracle!

**Nick Mason:** It's a good story. But it would have made more sense to have a generator.

**Adrian Maben:** Then, the evening before the shoot, Steve O'Rourke came to see me and pulled out of his briefcase a vinyl demo of *Meddle*, on which, for the first time, I was to hear 'Echoes'. 'That's what we want to do tomorrow,' he said in a very loud voice.

I pointed out that all my script work and timings had been for the earlier pieces as discussed and it would be impossible. After a certain amount of discussion, we agreed we would film 'Echoes' first, and then do at least two older Pink Floyd numbers.

So I borrowed a portable gramophone from the concierge at the Hotel Forum and worked all night with the script girl Marie-Noëlle Zurstrassen's stopwatch, a ruler and an exercise book trying to calculate the camera positions and movements. We dropped 'Astronomy Domine' and they did 'Echoes', 'One of These Days' and 'A Saucerful of Secrets'.

**Nick Mason:** When we moved all the gear in, I didn't think, *Oh, it's a thousand years on and instead of lions and Christians, here we are!*. None of us had worked out that the fact that it was outdoors and a bit gritty gave it a live quality that made up for the fact there wasn't an audience. There was something about the whole windblown outdoors that gave it a real live atmosphere.

**Adrian Maben:** 'Echoes Part 1', for example, was shot in four separate parts and 'Saucerful of Secrets' in three sections. In between each portion, the Floyd would stop playing and check the recording on an eight-track recorder which had been transported from Paris. If they found mistakes, then they would do it again until they were satisfied. They would then return to their original positions and do the next piece in the song.

**Nick Mason:** Every drummer has seen the bit during 'One of These Days' when I drop my stick. They think I practised it because the spare was so perfectly placed – no beat was lost. They showed all the drum parts in 'One of These Days' because the rumour was they lost the can of film which had David, Roger or Rick playing. So it became a triumph for me.

**Adrian Maben:** In 1975, the production company MHF, without my knowledge, deposited 540 cans of unused 35mm rushes with the Archives Françaises du Film at Bois d'Arcy near Paris. Several years later the production company ceased to exist and nobody knew where the rushes had been sent.

When the time came to start work on the director's cut, I promised David Gilmour and the others that I would search for the missing cans of film and they could be used in the new version.

Then came the devastating news. An official administrative paper arrived by post to inform me that everything had been incinerated ten years ago.

The previous director, a certain Mr Schmidt, wanted to make extra space on the shelves. He had decided that the cans of *Pink Floyd: Live at Pompeii* were of no interest to anybody and should be destroyed. Apparently, he had no clue as to who the Pink Floyd were.

**Colin Greenwood (bass guitarist, Radiohead):** Jonny [Greenwood, Radiohead guitarist] made us all watch *Pink Floyd: Live at Pompeii* and said, 'Now this is how we should do videos.' I just remember seeing Dave Gilmour sitting on his arse playing guitar and Roger Waters, with long greasy hair and dusty flares, stagger over and pick up this big beater and whacks this gong. Ridiculous!

**Adrian Maben:** There's a magical quality to the October light in Pompeii – the silvery blue light of the early morning, the harsh midday sun and that coppery glow of the sun's rays towards the end of the afternoon.

After Roger's dramatically loud gong-bashing, everything became strangely quiet. You found yourself in the middle of nowhere, in a sort of mental no man's land. I think that it was probably the tension between the music and the disquieting silence of the ruined city.

**Nick Mason:** Gongs are almost indestructible. We probably only had two or three in forty years or whatever of Pink Floyd's history.

**Adrian Maben:** It was clear we would never finish the shoot with the stock of 35mm film we had and it was too expensive to buy more. So

I came up with the idea of recording the numbers we'd agreed on, but leaving gaps in the film that could be filled in when the band came to Paris later in the year. Steve told me several times that Floyd *had* to leave Pompeii on 8 October.

At the hotel, Marie-Noëlle kept the cash in a padlocked metal box which she hid under her pillow for fear of being robbed – and because she needed every cent to pay the daily expenses of the four members of the group. But, on the last day, there was nothing left to pay the hotel bill.

I was politely but firmly requested to remain in the hotel, a reluctant hostage, waiting for more money to arrive from the producer to pay the crew's bills that had accumulated over the shoot.

It was an embarrassing situation and, drinking too much Pompeiian red wine, I tried to stop worrying and think about what to do next.

❀

*The Parisian production company finally sent the money by post and Maben escaped house arrest. But there was more work to be done on the movie.*

*In November, Maben and his crew filmed Pink Floyd performing 'Set the Controls for the Heart of the Sun', 'Careful With That Axe, Eugene' and 'Mademoiselle Nobs' ('Seamus' but with an Afghan hound called 'Nobs' understudying Steve Marriott's collie) on a soundstage at Studios de Boulogne in Paris.*

*Maben transposed images of Pompeiian relics and bubbling lava pools behind the band. Later, many of the film's viewers were too stoned or lost in the music – or both – to notice that Rick Wright's beard had disappeared after the first part of 'Echoes' before reappearing in part two.*

*In 2003, the director's cut edition of the film included Maben's interview with the group from Paris, and a sparring match as gladiatorial as any in ancient Pompeii.*

*'What I'd want to know David, is how you manage to stand working and living with Roger and with Nick and with Rick all these years?' asked Maben,*

*struggling to be heard over the sound of Pink Floyd eating oysters, quaffing beer and laughing.*

*'Pretty bloody difficult,' Gilmour replied, to a chorus of jeers and more laughter. 'I dunno, perseverance.'*

*'The laughter, the cutting remarks, the jokes ... somehow summed up the Floyd as they were at the end of 1971,' Maben told me.*

*A sixty-minute cut of the film received a limited cinema release in the summer of 1972. By then, Maben was convinced there was something missing, though it would be a while before he could do anything about it.*

*Meanwhile, Pink Floyd released their soundtrack LP for Barbet Schroeder's latest movie,* La Vallée, *starring Mimsy Farmer as a pampered diplomat's wife experiencing a spiritual and sexual epiphany in the Papua New Guinean jungle.*

*Floyd created their soundtrack in spring '72 during a sabbatical from making what would become* The Dark Side of the Moon. *They lived and worked at the Château d'Hérouville near Paris, where their road crew placed bets while challenging each other to brutal eating contests.*

*Production manager Mick Kluczynski took first prize for devouring a stomach-churning number of fried eggs. 'He did throw up, but he got twenty-eight down before he threw up,' recalled Waters. Meanwhile, Kluczynski's colleague Chris Adamson attempted to consume a stone of raw potatoes before giving up.*

*'To give him his due, he got through about two and a half pounds,' recalled Waters. 'Peeled and then sliced up with a bit of salt. They're full of starch so it would definitely have killed him if he'd managed to get them all down.'*

*'I'm used to raw vegetables,' explained Adamson. 'I eat all my vegetables raw.'*

*Folk, blues, West Coast rock and the sound of Mason playing 'electronic bongos' snaked through the title track, 'Childhood's End', 'When You're In' and 'Wot's... Uh the Deal' (the last two titles named after a couple of Chris Adamson's favourite sayings).*

La Vallée's *soundtrack was titled* Obscured By Clouds *(after a dispute with the film company) and released in June 1972. It was succinct and concise with only one song, 'Absolutely Curtains', exceeding the five-minute mark, and included chanting by members of Papua New Guinea's indigenous Mapuga tribe.*

Obscured By Clouds *made it to number six in the UK, with Schroeder mischievously suggesting the group didn't consider it a 'real Pink Floyd album'. Meanwhile, Syd Barrett had started to play live again...*

✣

**David Gilmour:** We had huge arguments about what exactly to do on those soundtrack albums. Some of us thought we should just put songs on them. Others thought we should turn the whole thing into a one-subject concept for the whole album.

**Roger Waters:** We wrote and recorded *Obscured By Clouds* at the same time. I was sort of just sitting at the side of the studio while we were putting down the backing tracks.

**Barbet Schroeder:** Pink Floyd's music was the biggest present to my movie because it really was fantastic. Personally, I think they should have made all their records like this one, spending two months on it instead of devoting a year of work.

**Nick Mason:** It's one of the annoying things that the difference between something we spent a week on and something that takes nine months isn't that great. The thing that takes nine months isn't thirty-six times as good.

**David Gilmour:** On *Obscured By Clouds*, there are one or two significant things. 'Free Four', for example, has got all that stuff about Roger's father being killed, which is where all *The Wall* and *The Final Cut* stuff came from.

**Barbet Schroeder:** There was a problem with the LP cover. It was a blurred photo from the movie where people were picking fruit from a tree or something. Storm and his people didn't make it look too good because the story I heard – and I don't know if it's true – was that they had another album coming out soon which was much more serious, so they didn't want their soundtrack to my little movie stealing the show.

**Aubrey 'Po' Powell:** Storm and I had pile of 35mm film slides which we were looking at for a cover image. One was an outtake of the film's male lead [Mark Frechette] in a tree. We were tired and being careless, jamming the slides into the projector, and one of them jammed, throwing the image out of focus. But we liked it. It's always reminded me of something by [the French artist] Georges Seurat.

**Storm Thorgerson:** Since we believed that the Floyd were obviously beyond normal reality, then out of focus was considered cool.

**Ron Geesin:** Syd Barrett was still around at this time. I remember Syd turning up one day to the studio when we were making *Atom Heart Mother*. But he span out again as quickly as he span in.

**Peter Wynne-Willson:** I saw Syd in Cambridge around 1970. I went round to his place and picked him up as we were having a Satsangi meeting at a local place and there were going to be some people there he knew. He came, but after a while he just got edgy and left.

**Nigel Lesmoir-Gordon:** I was back living in Cambridge in the '70s and I used to see Syd shopping in Sainsbury's. He spoke to me once, because I went up to him and said, 'Hello Roger'. And he replied, 'Hello. One day you won't be needing that beard.' I did have a beard at the time. God knows what he meant, but I suppose he was right. I did shave it off later.

**Syd Barrett (speaking to Mick Rock in May 1971):** 'That's all I wanted to do as a kid – play a guitar. But too many people got in the way ... I wasn't always this introverted. I think young people should have fun. But I never seem to have any.'

**Mick Rock:** In 1971, my first wife Sheila and I were living in Queensdale Road in Shepherd's Bush and Syd used to come and visit. He liked Sheila and she liked him. Syd knew me in a different way. We had a rapport that was to one side of anything he had going with other people. There was no pressure and I wasn't associated with Pink Floyd. We went to see him in Cambridge at his mother's house, which is where I did a small interview for *Rolling Stone* [in May] and Sheila and I took some photographs.

**Sheila Rock (music photographer):** Being American, I didn't know who the Floyd were or that there was an incredible mystique about Syd. What I found interesting was the family he came from seemed very conventional. It wasn't working class and it wasn't upper class. It was a kind of bland England – sort of lower middle class. I always remember his room in the house was so uninspiring. There was a *sink* in there and I found that very odd – to have a sink in one's bedroom. I'd never seen that before.

**Mick Rock:** He was quite coherent that day. His mum brought us tea and iced cake out in the garden. God knows what she thought of it all.

**Sheila Rock:** I thought Syd was very sad. He wasn't dynamic. I don't know if I'm saying the wrong thing here. He was very good-looking, but I saw him as kind of tragic. Perhaps the tragic poet thing is part of the appeal. Mick did French and German literature at Cambridge and it was all tragic poets at that time. He was very attracted to that, hence his fascination with all kinds of decadent rock.

**Jenny Spires:** I met up with Syd again in 1971. I was six months pregnant and living outside Cambridge in Graveley. He was at his mum's in the basement at number 183. Gala [Pinion] had fled. I'd learned to drive and was picking him up and bringing him over to visit. He still loved playing guitar and jammed with [bass guitarist] Jack Monck, whom I was living with at the time.

I was with Syd at 183 one day [26 January 1972] when Jack was playing with Eddie 'Guitar Burns' and Pink Fairies drummer John 'Twink' Alder at the King's College Cellars and Syd came along. We watched the set and afterwards he jammed with them.

I thought maybe Jack and Twink would go round and play with him some time. It would be fun and Syd had complained there were no musicians to play with in Cambridge. So we went over to see him at 183 and Win was delighted. She wanted him occupied.

**Jack Monck (bass guitarist in Barrett's group, Stars):** Twink and I also had the Last Minute Put Together Boogie Band, and we did a gig supporting Hawkwind at the Corn Exchange with Syd and Fred Frith from Henry Cow also on guitar. We relied on doing twelve-bar blues and some of Syd's songs.

**Nick Kent (author and ex-*New Musical Express* writer):** I encountered Syd after he'd formed that band with Twink. Syd turned up at the makeshift office of an underground paper called *Frendz* that I was writing for and didn't say much. He just stood there as if he was on a different planet. There was a young hippie kid there that day who asked him, 'Written any new songs, Syd?'. And Syd replied, 'I'm sorry, I don't speak French.'

✲

*After the Hawkwind gig, Barrett, Monck and Twink formed the optimistically titled Stars and began rehearsing in the cellar at 183 Hills Road.*

*The trio played for free at the Dandelion Health Food Café on East Road and on Petty Cury off Cambridge's Market Square. Then a local promoter booked them a headline date at the Corn Exchange for 24 February, with American garage rockers MC5 supporting.*

*The café and Market Square performances had been public rehearsals, free of pressure or expectation. But a headline date at an actual venue ramped up both.*

*Pink Floyd devotees arrived in droves and* Melody Maker *despatched a writer, Roy Hollingworth, to review the show. Barrett had dressed up for the occasion in some new velvet trousers, but his heart wasn't in the performance.*

*Stars were under-rehearsed, Monck's bass amp cut out and Barrett slashed his finger on a guitar string. MC5 were a couple of years past their peak, but the group's energy, exemplified by their signature song 'Kick Out the Jams', rendered Stars' performance feeble.*

*The trio played two days later at the same venue, opening for furrow-browed progressive types Nektar and noisy power trio the Groundhogs. According to one eyewitness, it was equally disappointing. Stars pulled out of another planned date at the University of Essex and never played together again. Syd Barrett's musical comeback had lasted barely a month.*

❦

**Clive Welham:** I went along to the Corn Exchange [the gig with MC5] and Syd just seemed to stand there, doing nothing, looking around as if to say, 'What's happening?'. I left the gig early. I was almost in tears. I couldn't stand to see him like that.

**Jack Monck:** Syd wasn't happy. He'd stop singing halfway through a line and his body language suggested he didn't want to be there.

**Roy Hollingworth (*Melody Maker* writer):** 'Syd played and played and played. No tune in particular ... but the tune was most certainly in his head ... It was like watching somebody piece together a memory that had suffered the most severe shell-shock.'

**Jack Monck:** Syd came round after the Corn Exchange show and said, 'I don't want to play anymore'. So that was it.

**Jenny Spires:** The initial few gigs had been good. It was the Corn Exchange that threw him. He hated it. It should never have taken place.

**Mick Rock:** In that interview, Syd told me he just wanted to play guitar. But he didn't want to be like the Rolling Stones forty years on, playing the same old songs. He was more like Charlie Parker, an improviser. He didn't want a formula that was repeated. God bless the rest of Pink Floyd, because if they hadn't gone on and sold so many records, I don't know if people would be that interested in what Syd did.

❦

*Pink Floyd's flirtation with the arts outside of rock 'n' roll peaked that year in France. In November 1972, the group and Roland Petit's Ballets de Marseille finally performed a residency at Marseille's Palais Des Sports, followed by dates in Paris the following year.*

*'It started off with grand ideas of a huge ballet of Proust's* À La Recherche Du Temps Perdu,*' recalled Gilmour. 'Meetings with Rudolf Nureyev, Roman Polanski, about making a film of it. But then it slipped down to a bit of old ballet danced to a bit of old music.'*

*In Marseille and at later dates in Paris, Petit's troupe performed their pas de bourrées to the likes of 'Obscured By Clouds' and 'Careful With That Axe, Eugene'. But Pink Floyd also discovered the restrictions imposed by choreography when they finished a song too soon or too late and left the dancers mid plié or just floundering.*

*'The reality of all these people prancing around in tights in front of us didn't feel like what we wanted to do long term,' admitted Gilmour years later.*

*There would be no more concerts in 2,000-year-old amphitheatres, art rock ballets or film projects for the group until 1980's* Pink Floyd's The Wall. *Everything in their world was poised to change.*

# 6

# 'HE WAS QUIETLY DETERMINED TO CATCH THE BIGGEST TROUT'

*'The shit you go through from birth to death', road rage in Northwood Hills, 'Everybody knows you're God Almighty' and the MGM lion roars...*

❦

It's 9 May 2017, but the scene is reminiscent of the one in Stanley Kubrick's *2001: A Space Odyssey* where the apes discover the monolith. Instead of prehistoric Africa, though, it's London's Victoria & Albert Museum, the launch of 'Their Mortal Remains: The Pink Floyd Exhibition', and the monolith is a hologram of the prism and spectrum from the cover of *The Dark Side of the Moon*.

This object exerts a magnetic pull on every visitor. Queen's royal couple Brian May and Roger Taylor, Rolling Stone Ronnie's ex-wife and organic food maker Jo Wood, and perma-smiling TV presenter Anneka Rice all stop and stare at the most famous record cover image in the world (after the Beatles' *Sgt Pepper...*, perhaps).

Of course, the image is famous because the album has sold somewhere between 46 and 50 million copies, apparently. Though a few million here and there now seems academic.

'When we'd finished it, we all knew it had what it took to be more successful than anything we'd previously done,' says David Gilmour, talking in his West Sussex studio, surrounded by the spoils of war. Among the arsenal is the worn-looking yellow Fender pedal steel guitar heard on the songs 'Breathe' and 'Us and Them'.

By 1972, Pink Floyd's albums were hits in the UK and parts of Europe, but the group didn't release singles or get played on daytime radio. 'So nobody had really heard of us,' said Nick Mason, 'until *Dark Side...*'

They were also no longer ex-students who'd dodged gainful employment to try their luck at music for a year or two. Mason and dancer Lindy Rutter, Roger Waters and potter/schoolteacher Judy Trim, and Rick Wright and model agency manager Juliette Gale had all wed in 1969, with the Masons and Wrights becoming parents. Meanwhile, Gilmour had met an American model, Virginia 'Ginger' Hasenbeim, on Floyd's 1971 US tour and had asked her to join him in England.

Making the album began as soon as *Meddle* was in the shops. At the end of November 1971, the group arrived at Decca Studios in Broadhurst Gardens, West Hampstead, to jam ideas and plunder what Gilmour calls 'the rubbish library'.

The recycled rubbish included a sombre piano piece rejected from the *Zabriskie Point* soundtrack and the lyric 'Breathe in the air...', previously used in the eco-conscious ballad 'Breathe' from Waters and Ron Geesin's soundtrack to *The Body*.

*The Dark Side of the Moon* would be recorded in fits and starts at Abbey Road Studios between May 1972 and February 1973, in between tours (including dates with Roland Petit's ballet) and the recording of *Obscured By Clouds*.

Waters and his wife were now living in New North Road, Islington, where Judy taught at the local girls' grammar school. Before that, though, they'd had a flat in Shepherd's Bush where Waters watched herds of commuters – all raincoats, briefcases and umbrellas – swarming towards the tube station. Whenever he boarded a train, he was struck by a piece of graffiti which reminded him of the view from his flat window.

'It was just after Goldhawk Road station,' he recalled. 'It said something like, "Same thing day after day ... Get up, go to work, do your job, come home, go to bed, get up, go to work..." It was on this wall and it seemed to go on forever and as the train sped by it would go by quicker, until, Bang! Suddenly you were in the tunnel.'

The message stayed with him and became the springboard for other ideas. Ultimately, *The Dark Side of the Moon* would be a Pink Floyd album for everyone, because it was about everyday subjects: money, religion, travel, violence, madness, death, good versus evil...

'It's all *Star Wars*,' suggested Waters, decades later. 'The light side and dark side.'

✣

**David Gilmour:** There was no deadline pressure from the record company. But we wrote some of *The Dark Side of the Moon* at Decca in Broadhurst Gardens and then we went to the Stones' warehouse place in Bermondsey to do some more work. Then Roger came in with the idea of putting the songs all together as one piece with a theme that linked it.

**Roger Waters:** I'm not sure how much writing happened there [at Decca Studios]: 'Let's play E Minor or A for an hour or two ... and we might get five minutes.'

**David Gilmour:** Writing was about jamming in the studio and hoping some little moment of magic would be formed that Roger could take away and write some lyrics for. The main focus of our endeavour was to try to create things together. Obviously old Rog did work all sorts of hours, writing the lyrics and writing the concept while the rest of us went home to enjoy our suppers.

**Roger Waters:** I remember sitting in Nick Mason's kitchen – he had a house on St Augustine's Road in Camden – and explaining what the record might be about. The year we made it was the year I had a sudden revelation, which was that this was *it*. Growing up, I had the strangest feeling that adolescence and one's early adult life are preparing you for something that's going to happen later. I suddenly thought, at twenty-nine, *Hang on, it's happening. It has been right from the beginning, and there isn't suddenly a line when the training stops and life starts.*

**Nick Mason:** I always took it to be about the pressures of modern life. We ended up with a piece of paper on which was written various subjects that would be covered and worked from there – travel, money, madness and so on.

**Richard Wright:** At the start, we only had vague ideas about madness being a theme. We rehearsed a lot, just putting down ideas and then, in the next rehearsals, we used them.

**David Gilmour:** 'Echoes' to me felt like the beginning of *The Dark Side of the Moon*. Roger's concept grabbed me. Nobody had problems with the concept of concept albums then. Their fall from grace happened much later.

**Roger Waters:** The lyrics in 'Breathe' – starting with 'Breathe, breathe in the air / Don't be afraid to care' – are an exhortation directed mainly at myself. It's about trying to be true to one's path.

Around the same time as the graffiti at Goldhawk Road was an advert in the tube. Not sure what it was advertising, a bank or building society or something and it said, 'Get a good job with more pay'. And I remember connecting those two images from the underground – and they sort of married in my mind. That's where the lyrics for 'Money' came from...

**David Gilmour:** Roger came in with 'Money'. I've still got his demo of him singing it with an acoustic guitar. Very funny. We did it pretty well the same as the demo, but did the twelve-bar bits for the solo in the studio.

**Roger Waters:** With 'Money', I was just fiddling around on the bass and came up with that riff. I thought, *Let's make a record about the pressures that impinge upon young people in pop groups, one of which is money*. I also had a two-track studio at home with a Revox recorder. My wife Judy was a potter and she had a big industrial food mixer for mixing up clay. I threw coins and wads of torn-up paper into it.

The first verse [in 'Us and Them'] is about going to war – how in the front line we don't get much chance to communicate with one another. I was always taken with those stories of 'the First Christmas' [during World War I], when British and German troops wandered out into no man's land, had a cigarette, shook hands and then carried on the next day.

**David Gilmour:** Roger was always the guy that drove it forward and had those ideas and concepts. None of us objected to that. From my perspective, I always thought I was the better musician. In a musical way, I wasn't willing to let go of that. But I wouldn't have dreamed of putting my oar in about the concept and the lyrics.

**Richard Wright:** Of the songs that Roger and I have written together, I would say that 'Us and Them' is my favourite.

**Nick Mason:** *The Dark Side of the Moon* was the first album we played live in front of an audience for months before we recorded it.

**David Gilmour:** You couldn't do that now. You'd be bootlegged out of existence.

✤

*Pink Floyd tried to perform 'Dark Side of the Moon: A Piece for Assorted Lunatics' for the first time at the Brighton Dome on 20 January 1972. The production matched the scale of the music, with a new 360-degree quad system. Over the next twelve months, the show would expand to include pyrotechnics and a mirror ball that opened out like a psychedelic flower behind Nick Mason's drum kit.*

*Unfortunately, the sound system malfunctioned at the Dome and the new piece was abandoned during 'Money'. The group stalked off stage, but returned later to strike up the fanfare to 'Atom Heart Mother'.*

*The music went off without a hitch on the following night and the tour culminated with four sold-out dates at London's Rainbow Theatre in February. A bootleg LP from the Rainbow worried Floyd's EMI paymasters as it was rumoured to be selling thousands of copies and the actual* Dark Side... *wasn't due until the following year.*

*However, the piece remained a work in progress during spring '72 dates in Japan and the US. 'The Great Gig in the Sky' was still known as 'The Mortality Sequence/Piece' or 'The Religious Section', an instrumental punctuated by the sampled voice of bible-bashing journalist Malcolm Muggeridge and a recitation from 'St Paul's Epistle To The Corinthians'.*

*The song's wailing wordless vocal, the pedal steel on 'Breathe', the synthesiser on 'On the Run', the alarm clocks on 'Time', the saxophone on 'Money' etc would all come later.*

*Even the grand finale, 'Eclipse', was composed after the group had started performing the rest of the piece live, as Waters recalled. 'I came in one day' – just before a date at Bristol Colston Hall on 5 February – 'and said, "Here, lads. I've written an ending..."'*

✻

**Roger Waters:** *The Dark Side of the Moon* means, 'If you feel that you're the only one, that everything is crazy, just know that you're not alone.'

**David Gilmour:** For a time [circa June '72], we had to call it 'Eclipse' because a group called Medicine Head had an album out called *Dark Side of the Moon*. But that didn't sell well. We felt a bit annoyed, though, because we'd already thought of the title.

**John Fiddler (vocalist/guitarist, Medicine Head):** Our *Dark Side of the Moon* came out about a year before theirs, and we'd written a song called 'Dark Side of the Moon' even before that. Their album is a beautiful piece of work and, bless 'em, they used the title, but I got there first.

**Nick Mason:** I've never quite got round to listening to the Rainbow recording. But I think some of the songs and themes were there, but the way it was constructed didn't come together until the end of the recording process. It was still feeling a bit unsorted to me, a bit over-extended.

**Jill Furmanovsky:** I was still a student when I was given a job as the Rainbow Theatre's official photographer. The venue had just reopened, I was eighteen years old and had more bravado than actual skills. I became a photographer on 14 January and Pink Floyd played a dress rehearsal there on 18 January. I then went to the Dome in Brighton and took some photographs of them backstage. This was unheard of, but maybe they let me in because I was so naive. I didn't do a terribly good job technically, but those pictures became important as they were of the first outing for *Dark Side…* and Steve O'Rourke bought some of them.

**Alan Parsons:** I'd helped mix *Atom Heart Mother*, but engineering a Floyd album was a huge deal for me. By the time they went into Abbey Road Studios, it was in good shape. But their working day depended on what else was going on. If *Monty Python's Flying Circus* was on TV, they'd finish early and leave me to do a mix. It was the same if it was a big night for football and there was a match on TV.

**Roger Waters:** At the time I used to go and stand on the south bank at Arsenal every week. I loved it.

**David Gilmour:** I don't think I contributed as much to the writing of that album as I would have liked. When I look at the credits [Gilmour has co-writes on just four of the ten tracks], it tells me I didn't have a lot of stuff in the can. I wasn't feeling that inspired, but I have no self-recrimination about the work I did in the studio.

**Alan Parsons:** They would often come in and just start improvising. David Gilmour's guitar solos were all improvised – done on the spot and played at a deafening volume. But I think the improv period had become a lot more structured. Nick would be very vocal at times, especially when it came to his drum sounds and sound effects. He was very much a part of that rototom section on 'Time' [the song's lengthy intro performed on tuned drums].

**Nick Mason:** We found those rototoms in the corner of Studio 3. Someone had left them there from a previous session. They became a big part of that song, but I'd never heard of them before.

**Alan Parsons:** The clocks ringing and chiming at the start of 'Time' was my idea. I'd gone to a little antique shop down the road from Abbey Road Studios and got the owner to stop each clock and then recorded all of them chiming. But it wasn't actually commissioned by Pink Floyd. It was for an EMI sound effects record.

**Roger Waters:** The idea in 'Time' is a similar exhortation to 'Breathe' – to be here now, this is it. Make the most of life. My upbringing was about, 'You're going to want to get a decent job and you're going to want to have a family, so you need to prepare.' Everything was always in order to prepare for real life, which was going to start down the road. It came as a great shock to discover I wasn't preparing for anything. I was right in the middle of it.

**Alan Parsons:** There was one proviso going in that it would be mixed in quad as 'quadraphonic' was the big word at that time. So things like the chiming clocks on 'Time' were on four tracks so that the sound could be all around you.

**David Gilmour:** I created 'On the Run' on a new piece of kit that EMS [Electronic Music Studios] had just given us, the Synthi AKS, and Roger's ears pricked up when he came into Number 3 studio at Abbey Road and heard it. I drove it through a guitar amp – to give it more of the punch and drive you hear on things like 'Time' and 'Obscured By Clouds'.

I came up with the tune – eight notes that last less than a second – and showed him how it was done. I had already put in the eight notes, doing all the treating and filtration, Roger then put in eight slightly different notes and said, 'That's better.' I said 'Okay.' That was it. But the take on the record and its treatment was my work.

**Roger Waters:** 'On the Run' was about travelling, moving. We all spent so much time in cars and on planes. Those footsteps you hear were recorded in the underpass at South Kensington tube station.

**Alan Parsons:** My assistant, the late Peter James, was the guy who ran around doing the footsteps and panting for 'On the Run', which we recorded when the band weren't around.

**Richard Wright (speaking in June 1972):** 'I just feel like I've been rushing around, not knowing where I am, living in hotels, on planes, on American tours – it all got highly confusing.'

**Nick Mason:** We had one particularly scary flight back from Japan in a thunderstorm. After that, someone said, 'You need to learn to fly' – which I later did.

**David Gilmour:** Nick has year planners from those days and every day is full. Record in the morning, drive up to Newcastle for a gig in the evening. Recording, gigging every day of the year. I didn't find it a problem – go off to America, come back, do three or four days' work on the album. I was used to it.

**Chris Adamson:** We played Big Surf, near Phoenix, Arizona [17 September 1972]. We were all staying in a Holiday Inn and having breakfast one morning, and there were a couple of motorbikes outside – and somebody said, 'I bet you wouldn't drive that motorbike in here.' All of a sudden the money's coming out and Dave Gilmour disappears, and comes roaring into the breakfast room on this motorbike. He stalled it in the middle of the restaurant and then drove out.

**David Gilmour:** Funnily enough, it didn't get any reaction at all. People were so frightened by it that they all stared very hard at their plates.

**Nick Mason:** No one took a blind bit of notice and it reminded us of why we didn't usually do that sort of thing. It was brought on by boredom driving through Middle America. We were going through a period of not enjoying flying, so we pretended that driving was just as easy, but it isn't.

**David Gilmour:** We did *The Dark Side of the Moon* at the Hollywood Bowl [22 September 1972] and it was a wonderful show. We didn't sell it out and the back part was partitioned off, but we had these great big lights outside like the ones they have at film premieres, shining into the sky. A lot of this was thanks to our new lighting director Arthur Max – a bit of a superstar and a lovely guy who invented a lot of the stuff that's now part of every person's travelling lighting rig.

**Nick Mason:** In hindsight, we should have focused on the record. But that wasn't how we worked at the time. We'd go off on these American or

European tours lasting three weeks and then come back and start work on the album again.

**Alan Parsons:** I was part of a new breed of engineer that didn't mind making criticisms and suggestions that normally would have been made by a producer. One evening, when the group were off watching a football game, I tried some sound effects from NASA – it was the dialogue from a space walk – over the top of 'The Great Gig in the Sky', which was still called 'The Religious Section'. I liked it, they definitely didn't.

Sometimes, as an engineer, you could argue that I should have kept my big mouth shut. Sometimes I did. Sometimes I didn't. More often than not it was welcome.

**David Gilmour:** We used to do very long extended jamming on stage – interminable, many people would say and rightly – and 'Any Colour You Like' came out of that.

We made up the cash register loop for 'Money' in the studio – a studio control room with tape machines and mic stands all over the place with huge great loops of tape all over the room and people breaking and treading on them.

We'd never used a sax before we used one on 'Money'. I'd played with Dick Parry in a Sunday night jazz band at the Dorothy Ballroom in Cambridge. There were several people we could have gone to, but it's nice to involve your friends, people you have some empathy with. One of my instructions to Dick was to play like the sax player in the cartoon band when they ran ads in the cinema.

On 'Us and Them', I wanted him to play like Gerry Mulligan with Beaver & Krause on an album. I can't remember the name of the album [most likely 1971's *Ganharva*] or the name of the track but it was very breathy.

✲

*David Gilmour also helped direct the album's backing vocalists, listed simply as 'Girls' on the studio tracksheets. These were Liza Strike, Doris Troy, Lesley Duncan and Barry St John, a tight-knit clique of session singers used by the Beatles and Elton John, and whose gospel voices had featured on John Lennon's 'Power to the People'.*

*The quartet added backing vocals to 'Time', 'Us and Them', 'Brain Damage' and 'Eclipse'. But they found Pink Floyd reluctant to offer much feedback beyond fingers parting hair to reveal poker faces and a mumbled 'That'll do'. 'I must admit the band would never be jumping up and down with joy even when things were going well,' admits Alan Parsons. 'It was all very* controlled.'

*Session vocalist Clare Torry experienced the same when adding her voice to 'The Great Gig in the Sky', arguably one of the album's most famous moments.*

✣

**David Gilmour:** 'The Great Gig in the Sky' started off as an organ progression of Rick's, but it was a track we didn't know what to do with. Someone – probably Roger – suggested some singing to make it more interesting.

**Alan Parsons:** When the subject came up of a female singer for 'The Great Gig in the Sky', I thought of Clare Torry because I'd heard her doing the Doors' 'Light My Fire' on one of those Woolworths-style covers albums that were popular at the time.

**Clare Torry:** Dennis, who worked at Abbey Road, paid all the musicians. At the end of the week, you had to sign for your money from Dennis and we always used to have a chat. He gave Alan Parsons my number, but when Alan rang me up about the job, I said I couldn't do it. I didn't know what the job was, but it was a Friday evening and I was going with my boyfriend, Mike, to see Chuck Berry at the Hammersmith Odeon.

So I told Alan I was working, but suggested Sunday evening instead. Then he said it was Pink Floyd, I was like 'Oh'...'. So I went there on Sunday and they explained to me that the album was about all the shit you go through from birth to death – and I did think it was rather pretentious. Inside I was thinking, *Oh no, really?*

**Alan Parsons:** Clare was bewildered by the whole thing, particularly when she was asked not to use any words. She did a whole take of 'Yeah baby' ad libs – and then they asked her to do it again without using *any* words.

**David Gilmour:** We'd been thinking of [the Rolling Stones/Dusty Springfield session singer] Madeleine Bell or Doris Troy, but Alan told us Clare was brilliant. When she opened her mouth to sing, it was unbelievable. But it was a hard brief: 'Get out there and wail.' There was one quiet take all the way through and one screaming take all the way through. I think we mixed it down from about four versions.

**Richard Wright:** Clare did this incredible screaming and was then very apologetic. We said, 'It's wonderful.' It was a magical improvisation and you could never repeat it.

**Clare Torry:** In the past, Rick Wright has said 'Clare was really embarrassed after doing the vocal.' I was, but that was because when I walked into the control room, there was no feedback. I thought, *My God, they hate it*. Had they said 'Clare, that was great', it would have been a whole different ballgame. But I later realised it wasn't just me. They were like that with everyone.

I remember in the car going back, I told Mike, 'They're never going to use what I've just done.' I went to see Dennis and put in an invoice for £30. It was normally £15, but I charged double as it was on a Sunday.

**Roger Waters:** The fear of death is a major part of many lives and, as the record was at least partially about that, that question was asked, but not specifically to fit into 'The Great Gig in the Sky'.

**Nick Mason:** The snippets of speech on the album were a late addition. Roger drafted a series of questions and I wrote them out on a set of cards. We then invited whoever we could find at Abbey Road Studios to read each card and give their answers.

**Roger Waters:** When it said 'When was the last time you were violent?', they would answer that and the next card said, 'Were you in the right?'.

The idea was to stimulate people to speak in ways which would provide essential colour for the record.

**Nick Mason:** We used a number of people that were in the studio with us, including some of our road crew.

*

*These disembodied voices gave listeners the impression of eavesdropping on conversations in another room. None of the speakers were credited and it was years before their identities became known to the public.*

*The opening sound collage, 'Speak to Me', was named after Parsons' instruction to the musicians whenever setting his sound levels in the control room. The piece contained cross fades of every song on the album over a bass drum loop mimicking a human heartbeat (apparently the real thing was deemed too fast), Chris Adamson declaring 'I've been mad for fucking years…' and fellow road manager Pete Watts' cackling laughter.*

*Later, Watts's future wife, 'Puddie' Deighton, responded to the question, 'When were you last violent and were you in the right?' with 'Yeah, I was definitely in the right. That geezer was cruising for a bruising.'*

*Anyone Roger Waters found at Abbey Road was fair game, including doorman Gerry O'Driscoll, whose philosophical bon mots, delivered in a crisp Limerick accent – 'Why should I be frightened of dying? No reason for it. You gotta go some time' – became almost as famous as the music.*

*But not everything worked. Paul McCartney's Wings were in the studio making a new album,* Red Rose Speedway, *and McCartney and his wife/bandmate Linda agreed to be questioned. Neither's contribution made the cut as their replies weren't spontaneous enough. 'Paul was trying to be funny, which we didn't want at all,' grumbled Waters.*

*Wings' guitarist Henry McCullough fared better, responding to 'When were you last violent?' with 'I don't know. I was really drunk at the time.'*

*When they finally sat Pink Floyd's most wayward roadie, Roger 'The Hat' Manifold, in front of a microphone, the cards couldn't be found and a rather stoned-sounding Waters conducted the interview himself.*

*'I mean they're gonna kill ya, so if you give 'em a quick, short, sharp shock, they won't do it again ... dig it,' offers Manifold, recounting a road rage incident in the London suburb of Northwood Hills in 'Us and Them'. 'Live for today, gone tomorrow,' he adds later. 'That's me.'*

✲

**Richard Wright:** At that time, Hipgnosis were doing all these psychedelic album covers with masses of stuff and images all over the place. I actually remember saying to Storm Thorgerson, 'Let's try to do something very simple and graphic for this one.'

**Aubrey 'Po' Powell:** We went to Abbey Road and listened to some of the new album. We'd given them a cow, we'd given them an ear and now they wanted something simpler. Rick even suggested something like the design on a Black Magic box of chocolates.

**Storm Thorgerson:** For me, that was a bit like saying, 'Dear Picasso, can you paint a Magritte?'.

**Aubrey 'Po' Powell:** We left feeling a bit depressed, to be honest, and worked on some different ideas. We kept a lot of old books and magazines in the Hipgnosis studio and at Storm's flat, and one day he dragged out this old American physics text book [1963's *The How and Why Wonder Book of Light and Color*].

There was a chapter called 'How To Make A Rainbow' and a drawing of a triangular prism with a ray of white light passing through and coming out the other side as a rainbow of multiple colours. We both said, 'That's it!'. As neither Storm nor I could do technical drawings, we asked our illustrator, George Hardie, to create a maquette to show the band. It was a good example of the sort of simple product design Rick had asked for.

We put together some other ideas to show the Floyd as well. Rather shamefully, they were to do with the moon and stars and all absolute crap, and another one based on the Silver Surfer from Marvel Comics. Then we went back to Abbey Road and presented them all.

**Roger Waters:** There was no argument. We were in the control room of Number 2 at Abbey Road and they came in with a few mock-ups and we all went, 'That one.' A unanimous decision. The prism was beautiful. But we made our decision without allowing Storm to bang on for an hour about his other ideas or his philosophical notions of what it all was or wasn't about.

**Aubrey 'Po' Powell:** It was Roger's idea to extend the spectrum of the rainbow into the inside gatefold. That made it like a graphic representation of the heartbeat on 'Speak to Me'.

**David Gilmour:** For me, the cover coming in was one of the things that tied it all together, though I don't really remember the other ideas.

**Aubrey 'Po' Powell:** Storm was actually annoyed they hadn't considered his other ideas. He felt quite deflated, again, when we left Abbey Road. But if any band had walked into the studio and seen them, they'd have chosen the prism. But we decided the package needed something else, which is why Storm suggested a trip to Egypt to photograph the pyramids for a poster and why we commissioned the stickers and postcards all for inside the sleeve – all paid for by the Pink Floyd of course.

**Storm Thorgerson:** The pyramids of Egypt were similar in silhouette shape to the prism and were appropriate symbols of vaulting ambition and madness.

**Nick Mason:** Hipgnosis were always very good at spending our money, but the cover for *The Dark Side of the Moon* turned out to be a wonderful bit of branding.

**Aubrey 'Po' Powell:** Did we ever think it would become one of the most iconic images of the twentieth century? No, and we were only paid £1,500 for it. But it changed Hipgnosis's fortunes because, next thing, we were designing sleeves for Paul McCartney and Led Zeppelin.

**Adrian Maben:** About a year after we'd filmed in Pompeii and Paris, I invited Roger to go fly fishing on the River Teme near the Welsh Borders. It was something we both liked, and Roger is good at fly fishing and methodically patient. He was quietly determined to catch the biggest trout.

At the end of the day, I asked him about the possibility of doing a third shoot. The film was out but I felt something was missing. I said, 'It's nice to see you standing in the middle of an empty amphitheatre playing extraordinary music, but we don't see how you create the sounds. We don't understand how you put them together, how you relax or argue. We need something more ordinary. Could we film the group in an English recording studio when you are in the process of actually making an album?'

There was an awkward silence, then Roger replied, 'I'll think about it, but I'll have to ask the others.' When I was back in Paris, I got a call. 'Okay, we will do it. Come over to Abbey Road next week. One camera only and no interference with the recording.'

**David Gilmour:** The filming at Abbey Road was done especially for Adrian's Pompeii film. All the shots are of us playing again over the tracks which were virtually finished at the time.

**Adrian Maben:** I returned to London and found an English crew. We arrived at Abbey Road without knowing anything about the Floyd's new record or what was going to happen. We were totally unprepared. It turned out that I had been asked to film the band making *The Dark Side of the Moon* and to record conversations in the canteen.

**Nick Mason (filmed at Abbey Road Studios canteen, 1972):** 'Could you get me a fruit pie and cream and not a corner piece? ... I'd like some pie and not the crust.'

**Nick Mason:** There's that film of us in the canteen, which I have been asked about ever since. But I try not to spend a lot of time going back to watch me demanding a piece of pie with no crust... or what was the other bit? Yes, 'eggs, sausage, chips and beans and a tea'.

**Roger Waters (filmed at Abbey Road Studios canteen, 1972):** 'Steve [O'Rourke] knows what rock 'n' roll's about, but he's got *no* idea what the equipment's about and he's got very little idea in terms of technicalities – what the music's about.'

**Steve O'Rourke (off camera at Abbey Road Studios canteen, 1972):** 'Everybody knows you're God Almighty Roger...'

**David Gilmour (filmed at Abbey Road Studios, 1972):** 'It's an image we'd like to dispel, I think. It was very heavy a few years ago ... not so bad since. But I still think most people see us as a very drug-oriented group... Of course we're not. You can trust us.'

**Roger Waters:** Some of the interview bits done at the canteen in Abbey Road are really funny. You can see we were fucking stoned. Dave and I were completely out of our brains. I was going through a stage where I was giving up nicotine, so I'd roll a joint every morning.

**David Gilmour:** I smoked plenty of weed. Well, actually, it wasn't weed. It was hashish from when I was about eighteen to when I was thirty, when it stopped working for me, and I gave it up.

**Nick Mason:** The shoot at Abbey Road was an afterthought – but a good one in hindsight. We didn't often allow other people in the studio, and when we did, they usually got bored and went away very quickly.

**David Gilmour:** The Synthi bits you hear in the Pompeii film are of a completely different piece of music [to 'On the Run']. It's quite a nice doodle and I don't know why we never went further with it, but it's not actually related to 'On the Run'. *The Dark Side of the Moon* was practically finished when Adrian Maben brought his cameras in. All of the filming of the *Dark Side*... stuff is staged.

**Adrian Maben:** In reality, a film is never finished and one's opinion changes over time. You try to find a method, and some money, to change the old version into something new that hopefully will be more contemporary. It's like the French painter Pierre Bonnard, who was well known for wanting to retouch his paintings, even when they were hanging on the walls of the Louvre [the extended *Live at Pompeii*, with scenes from Abbey Road, premiered in November 1973].

**Alan Parsons:** EMI gave me a leave of absence to go on tour with Pink Floyd [in January '73] while we were still finishing the record. The first tour, I was lumped in with the loading crew, [who were] working until midnight and then up at four the next morning for the next gig. Then I got promoted and started arriving with the band. They were using a quad sound system and I had a lot of fun putting the scream from 'Speak to Me' in all four of the speakers.

**David Gilmour:** We had some pyro by then in the live show. When we played the Cobo Hall in Detroit, someone put a cast-iron weight on top of an explosive cabinet by mistake, and when it blew, a one-pound piece of it whizzed past my head and hit someone in the audience. They were carted off to hospital, but came back for the encore.

**Alan Parsons:** When they had the question cards at Abbey Road, one of the questions was 'What do you think *The Dark Side of the Moon* is all about?' – and I had no idea. There had not been a word said to me about the concept and my answer was boring. Like Paul and Linda's, it wasn't sufficiently interesting to use on the album.

**David Gilmour:** On *Dark Side...*, as on all the records, [Waters and I] had massive rows about the way it should be. Sometimes Roger would be willing to sacrifice all sorts of musical moments to get across the message. My role – wanting the musical vehicles to carry this whole thing – was, in theory, complementary. We would prevent one another's worst excesses and indulgences.

We had opposite views of the way it should be mixed, which is why we got [former Beatles engineer] Chris Thomas in to supervise the mix. The idea was he should do it on his own, so that our arguments wouldn't happen. But Roger went in. I heard he was in, so I went in and we were hovering over Chris's shoulder all the way through to the compromise.

**Nick Mason:** At the risk of simplifying things, David and Rick felt more comfortable with a purer musical solution. Roger and I were drawn towards making more of the non-musical elements. Chris did it the way he thought sounded right.

**Alan Parsons:** I'm not sure there was a huge conflict on the way it should be mixed. Chris Thomas didn't turn the album from one thing to another and totally transform it. We were dealing with subtleties. As the engineer, I would have preferred it if my voice had been as loud as everyone else's. But Chris made his voice heard.

**Phil Manzanera:** When Roxy Music were recording [debut album] *For Your Pleasure* at AIR Studios, *The Dark Side of the Moon* was being remixed by Chris Thomas. Chris played us 'Money' and I just loved the solo. I sent David Gilmour a telegram, 'Just heard "Money". Fantastic. Guess what. I am in a band now called Roxy Music.'

**Alan Parsons:** I worked ridiculously long hours, making sure I never missed a session. I wanted everything to be right. I'm sometimes bitter I earned little or no money from the album [beyond £35-a-week staff wages], but I must be honest, it also did wonders for my career.

**David Gilmour:** One of the last things we did was 'Speak to Me'. Everyone put their oar in on that – Roger more than anyone else. But Nick didn't have a writing credit, so Roger gave it to him as a present.

**Roger Waters:** Apart from the songs that are credited to one person, it's a bit of a grey area. 'Breathe' and 'Any Colour You Like' are grey areas – and so is 'Time', because it was close to a real collaboration of all four members. I gave away a lot of the publishing and I wish I hadn't, but these things happen and that's how it is and that's how it will always be.

**David Gilmour:** It's easy to think that with all the bile and drivel that's gone on that there was never any companionship or joy to be shared amongst us. But there certainly was. We had really good times, quite a lot of the time.

**Roger Waters:** There was a residue of Syd in *The Dark Side of the Moon*. When you see that happening to someone you've been close friends with, it concentrates one's mind on how ephemeral one's mental capacities can be.

**David Gilmour:** 'Brain Damage' and 'Eclipse' were some of Roger's first lead vocals. He was very shy about singing and I encouraged him, absolutely. Occasions did come up when he tried to persuade me to sing for him, and I wouldn't.

**Roger Waters:** On 'Brain Damage', 'the grass' [as in 'the lunatic is on the grass'] was always the square of grass in between the River Cam and King's College chapel in Cambridge. The lunatic was Syd, really. It was very Cambridge-based, that whole song.

✣

*Years later, Waters talked about an experience in the Abbey Road canteen when he felt himself 'receding', as in the lyrics to Pink Floyd's 'Comfortably Numb'. Other people's voices became distant and objects shrank in size. Waters claimed the 'morning joints' weren't to blame, slunk off back to the studio and waited for the feeling to pass. 'But it made me wonder if I was going mad,' he ventured. 'There for the grace of God go I…'*

*Who were these 'lunatics on the grass' then, other than Syd Barrett? 'Brain Damage' could have been about several Cambridge characters, riding the group's coat-tails and struggling to make it on their own.*

*More than thirty-five years after the album, one of these, Iain 'Emo' Moore, is waiting for me on his bicycle outside a railway station on the south coast. I am about to embark on another of those peculiar blind dates beloved of biographers in search of stories.*

*In a past life, Emo and his friend Ian 'Pip' Carter had been part-time Floyd roadies and full-time jesters at the courts of King Syd and King David. Emo appears on the inside sleeve of* A Nice Pair, *a hasty reissue of the group's first two albums, wearing a pair of cosmonocles amid a pile of Marvel comics and Moroccan-style soft furnishings.*

*There's still a picture of Pip Carter, with his wire-wool hair and handlebar moustache, on Emo's living room wall. It's part of a mosaic of faded photos and Polaroids plastered floor to ceiling, like a hippie Bayeux Tapestry.*

*In the summer of 1967, Pip Carter dressed up as a Royal Navy admiral to hand out flowers at the Games For May concert. But his heroin use made him unreliable and the band had to let him go.*

*'Pip used to do the lights for the Floyd, but he had this romantic idea of being a junkie,' says Emo. 'But he fucked himself up with the junk. He stuck a bad needle into his artery. Dave sent him to Greece to have a cure and sit in the sun, but he was busted as soon as he got off the plane.'*

*A spell in a Greek jail weaned him off heroin, but he lapsed after returning to the UK. Carter was seriously injured in a motorcycle accident, and never fully recovered. In summer 1988, he was attacked in his Cambridge flat and died later in hospital. It was a tragic state of affairs. David Gilmour paid for the funeral – but he'd paid for a lot more by then.*

*One of Emo's old Cambridge associates informed me that he'd 'never done a day's work in his life'. But Emo had a job putting studs in leather belts at Ossie Clark's Quorum boutique and worked at the Sweet Shop, a King's Road emporium where models and pop stars tried on beautiful clothes and lounged about on velvet cushions. After that, he enjoyed a grace-and-favour lifestyle at Gilmour's country estate, before banishment in the '80s.*

*'Dave was very watchful over me and Pip. He always used to make sure we were alright, and if we were okay for money,' says Emo later. We're now sat on the seafront, drinking a bottle of wine and looking at the English Channel, when Emo suddenly opens his mouth to show me his teeth.*

*'Dave sent me to his dentist four times,' he confesses. 'The first new set of teeth I had done, I got beaten up a day later in a pub on the King's Road, and he had to pay to have them done again.'*

*And so it went. The 'lunatics on the grass' either died too soon, like Pip Carter and Syd Barrett. Or they became, like Emo, with teeth paid for by a rich rock star, pedalling his bicycle around an English seaside town and telling tales about the old days.*

❦

**Iain 'Emo' Moore:** To me, they were always Syd and Dave from Cambridge and I was just going to see them do their jobs. I roadied at the beginning with the Floyd, but after the gig, they'd all get in their cars and we'd be left to clear up. Dave would be teasing me and waving out the car window.

I was never a musician, but I was on one of Roger's songs, 'Grantchester Meadows' from *Ummagumma*. There was the sound of a child in the background – and that was me. I was with Roger in the studio, and he disappeared, so I went up to the mic stand and started singing like a kid. I looked up through the studio window and they were all watching, laughing, and I realised it was being recorded. But I don't think it was used in the end.

That was one of the last times I went. I was sick of the studio by the time they made *The Dark Side of the Moon*. Everybody just standing around...

**Roger Waters:** The rather depressing ending to 'Eclipse' – 'And everything under the sun is in tune / But the sun is eclipsed by the moon' – is the idea that we all have the potential to be in harmony with whatever it is, to lead happy, meaningful and right lives.

**Gerry O'Driscoll (Abbey Road Studios doorman, last voice heard on *The Dark Side of the Moon*):** 'There's no dark side of the moon, really. Matter of fact, it's all dark...'

**David Gilmour:** Every time we made an album, there's that moment when you do the last edit on the final track and join everything together and think, *Right, let's listen to the whole thing*. By then, you've heard all the rough mixes dozens of times. But there's nothing quite like that one moment when you hear it all joined together. I remember that first fantastic run-through of *The Dark Side of the Moon* and afterwards we all turned round and went, 'Fuck me, that's brilliant.'

**Nick Mason:** Everyone thought it was the best thing we'd done to date. But there's no way that anyone felt it was five times as good as *Meddle*, or eight times as good as *Atom Heart Mother*.

**Roger Waters:** I thought it was a pretty coherent piece of work and that there were lots of good bits in it that were very moving. I remember taking a half-inch tape of it home and playing it to my wife Judy and her not quite bursting into tears, but certainly welling up. I was convinced it was going to be very successful. It was so connected with itself and the outside world. But I could not have guessed that it was going to stand the test of time as well as it has.

**Alan Parsons:** There was a launch for the album at the London Planetarium [on 27 February], for which I produced the music. The band vetoed it, which I thought was a bit churlish. 'We are Pink Floyd. We want to do it our way!'

**Nick Mason:** EMI were using a sound system we didn't consider good enough. We didn't want it played on a sub-standard PA. Though it was probably a question of money.

**Aubrey 'Po' Powell:** They had cardboard cut-outs of the band stood in reception, which was considered out-fucking-rageous, as they'd snubbed the press. But Rick Wright turned up for five minutes, not realising the others had snubbed it. There was an urgent phone call – 'You're not supposed to be there.' Communication was never Pink Floyd's strong point, even then.

**Roger 'The Hat' Manifold (roadie, outtake from the spoken-word section on *The Dark Side of the Moon*):** 'Someone once said to me that a proper artist has got a right to be temperamental. I think I've been unfortunate in meeting every temperamental artist in the business.'

**Nick Mason:** Before *Dark Side...*, Steve O'Rourke told EMI we weren't prepared to continue with Capitol in America. Bhaskar Menon [Capitol

Records chairman] heard about this and came to Marseilles when we were doing the ballet with Roland Petit and convinced Steve to let him have the album.

**Bhaskar Menon (former Capitol Records and EMI chairman):** There was one more studio album on the Floyd's contract, namely *Dark Side...* The band were disappointed by their lack of success in the States, but Capitol struggled with their music – extremely long tracks, philosophical ruminations, very English themes – but were also intimidated by their rise in other countries.

Capitol tried some desperate strategies too, like releasing Floyd music on their Tower subsidiary, which meant it put the band even further from the mainstream and the company's mainstream resources. But with the success of *Obscured By Clouds* [number fifty-five in the US, their highest placing yet] I think the band were happily surprised.

**Jeff Dexter:** In 1972, I'd done well managing a group called America who'd had a hit with 'A Horse With No Name', but I got completely screwed over by their label Warners and by [record exec] David Geffen. Steve O'Rourke and Tony Howard told me to go and have a rest in Lindos, where the Floyd had rented a house for the summer. They were all there – apart from Nick – about twenty people, including [the feminist author] Germaine Greer. I always remember there was an argument as Roger's wife got a bit precious about how many people were staying at this house.

That summer of '72, Steve was negotiating a new American deal for the Floyd. I'd encouraged Joe Smith, the president of Warners, to get in the running. Steve and Tony were helping me with the group America by pretending they were interested in doing a deal for the Floyd with Warners. It wasn't underhand – they were just playing the game and letting people know things were up for sale.

**Bhaskar Menon:** I was aware they were talking to other people. Steve wanted to buy the Floyd out of their contract with Capitol, so he could take *Dark Side...* elsewhere. In Marseilles, we went to a Moroccan restaurant that looked like an Algerian brothel, and I had a bet with him. I wagered my Casio watch against his Rolex that he would never succeed in dividing the EMI empire. I finally concluded a deal for *Dark Side*... just after sunrise, saving Steve from the loss of his Rolex.

**Jeff Dexter:** Back then, there was only one phone in the village where we were staying on Lindos and it was half a mile from the beach. We called the guy that ran the phone office 'Yanni Ring Ring', because he'd stand at the top of the square and call to us to say there was a phone call. One day, we were lying on the beach and Yanni started shouting. It was a call for Steve O'Rourke from [Atlantic president] Ahmet Ertegun. Steve said, 'Jeff, you've got to talk to Ahmet and tell him to fuck off.'

**Bhaskar Menon:** I already knew they'd signed to CBS [in the US for a $1 million advance] for the next album after *Dark Side*..., but couldn't see any great value in sharing this information with the Pink Floyd or anyone else. A number of people at Capitol thought that how we fared with *Dark Side*... would be a test and the band would re-sign, but they didn't know what I knew. Some might have said, 'Why waste your energies on this?'. But it wasn't in my interest or Capitol's shareholders not to keep going, and I wanted this album.

**Glen Colson (former Pink Floyd publicist):** I used to work for 'Strat', Tony Stratton-Smith at Charisma Records, and he was pals with Steve O'Rourke. 'Strat' wanted to get rid of me because I used to argue with him so much. He'd sign all these crap groups and I'd tell him about these lovely pub-rock bands like Chilli Willi, Kokomo and Ian Dury's Kilburn and the High Roads.

So I went to work for O'Rourke, who kidded 'Strat' that Charisma could sign Pink Floyd because there was a period at the end of the contract where there was a bidding war. Years later, O'Rourke had a group called the Explorers, which was Phil Manzanera and Andy Mackay from Roxy Music – and he got a huge record deal from Virgin on the strength that he might give [Virgin boss] Richard Branson the Floyd. He was doing stuff like that all the time.

Steve was a fearless operator – bit of a cowboy. He told me, 'When you want something, go in there and tell them what you want and that's it. Don't fuck about. Take exactly what you want and leave if they don't give it to you.' It might have been an ignorant approach really, but it worked.

**Peter Jenner:** I've heard great stories about how Steve O'Rourke got every penny he could out of people for the band. All the people who did what they did after us did an incredible job. That's unarguable. Steve built it and built it.

**Nick Mason:** Bhaskar Menon told us, 'I'm going to make this record number one.' In the past, we'd always blamed the record company for *not* being number one, because we'd been with them for seven years and they hadn't worked out how to market us. Even to this day, there are a lot of Americans who think Pink Floyd started with *The Dark Side of the Moon*.

**Bhaskar Menon:** 'Money' was *the* song. But I had to work very hard to persuade the group and Steve O'Rourke that we should put it out as a single in America.

**Jeff Dexter:** I'm not blowing my own trumpet here, but I convinced Steve and Bhaskar that 'Money' would be a hit. At first, they didn't agree because the time signature was too unusual. But I showed them how it worked by playing it at the Roundhouse and seeing how people responded. It was my insistence and my experience as a disc jockey. I knew that song would burst the bubble for them.

**David Gilmour:** I had a bet that I couldn't lose with Steve O'Rourke. Pink Floyd had never been anywhere near the Top 10 in the States and I bet him *Dark Side...* wouldn't go Top 10 in the States, and he bet it would – and he was very right and, thankfully, I was very wrong.

✿

The Dark Side of the Moon *was released in the UK after the boycotted Planetarium launch on 1 March 1973 and a fortnight later in the US. At home, it peaked at number two, denied the top spot by* 20 Flashback Greats of the '60s, *stuffed with hits by the likes of the Kinks and the Searchers.*

*In the US, Bhaskar Menon delivered on his promise and* The Dark Side of the Moon *leapfrogged Elvis's* Aloha From Hawaii Via Satellite *to number one. Soon after, the single 'Money' became a mainstay of US AM Radio and went to number thirteen on the Billboard chart, despite its tricky 7/4 time signature.*

*Later, 'Money's lyrics – scorning the 'hi-fidelity first-class travelling set' – seemed bitterly ironic. Equally, 'share it fairly but don't take a slice of my pie' acquired greater relevance once Waters started complaining about his bandmates' generous writing credits.*

*Nick Mason didn't feel compelled to post another deadly jack-in-the-box, though. Press reviews were largely positive, even if* Rolling Stone *writer (and future TV food pundit) Loyd Grossman felt that some of Gilmour's vocals were 'weak' and that they should have left 'The Great Gig in the Sky' off the record.*

*What* The Dark Side of the Moon *had that Pink Floyd had never quite managed before was inclusivity. Waters has dismissed some of his words as 'sixth-form stuff', but lines such as 'hanging on in quiet desperation is the English way' were relatable to any lapsed '60s wild-child navigating adult responsibility and wondering where all the good times had gone. Or, indeed, anyone reaching their thirties and older in generations to come.*

*For all the window dressing – the spoken word bits, the screams, the frantic synthesiser on 'On the Run' – there were plenty of gorgeous backing vocals and loud guitar solos to keep it grounded. As Gilmour said when filmed soloing noisily at Abbey Road, 'Don't worry about that... Christ, where would rock 'n' roll be without feedback?'*

*By April 1973, the album had gone gold and descriptors such as 'underground group' became irrelevant. O'Rourke's company, EMKA Productions, worked doggedly to ensure the band made as much money as they could, by setting up Pink Floyd Music Publishing, which allowed them to collect royalties directly from overseas partners – a shrewd move as even the Beatles only owned part of their publishers, Northern Songs. An audit by Floyd's publisher*

*Pete Barnes discovered that EMI had failed to collect German royalties for the past three years amounting to a six-figure sum.*

*'We wanted to be rich, we wanted to be pop stars,' admitted Roger Waters. They were now on their way to achieving both.*

⁂

**Nick Mason:** I think we were 'underground' until *The Dark Side of the Moon* put the nail in that particular coffin. I think the album's success was down to a number of facets. There's some very good music on it, and the lyrics are astonishingly relevant to an age group that are now much older than the band was at the time. Roger's lyrics are probably more relevant to a fifty-year-old than a twenty-year-old. But it also became renowned for its engineering and was seen as the ultimate stereo test record. And then there were Storm and Po's graphics...

**Storm Thorgerson:** The prism and the spectrum are so universal and fundamental and don't really belong to Pink Floyd or anyone else. But I also think a bit of playfulness is needed. We're only talking rock 'n' roll here, not a military attack or tsunamis or AIDS....

**Aubrey 'Po' Powell:** *The Dark Side of the Moon* is not actually my favourite Pink Floyd album cover, though. But if you work on the principle that it's sold, I don't know, 60 million, then that means at least 120 million must have seen that image somewhere on billboards, CDs, T-shirts. There are probably a billion people around the world familiar with that image.

**Peter Jenner:** It never had the musical excitement for me after Syd left. I remember really pouring piss on *The Dark Side of the Moon* because I was comparing it to Syd. But I grew to like Pink Floyd again after I'd got over the initial cultural sour grapes.

**Andrew King:** I thought *Dark Side...* contains a lot of awareness of what was happening in the avant-garde across Europe, but synthesised in a way that made sense in a pop group.

**Nick Mason:** Anything a bit continental sounded a bit suspicious to us. If you mean Kraftwerk or Tangerine Dream, I think we probably thought they were a bit too odd.

**Clare Torry:** One day, I was walking down the King's Road and next door to the Chelsea Potter pub was a record shop, and there was a display in the window showing *The Dark Side of the Moon* cover with the prism. This was just after it came out.

I thought, *Is that the thing I did?*. I went into the shop, opened up the sleeve and my name was on it and they'd spelt it right too. I bought a copy and took it home and played it, but I didn't expect them to use the whole of what I did for 'The Great Gig in the Sky'. I still think it's a marvellous album.

Pink Floyd sent me two tickets for when they played Earls Court [in May]. I went with a girlfriend, and there were three backing singers [Phyllis and Mary Ann Lindsey and Nawasa Crowder] up on stage – and I cried when they did 'The Great Gig in the Sky'. I thought it was mine and I should have been up there doing it. Very strange.

**David Gilmour:** David Bowie had played Earls Court Arena immediately before us – and the sound was so bad, the reviews said nobody should ever play a show there again because it's such a barn. But I think our reviews changed that perception. We showed how it could have been done, and we did a full-on show with the crashing Spitfire [co-ordinated by future James Bond special effects technician Derek Meddings] and rockets fired out along wires into the crowd. There was a rather reckless disregard for people's safety then. Health and safety standards have been in place since.

**Jeff Dexter:** They'd honed their act into something special. In spite of everyone saying, 'Oh, all their early light shows were much better', Arthur Max took them to another level.

**Nick Mason:** We gave audiences something to ponder rather than figures on a stage. Before *Dark Side...*, we'd had light shows and slides and so on, but we'd had fuck all to do with them. They were done by whoever was around and they were whatever tricks they came up with – 'Let's try lighter fluid', 'Let's try acrylic'. After *Dark Side...*, we started having more input.

**David Gilmour:** Even more than the album, it was when 'Money' came out in America that we acquired a much larger following. We should be thankful, but some of them weren't versed in Pink Floyd's ways. We did two three-week US tours during 1973, where there were people at the front shouting, 'Play "Money"! Play something I can shake my ass to!'

**Storm Thorgerson:** I remember a story where Columbia were threatened with an audit and Dave telling me they'd found some unbelievable amount of money unaccounted for. I'm talking serious money, 5 million or something.

**Nick Mason:** The money seemed to come in gradually. You'd have a lunch and the record company would present you with another gold disc. But there was a moment where I thought, *Oh, I* can *buy that car*. I bought a 275 GTB Ferrari because I couldn't quite afford a GTO at the time.

**David Gilmour:** The fat royalty cheques took a while to arrive. But the difference was in the massive droves of people that now came to see us. It's the change in our status that comes to my mind thinking about that time. It was very rapid and enormous and shocking.

**Clare Torry:** 'The Great Gig in the Sky' hardly changed my life. I went back to singing commercials for Radox bubble bath, HP sauce and sweet pickle. I even sang 'The Great Gig in the Sky' again for a Nurofen TV ad.

**Richard Wright:** To my great regret, I did allow it once to be used in an advert for headache pills [in 1990], which upset the others, understandably. At the time, I thought, *Why not?*. I got paid a lot of money for it.

**David Gilmour:** That was Rick's decision. If my name had been on that track too, it wouldn't have happened. But I had no control over it.

**Clare Torry:** I thought over the years about doing something to get a songwriting credit on the song, but I couldn't afford the legal fees. Then, in 1996, I decided to act. [It was eventually settled in 2005 that the credit should now read 'Wright with vocal compositions by Torry'.]

**Storm Thorgerson:** Shortly after the release of *The Dark Side of the Moon*, I was walking down Bond Street with Steve O'Rourke when he put his arm around my shoulder, pointed to an expensive-looking sports car and asked why I didn't have one of those. I ventured, tentatively, 'If the Floyd would pay me more...' He withdrew his arm. 'Not a chance,' he said.

**Roger Waters:** I loved Storm. I adored Storm. But many years later, he asked us for 15 per cent of the gross receipts for *The Dark Side of the Moon*. Somebody had told him 15 per cent of its sales were due to the cover. We told him to fuck off.

**Aubrey 'Po' Powell:** We might have been creative people, but we were also in a service industry. You're asked to do the cover, you design an interesting piece of art, and at the end of the day you're paid for it. To turn around and say 'I want a piece of your profits', like Storm did... They laughed him out of the room.

**Storm Thorgerson:** EMI, in their infinite wisdom, decided to put the Pink Floyd's first two albums out again. I am sure the success of *Dark Side...* had an awful lot to do with [1974's] *A Nice Pair*, which was a dull and rather sexist title. We designed eighteen different cover ideas including a sexist one and ended up using all the images somewhere on the sleeve.

**Aubrey 'Po' Powell:** One of the photos on *A Nice Pair* had been taken in Belsize Park just before *The Dark Side of the Moon*. Pink Floyd hated having their photograph taken and turned up in scruffy clothes – David in his tatty velvet jacket. Storm and I had the opportunity to take their picture and they were in such good spirits – everybody started fooling about, pretending to be fashion models or putting their hands over their faces.

You got an infectious joyous feeling from this mysterious group who usually hid behind their light show and rarely gave interviews. I think they're the only photographs I've ever seen of Pink Floyd in the '70s where they look like a happy-go-lucky band who are enjoying each other's company. They were about to make this historic album, after which the relationships between them changed.

Money is a huge corrupter, especially in the rock 'n' roll business. Suddenly, you can afford a nice house and a nice car and you feel like, 'I don't have to spend twenty-four hours a day with these people anymore...'

❋

*In 1994, student journalist Charlie Savage went online at his college in Fort Worth, Indiana, and looked up 'Pink Floyd', after going to see the group in concert. Among the posts from other early net adopters was one claiming that if you listened to* The Dark Side of the Moon *and watched* The Wizard of Oz *with the sound off, the music and movie synced up.*

*So Savage rented a VHS of the film and synced it up with the album. Parts of it worked, sort of, and he wrote a fun article, 'Pink Floyd,* The Wizard of Oz *and Me', for the* Fort Worth Journal-Gazette. *'Put* Dark Side of the Moon *in your CD player and press play at the exact moment the MGM lion roars for the first time,' he instructed. 'The result is eerie, almost astonishing.'*

*There are certainly moments of great providence. 'Time''s lyric 'No one told you when to run' matches up with Judy Garland's Dorothy fleeing her house, and 'Don't give me that do-goody goody bullshit' from 'Money' accompanies Glenda, The Good Witch of the North's first appearance. 'And the wordless moan-singing on "The Great Gig in the Sky" is almost perfectly matched to the tornado scene,' suggested Savage. Best of all, Floyd's soundtrack ends after forty-two minutes and fifty-three seconds with the thump of a heartbeat at the very moment Dorothy puts her ear to the Tin Man's hollow chest.*

*Savage went on to win a Pulitzer Prize for his political journalism and has good-humouredly described the* Journal-Gazette *article as having 'barnacled itself to my career'. The band seemed to feel the same.*

*In 1999, Gilmour was asked: 'Is there any truth in the rumour that* The Dark Side of the Moon *doubles as a soundtrack to* The Wizard of Oz?'

*'If it does, then Roger never let me in on it,' he harumphed.*

*Still, time's a great healer and all that. In the summer of 2024, Gilmour appeared on* The Tonight Show Starring Jimmy Fallon, *promoting his new album,* Luck and Strange. *He was all beaming smiles and twinkly eyes, when Fallon asked him the Wizard Of Oz question.*

*This time Gilmour admitted that he and Polly Samson had tried it out. 'Now people have done the donkey work, and added it on YouTube, you can watch bits of it,' he said. 'And there are these strange coincidences.' He paused, cautious as ever. 'I'll call them* coincidences.'

The Dark Side of the Moon *was now like* The Wizard of Oz, *so entrenched in popular culture that Jimmy Fallon didn't need to explain what it was. Everybody watching the show just knew.*

# 7

# 'LOTS OF TROUBLE, USUALLY SERIOUS'

*Arsenal FC and white Alsatians,*
*'Oh shut up, Roy!', 'An intellectual vibration'*
*and a Suffering Bastard...*

✲

Another Sunday morning, another scrub of parkland doubling as a football pitch and the Pink Floyd First XI locked in sporting combat. Record company staff, members of the progressive rock band Family, Roland Petit's ballet dancers and comrades from the North London Marxists all played against the Floyd XI. After a bloody clash with the latter, David Gilmour was carted off to hospital to have stitches put in his bloodied tongue.

'David was a good player and so was Roger, who was very combative on the pitch,' recalls Nick Mason, talking inside the old Islington HQ of his motor vehicle company, Ten Tenths.

Most of the memorabilia is automobile-related and includes an actual racing car. But there's also a replica of Mason's illustration for *Relics*, and a model of 'Pink', the rock star anti-hero from *The Wall*, slumped at the end of an L-shaped sofa like a discarded child's toy.

Mason approaches any discussion of his sporting prowess with the same self-deprecating air as questions about his drumming. 'Rick and I were, shall we say, less committed,' he admits. 'The only people we managed to push really hard were Roland Petit's dancers, because they had to be so careful of their legs.'

'Roger was a better player than me,' says David Gilmour. 'He had more skill. I hadn't played at school because we did rugby instead, but I was a decent defender – Chopper Gilmour. I played regularly for years after that in a Sunday league team in parks around London.'

Football also offered an escape from the challenges Pink Floyd faced as musicians. 'The enormous success of *The Dark Side of the Moon* had rather scared us,' admits Gilmour. 'You think, *Is this a fluke... Is this it?*'

The group's final dates of 1973 were two performances in a day in November at London's Rainbow Theatre to raise money for Soft Machine's Robert Wyatt, recently paralysed in an accident. The following year, Mason snuck off to produce Wyatt's album, *Rock Bottom* – 'simply because it was nice to get out from behind the drums and be on the other side of the glass,' he says.

Meanwhile, Gilmour encouraged Steve O'Rourke to manage a rock group called Unicorn, whom he'd jammed with at the wedding of musician/publicist/old friend of Syd Barrett, Ricky Hopper. Unicorn came from Surrey, but played what critics later called 'Americana'.

'Their writer, Ken Baker, was very good. But they were so self-effacing, they were probably never going to make it,' says Gilmour, who'd go on to produce four albums for the band before they broke up.

What these outside projects offered them over the next year and more was a creative life away from Pink Floyd. But there was still the pressing matter of another album...

**Nick Mason:** Being wise after the event, we should have taken a gap year after *The Dark Side of the Moon*. But we went back in the studio [in December '73] because that's what we'd always done.

Steve had negotiated unlimited time for us at Abbey Road, but we didn't have a single idea between us. So we went back to the 'Household Objects' project, which had no musical ideas but a lot of ideas about how to make sounds. I remember hitting a piece of wood with an axe to create a percussive sound and hitting a cymbal and dipping it in a bucket of water.

**David Gilmour:** I can't quite believe the timescale involved. Bands today would take five or six years off after a hit like we'd just had. But then the Beatles knocked out their first album in an afternoon. I don't think we'd have known what to do with a year off.

So we went back to the studio and it was as if we'd set ourselves obstacles to overcome. Whose idea was 'Household Objects'? Not mine. Probably Roger's. We found a great sound you could make if you held a rubber band over a matchbox as it amplified the sound. Very silly. These days, you could get your sampler out, plonk these things in, tune them and do it in no time flat.

**Alan Parsons:** There were some nice moments. But it probably amounted to half an hour's music out of a couple of months. I remember the rubber bands stretched across a matchbox, making a rhythm with a witch's broom and feet tapping... I was actually disappointed it never came to anything. But there was the tuned wine glass which I remember working on.

**David Gilmour:** The tuned wine glass was successful because although that was created for 'Household Objects', it later became something we used on 'Shine On You Crazy Diamond' from *Wish You Were Here*.

**Nick Mason:** Everyone was committed to the idea. We did it for a couple of months and then decided, 'No more'. Looking back now, I think the whole thing was a delaying tactic, because we didn't really know what to do next.

**David Gilmour:** Two new songs, 'Shine On You Crazy Diamond' and 'Raving and Drooling', began in a little rehearsal room [Unit Studios] in Kings Cross [in January 1974]. I can't quite perceive why we would have put ourselves in that particular room. It was like the black hole of Calcutta – down an alley behind a pub – horrible, unpleasant, a shit-hole. I think the point of view was that if there was nothing else to distract us – no telly – the creativity would come.

**Nick Mason:** I remember that place in Kings Cross. It was rather grim and next to a Wimpy bar. Perhaps we were punishing ourselves.

**Roger Waters:** I think it was a guitar line of Dave's that sparked me off – a very plaintive phrase you hear at the beginning of 'Shine On You Crazy Diamond'. It's actually the signature tune from the [BBC] radio show *Take Your Pick*.

**David Gilmour:** Absolute bollocks! Someone made that connection later with *Take Your Pick* and it's something I will not have. But Roger explained the words to 'Shine On...' to us and we always accepted it was about Syd. With lyrics like 'you crazy diamond', it couldn't be about anyone else.

**Roger Waters:** I wrote and re-wrote and re-wrote that lyric because I wanted it to be as close as possible to what I felt. There's a truthful feeling in that piece.

**David Gilmour:** Right at the beginning of my time in the group, I was nervous and distracted by too much criticism and people saying I was a pale imitation of Syd and we were nothing without him. The trouble is, we'd all agreed we *weren't* as good without Syd. That feeling changed over time, but I think our love and respect for Syd outweighed any thoughts of wanting to be free of him. So I saw nothing wrong in singing a song about Syd Barrett.

**Nick Mason:** The whole 'They were better with Syd' thing niggled us, but for a time it felt true. Syd had been the frontman, he'd done all the writing, so what the hell were we doing trying to carry on without him? What we didn't know is how much Roger would step up. So I think we were a little thin-skinned about it, but we didn't agree with the critics.

**Nick Kent:** *NME* commissioned me to write a piece about Syd that year ['The Cracked Ballad of Syd Barrett', published in April 1974]. Whenever I used to bump into people, they would tell me Syd Barrett stories. Tony Secunda told me the one about him rubbing Mandrax into his hair. Then someone else would tell me the same story. As is the case with that sort of after-the-fact gossiping, it seemed that maybe 70 per cent of these stories were true, and sometimes there was other stuff added on.

Storm Thorgerson spoke to me and phoned up Dave Gilmour and told him one of the Floyd should put their side across. I had to write the piece on a Friday and, at seven o'clock in the evening that Friday, I met Gilmour in a pub two doors down from the *NME* offices in Covent Garden.

**David Gilmour (to Nick Kent in April 1974):** 'In my opinion, [Syd's] father's death affected him very heavily and his mother always pampered him, made him out to be a genius of sorts ... He functions on a totally different plane of logic and some people will claim, "Well, yeah man he's on a higher cosmic level", but basically there's something drastically wrong.'

**Nick Kent:** Gilmour was the most insightful, as he'd known Syd and had some insight into the family situation. He had a wife then called Ginger, an American girl. I could see they were going to have trouble. She was constantly bugging Gilmour to stop [the interview] and go to a restaurant with her – 'How long is this going to go on, Dave?' – and he was only there for forty-five minutes. I wrote all through the night and came back with the finished thing at ten o'clock in the morning. *NME* were pissed off because I'd missed the deadline.

A week after the piece came out, I ran into Jimmy Page at the Speakeasy. He wanted to know all about Syd and whether he might be brought back to work, as Led Zeppelin's own label, Swansong, was starting. Jimmy wanted to sign him.

**John Leckie:** Peter Jenner and Bryan Morrison encouraged Syd to go back into the studio that year [Abbey Road, August 1974]. Bryan was managing a group called Doctors Of Madness who I was working with. Syd came into Abbey Road by himself with a lot of new guitars, which he kept strumming, then unplugging and then wandering off. He had this vacant look in his eyes. Morrison was really pushing him. 'Come on Syd, get it together.'

**Peter Jenner:** It was upsetting because there were hints of something, and moments when John and I looked at each other and wondered whether we could get him to play whatever it was again.

**John Leckie:** Syd was going to make the album by doing different things every day – piano one day, drums the next, then bass and so on – from Monday to Friday. I don't think we made it to the piano. I don't think we got to Friday.

We used to watch him whenever he left the studio. If Syd turned left outside Studio 3, it was okay, he'd be back. But if he turned right, he'd be gone for the rest of the day. Back then, you could see the famous Abbey Road crossing from the studio window and we'd watch him cross. The story I remember hearing was that he was renting a flat in Chelsea, but actually staying in a hotel.

**Rosemary Breen:** My brother had left Cambridge and had a flat in Chelsea Cloisters [on Sloane Avenue], but he wasn't himself by now. He was there for a few years until he ran out of money and had to come home again.

**Storm Thorgerson:** Hipgnosis did the artwork for the Syd Barrett double album [a repackaging of *The Madcap Laughs* and *Barrett*]. We went to Chelsea Cloisters and tried to take a photo for the cover, and he wouldn't let me in. I tried twice, before thinking, *I can't be doing this. Here am I knocking on the door of someone I've known since I was fourteen and he won't let me in.* Part of me was angry – 'Screw you, I'll be off.' But there were many feelings, and I was also worried about him. But, as far as everybody was concerned, Syd was incommunicado now.

✿

*EMKA Productions' office at 69 New Bond Street was a hive of activity and inactivity, shared with, among others, Tony Howard, Jeff Dexter, the Floyd's publisher Pete Barnes and 'cocky young publicist' Glen Colson.*

*After* Dark Side..., *Pink Floyd's stock had risen in ways that would have seemed inconceivable a few months before. In early summer 1974, the band were paid handsomely for a photoshoot in the desert near Marrakesh. The offer came from a French soft drinks company, Gini, who believed Floyd's hip image would sell their range of bitter lemon tonic.*

*'Un goût, une musique étrange venue d'ailleurs' (translated as 'a taste, a strange music from elsewhere') declared a set of print ads showing the band squinting into the Saharan sun and looking windswept and dusty...*

❧

**Roger Waters (speaking in 1976):** 'I wrote a song about it at the time. I was going home from Morocco by plane and I felt very bad as a result of the episode with Gini. The song's called 'Bitter Love'. In the beginning, it was as if we were winning a prize. They wanted to give us £50,000 to take our photograph. Good God! Fantastic! It was only later that I told myself, "Who needs that?"'

**David Gilmour:** £50,000? It could have been that much. I just remember going into the desert in Morocco and being photographed. But I have a feeling that money went into a school for disabled children in France, or something like that.

**Nick Mason:** Against our better judgement, we wandered into that situation. It was a lot of money and we took it, and then realised that the commercial realities were more painful than we thought. So there we are with this fucking sponsorship roadshow – models and people dressed up as bikers waving huge Gini placards – at every gig on our French tour [in June 1974].

It was also a bad decision for our audience. The French respected us and thought we were an art band, and I think we rather brutalised that by having all this nonsense going on. Charity? No. We didn't give the money to charity. I think we might have put some of it towards the production, but, no, we were rather acquisitive back then.

**Glen Colson:** The story around the EMKA office was Roger would hide his cheques in a drawer by his bed because his parents had been Communists and he was embarrassed about earning money.

Roger and I played football together in Tony Howard's team, the World's End Wanderers. I played in midfield and Roger used to shout at me because I wasn't much of a tackler – and we once had a row in a pub about Keith Moon. Roger wanted a row with everybody, though. God knows how O'Rourke put up with him.

That office was a funny old set up – lots of bands in and out all the time like Family and Hawkwind. Ricky Hopper was always wandering around. He was very friendly with Syd Barrett and told me once that Syd used to pretend to be mad until one day he fucking was.

Ricky was always going on about this girl he'd discovered, who was his mate's younger sister. He said, 'Dave likes her. You've got to come down and see her.' And I did. Her dad was a doctor and she was playing piano in his surgery. It was Kate Bush and I just didn't get it all at first.

**Storm Thorgerson:** Around this time, I suggested to Nick Sedgwick, a friend from Cambridge, that we write a book about the Floyd. Nick was a schoolteacher and an aspiring writer, and because he got on well with Rog – they played golf together – I knew we would have access backstage, without being too noticeable.

**Roger Waters:** Nick Sedgwick ended up writing two pieces, which later became part of a book. The first one was about the summer of '74 when he went on holiday with my wife and I in Greece, and wrote about the beginning of the end of our marriage. Then he came on the road with Pink Floyd in winter '74, took a cassette recorder with him and recorded many conversations backstage.

✣

*By now, Waters had a villa in the Greek coastal town of Volos, along with a powerboat in which he zoomed around the local bay before mooring up for a Retsina-fuelled lunch. Back at the villa, he attempted to write songs in between arguing with Judy – a ritual faithfully recorded by Sedgwick, playing Boswell to Waters' Johnson.*

*During one heated discussion, Judy raised the subject of Waters cheating on her with a woman from Texas during an earlier Floyd tour. 'The way Judy put it, Roger fucked her up in much the same way as he fucked up his audience,' Sedgwick wrote. 'He was remote, invulnerable.'*

*Earlier, while driving through the former Yugoslavia towards Greece, the vacationing party's car was forced off the road in an attempted robbery. The bandit waved a pistol in Waters' face and, in Sedgwick's account, started 'rubbing his thumb and forefinger together in the Esperanto sign for "Gimme the cash".'*

*Nick and Judy were terrified, while Waters looked remote and invulnerable. 'I'm sorry!' he boomed. 'I can't understand a word you're saying.' The gunman fled empty handed.*

*Waters swapped marital disharmony for turmoil of another kind on a slog through Britain's provincial halls on Floyd's winter '74 tour. The group were joined by saxophonist Dick Parry and Humble Pie's backing vocalists Venetta Fields and Carlena Williams, whose silver platform boots and hip shimmies brought some pizzazz to the show. Both later sang on* Wish You Were Here.

*Floyd played three new songs – 'Shine On You Crazy Diamond', 'Raving and Drooling' and 'Gotta Be Crazy' – 'before the golden oldies,' explains Mason. There was more of Arthur Max's lighting effects and a forty-foot circular screen showing bespoke film clips, aircraft landing lights during 'On the Run', banknotes and Learjets in 'Money'... Yet technology ran up against human error, the band's collective unease and, soon, writer Nick Kent's mildly poisonous pen.*

✣

**David Gilmour:** That tour was eighteen dates in twenty-one days, which was going some. Roger didn't want to do any longer and he put his foot down about it. It might have been to do with his marriage – he was having difficulties in his personal life. But if one person was uncomfortable about something, we wouldn't make them do it.

**Alan Parsons:** Floyd offered me a full-time position as their permanent sound engineer. The salary was £10,000, a huge amount at the time. I needed a full week to consider the offer and, if it had come a few months earlier, I'd have taken it. But I was doing more production work and was thinking about making the first Alan Parsons Project album. One of my other reasons for not taking the job was I wanted a royalty on the next album and Steve O'Rourke said no.

**Nick Mason:** We had to take on a studio engineer [Rufus Cartwright] at short notice, who had no experience of a live concert environment and whose job was made more difficult as there were issues with the mixing desk.

**Roger Waters:** The circular screen may have been my idea or it may have been Arthur Max's. But I do remember Steve O'Rourke coming up to me and going, 'Um, bad news, you can't use the circular screen.' Why not? He said, 'Um, Emerson, Lake and Palmer used one at a festival.' I remember being a little bit snappy and going, 'What are you talking about? What does it matter if somebody used one before? Does that mean you can't make a movie because somebody once projected one on a rectangular screen? It's ridiculous.'

**Gerald Scarfe (artist and film-maker):** In 1971, the BBC had sent me to Los Angeles to make an animated film, *Long Drawn Out Trip*. So I made a film about everything I could think of going on in America – Mickey Mouse, Black Power, the Statue of Liberty – and peppered it with a soundtrack of Jimi Hendrix and Paul Simon and all the people around at the time.

Nick and Roger saw it on BBC2 and said, 'We should get this guy to do something for us.' I was aware of Pink Floyd, rather than being a fan. I used to go to UFO and once filmed Arthur Brown with his head on fire. But Nick invited me to see Floyd at the Rainbow with the Stuka diving into the stage and I was very impressed by the theatricality of it all.

**David Gilmour:** It was a large model aeroplane coming down at the end of 'On the Run' and disappearing into the dark and crashing into a great big wodge of foam rubber. Jolly entertaining.

**Gerald Scarfe:** We had a meeting at Nick's place and they told me to go off and do anything I felt like doing. They were coming up to doing *Wish You Were Here*, but I was confused about what they wanted. I left it for a long time before I did anything. I was on other projects and didn't quite know where to begin. So, for the time being, I ended up drawing a picture of the group for their tour programme. I sketched them while they were rehearsing in a dingy room in King's Cross. I remember they sent out for terrible hamburgers from the Wimpy bar next door.

**Nick Mason:** Gerald came to work with us, as did the director Peter Medak [who'd just made *The Life and Death of Joe Egg*] after Ian Emes, who made some wonderful films, including the flying clocks at the start of 'Time'. These were talented people. But the films were fantastically complicated because we had to work out how to sync them and we weren't using click tracks.

So the films were made in such a way they didn't have to sync too closely. But the projectionist still had to frantically spool backwards and forwards to make things match up. The shows on that tour were erratic. It was a learning process and we were soon getting a bit cranky with the technology.

**Richard Wright:** It was a massive headache because the equipment was pretty unreliable. The film would break or the projector would break down.

**Jill Furmanovsky:** I was working for Storm and photographing that tour. Venetta Fields and Carlena Williams were on the road – these two American girls with gospel and soul-singing backgrounds. It was an hilarious contrast to see them with their sexy frocks and sexy movements next to David Gilmour, the most dishevelled and reticent of English gentlemen. They were like 'Give it to me Dave!' – and he was hiding behind the amps, trying to be invisible.

**Chris Charlesworth (*Melody Maker* writer):** I'd seen Pink Floyd before, at the Bath Festival playing *Atom Heart Mother*, and all four of them in a doctor's waiting room at Harley Street, waiting to get inoculated. That day, I said hello and told them I was from *Melody Maker*, but they certainly weren't very sociable.

I don't know if they'd banned the press from covering the first show [at Edinburgh's Usher Hall], but they weren't encouraging them. So I rang all the hotels in Edinburgh asking if they had a 'Mr O'Rourke' staying there, because I thought band members would use false names. Once I found where they were, I booked a room, caught the train to Scotland and bought a ticket off a tout.

Later, I bumped into the promoter Harvey Goldsmith, whom I knew, and inveigled my way into an after-show meal. I sat down next to Steve O'Rourke and we started talking about fast cars. My granny had died and left me £1,000, which, instead of doing the sensible thing and putting down a deposit for a house, I spent on a second-hand Lotus Elan. Yellow, it was.

I told O'Rourke this and he said, 'Do you know what Lotus stands for? Lots of trouble, usually serious' – which made me laugh. Then Storm Thorgerson insisted he sit next to Steve because they had business to discuss and I was out.

What I really wanted was an interview, though, and Steve arranged for me to talk to Rick Wright the next day. What surprised me the most, though, was discovering that Roger Waters was such a keen golfer. Apparently there were some good courses in Edinburgh.

**Jill Furmanovsky:** It was a shock how sporty Pink Floyd were. It was incomprehensible to me. Roger would play golf and then squash at the hotel, and if a gig was running late, they would rush through it to watch *Match of the Day*. Storm was always ringing my room, 'Get your camera, Dave's playing backgammon.'

**Nick Mason:** Roger was the best golfer and we all played a bit of squash. We were probably more interested in that than sorting out some of the problems with the show, and we were more interested in playing squash than taking drugs – though we did both, of course. Maybe the drug dealer ran the squash court.

**Richard Wright (to Chris Charlesworth, November 1974):** 'We're not underground anymore ... At the UFO it was underground, but you can't be underground when you sell out every concert hall and your album goes to number one.'

**Chris Charlesworth:** I enjoyed the show. Out of all of them, I'd wanted to interview Roger, but Rick was probably the nicest. After we were done, I caught the train back to London and then, a couple of days later, Nick Kent wrote his famous review in *NME*, with all that stuff about David Gilmour's hair.

**Nick Kent (review of the Wembley Empire Pool show, *NME*, November 1974):** 'On 14 November 1974, approximately seven thousand people washed their hair and travelled down to the Empire Pool, Wembley... Almost everyone, that is, except David Gilmour – his hair looked filthy ... seemingly anchored down by a surfeit of scalp grease and tapering off below the shoulders with a spectacular festooning of split ends.

'At 8.20 p.m. or thereabouts the four members of Floyd saunter on stage. It is not a spectacular entrance. In fact they wander on rather like four navvies who've just finished their tea-break and are about to return slowly to the task of tarring a section of main road.'

**Nick Kent:** I'd always been a Syd fan. I saw him with the Floyd at Sophia Gardens in Cardiff when I was fifteen. The four of them had a sound before *The Dark Side of the Moon* and they can say what they like about it now, but those albums were what we used to call 'space rock' – they were the rich man's Hawkwind.

All those German bands ripped their sound off in the mid-'70s and all these punk bands that used to claim they hated them were there in the fucking audience – that's what John Lydon was going to see. But with *The Dark Side of the Moon*, they changed. Some of their roots audience – the hippies – liked it, but it moved them into sort of *Guardian* reader territory.

I admit the 'hair thing' in the Wembley review was a low blow on my part, though. But they'd look at each on stage the way workmen look at each other as if to say, 'Oh fuck, I suppose we better get on with it.' Waters, especially, was a very haughty guy.

**Richard Wright (to Nick Sedgwick, 1974):** 'It's not a review of the show. It's an all-out attack on the band. We can take fair criticism, but not this. What a cunt.'

**David Gilmour (speaking to *NME*, January 1975):** 'When I'm standing there, I'm consciously trying to give the most I can... And I don't need to have clean hair for that.'

**David Gilmour:** Nick Kent had every right to say whatever the fuck he likes. I was over-sensitive about my split ends... but to say I never washed my hair? Untrue, libellous, of course... The thing is that was an uncomfortable moment, because we didn't think that Wembley gig was up to much either – though I listened to it again years later and thought it sounded brilliant.

**Roger Waters (to Nick Sedgwick, 1974):** 'Kent's talking about a general attitude we do display, and we display it because we're confused, right. At least I'm confused, and that confusion comes out on stage because we don't quite know what we're doing there anymore. We do shamble out on stage, and we don't have any real connection with audiences.'

**Roger Waters:** Looking back now, I was scared of my own shadow, never mind about making contact with an audience. We were very disconnected.

**Nick Mason:** We always read reviews. When they were bad, we didn't retire, but we did want to be approved of and it was difficult to get the knockback, even if sometimes we understood why. What did Nick Kent say? That we looked bored? I don't think we were bored on stage. It's very hard to be truly bored on stage. But I do think the tour was slightly self-indulgent.

**Ossie Clark (fashion designer, diary entry 15 November 1974):** 'Pink Floyd. Seven o'clock suddenly loomed up and we were ready and dressed in furs to go to Wembley. The show was good, but not as good as the last. The crowd certainly really dug it and afterwards we went backstage for drinks. John Cale, very heavy, nasty roadies and lots of people I knew. Then we went to Gilmour's new house behind Westbourne Park Road to watch a pornographic movie and Monty Python on videotape.'

**Nick Kent:** Almost a year later, I bumped into Rick Wright at a party in Ladbroke Grove and he actually thanked me for that review. He told me it stimulated some intra-group discussion about where they were because they'd become so detached from each other.

❀

*There was dissent within some of the audience too.* The Dark Side of the Moon*'s success had brought Pink Floyd a teenage fanbase almost half the band's age. At Newcastle Odeon, one of them called out for T. Rex's hit 'Telegram Sam'. Waters replied with a long, exaggerated yawn. 'Play music!' shouted the heckler. 'We have been playing music for fuck's sake!' snapped Waters, whom Gilmour later accused of sounding like 'an old schoolteacher'.*

*The road crew, aka 'The Quad Squad', were unhappy too. Crew chief Pete Watts had been fired (he died two years later of a heroin overdose) and Arthur Max promoted. But lighting, rather than sound or man-management, were Max's forte. He soon clashed with front-of-house sound engineer Rufus Cartwright, and was always screaming at someone, including a hall manager who had the temerity to enter his venue while the group were soundchecking.*

*Things kept going wrong with the show too: the digital clock on the screen counting down 'On the Run' only showed seconds instead of tenths and hundredths of a second, and was abandoned on Waters' orders; the PA was either too quiet or so loud that it distorted; and mastering the new mixing desk seemed to be a dark art.*

*Sound engineer Brian Humphries, who'd last worked with the group on* Zabriskie Point, *attended the second night at Wembley and came home with a new job.*

❀

**Brian Humphries:** I'd been hired by the BBC to record one of the concerts at Wembley, so I went to one of the earlier shows to see what equipment we'd need for the mobile studio. The Floyd's tour manager, Warwick McCredie, took me backstage and I told the band I'd been doing a lot of live gig mixing. I'd just come back from America with Spooky Tooth and I got the bug for it – 'This is the life'.

The band asked me to sit with their sound mixer and tell them what I thought. They'd given me a brandy and orange juice, which wasn't a good move, and then I saw the engineer [Rufus Cartwright] – long hair, long fingernails, wearing sandals. No disrespect, probably a very nice person.

I sat next to him and you couldn't hear the bass drum or the bass and I thought, *What? You've got all this fucking power at your disposal...* I went back and told the band in the interval, who said, 'Yes, that's what we've heard. Could you take over tomorrow night and do the rest of the British tour?' And then it became full-time employment and working with them on *Wish You Were Here*.

**David Gilmour:** Really, the most difficult problem on that tour was Arthur Max, who wanted to be a fifth member of the band on equal pay. We said, 'Arthur, as much as we love you, but no.' He decided enough was enough and we decided enough was enough and he left on a train up to Liverpool.

**Nick Mason:** Arthur was a wonderful man, but a little over-excitable. We still have a fantastic recording of Arthur losing his temper with the follow-spot operators and he had to be smuggled out of the building at the end of the show because they were all looking for him. Of course, he's now enormously important in Hollywood.

**David Gilmour:** One night, I was clambering into bed, the TV was on and the credits were rolling for [Ridley Scott's 2000 movie] *Gladiator* and Arthur's name was in them [as production designer]. A brilliant guy, but his eccentricities got the better of him. The mood on the tour improved after Arthur left. But, in some ways, the inspiration in the visual department was diluted. All I have are mood memories – and the mood on that tour was on the dark side. I'm not trying to make a pun there...

**Jill Furmanovsky:** Pink Floyd were part of a network of people, which also included Storm, Po, Arthur Max... But you never quite knew who was considered persona grata, and who was persona non grata. The road crew were on an equal footing, record company people were barely tolerated backstage, and wives and girlfriends were just about allowed in. Storm used to hold court with Roger Waters. There was always an intellectual vibration going on after a gig and those two having a heated discussion.

**Glen Colson:** My behaviour was dreadful. O'Rourke was bemused by my indifference towards Pink Floyd. I saw them on [the last night of] that tour in Bristol and they'd laid on a load of limos. So we took one and picked up the backing singers on the way. They had a bar in the dressing room and I stayed there all evening. Afterwards, Nick Mason asked me what I thought of the show. 'No idea, Nick.' It sounds shameful now, doesn't it...?

**Nick Sedgwick (writing in 1974):** 'Roger and I walk to a waiting limo. The lights of Bristol and six weeks of noise and crowds shrink behind us as we slump in the back of the car ... As we pull on a bottle of Southern Comfort, a line from the *I Ching* pops into my head: "Difficulty at the beginning brings success; perseverance furthers."'

**Nick Mason:** At the end of that year, everyone in the band approached the management individually and said they were thinking of quitting. It's one of those things that one discovered much later. At the time, none of us had any idea the others felt the same. It was down to the pressure of following *Dark Side*... and Roger being at the point where he was starting to think he could do it all on his own.

**John Leckie:** I started engineering *Wish You Were Here* at Abbey Road [in January 1975]. It was the first session they had with the studio's new Neve mixing desk. Nobody knew how it worked – just turn it on and hope for the best.

I'd recorded a few takes of 'Shine On You Crazy Diamond' before Brian Humphries turned up unannounced, so there was a bit of a hoo-ha about that because Abbey Road didn't usually allow outside engineers. I stuck around for a day or so and then I went to work with Roy Harper.

**Brian Humphries:** Nobody knew how to use that bloody machine and a few times I had to beckon in the boffins. To start with, there was a bit of, 'Oh he's not Abbey Road', but once they realised I knew what I was doing, they accepted me. Peter James was my tape op assigned to me by Abbey Road, who'd worked on *Dark Side*... and was a fabulous guy. Peter drank too much... as did I.

**David Gilmour:** We did the backing track for 'Shine On You Crazy Diamond' over the course of several days, but it just wasn't good enough. So we did it again in one day and got it a lot better. Unfortunately, nobody understood the desk properly and someone had switched the echo returns from the monitors to tracks one and two. So we had to do it yet again.

**Brian Humphries:** Only one other person fiddles with buttons and stuff when he's not doing anything – and that's a certain guitarist. But, as it was four against one, I got the blame for that. Even the technical people at Abbey Road didn't know how the desk worked. I felt they were looking for any excuse to replace me with one of their in-house guys. This all happened on a Friday evening and I was expecting to get fired on Monday morning.

**David Gilmour:** It was an unusual practice to use an outside engineer, but we liked Brian. Apart from doing *More* for us, he'd done a lot of work with Traffic, which we liked, and he was a natural engineer.

**Brian Humphries:** As soon as I got the job, I told Pink Floyd I needed a company car because I lived in Tunbridge Wells and my wife needed our car to get to work. So they gave me a second-hand Cortina 2000, but that broke down on the way to work one day, so they had to give me a brand-new one. I had a personalised number plate – 'PF' and then my initials 'BH'.

The number of times I got stopped by the police speeding in the dead of night and they always wanted to know why my number plate was 'PFBH' – and every time this happened, they'd say, 'Oh, if you told us that at the beginning sir, we wouldn't have given you a ticket. I'm a Pink Floyd fanatic.'

**David Gilmour:** Brian was a very nice guy, but not a terribly strong person and being in a band situation with us was a bit like being thrown to the lions. We were a tough cruel bunch led by Captain Roger, the toughest and cruellest of the bunch. There always has to be a bit of alpha male-ing in life. Roger was the cruellest, but we all joined in quite heartily with the teasing and didn't realise that some people are taking it to heart more than you think. I think, in the end, Brian found it a bit hard to take.

**Brian Humphries:** They used to take the piss out of Rick as well – 'Have you got any ideas, Rick? Have you got any ideas, Rick?' If we'd been working late, rather than drive home I used to stay at Rick's, and he and I would talk. Rick had a lot of ideas and he'd take in a lot of what I had to say.

**David Gilmour:** 'Shine On...' is a personal favourite. I have always loved this song. I love the words. I love all the music in it. It has a real atmosphere to it and Rick was a big part of that. It was sometimes hard to define Rick's contribution. He always added something that was magical but unobtrusive, which could lead one to think he hadn't put himself about much.

**Brian Humphries:** There were days when they didn't do a thing – nothing – because I don't think they knew what they wanted to do. So we had a dartboard and an air rifle that shot these darts at the board. That came about because Roger wanted to do something like asking people questions again on the new record, as he'd done on *Dark Side*.... But it never got used, so someone suggested bringing a dartboard in. Hours were wasted.

**Nick Mason:** Before, I had enjoyed being in the studio and now we were in this place where nothing might get done. And you could be there from midday until midnight – and I had a wife and child. Consequently, we were getting unbelievably ratty with each other. We would get fantastically cross about people being late. It's not as if anything was going to happen, but it would become a personal affront. I was also under pressure to make my drumming less flowery.

**David Gilmour:** Nick had a particular style, which was great, but I had been nagging him going way way back to use that particular style to its best advantage in certain moments, but to stick to a regular groove. I nagged him about this, but I am still convinced he was the best person to be in our little combo.

**Roger Waters:** After *The Dark Side of the Moon*, it was a case of, 'Oh look, we're rich! We've achieved whatever we set out to achieve!' Then we did *Wish You Were Here* and there was all that argy-bargy about what to do. It was torture, torture, torture! And, of course, it all came to a head when I suggested we lose 'Gotta Be Crazy' and 'Raving and Drooling', and keep 'Shine On…'. I would go away and write more songs in keeping with the theme of absence, which had some relevance to the state we were all in. This led to a disagreement between Dave and myself.

**David Gilmour:** I have read that I disagreed with getting rid of those songs and, yes, guilty as proven. But I was wrong. Having argued my side fairly vociferously, I then got on with it. 'Shine On…' was originally going to be the whole of one side of the album, but a decision was made to split it into two and it would begin and end the record and the new songs ['Have a Cigar' was the first to be performed] would slot in around it.

**Nick Mason:** I always liked Roger's lyrics, but he was starting to get very cross about the music industry. 'Have a Cigar' started off with a much slower tempo, but lyrics like 'By the way, which one's Pink?' were all things we had been asked or heard from people at record companies.

**David Gilmour:** Memory is a fickle friend, but my memory is Roger wanted to sing 'Have a Cigar' and he had a go at singing it and one or two people were unkind about his version. Then one or two people asked me to have a go at singing it – and I did, but I wasn't comfortable. It's nothing against Roger's lyric, but there are areas of tonality when you know your own voice.

Roy Harper was recording his album, *HQ*, in another studio and we were sitting in the control room of number three arguing, and I can remember Roy leaning on the side wall of the outside building, saying, 'Go on, let me have a go. Let me have a go.' 'Oh, shut up Roy…' But then, eventually, we said, 'Go on then, Roy. Have your bloody go.' Most of us enjoyed it, though I don't think Roger ever liked it.

**John Leckie:** Roger said to Roy, 'We must make sure you get a payment for this' and Roy said, 'Just get me a life season ticket to Lord's [cricket ground]'. It never came. About ten years later, Roy wrote a letter to Roger and decided that, due to the success of *Wish You Were Here*, £10,000 would be adequate. He heard nothing back at all.

**David Gilmour:** Roy's claim to a life season ticket to Lord's was a new one on me when it raised its ugly head a few years ago. There's no way that Roger would have agreed to that.

**Roy Harper:** The original joke was they'd give me a life-long season ticket to Lord's in return. I took the song away and changed it a little bit to suit myself.

**Roger Waters:** I regret it. To me, it doesn't feel very natural him doing it. I think if I'd persevered with it, I would have done it better than that. If I'd sung it, it would have been more vulnerable and less cynical.

**Roy Harper:** That song would have been good whoever sang it. But it seemed to take an age and I have this vision of me being in and out of the studio and nothing progressing. They'd take breaks and all that happened was a conversation about football – Arsenal, generally.

One of the guys at the time was breeding white Alsatians, and one day the conversation drifted from football to white Alsatians – and Nick Mason had been asleep, lying flat out on one of the benches at the back of the studio, and he turned over. It was the first time he'd moved for an hour, so we could see his face and he just said, 'Oh God... sport and animals.'

**David Gilmour:** On 'Welcome to the Machine', Roger came in with that thumping VSC3 synthesiser on a delay, and we worked on it from there. There was one line – 'You know where you've been' – that I couldn't reach, so we slowed the tape down. You can't get as high in the studio as on stage. Don't know why, maybe it's the air in the room.

**Roger Waters:** The dream is that when you're successful, when you're a star, you'll be fine, everything will go wonderfully well. 'Welcome to the Machine' is about the business situation I find myself in. One is encouraged to be absent because no one is encouraged to pay any attention to reality.

**David Gilmour:** We were all a bit absent – as Roger says. It was a tricky time and we had to sit around and assess music and life. But I had reached the assessment that whatever faults there were in the music business, I am a musician. And I liked being a musician.

**Storm Thorgerson:** I heard a lot of the music, as Abbey Road was very near to my house and I could leg it in and out. They did a lot of talking to try to work out what was going on. Roger, who was usually quite clear about things, didn't have a clue either. So it took a long time to find the theme.

The magic word was absence: an absence of Syd, an absence of wives and, to some extent, an absence of commitment from the band themselves. Having been extremely successful with *Dark Side...*, there might have been a great temptation not to go to work. There was also the nice problem of, how do you follow a million seller? Hard for the cover too. *Dark Side...* wasn't my favourite, but it was clearly successful. So how do I follow that?

I'm interested in numerology and became fixated on the number four, and there were four people in the band. I decided on a cover with the four elements. Water would be represented by the postcard of the diver in Lake Mono, air in the form of wind with an image of a red veil, earth by a faceless record company executive standing in the Yuma Desert and fire, which came out of a conversation with [illustrator] George Hardie, who said, 'Let's draw a man on fire' – to which I said, 'Oh no. We'll set a man on fire.'

I was very nervous about the presentation at Abbey Road. There were almost twenty people there, including Steve O'Rourke, all sat at a long table. Of course, I took a long time to get to what I wanted to say and they were all laughing and jeering and asking, 'Are we paying you for this?'. But it went down really well. They thought my ideas were fantastic and gave me a round of applause. Have I had that since? What, with the Floyd? Of course I fucking haven't.

**Roger Waters:** In those days, you bought a vinyl long-playing record, you studied the sleeve, read the lyrics and looked at all the pictures and went, 'Wow'. That cover was to some extent developed from conversations between me and Storm about what the record was about. He got it. Storm was interested. The others weren't.

**Storm Thorgerson:** I got an email once from a fan who'd studied the sleeve for *Wish You Were Here* for years and said he knew what it was all about. 'It's about the devil,' he said. We wrote him a nice letter back, because if that's what he saw, that's what he saw.

**Aubrey 'Po' Powell:** I went to Los Angeles and arranged the shoots for water, earth and fire. Personally, one of favourite images was the diver in Lake Mono. We'd hired one who could hold his breath underwater for ninety seconds, until all the ripples in the lake had subsided.

The front-cover photograph of two businessmen shaking hands with one going up in flames was about people being ripped off by the music business – 'Oh, man, I've been burned' was a saying at the time. Hey, it was the '70s.

We hired two stuntmen and shot it on an back lot at the Warners Studio in Burbank. Ronnie Rondell and Danny Rogers had both been in the [hit disaster movie] *The Towering Inferno* and were experts in the field. But Ronnie's moustache and eyebrows still got singed when the wind changed direction, and his assistants had to smother him in blankets and foam. I kept shooting. We had an edict at Hipgnosis: 'the art always comes first'.

**Glen Colson:** One day, O'Rourke asked me to take the record exec Colin Miles up to Abbey Road and give him a bit of a vibe, because Pink Floyd were making a new album there. O'Rourke said: 'The only person in EMI that the Floyd will talk to is Colin Miles. They hate everyone else.' Colin had been involved with the Harvest label and was a bit posh, and I always thought a fish out of water in the music business.

Anyway, when we got to Abbey Road, there was this figure sat on the couch, overweight, saying nothing, just staring. I was quite tight with Mick and Sheila Rock at the time, and all I remember is this Syd Barrett looked nothing like Mick's photos of Syd Barrett.

**David Gilmour:** I remember seeing him wandering in and out and thinking he was a house engineer and then he came into a control room and someone said, 'That's fucking Syd.' I think it was me, Roger thinks it's him... and so on. We tried to engage him in conversation and he wandered off down Abbey Road and that was the last we ever saw him.

**Aubrey 'Po' Powell:** That day, he'd showed up unannounced at the Hipgnosis studio first. I didn't recognise him to begin with. I had to look closely into his eyes – 'Syd is that you?'. I offered him a cup of tea but he refused. He was looking for Storm and I told him Storm was with the Floyd at Abbey Road.

**Brian Humphries:** I just saw the control room doors open and in came this fat, bald guy wearing a trench coat. He just stood there while we all looked around at each other. He had his acoustic guitar with him and I remember Roger taking him aside.

**Roger Waters:** This great fat, bald, mad person... The first day he came in, I was in fucking tears.

**Richard Wright:** Roger said, 'You don't know who that guy is, do you? It's Syd.' He kept standing up and brushing his teeth, and then putting his toothbrush away, and sitting down ... Syd stood up and said, 'Right, when do I put the guitar on?' And we said, 'Sorry Syd, the guitar's all done.'

**Nick Sedgwick (writing in 1975):** 'Syd drank orange juice ... chewed Amplex tablets, and observed the action. I asked him what he thought of the music. There was a prolonged pause, then he answered. "It's all... all a bit Mary Poppins," he said. It was the last I saw of him.'

**Nick Mason:** We were working on 'Shine On You Crazy Diamond' at the time and later Rick played a bit of 'See Emily Play' on the fadeout. If you listen *really* closely, you can hear it on the record.

**David Gilmour:** People love to be involved with a moment. People have said we were working on 'Shine On You Crazy Diamond', but I can't remember what song it was. I have heard people say Syd came for two or three days. I don't think that's true and I don't think he said any of the things people think he said. That's more fiction than fact.

**Roger Waters:** 'Shine On You Crazy Diamond' couldn't have happened without Syd. On the other hand, Pink Floyd couldn't have gone on with him.

✿

*Photographs published of Syd Barrett at Abbey Road suggest he was there more than once, as he's wearing different clothes. But who knows? Peter Jenner and Andrew King certainly remember him at a band meal in the studio canteen prior to Floyd's next US tour. When asked why he was so fat, Barrett reputedly blamed it on the pork chops he'd been eating.*

*At least he seemed jovial. Around this time, Syd often appeared at his publisher Bryan Morrison's office in Bruton Place, asking for an advance on his royalties. Morrison insisted Barrett sign a receipt for these sums. When a royalty cheque for £20,000 finally arrived, Morrison asked Syd to reimburse them the few hundred pounds he'd borrowed against it. Barrett denied borrowing any money and, in the ensuing argument, apparently bit one of Morrison's fingers almost down to the bone. Morrison responded with what he later called 'a humdinger', knocking Barrett on his back, after which Syd started laughing, with 'an increasing pitch of hysteria'.*

*Pink Floyd's US tour was split into two legs that summer. After the final night in Hamilton, Ontario, the crew detonated leftover dynamite from the crashing aeroplane sequence. They'd underestimated the firepower and the subsequent explosion blew out the Ivor Wynne Stadium's illuminated scoreboard and windows in several neighbouring houses. In some ways it was a metaphor for the tour.*

*Nick Sedgwick had submitted his account of the winter 1974 dates prior to flying to the US. Waters and Mason approved, but Gilmour and Wright didn't, and Sedgwick felt distinctly unwelcome backstage.*

*Aptly perhaps, Waters' favourite cocktail during this jaunt was a gin, brandy and angostura bitters concoction named a Suffering Bastard. On 10 April, before a date at the Seattle Center Coliseum, he telephoned Judy at home and a man's voice answered. Merging art and real life, he later recreated the incident on 'Young Lust' on* The Wall.

*Back home, on 5 July, Pink Floyd headlined the Knebworth Festival (alongside the Steve Miller Band, Roy Harper, Captain Beefheart, Linda Lewis and Monty Python's Flying Circus) in the grounds of Baron Cobbold's stately home in Hertfordshire. Here, Waters was accompanied by his new partner Carolyne Christie, niece to the third Marquis of Zetland.*

❋

**Roger Waters:** First of all, if I'm honest, I have to accept that, at that point, I became a capitalist. You can call yourself what the fuck you like, but if you suddenly get a lot of money, the impression is that you're a capitalist. You can't pretend ... you can still espouse humanitarian ideas, which I still do, but things are that bit more complicated.

**Nick Kent:** I knew Carolyne fairly well. She was an aristocratic woman and the first time I met her she was an acting press officer for Bob Ezrin who was producing Lou Reed's album, *Berlin*. She was often around rock stars. I later saw her in LA, hanging around Led Zeppelin with Boz Burrell from Bad Company. If you read Rock Scully, the manager of the Grateful Dead's book, he claims Scully married Carolyne in 1974 so she could come to America. Carolyne came from another era of entitlement – 'I just arrive and the doors open.'

**Peter Jenner:** All the Floyd's wives were strong women. Roger's first wife Judy was very nice and, I subsequently discovered, also a screaming Trot. But I always felt Roger was very influenced by his women. Judy kept him left wing and committed, and she didn't put up with his shit because she'd known him since before the Floyd. Then he had the second wife...

**Jeff Dexter:** In the 1940s, there was a film about swing musicians and their wives called *Orchestra Wives*. Think of Ozzy Osbourne today, who wouldn't be able to piss without his missus. Two of Pink Floyd had influential wives. One was benign, the other one wasn't. Suddenly, it was all wives, money, property and ego.

**David Gilmour:** A lot of money changed hands on one of those tours. Roger had this card game called Klaberjass, which he used to play against Tony Howard. We also had a poker team going when we were on the plane flying between gigs in the States – five-card drawer poker. I remember having an envelope, which started with a couple of hundred dollars and, by the end of the tour, there was considerably more than that inside it.

**Storm Thorgerson:** I went to the States to try to continue the book with Nick Sedgwick. I remember a fantastic gig in San Francisco at the Cow Palace. The theatrical live music experience was just unbelievable – 'Shine On You Crazy Diamond' and all that. I sat in the wings and thought to myself, *I'm a lucky guy. I'm witnessing something special.*

**Brian Humphries:** I think going on tour twice, on the West Coast and then the East Coast, in the middle of making *Wish You Were Here*, gave the band some inspiration. The interruptions worked in their favour when we went back to the studio.

**Storm Thorgerson:** The Nick Sedgwick book petered out, though. Roger was getting a divorce, and there were various – how shall I put it – indiscretions, some might say, that occur on foreign tours rather than domestic tours, and it might not have gone down so well if reported. And we would have been very likely to report them.

**Brian Humphries:** The Floyd once said to me, 'You told us you'd never go on tour because it would upset your wife.' It was true. She was always telling me to get a proper job, but after Spooky Tooth, I got a taste for it. Then things started to go wrong in the marriage and I became involved with one of the women on the Floyd tour. When you're in America on your own, and she's on her own... Dave's [soon-to-be] wife Ginger was a friend and she used to have to listen to me talking about it. But then the band really put me in a position when they flew my wife out onto the tour as a present for her fucking birthday.

**Roger Waters:** Nick Sedgwick produced a document – the story of the '74 tour; it didn't have all the stuff about the breakdown of my marriage in Greece – which was distributed to all of us. Everybody read it and went, 'This is great.'

Then Gilmour had a delayed explosion. Reading that manuscript was like lighting the blue touchpaper. Boom! He was saying, 'if this reflects the way this band is, I may as well not be in it and Roger decides everything.' But that is the truth and that's how it worked. It's all in there and verifiable on a set of cassette recordings which still exist.

**Nick Sedgwick (writing in 1975):** 'One truth, which might come hard for the others to accept, is their current reliance on Roger... Ask anyone who is at all in the know – and he'll answer without hesitation that Roger rules.'

**Nick Mason:** The trouble is Nick Sedgwick was very much Roger's friend. Even if the book wasn't slanted towards Roger, there was a perception that it was.

**Storm Thorgerson:** I don't think the book was particularly revelatory, but at times people may have said things they wish they'd never said. The way Nick tried to write was to add some psychological weight to it, rather than just report verbatim what was said or done. Instead, we went into the power dynamics – who was more outspoken and/or for what reason. Not sure David stopped it. These things often don't happen because something else happened. *Wish You Were Here* was an issue, Roger getting divorced was an issue. To some extent the book didn't get followed through because we didn't follow through.

**David Gilmour:** I felt aggrieved by it and I didn't think it portrayed us accurately and certainly not kindly. I haven't read it forever. But I probably did manage to get it canned [the book, *In The Pink*, was published by Waters after Sedgwick's death].

**Nick Mason:** Has anyone talked to you about the floating pyramid? It was Roger's idea – a pyramid-shaped stage with an inflatable roof making it weather-proof. At the end of the show, the pyramid would float up into the heavens on the end of a rope. There was a helium balloon inside the tip of the pyramid.

**Roger Waters:** I think, in Pittsburgh at the Three Rivers Stadium, it went up for a bit, tipped on one side, tore open and the helium sphere came out of the rip.

**Nick Mason:** The bladder came out of it to screams of astonishment from the audience, one of whom shouted 'My God, it's giving birth!'. So this very large and now empty carcass fell into the car park to be ripped to shreds by souvenir hunters. Once the pyramid was gone, we were a bit short of visuals. We were stuck with the films which were great for arenas but not stadiums.

**Michael Palin (*Monty Python's Flying Circus*, writing in 1975):** 'Steve O'Rourke, Pink Floyd's manager, is very keen to get us on the bill for their prestigious open-air gig at Knebworth. We'd said no, but O'Rourke has made us a new offer. For five of us, a half-hour cabaret appearance, £1,000 each in notes, no questions asked... It's like an offer from the underworld.'

**Graham Chapman (*Monty Python's Flying Circus*, addressing the Knebworth crowd):** 'Now we've got all you hippies right where we want you, you are surrounded and there is no escape.'

**Nick Laird-Clowes (songwriter, future Pink Floyd lyricist):** Jeff Dexter and Tony Howard were managing my first group, Alfalpha, and Steve O'Rourke was bankrolling us, because rich bands had money they had to get rid of in certain ways. I used to go to the New Bond Street office and the first time we were given backstage passes was for Knebworth.

I'd been a fan since seeing Syd on *Top of the Pops* and *Atom Heart Mother* at Hyde Park. I couldn't believe how casual it all was backstage, David Gilmour with his first wife Ginger, everybody sat on the grass. At Knebworth, they did most of *The Dark Side of the Moon*, but also most of the new album, which nobody really wanted to hear, because it wasn't out yet. My mind was still blown.

**Nick Mason:** We rushed back from the States for that show at Knebworth and Rick's electric keyboards needed retuning. They sounded frightful. Still, we managed to arrange a flypast with two wartime Spitfires just before the show began and Roy got up on stage with us and sang 'Have a Cigar'.

**Freddy Bannister (Knebworth Festival promoter):** One of Roy Harper's retinue had forgotten to take Roy's stage clothes from the boot of his chauffeur-driven car before it was removed to a place of safety. Another story goes that he was annoyed he couldn't ride his horse onto the stage. Whatever the reason, Roy threw a moody and smashed up his dressing room...

**David Gilmour:** The main problem for us was the generator – the Hammond organ runs off a different frequency in England to the US, so Rick's was a tone and a half flat. Anyone sharp or quick enough would have sorted it out or just got Rick to play his Farfisa instead, so there was a lot of out-of-tuneness, which was pretty uncomfortable.

**Gerald Scarfe:** I went to Knebworth with some film we'd just made. Beforehand, the animators said, 'We can't do this. We need some music.' I said, 'It doesn't exist.' And then I said to Roger, 'We can't get them to do anything as there are no tracks.' He said, 'Just get them to do anything. I'll make it fit later on.' Sure enough, we did some surreal bits and pieces, and it did fit alongside certain passages. What was frustrating was I knew it could have been better. I suppose it was an artform in its own way.

**David Gilmour:** Overall, I remember a jolly day. Backstage with Roy Harper's horse, the Monty Pythons were good fun and the Steve Miller Band played at our invitation. Did I get married two days later? July 7? Then, yes, I did.

**Nick Sedgwick (writing in 1975):** 'Two years ago [Roger] would whip off a lyric with what he referred to as his "songwriter's kit" – a notebook, pencil, a hunk of dope and *Walker's Rhyming Dictionary*. Six months later, this changed. He began to work at them, all the while searching for connections and correspondences in accord with the patterns of his own life...'

**Roger Waters:** Usually the music comes first and the lyrics are added or the music and lyrics come together. Only once have the lyrics been written down first and that was 'Wish You Were Here' ... It's a love song and still one on a very general and theoretical level.

**David Gilmour:** When I strummed the introduction to 'Wish You Were Here', it was the same as when I'd played the four notes at the beginning of 'Shine On You Crazy Diamond'. People said, 'You've got something there.'

**Roger Waters:** In a way, it's a schizophrenic song. It's directed at my other half ... the battling elements within myself. There's the bit that's concerned with other people, then there's the grasping, avaricious, selfish little kid.

**Nick Mason:** We paid [French violinist] Stéphane Grappelli, who was working in another studio, to play on the song, and I thought his version was wonderful. I don't know why we didn't use it instead of the one we did. Perhaps we thought, *This is Pink Floyd making a record, not Pink Floyd and special guests*.

**David Gilmour:** The classical music at the beginning [Tchaikovsky's Fourth Symphony] of 'Wish You Were Here' and the first guitar is meant to sound like it's coming out of a radio. We did that by knocking out all the bass and most of the high top. The interference was actually recorded on my car's cassette radio.

**Roger Waters:** The record company said, 'Well, it's very nice, but there's something wrong with the pressing – the guitar sound at the beginning of the song, it's really thin, it sounds like it's coming out of a little radio.' Which was exactly what it sounded like – that was exactly the intention.

**David Gilmour:** I know that the words to 'Wish You Were Here' were more general and less specifically about Syd, but I am sure he was included in it somewhere. When I sing it, I think about Syd.

**Nick Mason:** *Wish You Were Here* wasn't made with the same white heat of enthusiasm with which *The Dark Side of the Moon* came together. I think it's a wistful, romantic album and it has a number of qualities, which include that thing of abstraction – allowing the listener to paint their own picture over the music.

The other records are much more specific. With *Wish You Were Here*, people can make up their own ideas and we still hear it from people. They say, 'I know what it's all about. I've got it.' And we still say, 'Yes, okay, if you say so.'

**Roger Waters:** Personally, I think Floyd hit two real peaks in terms of creativity. *The Dark Side of the Moon* and *The Wall* were the most complete albums we ever made. *Wish You Were Here* came close without being a complete classic.

**David Gilmour:** It seems ludicrous to say that I felt some of the musical moments on *The Dark Side of the Moon* were slightly lightweight ... But I pushed for a slightly looser framework for the following album. I wanted every bit of the music to be every bit as good as the words. I was pushing towards that end and I love *Wish You Were Here*.

**Richard Wright:** I think it was the last album where we worked well together. When we started off, we weren't putting our hearts into it. But I still think it's our best record. I love it for the lyrics and I love it for the music.

*After a long, tortuous gestation,* Wish You Were Here *arrived in September 1975, swaddled in a black cellophane wrapper. 'Not only was the theme absence, but the cover was absent,' said Storm Thorgerson. 'The band thought that was funny, especially when it upset EMI.'*

*'*Wish You Were Here *sucks,' declared* Melody Maker, *but it became Pink Floyd's first UK and US number one album, and has now sold some 23 million and counting. Despite critics obsessing over Syd Barrett and the group writing songs about him, most of* Wish You Were Here *sounds divorced from the Barrett era.*

*It contains their greatest simplest love song (the title track), several bedroom-mirror guitar solos (most of 'Shine On You Crazy Diamond, Parts I–IX') and 'Shine On..., Part VI' is the kind of electronic instrumental that later inspired the dance duo the Orb to invite Gilmour to collaborate with them (on 2010's* Metallic Spheres*).*

*Fast-forward to July 2011, though, and the music industry's beleaguered warhorse, EMI, has just issued a box set of* Wish You Were Here. *'That should keep the company going for another two weeks,' suggests Nick Mason.*

*This version includes the tuned wine glasses from 'Household Objects', Stéphane Grappelli's version of the title track and some of the Wembley Empire Pool show that so upset Nick Kent, but sounds magnificent.*

*Today, I'm with the brilliant if infuriating Storm Thorgerson in his favourite restaurant Limonia in Primrose Hill. Thorgerson's body now operates at reduced capacity after a stroke, but his brain still moves at 100 mph.*

*He's telling me why he promoted the picture of the faceless businessman in the Yuma Desert to the cover of the box set, but gets distracted. Instead, he opens the box and shows me a velvet pouch containing three marbles. The previous* Dark Side... *box also included marbles.*

*What for? 'Because you must have lost your marbles to pay for these expensive box sets, so we're returning them to you,' Thorgerson chuckles.*

*How much is this costing EMI and Pink Floyd, I wonder? Almost on cue, one of the marbles rolls off the table and lands on the floor, where a waiter picks it up and pops it back in the bag. A few months later, EMI is sold to Universal Music for £1.2 billion. All the Pink Floyd box sets in the world aren't enough to save the company.*

# 8

# 'IT'S UNLIKELY THEY RECEIVED ANY SALIVA'

*A dog called Tina, 'Oink, oink, woof, woof, baaaaa', tranquillising the elephant and 'Earl Grey and hot buttered muffins'...*

❦

'Let me tell you something...' begins Roger Waters in that familiar schoolmasterly voice. 'If you're lucky enough to be in a band with somebody who can write something interesting or cool or that rhymes *even*, you don't rock that boat. You go, "Phew, thank God for that! He's written another song." Rock bands absolutely live or die by whether there is anybody who can write anything.'

We're back in the Azure Suite of London's May Fair Hotel, and Waters' people still haven't found the corkscrew. No matter. He closes his eyes and places his palms together in a meditative pose, before continuing our discussion of Pink Floyd's *Animals*.

According to the sleeve notes, Waters composed almost everything on the group's tenth studio album. Four of the five compositions are solely credited to him; the other to Waters/Gilmour. Wright and Mason aren't mentioned anywhere. But the credits don't tell the whole story...

*Animals* was created in a different environment. Pink Floyd had instigated a six months on/six months off rule, allowing more time for parenting. Ginger Gilmour gave birth to the Gilmours' first daughter, Alice, and Waters and Carolyne Christie had their first child, Harry, while making the record.

Waters had a townhouse south of the Thames near Clapham Common and the Masons had moved to upmarket Hampstead. Elsewhere,

Gilmour and Wright were enjoying country life, with the Wrights in the Grade II-listed Old Rectory in the Cambridgeshire village of Therfield.

Meanwhile, the joke working title for *Wish You Were Here* – 'An Afternoon At Home With the Duke of Roydon' – referred to the Gilmours' farmhouse near Roydon in Essex, which the family shared with horses, dogs, chickens, a peacock and Emo.

Waters also berated Wright for buying his country house. 'He said, "I can't believe you've done this. You've sold out,"' recalled Wright. A year later, Waters acquired a country pile near Horsham in West Sussex, but insisted it was Carolyne's idea, not his. In time, he'd replace this with a Georgian mansion in the Hampshire village of Kimbridge, situated on the River Test, where Waters could fish trout to his heart's content.

The band also expanded their collective portfolio with a three-storey church building at 35 Britannia Row, Islington. Using a supposed wonder brick called Lignacite, the space was converted into an office, a storage facility and a studio while Pink Floyd were making *Wish You Were Here*.

The idea was to phase out Abbey Road (the group's unlimited studio time deal had ended), lease their equipment to other artists and keep their crew employed all year round. However, many bands didn't need, or couldn't afford, quadraphonic mixers and genie lighting towers.

Mason and Waters' old Regent Street Poly friend, architect Jon Corpe, oversaw the build. According to Waters, the functional but spartan studio and control room resembled 'a fucking prison'.

*Animals* was recorded over the spring and summer of 1976 and reflected the austerity inside and outside the bunker. Unemployment was at a high of 7.8 per cent, police and striking workers clashed during an industrial dispute at north London's Grunwick film processing plant, and racial tension spilled over into bloody violence and arrests at the annual Notting Hill Carnival.

The lyrics on *Animals* addressed corporate greed and man's inhumanity to man, with Waters splitting the human race into subservient sheep, tyrannical pigs and authoritarian dogs. Orwell's 'Animal Farm: The Musical', then, but bookended by two verses of a love song, 'Pigs on the Wing', which Waters said at the time was written for Carolyne. Having divorced and remarried three times since 1977, though, he's reluctant to go there now. 'I can't remember who it's about.'

*Animals* is a very angry album. It's all about politics, isn't it?

'Yes,' says Waters, 'and the sheep, pigs and dogs are still with us...'

✣

**Nick Mason:** Britannia Row took over a year to build. We used a new brick called Lignacite that was supposed to absorb sound and the floor had rubber mounting points, so it sort of *floated*, which ensured lorry noise from Essex Road didn't impinge.

**Brian Humphries:** Nick and Roger's architect friend knew nothing about recording studios. I knew that, David knew that, but Nick and Roger used to say, 'Oh he'll get around to fixing it.' The number of times they had to rethink the baffling for soundproofing. Me being the engineer, I'd sit there, not say anything, and let them get on with it. After Abbey Road, the whole place was pretty pokey.

**Nick Mason:** We put in a mixing board and a 24-track recorder. Our thinking was it had to be easy enough to use so one of us could work it without having an engineer there. But there was also a snooker table upstairs, which Roger supervised. Snooker was integral to the whole process. But we didn't make it easy for ourselves. Normally the control room in a studio has a sumptuous sofa, but we had a bench. When you sat on it, you felt like you were part of a hockey team – 'Alright number seven, you're on...'. The whole place was curiously bleak.

**Nicky Horne (radio presenter, host of Capital Radio's *The Pink Floyd Story*):** I met Nick Mason in the green room after a gig at the Hammersmith Odeon. He said, 'I'm Nick Mason, I'm with you know who and I know you play us on your programme [*Your Mother Wouldn't Like It*]. I wanted to say, "Thank you, here's my number, come round and have tea?"' I was surprised to say the least. It was so incongruous, the fact that he was being so hospitable and yet, as a band member, he was completely anonymous and distant.

So I went round to his house, which was near where my mum lived in Hampstead. Nick had a miniature Bugatti that he drove around his garden and we had tea and it was all very English. I'd only been on air for a year or so and was quite green, but I said, 'I'd really like to do the definitive Pink Floyd story.' He told me they were about to start recording *Animals*, so I suggested we structure it so the story finished with the release of the album.

Over a period of about three months, we had various meetings, with the programme director at Capital, Nick and Steve O'Rourke. I didn't meet David or Roger. But they agreed to do this programme and said we could have full access to them, but they would have pre-approval of each programme before it went out.

**David Gilmour:** With *Animals*, it's hard for me not to fall back on well-known tracts of information that I'm not sure I ascribe to, about being influenced by the advent of punk, and feeling that things needed to be more live and raw. *Wish You Were Here* was a sumptuous album and we moved towards a tougher sound on *Animals*. But Britannia Row was a stark rough place – and that all fed into the whole thing.

**Roger Waters:** *Punk?* When was punk? I wasn't remotely aware of punk.

**Aubrey 'Po' Powell:** The Sex Pistols moved into a rehearsal room in the courtyard behind Hipgnosis's studio in autumn 1975. I don't think they'd even played a gig yet, but I can't vouch for that. They just seemed very young and ordinary, and we used to hold the door open for each other as they had to walk through the building to get to their place. Then the relationship changed. They rehearsed loudly – all these old Who and Monkees songs – and the noise started disturbing us in the studio.

Then one day I was walking down the communal hallway and passed one of them, John Lydon or 'Johnny Rotten' as he called himself, wearing a Pink Floyd T-shirt and above the name 'Pink Floyd' he'd written 'I Hate'. I said, 'Are you having a go at us?', because they knew we worked with Pink Floyd, and John said, 'Yes, you and all those other cunts you listen to.'

I was appalled. But pretty soon I started to get this sense that the tide was turning. There we were, making album covers for the Floyd, Genesis, Yes and Wishbone Ash, and this was something new.

**Rob Brimson (Hipgnosis photographer):** The Sex Pistols' rehearsal place was in the courtyard behind the studio, which they got into by climbing a ladder to the first floor. I remember seeing them from our dark room window, climbing up there with their girlfriends following behind, and then disappearing. I heard all their early practices and they were pretty terrible. I was still this unredeemed hippie with long hair. Then one day, suddenly, I thought, *Oh this sounds alright*.

**Richard Wright:** Punk brought me back to the UFO club days. *At last*, I thought, *there was something that had come along and was really pushing the boundaries*. Unfortunately, I didn't like the music, but I liked the whole movement and people like Malcolm McLaren and Vivienne Westwood. I was quite flattered when the Floyd were criticised by some of the punk bands. It didn't bother me.

**David Gilmour:** I thought the Sex Pistols were rather good. I've been on a show with Johnny Rotten at Sadler's Wells, and he said he never really hated Pink Floyd and actually he was a bit of a fan. I confess to not having entirely believed it in the first place.

**Roger Waters:** Of course, the whole concept behind *Animals* was Orwellian. Orwell's idea of *Animal Farm* and pigs, dogs and sheep characterised anthropomorphically seemed kind of neat. We are in the same monetary merry-go-round today as we were in the '70s. It's still with us now, so all those ideas in the songs 'Dogs', 'Pigs (Three Different Ones)' and 'Sheep' are still relevant today. In my head, the brief was clear – and it was easier to do and better than *Wish You Were Here*.

**Gerald Scarfe:** Roger asked me to create some designs for *Animals* and I actually did a lot of work on it. But I'm not sure I ever showed any of it to the band. Roger doesn't remember now, but he was distracted – his first marriage was breaking up.

**Roger Waters:** Drawings of animal masks? No, I don't remember anything about that.

**David Gilmour:** Curmudgeonly old me, I can remember thinking Roger's idea of *Animals* was a bit contrived, but I am just a humble musician and here to do my job. I'm not sure I'm wholly subjective, but I think how he ascribes these animal features to political situations is brilliant. It was very well done, but for me not as focused as *The Dark Side of the Moon*.

Part of the problem I had was with the lyrics to the two songs left over from *Wish You Were Here* – 'Raving and Drooling' and 'Gotta Be Crazy' – which became 'Sheep' and 'Dogs'. I'd complained about them on the tour as there were too many words in them. I said to Roger, 'I can't get 'em out, Rog, I can't do 'em fast enough. Can we change 'em please?' So he rewrote some of them.

**Roger Waters:** Let me think, 'Raving and drooling I fell on his neck with a scream ... a look of terminal shock in his eyes...'. Raving and drooling in 'Sheep' was the idea of being led to slaughter, so what was going on in my life then? I think I was somewhat disturbed. It was around then that my first wife left me in the middle of a tour.

What are the lyrics to 'Pigs on the Wing'? 'If you didn't care what happened to me...' and 'Zigzag away through the boredom and pain...'. No, I don't think it's a love song or about someone specifically. My feeling is it's a song saying that if we don't care for one another and have empathy, then all that's left is this crap, and learning to smile and shake hands in order to get something before you get 'the chance to put the knife in' – which is 'Dogs'.

**David Gilmour:** The ideas behind *The Dark Side of the Moon* and *Wish You Were Here* I am in sympathy with. With *Animals*, I could see the truth of it, though I don't generally paint people as black as that.

**Roger Waters:** David played that descending guitar part in 'Dogs', which is very important, great in fact. But apart from that...

**David Gilmour:** The last 20 per cent of 'Sheep', I wrote, I recorded and I played the bass on. It's basically a fade out, but it's two minutes long. It's a dark song and I gave it an uplifting coda, which I think turns it around. My view at the time, which may have changed a little bit, is that it was substantially Roger's song. But at the same time, when people say, 'Roger wrote that all on his own', it irks me a bit. I'd like him to be more truthful. At the time, though, I was perfectly happy because it seemed like we were in a fairer world back then.

**Brian Humphries:** That's my dog Tina, a golden retriever who I loved very much, barking on 'Dogs' and me whistling on 'Sheep'. Roger and David wanted to listen to the twenty-four tracks of 'Dogs', and there are some drum things in the middle eight – that wasn't Nick, that was David. Nick and Roger wanted some sound effects as well, which we got from one of those BBC sound effects records. I was letting them get on with the twenty-four tracks, and they wiped the over-dubbed drums and David had to re-do them.

**Nick Mason:** *Animals* was tricky because although we had Brian Humphries, we didn't have the perfect sound we'd had at Abbey Road. So it wasn't as well-recorded as everything else we'd done.

**Roger Waters:** I do remember there was something cool about putting pig sound effects on things. I don't recall any objection from the others to 'Pigs' ['Pigs (Three Different Ones)'] and the lyrics about [pro-censorship campaigner] Mary Whitehouse. At that time, she was everywhere, pontificating on TV and interfering in everybody's life and trying to drag English society back to an age of Victorian propriety.

But people still misinterpret the lyrics, because they always did back in 1977. In America, nobody had any idea who Mary Whitehouse was. They did in England, but not in the United States. Everybody there assumed it was an attack on the government, the president, Washington, the White House...

*Animals* may well have been inspired by some of what was happening in the country, but I can't specifically say what it was about that. The lyrics I come back to the most are on 'Pigs on the Wing, 2': 'Any fool knows a dog needs a home, a shelter from pigs on the wing...' That nods towards the idea of safety and succour in the arms of a loved one and the idea of not being alone, which you can expand into society and the idea we are all in this together and have a responsibility towards one another.

**Nicky Horne:** I did interviews with all the band members, in different places, and spliced them together. But the approval thing could be a fucking nightmare. There were times when we were biking tapes across London to get Steve O'Rourke's permission before broadcast and then he had to get all the band to listen to it and one of them couldn't be found.

I remember Rick Wright being reticent. A couple of the sessions we had he talked quite a lot and quite deeply, but most of the time I got the feeling he didn't really engage. David Gilmour did. Gilmour liked taking the piss out of me, gently. But there were several sessions where they were all together and Gilmour would start and then they would all jump in. It was like a feeding frenzy. But I was used to it by then.

**Richard Wright:** *Animals* was difficult because that was when Roger really began to start believing he was the sole writer of the band. With regards to that album, it was partly my fault, because I didn't have much to offer. Dave, who did have something to offer, only managed to get a couple of things on there. I like my playing, but it wasn't a fun record to make. *Animals* was a slog.

**Brian Humphries:** If you listen to the beginning of 'Sheep', that Fender Rhodes solo was done by Rick and it was just me and him on our own at Britannia Row. I put the lights down and told him to just play, do his thing.

**Nick Mason:** Rick suffered because the problem is there are never enough credits to go round in bands. Doesn't matter who you are. Even the

Beatles ended up arguing the toss about where the credits should come on the albums, didn't they?

**David Gilmour:** I don't remember *Animals* as a bad period and I didn't feel remotely squeezed out of the album. 'Dogs' was almost the whole of one side of the album and the main chord structure was 90 per cent my thing. There was some tension, though, because Rick didn't seem to be pulling his weight.

But this was Roger's natural dominance. I don't think he consciously wanted to do people down. It's just the way people have their own particular character and it's hard to be sensitive to how much it can be affecting other people. Roger and I were both quite tough. I'm like a mule. I can be knocked down, but I get up again... like in that song [Chumbawumba's 'Tubthumping']. Rick was thinner skinned and he got knocked down and didn't find it so easy to get up again.

**Nicky Horne:** I did an interview with Roger at his place in Clapham and I was there all day. I expected them all to be reticent and bolshie and guarded. But Roger, particularly, when you started to peel away the layers, the core was quite close to the surface. There were some things he said that shocked me – the stuff about Syd Barrett. One of those sessions was like a therapy session about Syd. I'd say, 'Talk about guilt' and then not say anything for twenty-five minutes and just let him fill the gaps.

**Roger Waters:** Did I really say to you that *Animals* signalled the end of the band? Nowadays if you asked me, I'd say *The Dark Side of the Moon*, because by then we'd achieved what we set out to achieve. But I'm glad we didn't break up then. Going through all that pain, we came up with some good works and I think *Animals* is a good piece of meat.

**Nick Mason:** One of my jobs on the album was doing all the lettering – the band name and the album title on the back cover – and writing out all the lyrics for the inside sleeve. Nobody knows that? Not like Roger not to mention my contribution...

**Nicky Horne:** During the last episode of *The Pink Floyd Story* [broadcast 21 January 1977], we made a big deal of having the exclusive on playing the whole of *Animals* the next night. The day before we were meant to be doing it was a Thursday and I was driving home and listening to [rival BBC DJ] John Peel, and Peely said, in his inimitable style, 'We play tomorrow's hits today…'. And then he played side one of *Animals*.

I couldn't believe it. Someone had given him the album. Gilmour, I think. After six weeks of going on and on about our exclusive, we'd had our comeuppance. Of course, I'd have done exactly the same thing if I was him.

**Aubrey 'Po' Powell:** Roger Waters and Storm fell out, I can't remember what about. But by the time we got to *Animals*, they just weren't getting on, which affected us as Hipgnosis. After all, we'd done all the Floyd's covers since *A Saucerful of Secrets*.

**Roger Waters:** Storm and I played squash at least once a week year after year until I couldn't stand it anymore. Not the defeats, of which there were many. I just couldn't take the fact that he was always late. Storm was always at least five minutes late and sometimes more. One day, I was there for twelve minutes waiting, so I took my squash kit off and changed back into mufti.

Then Storm rushed in and said, 'Come on, get changed. What are you doing?' I said, 'I am sitting here. What are you doing?' 'We are meant to be playing squash,' he said. 'No, we *were* meant to be playing squash,' I replied. 'But I have since changed back into my street clothes. We are never playing squash again. If this is a test to see whether I love you so much I don't care if you're late, then I failed the test.' We never played again.

**Storm Thorgerson:** The main thing about Roger is that he tends to be more fixed than you might expect in a view. And once a view or decision is taken, he doesn't deviate – and that, of course, is quite virtuous in some ways.

**Aubrey 'Po' Powell:** Roger, for some reason, didn't like Storm's cover idea for *Animals*, which was a little boy clutching a teddy bear, opening his parents' bedroom door and finding them fucking. Not Hipgnosis's finest hour.

**Storm Thorgerson:** They turned down what I thought was a brilliant idea – the child watching his parents fucking, like *animals*, get it?! I also nailed three ducks to a wall and took a picture of that, but they didn't like it either. So I have mixed emotions about *Animals*.

**Roger Waters:** The drawing of the kid looking at his parents fucking was one of several cover ideas and certainly the most shocking, but I didn't like any of them. When I told them that, all eyes turned to me, and Gilmour said, 'Well, why don't you do better?'. So I got in my car and drove to Battersea Bridge from Clapham Common where I lived and saw the power station and thought, *Hang on a minute*... I had already thought about flying a pig on the *Animals* tour and had commissioned a maquette for it, so I thought the power station would be a cool place to fly one.

**Aubrey 'Po' Powell:** Instead of Storm, Roger invited me to his house in Clapham one Sunday afternoon. We had Earl Grey tea and hot buttered muffins and he told me about his idea for the pig. After we'd eaten, we jumped in his Range Rover and drove to the power station. In those days, you could just wander around. It was a dump and in the middle of an impoverished area surrounded by old working-class Victorian cottages. But it was an amazing building, so we took some photographs and worked out how and where we were going to fly Roger's pig.

**Roger Waters:** I drove past the power station all the time on my way to Britannia Row and always liked the building and its symbolism, because there's something menacing about it. I also liked it as a symbol for the band – maybe it's the architecture student in me – but there are four chimneys like four phalluses for the four members. I presented the idea to the other three and even Dave begrudgingly said, 'Oh that's good.' So Storm and Po offered to get the photographers together.

**Aubrey 'Po' Powell:** Roger had already commissioned a company in the Netherlands to design a forty-foot-long inflatable pig – made out of the same material they'd used to make Zeppelin airships in the First World War – for the tour. It was a collaborative effort, but Storm wasn't keen because it was Roger's idea.

A decision was taken to fly the pig, which we nicknamed 'Algie', between the chimneys and to take pictures from various vantage points and film the whole thing. Steve O'Rourke wrote to the station manager asking for permission and it was granted. We told the Metropolitan Police what we were doing and their one condition was we hired one of their marksmen to shoot the pig down if it broke loose.

On the day, we had eight photographers positioned on Battersea Bridge, on the roof of the power station, on a nearby tower block, by the railway line and others filming the action from a helicopter. The pig turned up attached by a winch to the back of a truck, but it wouldn't inflate because there was a problem with the gas.

**Nick Mason:** We arrived for the launch and hung around in the cold for hours and nothing happened. There was this whole thing about having a marksman. But I'm not sure whether a bullet hole in the fabric of a Zeppelin would have done that much damage unless it was an incendiary bullet.

**Aubrey 'Po' Powell:** The next day, everybody came back again, the pig inflated – all good – and then... 'No!' The iron ring attached to the cable snapped and the pig zoomed off into the heavens. There was nothing we could do to stop it and I had forgotten to re-book the marksman. Steve O'Rourke and I both started laughing until we realised the seriousness of what was happening. I'll always remember the look of schoolboy glee on Roger Waters' face and then the whole band jumped in their cars and pissed off. 'Oh you sort this out, Po.'

**Nick Mason:** Of course we did. That's one of the benefits of being higher up the food chain. We had a secretary, Linda, whose job was to type out all the carnets so every item on the trucks was itemised for customs officials when we toured abroad. Linda watched the pig disappear and said, 'Oh my God, it hasn't got a carnet!' She was worried it was going to cross borders without permission. In fairness, it could have been a disaster.

**Rob Brimson:** I was on standby to go to the helicopter at Battersea heliport to do the aerial shots. I leapt into a van with my cameras and headed to the heliport through the morning rush hour, jumping lights and frequently on the wrong side of the road, then into the helicopter and off on the pig hunt. But it was travelling too fast for us.

**Marc Wolff (helicopter pilot):** We were in radio contact with Heathrow. Air traffic controllers tend to be very dry, so it was hilarious having to tell them an inflatable pink pig was rising into their airspace. The trouble is the pig went much higher than we could and kept disappearing into the clouds. The pig wouldn't show up on air traffic control's radar, but we had a transponder in the helicopter, so they could track it by tracking us.

**Aubrey 'Po' Powell:** I called 999 from a phone box and warned them about a flying pig. The police called the authorities and stopped all flights into Heathrow, put out requests for information on the TV and radio, and sent up a police helicopter to try and chase it.

**Nick Mason:** Many years later, I was introduced to the police pilot sent to chase the pig. He told me he didn't have a hope in hell as the pig was climbing at a greater rate than the helicopter. It could have caused a major air disaster.

**Aubrey 'Po' Powell:** Storm and I were given a police escort back to the studio and were told to wait by the phone. We had several hoax calls until I answered one at about nine o'clock in the evening and this voice with a deep country accent said, 'Are you looking for this pig? Well, it's come down in my field and it's scaring my cows…'. As the air pressure outside increased, the helium had started to leak out and the pig had landed in a farm in Kent. Pink Floyd's road crew were sent out to collect it.

**The *Kentish Express* (10 December 1976):** 'An enormous pink porker put in an appearance over James Stewart's farm at East Stour on Friday afternoon. "I didn't believe it at first so I went to see for myself," he says. "We caught it, and tied it to the barn before phoning the police."… The pig was seen 18,000 feet over Chatham, but carried on drifting before one of its trotters began to deflate and it descended, presumably to save its bacon.'

**Aubrey 'Po' Powell:** The next day, the third one, we went back and did it all over again, with a marksman and everything went off without a hitch. The problem was the sky was too bright and sunny. On the first day, when the pig wouldn't inflate, we'd had this beautiful stormy sky like something out of a Turner painting. So we cut out the pig from the third day and stripped it into the sky from the first day – and that became the cover. We could have saved ourselves and the Pink Floyd an awful lot of money.

**Rob Brimson:** What was the concept? I'd heard some of the conversations and it seemed to be a comment on greed, money and power. I was always amazed the power station agreed to that image. The pig represented corporate greed and for a power station to allow a big inflatable pig to be flown over it showed a certain naivety. It was such a dangerous thing to do on a number of levels too. These days, the security would be immense, questions would be asked in the House of Commons. It was a different world.

**Storm Thorgerson:** A lot of people have asked me over the years if losing the pig was a publicity stunt. No, it wasn't, because it wasn't our pig to lose. I can't say that I care for *Animals* very much. Compared to *Wish You Were Here*, I find it too angry. In terms of the cover, it's my artwork maybe, but Roger's idea wholly, and I now realise that the word 'iconic' suits that picture.

✣

*In 2010, the* Guardian*'s cartoonist Steve Bell drew the then UK prime minister David Cameron as a corpulent blob floating over Battersea Power Station. Readers recognised Bell's inspiration – Pink Floyd's pig almost rivalled the* Dark Side... *prism in the public consciousness – but fewer knew the music.*

*'There's not a lot of sweet, singalong stuff on* Animals,*' admitted Gilmour.*

*'It got a bit lost coming after* Wish You Were Here *and before* The Wall,*' said Mason.*

*'Oink, oink, woof, woof, baaaaa,' trumpeted the press ads when* Animals *was released in January 1977, vaulting to number two in the UK, five in the US and number one in Germany. It looked and sounded like the anti-*Wish You Were Here*: the former's picture of a gorgeous Lake Mono replaced by photographs of barbed wire and slag heaps, its lush soundscapes by honking pigs, and Gilmour singing about 'a sad old man all alone and dying of cancer'.*

*There was beauty in its bleakness, though, and 'Sheep''s bastardised take on the 23rd Psalm ('He converteth me to lamb cutlets...' etc) and the 'fucked-up old hag' in 'Pigs' delighted kids who parroted hymns in school assemblies and missed seeing Sex Pistol Steve Jones swearing on daytime telly.*

*However, Waters' decision to chop 'Pigs on the Wing' in half upset the others as it doubled his royalties, while the heavy metal guitar riff at the end of 'Sheep' should have qualified Gilmour for a co-writer's credit.*

*Recreating some of the album's overdubs required another pair of hands and Terence 'Snowy' White, a blues guitarist in thrall to Fleetwood Mac's Peter Green, was asked to join Pink Floyd's 1977 tour. White hadn't even heard* The Dark Side of the Moon, *but he played bass and guitar on a jaunt which began in Europe in January and ended with American and Canadian stadium dates in the summer.*

*'David and Roger had an argument in front of me the first time we all met,' recalled White. 'I had to walk out on my own and start the show, and most of the audience probably didn't know who I was. My cue was an aeroplane flying over the top of the stage.'*

*When the In the Flesh tour rolled into the US, stadium audiences experienced what* Rolling Stone *called 'a sensory banquet': planes, flying pigs and parachuting sheep, an inflatable nuclear family (mother, father and 2.4 children), with the spoils of their consumerist lifestyle (a sofa, a car and a fridge, which opened to reveal worms and rotting comestibles), plus Gerald Scarfe's animated steel insects, skulls, reptilian robots, seas of blood....*

*Since the last tour, though, Pink Floyd had gone from playing 12,000-seaters to arenas built for up to 80,000 people, some zonked out on quaaludes, others drunk on ripple wine and waiting impatiently to hear 'Money'. 'In the old days, you could hear a pin drop during the quieter numbers,' remarked Gilmour. 'Not now.'*

*Inevitably, promoters shipped in real animals as mascots. A vegetarian Ginger Gilmour insisted promoter Bill Graham release the pigs backstage at the Oakland Coliseum. Ginger also liberated a piglet from a nightclub in Frankfurt and smuggled the animal back to the hotel, where the distressed beast cracked a wardrobe mirror and shat all over tour manager Warwick McCreadie's room.*

✲

***Melody Maker* (review of *Animals*, January 1977):** 'Here is a memo to Sir John Read, head of the EMI group. You are about to release an album which features obscenity, profanity and a dastardly attack upon a well-known public figure ... Perhaps they should re-name themselves "Punk Floyd".'

**Karl Dallas (*Melody Maker* writer):** I used to hang out at UFO when Pink Floyd were the house band, and talked to Roger and Syd in the refreshment bar, but I thought their music was boring. Floyd would be playing and somebody would be projecting a film onto them and I tended to watch the film.

There was a playback for *Animals* and nobody else wanted to go, so I did, bootlegged the album and wrote a rave review. Then EMI said they were taking some journalists to Frankfurt for the opening night of the tour and did I want to come. I had dinner with the band afterwards and Roger sat at one end of the table refusing to speak to anyone.

We were on the same plane back to England – though, obviously, he was flying first class – and he completely ignored me again. But a few days later, I received a letter from him which began, 'I don't usually communicate with members of your ignoble profession...'. Since coming back from Frankfurt, he'd read my review of *Animals*. 'It's nice to know somebody really understands what we're doing.'

A couple of weeks later, I went to see Alan Price at Wembley, and who should be sitting behind me but Roger. So I thanked him for his letter and said, 'If you think I am different from other journalists, why don't you give me an interview?' He told me they weren't doing any interviews, but assured me that when they did, I would be the first. He kept to that for the next two years.

**David Gilmour:** The thing is if we could get away without talking to the press, we would. It was never something we particularly enjoyed doing.

**Roger Waters:** We were dots on a stage in some of those places. The idea on that tour was to make the show a 3-D theatrical experience – like a circus – rather than something that happened in a football stadium but really wasn't meant to. Besides the main pig, we had a bunch of other pigs because we'd destroy one at every show. They had helium and propane in their legs and little squibs in their feet which were detonators.

**Brian Humphries:** I was fine with the pig, but every time that crashing plane flew over, I used to duck. It started on my first tour with the band, and I was convinced it was going to crash right onto the mixer.

**Roger Waters:** [Set designers/architects] Mark Fisher and Jonathan Park made the inflatable nuclear family for that American tour. We were thinking about the family as a target for consumer advertising – the concept of a rich wage slave – which tied in with *Animals*. We had a man and a woman and 2.4 children, so one of the kids was cut in half.

I had no idea where the fridge came from, but worms came out of it – the first worms we used before doing them again for *The Wall*. Best of all was the sheep, which was a parachute in the shape of a sheep with little lead weights in each foot that we fired out of a mortar. It really did look like sheep floating down on the audience.

**Mark Fisher (architect, speaking in 2000):** 'I realised something was going on in this business. It was beginning to create an architecture which was consistent with what the band were trying to do – in the Floyd's case particularly, developing ideas of a sort of dream world.'

**Nick Mason:** The great thing about these inflatables was there was something else on stage as well as the films, because the films were inadequate if there was daylight, which there often was on the American tours. The big problem with stadiums is trying to entertain 90,000 people or whatever. Seventy per cent of the audience are interested, but then there's 10 per cent who are dealing with drug overdoses and another 10 per cent who are playing frisbee at the back...

**Roger Waters:** I was getting ready to do a gig [at the Philadelphia Spectrum, 29 June] and I had terrible stomach cramps. We had a doctor come to the hotel and he gave me a shot, and to this day I don't know what it was. But it came out of a dart that felt like it was used to tranquillise an elephant. We did the whole show and I was barely able to stand. And that's where the term 'comfortably numb' came from.

**David Gilmour:** When there's a great big thing in a stadium, there's a lot of people who just want to go along and be part of the experience, and maybe enjoy the music. They want more stuff to *boogie* to. That was one of the phrases that irritated the hell out of us.

**Roger Waters:** I loathed playing stadiums. I kept saying to people on that tour, 'I'm not really enjoying this, you know.' And the answer to that was, 'Oh really? Yeah, well, do you know we grossed over 4 million dollars today?'

**David Gilmour:** I don't think any of us got used to the stadium shows and there was an awful lot of them on that tour. You gain a lot, but you lose a lot and you feel like you're providing the music at someone else's party. Roger felt completely cut off from it. I had a different view, but that was hard to hang onto at times. It made us change our music too, because we couldn't do the quiet stuff without firecrackers going off in the middle of it.

**Roger Waters (addressing the audience at Montreal Olympic Stadium, 6 July 1977):** 'Oh for fuck's sake, stop lighting fireworks and shouting and screaming. I'm trying to sing a song ... If you don't want to hear it ... Fuck you ... If you want to light your fireworks, go outside.'

**David Gilmour:** I remember being in this huge stadium [in Montreal] with a great big crane stuck inside because they couldn't get it out after they'd finished building the stadium for the Olympics. It was a shame to end the tour on a not very good concert. Roger was so disgusted that he had let himself go sufficiently to spit at a fan [who was trying to climb on stage towards the end of the show].

**Roger Waters:** He was climbing up the barrier or some chicken wire when I spat at him. I am sure I felt remorse, because what a terrible place to arrive at. Not very nice.

**Nick Mason:** What sent Roger over the edge was that complete non-comprehension from both sides: the audience who wanted to bay and shout, and Roger who wanted to play them a quiet song and ended up spitting at them. Except, with the size of the gap between audience and stage, it's unlikely they received any saliva.

**David Gilmour:** I was so unenamoured by the whole thing I sat at the mixing desk for the encore. The band played a blues with 'Snowy' White on guitar. I think Roger felt he'd grown apart from the fans and the contact that he had with his fans wasn't real.

**Bob Ezrin (music producer):** After the show, Roger cut his foot after getting in a little tussle in the toilets [a play fight with Steve O'Rourke], so we had to take him to the emergency room. It was a wonderful adventure. There was me, Roger, Carolyne and a psychiatrist friend of mine. I always thought it was a wonderful coincidence that I had a psychiatrist with me that night.

So we drove Roger to the emergency room to get his foot looked at and then, as we're heading onto the hotel, he starts talking about his sense of alienation on the tour, and how he sometimes felt like building a wall between himself and the audience. My friend, the shrink, is fascinated. And, for me, there was a moment's spark. I don't know whether it was me or Roger or the shrink that said it first, but one of us went, 'Wow! You know that might be a really good idea.'

**Roger Waters:** On a plane or in a bar somewhere, I got a piece of paper and drew a picture of this wall across an arena with a stage – and when I did that, I got very excited.

❁

*During the In the Flesh tour, Rick Wright flew home, threatening to leave the group. 'I said, "I don't want any more of it". But Steve O'Rourke said, "You can't, you mustn't..."' Wright returned and stayed put. They all did.*

*'The name "Pink Floyd" is worth millions of pounds,' said Waters at the time. 'The name is probably worth one million sales of an album. Even if we just coughed, a million people will order it simply because of the name. And if anybody leaves, or we split up, it's back to our own resources without the name.'*

*In the aftermath of* Animals, *everybody except for Waters embarked on outside projects. Instead, Waters became a new father, to daughter India, and started writing not one but two new albums.*

*Meanwhile, Mason produced records for hippie royalty Steve Hillage and punk newcomers the Damned, Gilmour was listed as a co-producer on Kate Bush's debut* The Kick Inside, *and he and Wright recorded their first solo albums. Wright hired 'Snowy' White to play guitar, and Gilmour recruited his old rhythm section, Rick Wills and 'Willie' Wilson.*

*The albums,* Wet Dream *and* David Gilmour, *were recorded at Super Bear Studios in Berre-Les-Alpes, France. Both musicians now had villas and boats on the Greek island of Lindos; Gilmour's album had a song named after his seafaring vessel* Mihalis, *while* Wet Dream*'s cover recreated the sun-dappled Aegean, with Po's girlfriend floating topless in the water.*

*Rock stars on holiday wasn't a popular look in 1978. However, both albums were darker and better than that, but also contained several instrumentals, suggesting neither party was keen on writing lyrics. Wright hymned the joys of island life, but also addressed his marital difficulties, while Gilmour explored his favourite theme, mortality, on 'There's No Way Out Of Here' and 'I Can't Breathe Anymore'. Neither albums were hits, though, suggesting Waters' prediction was already coming true.*

✲

**Nick Mason:** I had great fun producing records, but just as I had with Robert Wyatt and Steve Hillage, I didn't want to commit to something that was going to take six months. The Damned wanted Syd Barrett to produce their record, but he wasn't available. I enjoyed it, but I think I got more out of it than the Damned did.

**Captain Sensible (guitarist, the Damned):** We had the same publisher as Syd Barrett, Peter Barnes. I think they wanted to coax Syd back into the studio and thought producing us [1977's second Damned album, *Music For Pleasure*] would be the best way of doing it. I fully expected to see him walking through the door at Britannia Row, until Nick Mason walked in. He said Syd couldn't make it – 'He's not well.'

Not that Nick was an unpleasant bloke, but there just wasn't a meeting of minds. Here we were, bunking the tube everyday and saying, 'Fucking hell, Nick. I nearly got caught by the ticket collector this morning.' And all he could say was, 'I came in my Ferrari.'

**Nicky Horne:** Of course, I wanted Syd Barrett for the radio story and Dave Gilmour told me that he was living at the Playboy Apartments in Park Lane. But when I got there, they told me he'd moved into the Hilton. So I rang Dave who came back and said, 'Yeah, he's staying in Room So-and-So at the Hilton in Park Lane.'

So I turned up at the Hilton with my tape recorder and knocked on the door – and the door's opened by this big, big guy, like a bouncer. I said, 'Dave Gilmour sent me to talk to Syd', and this guy looked down at me and, with immense difficulty, contorted his face and said, 'Syd ... can't ... talk' and closed the door. I went downstairs and rang Dave again and told him. He asked what the guy who answered the door looked like. When I told him, he said, 'No, that *was* Syd.'

**David Gilmour:** Kate Bush was fifteen when I first met her, warbling away and playing piano and I thought she was amazing, but there was no way a record company would get what she was doing. They were all cloth-eared gits. So we did a demo for her in my home studio with Unicorn as a backing group. But we needed more, and I ended up getting [orchestral arranger] Andrew Powell involved and doing masters for a whole album. A couple of guys from EMI came down when we were finishing *Wish You Were Here* and I played them the tape and they signed her. I helped get her started and I'm very proud to have been involved.

**Richard Wright:** *Wet Dream* was rather amateurish. It wasn't very well produced and the lyrics weren't very strong, but at the end of the day, I think there's something rather quaint about it.

**Roger Waters:** In Pink Floyd, Rick was playing less and less and just wasn't interested. If he thought he'd written a good keyboard part, he'd hold on to it and put it on one of his awful solo albums. He didn't want to share anything with anybody. He just got really anal.

**Richard Wright:** It always used to be a joke that you saved your best stuff for your solo album, but I know that isn't the case with me.

**'Willie' Wilson:** We did some tracks for Dave's solo record at his house in Essex and some more at Britannia Row. We'd sit in the games room upstairs, having a few beers and playing snooker.

**David Gilmour:** We all needed time off, and I was persuaded by Rick [Wills] and Willie, who said, 'Come on, let's just do it.' I like some things on the album and I'm excruciatingly embarrassed by others. 'There's No Way Out Of Here' was written by the very talented Ken Baker from Unicorn. But I never saw the album as being the beginning of anything. It was about wanting to make some music in a light, relaxed way – as our stuff was getting so drawn out.

**'Willie' Wilson:** We had to go to Super Bear [in France] to re-record the album. There was something going on, maybe a tax thing, I don't know. The idea was we were going to go out and tour, and we rented the Roxy in Harlesden and filmed three or four songs for a promo video. Then we all went on holiday together to Greece.

**Jeff Dexter:** Rick had a beautiful house in Lindos – him and Juliette were in Greece before any of us – and he was also passionate about sailing. There was an annual regatta on the island and Rick had started to win because he was a very good sailor. Dave got the passion as well. That summer of '78, they both had Hobie Cats, these very nifty catamarans, and Dave was determined to beat him in the regatta. I was his crew member, but Rick beat us, only just.

**Nick Laird-Clowes:** I went to Lindos that summer. Tony Howard managed Marc Bolan and, when Marc died our band, Alfalpha, got dropped. Jeff said, 'Come to Lindos for six weeks.' *Six* weeks? I couldn't believe it. David Gilmour was there and, after a few weeks, I spoke to him. He said, 'I'm here for three months, we're writing a new album.' I thought, *Three months? God, so that's how it's done.*

**'Willie' Wilson:** It was when we were in Greece that Roger presented David with a cassette of his demos for *The Wall*, so that was the end of us planning to tour his solo album – and then I was asked to do the Wall tour as part of the surrogate band.

**Brian Humphries:** By the end of *Animals*, there was a mutual decision that they were going to use someone else for the next album. They were thinking about computers, and computers were out as far as I was concerned. I was old school. Roger already had [*The Wall* engineer/co-producer] James Guthrie in the wings at Britannia Row.

I was given a sheet of paper which Rick and Nick had written out, saying, 'Thank you very much Brian for all your hard work.' I thought, *Oh, thanks very much.* Then I discovered that while Roger and David wanted me to keep the company car, Nick had allocated it to somebody else.

**David Gilmour:** Brian had a rag that he used to wipe the chinagraph marks off the desk. It was white cotton that eventually became black – and it was always the same one. Eventually, we had it mounted in a picture frame so Brian wouldn't lose his rag. Typical stuff, but when you get older you look back and think, *Blimey, we were quite unpleasant.*

**Roger Waters (speaking in 1970):** 'I want to stop going out and playing the numbers. I would like to be creating tapes, songs, material, writing, sketches of sets – whatever is necessary to put on a complete theatrical show in a theatre in London ... I have great faith in giving the audiences more than music. There is just so much more that you can do to make it a complete experience, rather than watching four long-haired youths leaping up and down beating their banjos.'

***New Musical Express* (news report, November 1978):** 'No release date has yet been set for Pink Floyd's next mega statement, but already mystery surrounds the idea behind the long player ... [we] are told by a reliable source that the title of the new Floyd waxing is "Walls" and that to present the piece, the band are planning to delve deep into the realms of "environmental theatre".'

✣

*It's 2016 and a pile of what Aubrey 'Po' Powell calls 'perished pigs' have just been rediscovered in a warehouse in Paris. This is a significant find. Following the death of Storm Thorgerson, Po has been appointed Pink Floyd's creative director and is gathering exhibits for the upcoming 'Their Mortal Remains' exhibition.*

*While Thorgerson was brilliant and difficult, Po relies on charm, pragmatism, sleight of hand and a support network of aides willing to rummage through old warehouses on his behalf. He's also the only conduit between Gilmour and Waters, who aren't talking and who once fought a legal battle for ownership of the group's flying mascot.*

*Po's role has made him the pig's custodian then, recounting the story of its escape when anyone asks, including the BBC. A year later, to publicise 'Their Mortal Remains', the Beeb's flagship magazine programme,* The One Show, *is flying the pig over Broadcasting House, while Po and Nick Mason are interviewed by cricketer-turned-TV host Phil Tufnell outside Battersea Power Station.*

*Tufnell points at the photo of the pig. 'It's a whopper!' he exclaims.*

*'It is a whopper,' confirms Mason.*

*Away from the power station's phallic chimneys and stormy skies, though, the pig now looks a little cute, a bit Walt Disney even. But this is not the case when Waters takes his version on tour later that year. His beast is daubed with images of Donald Trump (in his first term as US president), dollar signs and the words 'Piggy Bank Of War'.*

*Waters' message on* Animals *hasn't been diluted. If anything, it's stronger.*

*'Trump is bizarre,' says Waters at the May Fair Hotel. 'But a lot of people voted for this. It's like Brexit. You think, "Why?" And then you realise that all those dirty foreigner feelings are very close to the surface. Scratch a Little Englander and there is an instinctive mistrust of the French, never mind anybody from the Middle East. We haven't progressed much, have we...?'*

# 9

# 'I WANT TO BE ALONE IN THIS COCOON'

*1979's vegetarian Christmas dinner, 'An awful lot of Carlsberg Special Brew', a middle-class wanker listening to Tchaikovsky and 'I still have my mask of Roger's face'...*

❁

It's Saturday night, 9 August 1980, and Pink Floyd's 'Another Brick in the Wall, Part 2' has become the subject of some tall storytelling among a bunch of west London teenagers. We are waiting for Pink Floyd to perform *The Wall* at Earls Court and some of our party are claiming that their mate's half-brother or best friend's sister's next-door neighbour is one of the kids' choir chanting, 'We don't need no edu-kay-shon' on the hit record. All lies.

Nevertheless, we are sat, shoulder to shoulder, in the concrete arena's cheapest seats (£7.50 each), squinting at the wall through a fug of Benson and Hedges cigarette smoke with top notes of marijuana, courtesy of an Afghan-waistcoated Jesus doppelganger two rows in front.

It might be 1980, but the '80s haven't started here. Earls Court is awash with males of no-fixed hairstyle and semi-stoned thousand-yard stares, sporting Dunlop green flash trainers and lots of double denim. It really is like punk never happened.

*The Wall* is Roger Waters' baby. How could it not be? Its anti-hero 'Pink' grows up with an absent father and an overbearing mother, becomes a famous rock star, but is restrained by his psychological and emotional walls and seeks answers from within.

Schoolteachers, managers, groupies, wives, even the doctor who'd shot Waters up with a tranquilliser on their last tour appear in his story.

So too does Syd Barrett (in real life, holed up in a flat not far from tonight's venue): he's there in the album's flashbacks to 'Pink' with his 'obligatory Hendrix perm' and 'little black book with me poems in'.

Twelve years later, I meet Roger Waters for the first time. '*The Wall* is stupefyingly good,' he tells me. 'Christ, what a brilliant album that was.'

✤

**Roger Waters:** The germ of the thing, and I still have it somewhere, is a sketch on a piece of A4 lined paper of an arena with a wall across it. It looks exactly as it looked in the show. That was always the idea. The personal stuff appended itself to the basic idea with almost no effort.

**Gerald Scarfe:** Roger worked on the music and lyrics until the day we sat together in my studio in Cheyne Walk and listened to his demo. It was very raw and, not being a musician myself, I didn't see the potential. To me, it just sounded like Roger rasping away over synthesised notes. When it ended, he asked what I thought. 'Great,' I said. There was an awkward silence before Roger said, 'I feel like I've just pulled down my pants and taken a shit in front of you.' I knew how he felt, though. I'd experienced the same when presenting my work to critical newspaper editors.

**Richard Wright:** Dave and I were in Greece that summer when we listened to Roger's demos for *The Wall*. I was being lazy and I can't speak for Dave, but I suspect he would say the same: the demo tape was awful, really bad. But there were some interesting things there.

**David Gilmour:** As far as I recall, we met up in a studio in London before summer 1978, and Roger said he wanted to make one of the two projects that he had been working on at his home studio. He came in with two demoed ideas. One of them was *The Wall* and one was what became his first solo album [*The Pros and Cons of Hitch-Hiking*], which had one nice tune but was too much the same. *The Wall* had more scope.

**Roger Waters:** Steve O'Rourke was strongly in favour of *The Pros and Cons of Hitch-Hiking*, but the other three, to a man, preferred *The Wall*.

**Gerald Scarfe:** Right from the day he played me the demo, Roger said he wanted *The Wall* to be an album, a live show and a film, and he wanted my illustrations and animations to be used across them all.

We used to play an awful lot of snooker and drank an awful lot of Carlsberg Special Brew round his house. I remember him saying to me, 'I'll never be in this position again Gerry, I'll never have this…' – meaning his hand on the steering wheel. He had the whole thing mapped out in his head, which of course caused problems, as one member of the band had in effect hijacked the whole thing.

**Aubrey 'Po' Powell:** Hipgnosis had published a book of our designs called *Walk Away Renée*. We'd included *Animals*, but hadn't credited Roger for the idea of the pig over the power station. Roger and Storm were not getting on anyway, so we were told Gerald Scarfe would be designing their next album. I was fine with that decision, as we had plenty of work, but I think Storm took it rather badly.

**Roger Waters:** People aren't content with what they've got. I thought the work Storm and Po did for many years was great, so why did they steal my little contribution to album design?

**David Gilmour:** We worked on the band demos of *The Wall* at Britannia Row for the period between September and Christmas [1978]. Around the end of that period must have been when we realised we had this financial problem.

**Roger Waters:** We were involved with a company called Norton Warburg. Their idea was to take gross income and run it through a finance company to protect it from the immediate payment of tax on the grounds that it was being used to finance venture capitals. It was legal. But what Norton Warburg did was move money from account to account and take huge management fees each time.

**David Gilmour:** That would have been okay as long as their venture capitals always made a profit, but as soon as things started going downhill, you couldn't trade them on – and you had to trade them on in order to prove you were trading, not investing.

We had a Belgian skateboard company, Benjyboards, that was big for a while, but then the craze stopped. There was a hotel somewhere [Moorhead Hotel, Devon], where they would make chutney in the winter to sell in the holiday season. There was also Carbocraft that did well for a while making rowing boats for the Oxford and Cambridge boat races, then a chequebook printing company.... But these venture capital things were a bit too venture for my tastes.

**Roger Waters:** We lost a couple of million quid – nearly everything we'd made from *The Dark Side of the Moon*. Then we discovered the Inland Revenue might come and ask us for 83 per cent of the money we had lost – which we didn't have.

**David Gilmour:** That made us take the decision that we'd better make *The Wall* in France and America to minimise our tax liabilities on it so we would have some funds to pay our *other* tax liabilities. The people who ran this scheme had been passed by the Bank of England and other regulatory boards, but were subsequently jailed [in 1987].

**Roger Waters:** I could see *The Wall* was going to be a long and complex process, and I needed a collaborator. There was nobody in the band you could talk to about any of this stuff, for one reason or another – Dave was not interested, Rick was pretty closed down and Nick was interested, I think, but a bit more interested in his racing cars. So I needed somebody who was musically and intellectually in a similar place to where I was.

**David Gilmour:** I thought it was a very good concept at the time. I don't like it quite as much as I liked it at the beginning conceptually. With the benefit of hindsight, it was a bit self-pitying – whingey, if you like. But I don't have any regrets about the concept. Roger was the one who had something lyrically he wanted to say and I didn't have a problem with that.

But it's not true to say it's about a rock star's alienation. That's one small part of it. This is about everyone. The symbol of the wall as something that cuts you off from other things in life covers an enormous amount of things: one's lack of communication with one's parents, one's partner in a long-term marriage or relationship, the lack of communication that can arise after years about being in a pop group. Many many things.

**Nick Mason:** We'd burned out Brian Humphries and were recommended a great young engineer called James Guthrie. But although we'd produced all our albums ourselves after *Atom Heart Mother*, Roger decided to bring in Bob Ezrin as a co-producer and collaborator.

**Bob Ezrin:** I met Roger through his wife, Carolyne, who worked for me. But it was Alice Cooper that turned me on to Pink Floyd when I was working with them in 1970. I produced their records and did the sound for their live tours and travelled with them to radio stations. When the DJs asked what we were listening to, we would always say Pink Floyd. I remember we played 'See Emily Play' at a station in Detroit and they got on to it years after it was released. After that, you could say I went to Floyd University, studied the band and became a full-on fan.

*The Wall* was Roger's project, and it might as well have been a solo album. His initial concept was that it was all his songs, his stuff. And I was brought in to handle 'the muffins' – that was literally how he referred to them. That was my job. But very early on, it was clear to me, and then to Roger, that this needed to be a Pink Floyd project, and there were some amazing things that they as a band could do that nobody else could. So it quickly became my job to be the liaison ombudsman, or whatever you want to call it, and broker a collaboration. But there was confusion at the beginning over who was making this album.

**James Guthrie (*The Wall*'s engineer/co-producer):** Steve O'Rourke didn't tell me about Bob Ezrin and Bob wasn't told about me. So when we arrived, I think we both felt we'd been booked to do the same job.

**David Gilmour:** Bob Ezrin was also there partly as a man in the middle to help smooth the flow between Roger and I.

**Gerald Scarfe:** Roger asked me to draw the characters for the story. He had the idea of the main character being called 'Punch' and his wife would be 'Judy'. I must have done a couple of months' work on 'Punch' and

'Judy' before Roger decided 'Punch' wasn't right so he came up with the idea of 'Pink' to replace him.

I didn't want to do a standard cartoon of a realistic little man, his mother and his teacher. They had to be bizarre and memorable and bear repetition in a year's time. There was a bit of pressure to come up with those characters before we had worked out what was going to be in the show.

I chose the predatory praying mantis as a model for my depiction of 'The Wife', who looked more like a scorpion, but it wasn't based on anybody's wife in real life. Weirdly enough, Roger has said to me that I am getting to look more and more like 'The Mother' in *The Wall*, and there's an element of truth in it. Make of that what you want psychologically.

**Roger Waters:** The mother [in *The Wall*] is over-protective, which most mothers are. If you can level one accusation at mothers, it is that they tend to protect their children too much and for too long. That's all. This isn't a portrait of my mother, although one or two of the things in there apply to her as well.

**Bob Ezrin:** *The Wall* started out as a completely autobiographical work. It was the Roger Waters story and I felt really strongly that we should not age him. Roger was thirty-six at the time. My sense was that our audience was not that interested in a 36-year-old rocker who was complaining. But they might be interested in a gestalt character, 'Pink', that was a composite of all the dissipated rockers we have known and loved. And that would allow us to go beyond Roger and get into some real crazy stuff.

If you look at some of the lyrics from the original, he was being fairly honest about his fear and his pain, but when we turned him into Pink, we were able to give him even more fear, alienation and isolation. Because if Roger had claimed that level of isolation, then it really would have been unacceptable. It would have been posing and it would have been wrong and they weren't posing at all.

I stayed up all night and wrote the album out in filmic form. I wrote notes about what each song was about and chords and ideas. Then we all sat around and read it – and that was the moment we had a blueprint. The final result was not the same as what Roger originally perceived. A lot of it is stuff that he had on those demos, but embellished, and a lot of it is a result of invention in the studio and the input of the other guys.

**David Gilmour:** 'Hey You' I think was the first track we recorded for *The Wall*, or the first track we had a go at in Britannia Row without Roger even being there. I did the high-strung intro thing, which is at the beginning and is also the middle breakdown section. The fretless bass I played later. I think we added that at Super Bear.

**Roger Waters:** Quite a lot of the other songs changed a lot, others didn't change at all. 'Don't Leave Me Now' and 'Is There Anybody Out There?' and 'Mother' are almost exactly as they were originally.

**David Gilmour:** There are three sections of making *The Wall*. The first bit we did in Britannia Row, which involved going through everything, having ideas, demoing it all up; then there was the period in France when we actually made the bulk of the album; and the next section in Los Angeles where we finished it up and mixed it.

**Bob Ezrin:** There was a public-school atmosphere, with Roger as the head boy. Sometimes he was alright and sometimes he was a bully. But I was the new kid, so I got tortured from time to time. But I also felt that I formed a bond, particularly with Nick and, as time went on, with Dave and Rick too. They appreciated me because someone was finally standing up to Roger on certain things.

I came to London with a New York punk attitude and early on in the sessions there was a moment where Roger was pushing me around – I don't remember the exact circumstances – but I turned around and said, 'Read my lips, motherfucker. You cannot talk to me like that.' And the whole band were onside, going, 'Yes'. I think that held me in good stead from that point onward.

Knowing Roger's personality as I do, I think that if I'd just caved in, he'd have dispensed with me quickly. But the thing I learned about him is that he's as tough on himself as anyone. He takes that perfectionism and harshness and applies it to himself and other people, which is sometimes not the right thing to do.

**Nick Mason:** Bob was going through what can only be described as an unreliable phase of his life. He was staying down in Nice, we were all up in the hills, and he'd drive down there when he finished work and have a wild time and then be astonished when we were pissed off when he'd arrive back the next morning late.

**David Gilmour:** When I look back at it, it's amazing how much we got done in a comparatively short time. We were in France for three months and we didn't work seven days a week. We didn't work evenings even – we were trying to keep civilised hours because we all had families living with us.

But at one point we were using two studios. Super Bear is up in the mountains and notorious for being difficult to sing there [due to oxygen levels]. Roger had a lot of difficulty singing in tune – he always did. So we found another studio, Miraval, where he'd go and do his vocals with Bob.

**Nick Mason:** I finished most of my drum tracks early, which allowed Steve O'Rourke and I to compete in Le Mans [the annual 24-hour sports car race] where we came second in our class.

**Roger Waters:** Up until then, we always had 'Produced By Pink Floyd' on the records, but it would have been done by me and Dave. So I put it to Nick and Rick that Bob Ezrin would be producing the record with me and Dave, and with all due respect to those guys, they wouldn't, because they never had. We thought it was fair that we got a producer's point, one per cent, and that would come off the top and then we would divvy up the rest of the deal four ways.

Nick went, 'Fine, no problem', but Rick went, 'But I can produce the record. I can help.' I said, 'I don't think you can, Rick. You never have in the past.' He said, 'Yes, I have.' So I said, 'Okay, let's make the record and if you seem to be producing, you can have a point too. Is that fair?'

**Richard Wright:** I did have reservations about bringing in an outside producer. Not because of losing production points, but because I felt that the band was losing one of its strengths, which was that Pink Floyd would fight each other sometimes, but it was all hands together as a group. I think our best work was created that way.

**Roger Waters:** After we've been working for a few weeks, Rick would be in the studio all the time from the moment we started in the morning to when we'd finish at night. One day, Bob Ezrin asked me why and I said, 'Don't you get it? He thinks he's producing the record.'

He replied, 'Don't be ridiculous.' And I said, 'He does. He wants the point. Have you noticed occasionally he goes, "I don't like that"?' And Ezrin said, 'Yes, it's rather irritating.' I said, 'He thinks that's record producing. You ask him.'

He came back and said, 'You're absolutely right. Well, I told him he's not producing.' And after that, Rick never came in unless we needed a keyboard part. He got the hump, played less and less and less, and generally just wasn't interested.

**Bob Ezrin:** Roger was very unforgiving because he had given a lot more of himself to the project than the others and every time he saw someone giving what he thought was less, he was very vocal about it and very cutting.

Everybody had some things they'd been working on, but nobody knew what the concept was going to be until quite late in the game. So Rick wasn't prepared because he didn't know the songs and was not a guy who performs well under that kind of pressure. He was a wonderfully intuitive and improvisational player. But if someone came in and said, 'You need to play an A flat seventh here', that wasn't his way of doing things.

**Richard Wright:** Once I got to know Bob, I thought it was good that we had him there, because there was so much friction in the band. Various issues came up, namely that I sat in the studio not really doing anything but because I wanted to get producer's points. But Roger made it extremely difficult for me to work. This idea that I was sitting around, wasting my time, is not really fair. On the other hand, I was slightly depressed, maybe really depressed.

**David Gilmour:** On *The Wall*, Roger and I had a good working relationship. We argued a lot, sometimes heatedly, but overall we were still achieving things that were valid. But Rick at the time didn't come in and offer anything up for the project. He was at a rather low ebb.

**Jeff Dexter:** Everybody was doing cocaine back then. But Rick had one incredible friend who was a major player and became his bosom buddy. It was on tap. If you wanted to know where it was, you'd go and visit Rick and his pal, and his pal was doing very well and had a couple more boats than him. It took its toll on lots of people.

**Richard Wright (speaking in 1999):** 'The band has never had a cocaine problem, none of us. It was being used, but that wasn't the problem. The problem was Roger and I did not get along and he wanted to be the leader of the band.'

✲

*'Margaret Thatcher saw it as a problem, but who gives a shit about her,' declares Alun Renshaw, who's lived in Australia since 1980 but hasn't lost his Yorkshire accent. Renshaw was the head of music at Islington Green School, whose pupils sang on 'Another Brick in the Wall, Part 2'.*

*Islington Green was a struggling state school whose headteacher, Margaret Maden, was determined to reverse its poor reputation. (Years later, local resident and future prime minister Tony Blair refused to send his children there.)*

*Day after day, Miss Maden stood at the gates, making sure the teachers arrived on time, and performed an afternoon check on one who'd recently set his classroom curtains alight after a lunchtime drinking session.*

*Alun Renshaw took a unique approach to education. 'I thought it was important that we made music relevant to the kids,' he tells me, down the phone from his adopted home in Webbs Creek, New South Wales. 'Not something where you sit down like a middle-class wanker and listen to Tchaikovsky. I wanted to make it practical and vocational and relevant.'*

*Renshaw led the school choir and orchestra, but also encouraged his pupils to 'go outside and draw the sound of the traffic' or create music from everyday items, such as dustbin lids and brick walls – a bit like Floyd's 'Household Objects' project, then.*

*In autumn 1979, Britannia Row's engineer Nick Griffiths approached Renshaw looking for children to sing on 'Another Brick in the Wall…', in which Waters' anti-hero Pink is brutalised by a tyrannical schoolmaster.*

*Renshaw was unaware of the subject matter when he ferried a group of pupils to nearby Britannia Row. The lunchtime recording sessions ran over, meaning the kids missed afternoon lessons – and nobody knew what they were going to be singing until it was too late, after which Miss Maden was hauled up before the authorities. 'Honestly,' says Renshaw. 'I had no idea it would cause so much trouble.'*

✿

**Caroline Greeves (former Islington Green School pupil):** Alun Renshaw was a fantastic guy, doing a great job in a pretty grim school. He was very creative, slightly mad and didn't give a stuff about the other teachers. In the music room, there was a poster for the Sex Pistols' *Never Mind the Bollocks* on the wall. Half the school thought Alun was a wanker, the others thought he was the best thing ever.

**Bob Ezrin:** There weren't any drums on Roger's demo for 'Another Brick in the Wall', as I recall. It was just delayed guitar and synthesiser and his voice on top. We decided to dress that song up when it came to the recording.

**Nick Mason:** The original always reminded me of some old kids' song that went 'A woman sat in a graveyard … ahhh … ahhh … ahhh'. Dirge-like might be too disparaging, but it was a funereal, gloomy old thing.

**Bob Ezrin:** Before *The Wall*, I'd been working with Nils Lofgren at the Power Station in New York. Next door to us were Chic and I used to stand in the hallway listening because what they were doing was so damn funky – and then I was going to England to work with some white people who weren't very funky at all and thinking, *Damn! Maybe we can do some of that.*

**Nick Mason:** I thought turning it into a disco tune was great. Some of the others were rather less enthusiastic. But it was nice for me as I have a slightly more simplistic approach.

**Bob Ezrin:** The minute I heard the song with the beat on, I said, 'This is a smash.' And we already had Dave's fantastic guitar solo at the end. But Roger said, 'Fuck it, we don't want a single.' I was pleading. And he was like, 'No! I'm not going to be told what to do.'

The problem was the original song was only one verse and one chorus long, so we copied it, found a small disco break that we picked out of a verse, stuck it in the middle and tacked the ending back on. When they went home one night, James Guthrie and I cut this thing together, and played it to Roger the next day.

There's some controversy over who said, 'Let's put children on it.' James thinks it was Roger's idea, and I think it was mine, because I was the kid guy who'd used children's voices before [on Alice Cooper's 'School's Out' and Lou Reed's *Berlin*].

We sent a 24-track reel with twenty tracks open from the studio in France to Nick Griffiths and said, 'Please find us some kids.' He went to the school round the corner. I told him, 'Just fill up the tracks and have them do it every way possible – cockney, posh, angelic, nasty...'

**Caroline Greeves:** I was part of the school choir, which was a choir in the very loosest sense. We didn't get any notice. We were just hanging out in Alun's office during break and he rounded up whoever he could find, and some of us had sung before on Alun's own composition, 'Requiem For a Sinking Block of Flats'.

At first we sang in our best choir voices, but were told by the engineer to shout and make it more cockney. I went home that night and told my older brother, who was a huge Floyd fan, that not only had I sung on one of their songs, I'd heard unreleased Pink Floyd music.

**Bob Ezrin:** When Nick sent the tapes back, I threw it up on the console, put the faders up and that *gang* came back at us. I balanced it up so the cockney was at the forefront and we had an instant army of children. Those kids were spectacular.

**Nick Mason:** People get starry-eyed trying to work out who came up with which idea. But I think Nick Griffiths interpreted the instructions he was given in a very creative way. I thought it sounded terrific and I don't recall there being any dissenters.

**David Gilmour:** Roger was pretty good about criticism during *The Wall*. Someone would say 'I don't like that one very much', Roger would look all sulky and the next day come back in with something brilliant. I can remember he'd gone off in a sulk the night before and came in the next day with 'Nobody Home', which we thought was fantastic.

**Roger Waters:** I didn't get Dave's chord sequence for 'Comfortably Numb' until quite late on when Ezrin and I realised we needed a piece for 'The Doctor'. By then, the story was beginning to unfold in the hotel room. At that point, Dave gave me this chord sequence he'd got left over from something or other [his solo album] and I wrote 'Comfortably Numb' to that.

**David Gilmour:** For 'Comfortably Numb', I banged out five or six solos. From there, I followed my usual procedure, which is to listen back to each solo and make a chart, noting which bits are good. Then I created one great composite solo by whipping one fader up, then another, until everything flows together.

**Nick Mason:** Whenever there is one of those polls for Pink Floyd fans' favourite songs, it's usually 'Shine On You Crazy Diamond' or 'Comfortably Numb'. Both songs have that moody aspect that appeals to the fans, or at least the ones that vote for these things.

**David Gilmour:** With 'Run Like Hell', there was only one section and Roger said he had some words that didn't fit and showed me how he wanted his words to go, so I had to write a second part. With 'Young

Lust', Roger had a song that we didn't think was great and he said, 'Well, go and do something better then.' So I went home and wrote the music for the verses.

**Roger Waters:** We'd renegotiated our deal with CBS to get a few more royalty points if they could have the album out for Christmas. But their end of the deal was that they'd definitely get the record at the end of October.

We all took a holiday in August and I wrote out a schedule for when we reconvened on September 5, and realised it was impossible. I asked Ezrin if he could do the rest of the keyboard parts with Rick for the week starting August 28 and he went, 'Oh my God, okay.'

So I got Steve to call Rick to see if he'd come earlier. He found Rick in Greece and Rick's message was, 'Tell Roger to fuck off'. So I gave him an ultimatum to do as he was told and finish the record, keep your full share and leave quietly afterwards, or I'd see him in court. He very wisely accepted the former proposal. In any event, I wasn't working with him anymore.

**Richard Wright:** We all agreed to have a holiday and I had specific time with my children [Gala and Jamie], whom I was missing very much – the others had their kids living with them in France – and there was no indication to me that we were that much behind schedule.

Then I had a call from Steve to come back now and start recording. And my reaction was, 'No, he's been sent to do this. He's testing me. We've all agreed.' Steve said, 'Will you come now?' 'No, I'm coming on the agreed date.' But I didn't tell Roger to fuck off. I wouldn't say that. And that was the last I heard of it, until I arrived in LA and Steve said, 'Roger wants you out of the band.'

**Roger Waters:** It was at this point that I had a meeting with Dave where he famously or infamously said, 'Why don't we get rid of Nick too?'. And I was like, 'Steady on Dave, he's my mate.'

**David Gilmour:** Roger says that, but I don't have any memories of that, apart from joking about off-loading and getting on with it. Nick was working very hard and had learned how to read drum music.

**Nick Mason:** I've broached this subject with David and I am happy to say that everyone denies even considering getting me out of the band. But I'm certainly not going to undertake a forensic investigation into the matter.

**David Gilmour:** I can remember being in Ireland on our break, before going to LA. I phoned Roger because I had heard he was throwing Rick out of the band. I called him from a phone box in Chapelizod just outside Dublin – because the flat I was staying in didn't have a phone – and me saying, 'You can't do that. He's been in the band all the way along. If you don't like it, your choice is to leave. It isn't to throw someone out ... You're letting this get very personal, aren't you?' I won't quote what he said.

Later in Los Angeles, Rick asked me to go for a drink and he said, 'What do you think about all this?' I replied, 'Well, you haven't pulled your finger out at all. You haven't really done anything to say why you should stay within this band. You're a founder member and as far as I'm concerned, it's a sacrosanct right for you to stay in it as long as you want to be. But you have to make up your own mind about this.'

He said, 'Do you still want me to be in the band?', I said, 'Not particularly, because you're not doing anything, but I'll support your right to be in it 'til the end.' I was never part of a movement to throw Rick or Nick out. It's not my position.

**Nick Mason:** Roger carried out a brilliant campaign to get what he wanted by a certain amount of cajoling and threatening. Looking back now, I should have stuck up for Rick, but I utterly failed to do so and aligned myself with the forces of safety.

**Richard Wright:** I shut off the whole idea that I was leaving the band. I actually fooled myself that I'd play as well as I could on the tour and maybe Roger will admit he was wrong. So I put everything into it.

❊

*It was Dick Asher, the head of CBS Records, who'd promised the band an additional percentage if they could complete* The Wall *in time for Christmas. With*

*Floyd's accountants picking through the debris of the Norton Warburg deal, they were unlikely to refuse.*

*Recording and overdubbing began at Cherokee Studios and Producers Workshop in Los Angeles. It was here, during eighteen-hour working days, that Waters' hysterical Scottish-accented schoolmaster ('If you don't eat ya meat, ya can't have any pudding…'), the sound of smashed television sets, deep breathing and whirring helicopter blades were added to the mix. 'I also recorded the sound my fridge made when I kept opening and closing the door,' recalls Mason.*

*Everybody wanted the Beach Boys to sing back-up vocals, but had to settle for just Bruce Johnston, his favourite session singers, and soft-rock husband-and-wife duo Captain & Tennille.*

*Elsewhere, film composer Michael Kamen helped score the orchestral players on several tracks, including 'Comfortably Numb'; session drummer Jeff Porcaro tackled the 5/4 time signature on 'Mother' ('If something's right for a track, and I can't do it, then so be it,' says Mason) and Alice Cooper's hired gun Fred Mandel was among those playing keyboards in Wright's absence.*

*'Right through the making of* The Wall *album, Roger and I had worked together extremely well,' says Gilmour, picking away at one of his signature Black Strats. Then came 'Comfortably Numb', 'which was when we had a major row…'*

✤

**David Gilmour:** There was a drum and bass backing track for 'Comfortably Numb' that Roger and Bob liked and I thought it was too loose, too sloppy. We did another one to a click track and I thought it was better. Both Roger and Bob dug in their heels and didn't think it was as good.

All these tapes went off to Los Angeles and we went out and had dinner in an Italian restaurant. Me, Bob and Roger shouted at each other all night about this fucking stupid point and I don't think I could tell the difference today. We wound up making some feeble compromise. You get over-obsessed by ridiculous things at times.

**Bob Ezrin:** David had a different idea that didn't include the orchestration in the body of the song and was a little harder. There was an arm wrestle over that, until finally there was a compromise, where Dave's original harder track was confined to the outro and the final solo.

**David Gilmour:** I loved all the orchestration, but I wanted to make the parts with Roger singing on darker and the parts with me singing lighter. I wanted more of a grungy guitar and Roger and Bob wanted it just drums and bass and orchestra. You focus in on certain things so tightly because you want it to be as perfect as you can get it. Now I don't think any of us would know the fucking difference.

**Bob Ezrin:** The song itself had that dreamlike, *pillowy* approach – and I'm still glad we did that. It sounds like being in bed with a comforter pulled up around your ears and a pillow around your ears, saying, 'Leave me alone. I want to be alone in this cocoon.'

**Nick Mason:** The record company said, 'We want to do "Another Brick in the Wall..." as a single' and we said, 'Oh well, if you *have* to', because we'd been rejected by the singles-buying public after 'Apples and Oranges' and 'Point Me at the Sky'.

**Gerald Scarfe:** Roger told me we had to make a video for the song. I said, 'How on earth can I do that by next Wednesday? Today is Tuesday.' He said, 'Just go and find some kids...'

**Caroline Greeves:** There was a huge hoo-ha with the headmistress when the single was released. I also remember being cross because they had different kids singing in the video. We were told we couldn't do it as we didn't have Equity cards. Some of the children at the school were working on [BBC school drama] *Grange Hill*, so we knew about Equity cards. I now think it was because the school didn't want any more adverse publicity.

**Alun Renshaw:** Maybe I was naive, but the song wasn't saying 'Kids don't need education'. It was about this guy who was going through life and this is what happened when he went to school. I didn't see it as a political statement, but it marked the boiling point of conservatism and everything changing. The headmistress was an amazing lady who gave me free rein. But within four weeks of the song coming out, I was in Australia. It had nothing to do with the song as I'd been invited out there for a job. But it meant they couldn't get to me.

**Gerald Scarfe:** We all had bastard teachers at school, those shits who used to get at you because you were vulnerable. I didn't base my image of the teacher on a specific one. It was based on that genre of teacher Roger and I and everyone knew – the kind that was visiting all the misery of their lives on the kids.

**Nick Mason:** The song came in for a lot of criticism. Clive James wrote something in the *Observer* about how awful it was to encourage children to think negatively about education – which is not what it was about.

**Gerald Scarfe:** Roger wanted a pure unadulterated wall for the album cover. We experimented with black bricks and white lines and different sizes of bricks, before going back to the plain white one.

On the inside, we had different characters from the story peeping out and popping out from behind the bricks. Then the powers that be on the commercial side said we had to have some lettering. So we compromised with a sticker on the cover. But if you think about it, Storm Thorgerson had gone to Cairo to shoot images for inside *The Dark Side of the Moon* and I did the final artwork for *The Wall* on our kitchen table.

**Storm Thorgerson:** I was miffed, but not surprised not to be asked to do *The Wall*. It was very different and I couldn't do something like that ... I think they did the wrong thing, though. I think they should have used Gerald's drawings of the characters on the cover.

✢

*'Another Brick in the Wall, Part 2' was Pink Floyd's first UK single since 1968. The video showed its teenage choir alongside Scarfe's animated hammers and a boggle-eyed schoolmaster feeding schoolkids into a mincing machine.*

*It sounded like Lionel Bart's 'Food, Glorious Food' from* Oliver! *reimagined for Thatcher's Britain and became the unlikeliest Christmas number one. Floyd had donated £1,000 to Islington Green, but following a change in copyright law and a legal campaign, Alun Renshaw's choir became eligible for modest royalties this century. 'At the time, we got a free copy of the single, the album and tickets for the show at Earls Court,' recalled Caroline Greeves.*

*Nick Mason remembers a playback of* The Wall *at CBS's headquarters where an executive threw up his hands in despair ('He said, "This is dreadful..."'). His fears proved unfounded when the album topped the US Billboard chart. At home, though,* The Wall *was held off the pole position by greatest hits collections from Rod Stewart and ABBA.*

*After punk's year zero, concept albums had been denounced as passé by critics. Less so by the record-buying public.* The Wall *was in for the long haul, shifting a million in its first two weeks and marching onwards, like Gerald Scarfe's goose-stepping hammers, to 30 million sales and counting.*

*In 2011, some of Waters' original demos featured in a* Wall *box set. They began with Vera Lynn crooning her wartime hit 'We'll Meet Again' and gave a great insight into his creative process and how much the others and Bob Ezrin brought to the table.*

*Gilmour's observation about the light and shade of 'Comfortably Numb' also applied to the rest. It was all about the yin and yang: how it flitted between Gilmour's honeyed tones on 'Goodbye Blue Sky' to Waters' delightfully neurotic voice on 'Don't Leave Me Now'; the juxtaposition of brutal synths and harmony vocals; background TV babble and bluesy guitar solos.*

*However, both Wright and Mason's names were absent from* The Wall's *original pressing – although the drummer had his reinstated soon after. When tickets for the show went on sale, nobody outside the group and its inner circle knew Wright was no longer a member of the band.*

❖

**David Gilmour:** Originally there was an idea to stage *The Wall* inside a giant slug – some sort of inflatable building – a tent-like thing that looked like a huge slug – that was going to be packed up and moved to other places around the world and set up again – one of the many bright ideas that, for all sorts of reasons, didn't reach fruition.

**Roger Waters:** I had the idea to build a wall physically between me and the stage in order to express the sense of fear and alienation I was feeling. There's something about the screaming that goes on in very big rock 'n' roll audiences, as if a certain segment of the audience want the experience to be as uncomfortable as possible, so they're demonstrating a masochism and the band are providing them with the sadistic counterfoil.

**Gerald Scarfe:** Everybody, including Bob Ezrin, said to Roger, 'You can't invite the fans into Earls Court and then shut them out.' There were also a lot of discussions about the band doing an encore, and Roger said, 'No, this is a piece, a concept. I don't want other songs tacked on the end.' Eventually, the others persuaded Roger to compromise, to at least have some holes in the wall.

**David Gilmour:** Obviously, when someone says, 'in the first half of the show, we're going to build this fucking great wall across the front of the stage, and we're going to be playing behind it, and the audience are going to be in front, looking at it', you go, 'Hang on a minute. I'm not sure I want to be in that audience.'

**Gerald Scarfe:** Roger also told me he dreamed of having a surrogate band playing all the gigs so he could avoid the tedium of long tours and play golf instead.

**Roger Waters:** The surrogate band are portraying what we become when we succumb to the trappings of power and turn into this fascist machine – wearing masks of us and dressed in black uniforms for the opening of the show.

✲

*Between them, Waters, Scarfe and architect Mark Fisher devised the idea of using 500 foldable cardboard bricks to construct a 33-foot-high by*

*260-foot-wide wall. The bricks slotted around a steel frame, incorporating three stages: one at the front to support theatrical effects and extra musicians; a back stage behind the wall for the main players; and a third rostrum inside the wall itself. Designer Jonathan Park helped turn the concept into a reality.*

*'It was a piece of rock 'n' roll touring theatre,' explained Fisher. 'It was taking the show and the arena and saying, "These things together are the experience of the evening".'*

*Scarfe's drawings were then transformed into marionettes, inflatables and animations: his ghoulish schoolmaster, the mother, the wife and despondent Pink brought to life against the wall's blank canvas. It was an extraordinarily ambitious undertaking – even more so in a pre-digital age.*

*Pink Floyd would be joined by a different host in each city (a radio DJ or actor whose job was to antagonise the audience in a comic pastiche of a typical MC), four backing vocalists and additional musicians, known as 'the surrogate band'. This comprised of Thin Lizzy's moonlighting guitarist 'Snowy' White (later replaced by Andy Roberts), bassist Andy Bown (on the lam from his day job with Status Quo) and ex-members of Sutherland Brothers and Quiver, drummer 'Willie' Wilson and keyboard player Peter Wood.*

*Besides fleshing out the sound behind the wall, the surrogate band posed as Pink Floyd during the show's key moments, including the opening number, 'In the Flesh'. To enable this, each one wore a latex mask moulded on the face of their opposite number in the band.*

✲

**Andy Bown (the surrogate 'Roger Waters'):** I got the job because I knew [Foreigner's bassist] Rick Wills, who was a friend of David Gilmour's. I recall David taking twelve of us out to a Japanese restaurant one night and picking up the bill. Then we went back to his house for a party and it turned out Rick was living there.

David offered Rick the job, but he was up to his neck with Foreigner and told him, 'If you want someone who's done a bit of singing, bass playing and acting, then Andy's your guy.' I was playing keyboards with

Status Quo, but they jogged their tour forward by three weeks to let me do the shows.

**'Willie' Wilson (the surrogate 'Nick Mason'):** I had been around Pink Floyd for years, I'd been to gigs, I'd soundchecked with them. But it was very weird wearing a mask of Nick Mason's face. Although I was a mate of David's, the surrogates stuck together. We all became one big family.

**Andy Bown:** I accepted the job, and moved my wife and two children – one of them thirteen months, the other one two years old – to a rented house in the Santa Clarita Valley. We were due to start rehearsing in LA and Culver City.

Two weeks after that, the cassettes arrived by courier so I could listen to what we were doing. It was only then I realised it was called *The Wall*. When I was offered the job on the telephone, I thought it was called *The War*. I had no fucking idea. I moved the entire family for this. But I wasn't a Pink Floyd fan.

We rehearsed for a couple of weeks and took a break for Christmas. David's wife Ginger cooked us all a soya turkey, which was ahead of its time for 1979. She made a rather good veggie burger as well. After Christmas, we started rehearsing again and I could see the tension building, as soon as David said, 'Roger's coming down next week.'

People started quaking a bit. Roger had been elsewhere working on the production and the show, but it was obvious Roger was the boss. Anyway, he arrived, and he and I started playing together on the bass and he made a terrible mistake. I said, 'Look, if you're going to play like that, I want smaller billing.' And he and I really hit it off from that moment.

**Richard Wright:** I loved the idea of the other band appearing in masks and not being us. 'Oh, there's Pink Floyd on stage!' Then there's another Pink Floyd. That's theatrical.

**Andy Bown:** I remember standing at the back of one rehearsal in Culver City and Steve O'Rourke said to me, 'I hope this fucking works Andy, because we're $2.8 million down the pan already.'

**Nick Mason:** The thing is that once you've committed to something like that, you can't back out. You can't say, 'Oh, let's go and do *The Dark Side of the Moon* instead.'

**Bob Ezrin:** I was asked to be involved with the show but couldn't commit. I was going through a divorce and fighting for custody of my children. Then, in my naivety, I took a phone call from a friend, a journalist, who teased information out of me weeks before the first date. A spoiler article appeared in the press, Roger went nuclear and had me banned from seeing the show.

**Cynthia Fox (MC, Los Angeles Sports Arena, 7 February 1980):** 'Hoo-ya, hoo-ya, good evening Los Angeles ... Are you starved for rock 'n' roll? Are the drugs happening or what? ... Guess we're all gonna make a lot of money off you guys...'

**Gerald Scarfe:** At the first show in Los Angeles, a drape caught fire. Roger called a halt, but had to convince the crew it was an actual emergency. Once they understood it wasn't part of the show, two roadies launched themselves up into the air trying to beat out the flames while burning cloth floated down to the stage below.

**Nick Mason:** Roger had to call a halt and wait while the riggers put it out. Since the shouted command of 'Stop! Stop!' was an integral part of the show, it took Roger some time to convince the crew that this time it was an emergency.

**Gerald Scarfe:** On the last night in LA, we were shocked to see the dummy of Pink, which usually lay at the bottom of the wall, get up and walk away. One of the road crew had removed all the polystyrene chips and somehow managed to squeeze inside.

**Gary Yudman (MC in New York and London):** I was doing things like *Saturday Night Live* and stand-up comedy and rock 'n' roll impressions, imitating people like Dylan and Bowie. I had done a number of things for Pink Floyd's New York promoter, Ron Delsener, who told me the band were looking for someone to do fifteen minutes of MC-ing [at the Nassau

Coliseum] to get the audience riled up before the surrogate band came on stage. The first night went well with lots of boos and cheers.

**'Willie' Wilson:** We could see through these masks and could see the surprise on the faces of the first five or six rows. They all thought we were the band. As soon as we stopped and the lights went up, you could see their faces as if to say, 'Who are you?'. It was weird but amusing. The first number stopped, the other surrogate band members went off and I was on a drum riser which disappeared under the stage during the next number.

**Andy Bown:** After the first number, we were playing around the back, behind the wall. Roger didn't really play much bass, to be honest. It didn't go out through the front PA.

**Gerald Scarfe:** It always amazes me to see the end result of what started as a few scribbles on a piece of paper. Roger and I had sat for hours, planning the show in detail, and here it was in reality – a gigantic Roman circus.

**Richard Wright:** The trouble is, as we were playing, you had roadies running around, putting bricks up. I never saw most of the show because we were hidden behind the wall. It was bizarre, but also funny to be playing with an audience that couldn't see you, and all the road managers casually walking around and having a chat and it didn't matter because nobody could see them.

**Gary Yudman:** There was a timing for everything and there was stuff going on the whole time backstage – an inflatable schoolmaster being blown up, people prepping the wall, getting the bricks ready...

**David Gilmour:** I had a six-foot-long cue-sheet draped over my amplifier for the first few shows. Someone out front would press a button and, ten or twenty seconds later, something would start happening. So you had to know what you were doing and stick with the programme.

**'Willie' Wilson:** You were playing the same thing every night to a click track and it had to be in time to the films or the projections of hammers and flowers. I had to wear headphones with the sound of David counting bars off. There wasn't much room for inspirational ad-libbing.

**Gerald Scarfe:** The marching hammers idea just came to me. Roger talked about the forces of oppression and I thought of the most oppressive, unforgiving instrument – and it was a hammer. They were simple in animation terms, as they were only seven drawings on repeat. But the fucking flowers took forever because each one took a couple of days and there were twelve drawings a second.

**Gary Yudman:** Roger took me aside after the first night and showed me a script. It said: 'The MC comes out and talks to the crowd and gets them so pissed off as they want to see the band.' Roger said, 'I want this, Gary. Can you make them angry? Can you do it?'. I said, 'I am an actor. I do this for a living.' So, the next night, I started reading out all these regulations, like, 'Please no fireworks. There will be enough explosions in your mind.' But I talked really, really slowly, so everything I said took three times as long as it should, and it went on and on and on… and got everyone pissed. Roger seemed delighted.

✤

*The wall was slowly built, brick by brick, as Pink Floyd and their understudies performed 'Another Brick in the Wall, Part 2', 'Mother', 'One of My Turns'…. Before 'Young Lust', Waters summoned Floyd's inflatable pig down from the rafters to glide over the masses, looking porky and malevolent.*

*The first half ended with 'Goodbye Cruel World'. As Waters uttered the final line, the last brick was slotted into place and the house lights came up. The audience were confronted with a wall obscuring the stage and spanning the entire width of the arena.*

*The backstage landscape of astroturf, picnic umbrellas and plastic chairs was broken up by four caravans – one for each band member – with their entrances all facing in opposite directions; the perfect metaphor for a group that was falling apart.*

*The second half began with Waters backstage, singing 'Hey You' to a brick wall. 'It was nice to be able to stand a foot from a solid cardboard thing, singing at it. I liked that. To have that wall there made the song more powerful.'*

*During 'Nobody Home', bricks were removed to reveal Waters as Pink, in a mock-up of a motel room, complete with a flickering TV set and an armchair liberated from West Hollywood's Tropicana Inn.*

*The second part's big production number followed. During 'Comfortably Numb', in which Pink tumbles into a narcotic haze after his injection, a spot-lit David Gilmour appeared on the top of the wall. To get him there, the crew created 'Dave's Pulpit', a wooden box acting as a platform with a smaller box as a step, on top of a hydraulic lift. A safety rail was added as a cursory nod to health and safety, but the rules were looser then.*

*The pulpit ascended as Waters sang the opening line. Then a single white light picked out Gilmour voicing the second verse – 'There is no pain, you are receding...' – more than thirty feet up in the air while his guitar tech, Phil Taylor, crouched below, like a roofer's mate holding a ladder.*

✣

**Roger Waters:** The audience must have been looking at this wall and thinking, *Fucking hell! What's going to happen now?*

**Bob Ezrin:** Roger couldn't stop me seeing the show. I still went to the Nassau Coliseum, but I had to buy a ticket. New York was my territory, so when Pink Floyd's security said 'He can't come in', all the security who knew me from working with Kiss said, 'Like hell he can't!'. I went backstage in the interval and I think Roger hid in his dressing room.

**Roger Waters:** Backstage was pretty separatist – separate trailers, none facing each other – with all our little camps. The atmosphere was awful, but the show was so important that I don't think that affected me at all.

**Richard Wright:** Why did I agree to play the tour? Maybe I couldn't handle the idea of just standing up and saying, 'Right, that's it. Bye-bye.'

I thought, *If I'm going to leave, at least I know I've got another month or so to carry on working* – possibly with the hope that things might change.

**Andy Bown:** I didn't have to worry about the politics, but the politics grew on me. It was a bit tense. Rick was really nice, but he was on the outside.

**Roger Waters:** I wouldn't do the Philadelphia shows [promoter Larry Maggid offered the band $1 million to stage *The Wall* at Philadelphia's JFK Stadium] and I had to go through the whole story: 'You've all read my explanation of what *The Wall* is about.' It's three years since we did that last stadium [in Montreal, 1977] and I always said we'd never do it again. So there was a lot of talk about whether Andy Bown could sing my parts, but in the end they bottled out.

**David Gilmour:** Going on tour without Roger never got beyond a band fantasy/joke. We never seriously considered doing *The Wall* without Roger.

**Gary Yudman:** I saw some friction, but most of the time they were just polite English gentlemen. Each had their own trailers, but we sometimes had dinner backstage, like a theatrical troupe. I went there expecting drugs and saw none of that. One night, I saw Nick and Rick eating cheese sandwiches in the hotel lobby. I remember Andy Bown saying to me, 'Roger really likes you, and respects what you do.' Roger must have thought it worked well enough for them to invite me to England, to MC when they played Earls Court.

**David Gilmour:** It was a fantastic moment, standing up there on top of the wall for 'Comfortably Numb'. Every night there'd be this sort of gasp as the audience looked up and saw me.

**Nick Mason:** At a normal gig, when the audience responds, you know you're getting through. Here, we couldn't always see the audience. But when the spotlight picked out David on top of the wall, you could feel the thrill, even backstage.

**Gary Yudman:** My cue to go on stage again was 'Comfortably Numb'. I would come on for the second half with my hair greyed out and my face covered in death make-up. Roger and I always passed each other in the wings as he came off. One night he glanced up, and just said, 'You're very *weird*, Gary.' I took that as a huge compliment.

**Andy Bown:** It was exciting being behind the wall and playing, but it came down at the end [during 'The Trial' and the chanting lyric – 'Tear down the wall']. It collapsed badly one day. We were in scaffolding cages and when it collapsed, a bit of metal came down. David grabbed me by the neck and pulled me out the way as a scaffolding pole whizzed past my earhole.

**Gary Yudman:** Some nights the wall would be taken down with great pride and other nights it was, 'Ah, fuck it!', and the whole thing was physically shaken down.

**Allan Jones (reviewing the Earls Court show for *Melody Maker*, 8 August 1980):** 'If Roger Waters had hung around much longer, I'd have been down the front with a trowel and a bowl of cement, helping the bugger brick himself up.'

**Guy Pratt (Pink Floyd's session and touring bassist):** I was eighteen and dressed like I was in the Clash, but I got in to see *The Wall* for free because I used to drink in the same pub as the hall manager at Earls Court – a Geordie lad called Neville. He could get you into anything, whether it was the boat show or Pink Floyd.

This was post-punk London and I was very much on the other side of the fence, but I loved *The Wall*. The first time I heard 'Run Like Hell' was on the John Peel show, and I remember thinking, *Oh, maybe it is okay to listen to Pink Floyd*. But the one thing I remember from the show was Roger having this big tirade against Allan Jones of *Melody Maker*. I thought, *Wow, he's really playing this vicious rock star character well*.

**Roger Waters (speaking to the audience, Earls Court, 8 August 1980):** 'Gonna do a song in a minute for all the disco freaks in the audience, also for the paranoids and the psychopaths, also for Allan Jones of the *Melody Maker*, you stupid shit...'

**Nick Kent:** At one point, Waters did this splenetic rant along the lines of, 'This is for all the people that like disco...' – as if anybody that liked that kind of music was some kind of leper, as if to say, 'What I am doing is high art. Now get this – all you peasants.' When you saw Waters, his sense of contempt for the rest of the world was very palpable. His eyes were just burning with disdain.

**David Gilmour:** I know things like *Spinal Tap* came out later with their wonderful Stonehenge set, but *The Wall* all seemed to have a meaning and a point, and if mockery was going to stop us it would have stopped us many years before.

❦

*There were changes when* The Wall *shows resumed in the new year. On 8 December 1980, John Lennon was shot dead outside his New York apartment building. When* The Wall *began an eight-date run at Dortmund's Westfalenhalle in February 1981, Waters was accompanied by two bodyguards, adding to the growing sense of dislocation and paranoia.*

*'Snowy' White had also left the surrogate band to resume his position full-time with Thin Lizzy. He was replaced by former Liverpool Scene guitarist Andy Roberts and the German comic actor Willi Thomczyk was hired to MC in Dortmund. Thomczyk failed to impress the band and Gary Yudman returned for further dates at Earls Court in spring 1981. The shows were filmed so that footage could be spliced into a forthcoming* Wall *movie.*

❦

**Gary Yudman:** I heard it didn't go so well with the German MC. Apparently, he took himself a little too seriously and got a pie in the face on the final night.

**Roger Waters (on stage to Willi Thomczyk on the final night in Dortmund):** 'We have a little surprise for you, wanker!'

**Andy Roberts (the new surrogate 'David Gilmour'):** I met David at the end of 1980 when I was playing the Dominion Theatre with Roy Harper. He liked my Cadillac-green Gretsch and rang me the day after and asked if I was available to take over from Snowy in February. It took me one-and-a-half seconds to say yes.

When I joined, they said, 'We have been offered so much money for these dates in Germany, we can't refuse. It's not a tour, but we set up in Dortmund. That's it, play and go home.' I got £500 a show – a heck of a lot of money back then.

But there was a lot of weird delusional stuff going on. The great unwashed had no idea who Pink Floyd were as people. But a couple of security guards had been hired to look after Roger. So you had these great big blokes with earpieces sat there waiting around the hotel. Then Roger's wife, Carolyne, would ring down and ask them, 'Er, can you take the kids shopping?'

**Roger Waters:** The album was so successful that any downside in terms of the show was irrelevant. We always knew it wouldn't make a profit. You can't put on a performance like that for fifteen shows and expect to make money.

**Andy Roberts:** I think we became the tenth biggest industry in Dortmund. They even threw a civic reception for us with the mayor. The scale of the thing was monstrous. They had 160 people running the show and four of them were accountants. But each night was different. They block-booked the place to a different country. One day they'd sell all the tickets in France, the next Spain, Portugal and so on.

At the end of the run, I sat down with one of the accountants as he did his calculations. He said, 'Okay, I'll make the deductions for room service, phone calls and DB…' I said, 'DB?' 'Yes, drugs bill.' It was all on account. If you wanted a bit of weed or Charlie, one of their guys would come along and charge it to your bill.

Then the accountant said, 'How do you want to be paid? Pesetas, lira, sterling?' 'Er, what do you recommend?' 'Well, the exchange rate is very good on the Deutschmark. Why don't you take it in that?' Okay, fine. I'd stepped up a division, I'd gone out with an arena stadium band. But I still came home from Germany with my jacket pockets bulging and this was the days when thirty quid was your maximum takeout. If you came back with thousands, they thought you were a drug baron.

**David Gilmour:** Alan Parker [*The Wall* movie director] and the film people came to see the show in Dortmund. Having done that, they wanted to use stuff from the show, so we went back to do the whole thing again at Earls Court to get film for *The Wall*.

**Gary Yudman:** Willie Wilson collapsed sick on the first night back at Earls Court and his drum roadie took over. That was like something out of a Hollywood movie. The show must go on!

**Andy Roberts:** Willie was sat backstage, then he went rigid, his seat tipped back and next thing he was on the floor. But I don't know who looked whiter – Willie or Nick Mason's drum tech Clive [Brooks] when Roger called him to his caravan and said, 'Clive, put this shirt on now.' Of course, Clive knew the show better than any of us. He was note perfect.

**Gerald Scarfe:** At one point, I was meant to be directing the movie with Alan Parker as the producer. We filmed Earls Court and it was very uncomfortable because every time I put my lights on to film, fans would start shouting that I was spoiling the show.

**Andy Roberts:** At the time, we were told that *The Wall* [the film] was going to be the concert cut in with some other dramatic footage. To make it an economic reality, they had to go back to Earls Court for these extra dates. Every night, I used to start the second part of the show playing a solo on an acoustic guitar. My cue to start playing was a camera crane on a cherry picker that swept over the wall and down into the audience. It was all about the film.

**Alan Parker (*The Wall* movie director):** The concert was rock theatre on a mammoth scale – a giant, raging Punch and Judy show. The sound was awesome – Roger's primal screams, the fears of madness, oppression and alienation cutting through the cordite smoke like fingernails on a blackboard.

**Richard Wright:** I put everything I could into the performances and I think Roger approved of that – and we would talk civilly to each other.

**Nick Mason:** I think it's a shame and looking back I feel guilty. The one thing about it was that Rick was the only one to make any money from *The Wall* shows. We had to stand the cost of the shows and Rick was paid a fee for doing them.

**Richard Wright:** I made a little money – $5,000 a show or something.

**Gary Yudman:** I was so impressed by the theatricality, the masks, the crashing aeroplane, Roger in his lonely little room, David on top of the wall. But it was also disorientating. I went to *The Wall* movie premiere and Steve O'Rourke told me, 'Your voice is in the background, Gary.' You sort of hear it, but mixed in with something else when Bob Geldof [the musician/actor playing Pink] is lying on the floor of a bathroom.

After we were done, I went back to New York, went about my business and later became a voiceover artist. I used to get Christmas cards from David Gilmour for a while. Then I was in a music store in LA a few years ago and there was a live album of *The Wall* [2000's *Is There Anybody Out There?*] playing and I heard my voice. I was like, 'Should I get money for that?'. I spoke to the authorities and they said I'd signed something twenty years earlier. Damn! The remuneration may be lacking, but I have never ever seen a musical production like it, before or since.

**Andy Roberts:** At the end of the run, the accountant paid me the rest of my fee out of the petty cash box and gave me one of those pink cash slips you buy in WH Smiths. I stashed the *Wall* money in a shoebox under my bed and bought groceries with it for the next five years. *The Wall* was a once-in-a-lifetime experience. After it was over, I was back to my regular gig, playing in the pub with Hank Wangford.

**Andy Bown:** Three days after Pink Floyd, I went out on tour with Status Quo. But *The Wall* was the best live show I have ever been involved with. I hadn't done any acting since *Toad of Toad Hall* at school. I still have my mask of Roger's face. In fact, it's sitting on my mantelpiece and I'm looking at it while I talk to you. Do you know anyone who might want to buy it?

✲

*One of Gerald Scarfe's next projects after* The Wall *was an animated opening sequence for the BBC's new political satire,* Yes Minister. *Since then, his art has skewered countless politicians, including Margaret Thatcher, Bill Clinton and Donald Trump. But his association with Pink Floyd endures and, in his words, 'changed my life'.*

*Some years ago, Scarfe received a letter and a VHS tape from the US. 'This guy had filmed himself having one of my images from* The Wall *tattooed on his arm,' says Scarfe. 'Apparently he had my drawings all over his body. You could see someone mopping up the blood running down his arm, but he wanted my signature so he could have that tattooed as well.'*

*The Scarfe superfan was in the military and had recently served in the Gulf War. 'He said, "Your images and the music helped me to survive that awful place." And at the very end, he said, "In honour of your great work I want to send you my Gulf War medal." And he did. He sent me his Gulf War medal.'*

*Scarfe immediately sent the medal back. 'I told him, "I'm just the artist". But it showed me the effect the music and the images have had on people. It's so evocative.'*

# 10

# 'THEN ONE DAY YOU BECOME THE CHAIRMAN OF COCA-COLA'

*'Where are my* towels?'*, banana cakes at night,*
*'Your rib cage wouldn't allow it', and sex with Arabs...*

✲

Sometime in 1980, Gerald Scarfe visited Roald Dahl at his house in Buckinghamshire and asked the famous children's author if he'd write a script for the movie *Pink Floyd – The Wall*. Dahl had never listened to Pink Floyd and, after weeks of umming and aahing, offered Scarfe an unused synopsis for a different film with the words, 'Could you use this?'

What, though, would the author of the children's fantasies *Charlie and the Chocolate Factory* and *James and the Giant Peach* have made of *The Wall*? After all, Scarfe's scorpion wife alone could have come straight out of Dahl's twisted imagination. Sadly, we'll never know.

The original plan was for Scarfe and cinematographer Michael Seresin to direct the film, with the acclaimed British director Alan Parker producing. Brainstorming sessions at Waters' house resulted in what Parker called 'a lunatic storyboard', where *The Wall*'s music and lyrics drove a movie that 'fused different cinematic techniques, live action, animation and no conventional dialogue'.

However, when Scarfe and Seresin clashed and investors proved reluctant to invest, Parker assumed the role of director. Scarfe and Waters agreed to this, but quickly realised they'd given up control of the movie. In their minds, 'The Wall' stage show was the spine of the film, around which other elements would emerge. Fresh from making the Academy

Award-winning prison drama *Midnight Express* and kids' caper *Bugsy Malone*, Parker had other ideas.

Filming began in September 1981. Bob Geldof, lead vocalist with the Irish new-wave group the Boomtown Rats, was cast as Pink, alongside Bob Hoskins as his manager and Alex McAvoy as his nightmarish teacher.

Geldof's first acting role proved to be a baptism of fire: he had his eyebrows shaved with a cut-throat razor; was dressed as what Waters called 'a fascist demagogue' wearing Nazi-style insignia and trailed by skinhead disciples; smashed up a hotel suite with bloodied hands; and almost drowned in a swimming pool.

Meanwhile Burnham Beeches in Buckinghamshire became the Anzio Bridgehead, where Pink's father, like Eric Fletcher Waters, was killed in action; a gang of south-east London skinheads were recruited to riot at the Becton Gasworks; and the wall itself was finally destroyed by an air cannon borrowed from the latest James Bond film set...

✿

**Official synopsis, *Pink Floyd – The Wall*:** 'Pink sits locked in a hotel room somewhere in Los Angeles. Too many shows, too much dope, too much applause, a burned out case on the TV and all too familiar war film flickers on the screen. We shuffle time and place, reality and nightmare as we venture into Pink's painful memories. And inevitably, into his madness...'

**Roger Waters:** The original scripts were about the story happening around a rock 'n' roll show and us performing and bombing the audience – a strange, surreal thing – and it wasn't until Alan Parker became involved that we dropped the idea of using any live footage.

**Gerald Scarfe:** Alan Parker took over because he had the clout in Hollywood. If he directed, they would put the money in. So I stepped aside and was relieved, as I had enough to do with the animation.

Parker was always very complimentary about my work. He was once quoted as saying the reason he wanted to make the film was because of my flower sequence in the show. I had nothing against Parker to start with. But Roger and I had worked on *The Wall* since it was a baby. So when it came to the film, Roger and I didn't want to relinquish power and Parker, quite naturally, didn't want two other people sticking their oar in. We all lived together rather uncomfortably.

**Bob Geldof (musician/actor):** The Rats were in Ibiza making [their fourth album] *Mondo Bongo* when Alan Parker called. I thought it was a bit weird and very flattering. But I was reluctant. If the Rolling Stones had rung and said, 'Would you be in a movie of *Exile On Main Street*?', I'd have still said no.

I told them, 'I'm not crazy about the record, I don't want to be in a film, the money is shit, plus I'm in a punk-rock outfit and this is going to damage our credibility.' But Parker kept on and on...

I eventually said to my manager, 'I'll open this script at any page you like. I'll read it and if you don't laugh, I'll do the film.' And he starts laughing because I read it in a stupid way. I said, 'That's it' and threw the script at him.

**Roger Waters:** Bob was in a taxi at the time and told his manager 'I hate Pink Floyd' and his manager said, 'I think doing this film will be good for your career.' What he didn't know was that the taxi driver was my brother.

**Bob Geldof:** Yeah, it was a random black taxi and the driver was Roger Waters' brother. So I agreed to do a screen test ... Roger was pleasant enough when we met, but he wasn't all 'Hail fellow well met'. Afterwards, we went back to his beautiful house and there were fifteenth-century portraits on the wall and a snooker table. We played snooker and my memory is I kept winning, much to his annoyance. So we kept playing until he won a game and then it was 'Oh, time for bed...'.

**Alan Parker:** Geldof had his first taste of filming sitting in a chair in an alien landscape, choking on our smoke machines. Destroying the hotel room took no time at all. Bob launched himself into each take with equal ferocity, cutting his hands quite badly until there was little left to break and we stopped to patch him up before he lost too much blood.

**Bob Geldof:** When I had to throw a telly out of the window, I said to Parker, 'Listen, if it doesn't break can I keep it?'. And he said, 'Yes, if you want to.' So I put two mattresses under the window and if you look at the scene, I'm throwing it very gingerly.

**Roger Waters:** The skinheads section was supposed to show how a character disintegrates when he becomes isolated, and how society disintegrates if we allow ourselves to become isolated from one another.

**Gerald Scarfe:** I worried about the skinheads because I was worried I had invented this Hitler-like symbol, because they were cutting the crossed hammers into their hair and having it tattooed onto their arms. But I was railing against the things I was drawing. I was saying, 'This is completely wrong'.

**Alan Parker:** I do ask a lot of the audience. The mind will constantly work to keep up with the eye. It's difficult to juggle all the language of film we use in *The Wall*.

**Gerald Scarfe:** It wasn't pure vitriolic hatred all the time. But there was Parker on one side and me and Roger on the other, and Parker did things we didn't like, and that was when the war started. I used to drive to Pinewood Studios at nine in the morning with a bottle of Jack Daniel's on the passenger seat so I could have a slug before I went in – and I'm not a heavy drinker. People also tell me I started swearing a lot.

**David Gilmour:** Alan Parker and Roger rowed so badly during the making of the film that Parker walked out. We had to persuade him to come back because there was big money invested. The entire film crew at Pinewood were going to remain loyal to Alan Parker because he's a film-maker, and not to Roger Waters.

In my view, then and now, it wasn't workable. But we had to go through this ridiculous power thing. The film is the least successful of the three ways of telling that particular story. Roger may have been right in as much as it wasn't going as well as it should have done, but that doesn't alter the fact that it was unworkable to stop it and for Roger to take over.

**Alan Parker:** Roger and I were both obdurate to a fault. Or, as my long time producer, Alan Marshall, eloquently put it, 'two egotistical, opinionated fuck-pigs'.

**Roger Waters:** The rest of the guys in the band had criticised 'When the Tigers Broke Free''s inclusion on *The Wall* on the grounds that it was too personal to me. It's very specific about time and place, and would have made it clear that *The Wall* was about me. [The song, about Waters' father's death, was used in the film and released as a single in July 1982.]

**Bob Geldof:** They said they wanted me to sing 'In the Flesh [Part 2]' for the film because it made no sense me miming it. I said, 'I'm not going to sing a Pink Floyd song. I sing Boomtown Rats songs ... I am not doing it unless I get more money.' This went on and I didn't show up for a couple of days. Eventually, they agreed to a bit more money.

I went down to Dave Gilmour's studio and James Guthrie was there. I said, 'Do you want me to sing it like Roger?' 'No,' they said. 'We want you to sing it as you would sing it.' I wasn't familiar with the album, but I'd heard the song many times and I'd learnt it. The control room was up high and I had to look up at the glass to see them. I said, 'What attitude do you want from this?' 'The way you do it in the role,' they said.

So I did it. Silence. 'Just do that again.' So I did it again. Silence. 'Is that the way you'd normally sing?', they asked. I said 'Yeah'. They said, 'It sounds a bit weird.' I said, 'That's what I normally do in the Rats. Do you want me to do it a different way?' 'No, do it a few more times.'

So I did it a few more times and I could see Gilmour and Guthrie staring down. Then they said, 'I don't think this is working. Could you try it more with Roger's attitude?' I was pissing myself laughing. They didn't want to say, 'Could you do it a little less Irish?'

**Alan Parker:** I never had the advantage of going to film school, so this is probably my student film – the most expensive student film in history.

**Bob Geldof:** I was looking at the film through parted fingers thinking, *God, I look such a cunt ... I could have done that much better.* I didn't like myself in it. But I'm forced to admit Pink Floyd are an extraordinary band. If you torture me, I am prepared to say that *The Dark Side of the Moon* is one of the seven pillars of rock 'n' roll.

❈

*On set, Alan Parker blasted out songs from* The Wall *to keep his actors and crew in the moment. He also borrowed ideas for some of the hand-held camera shots and close-ups from the French director Abel Gance's pioneering silent movie,* Napoleon.

*While cinematically brilliant,* Pink Floyd – The Wall *became a series of set pieces, resembling one long ninety-nine-minute pop video. What did it all mean? 'It's about a mad bastard and his wall, innit?' said one senior member of the production when asked.*

*The film cost £7 million and received its first public screening at the Cannes Film Festival. Pink Floyd's crew had installed a sound system into the Palais cinema; so powerful that flakes of paint and plaster rained down from the ceiling like shrapnel once the music began.*

Pink Floyd – The Wall *opened at London's Empire Leicester Square in July 1982 and a month later in the US, where it earned $22 million in a year.* 'The Wall *is a stylised work of satire and caricature,' Waters told Karl Dallas. 'And an attack on parts of myself that I disapprove of, a sort of exercise in self-flagellation.'*

*A plan to release a new album, with the working title* Spare Bricks, *with songs from the film and new material, was modified when an actual war broke out. In April 1982, Argentinian military forces claimed the neighbouring British province, the Falkland Islands, as their own. Prime minister Margaret Thatcher sent the British military to the South Atlantic to take the islands back by any means necessary.*

*Argentinian forces surrendered after seventy-two days of bloody conflict. The sinking of the Argentine cruiser, the* General Belgrano, *and the deaths of 368 crew members was celebrated in the right-wing newspaper the* Sun *under the headline 'Gotcha!', as the government stoked the flames of nationalism before the following year's general election.*

Spare Bricks *evolved, as Waters funnelled his rage about Thatcher, his father's death, the Falklands War,* all *wars and the parlous state of the world into a new song cycle.*

*Now called* The Final Cut, *and subtitled 'A Requiem for the Post-War Dream', the album was created in eight different studios between June and December 1982. Waters used the Billiard Room studio at his house in south-west London, and Gilmour his home studio at Hook End Manor, an Oxfordshire country pile purchased from Ten Years After guitarist Alvin Lee.*

*By the end of the project, Waters was working in one room with one engineer; Gilmour with another, and Nick Mason was kept busy recording church bells and skidding cars to showcase the album's immersive Holophonic sound effects system (it didn't catch on).*

*Michael Kamen, various session players and the National Philharmonic Orchestra helped get the album Gilmour called 'The Final Straw' over the finishing line...*

✲

**Roger Waters:** Argentina invaded the Falkland Islands and Margaret Thatcher, in spite of the fact that there were political manoeuvres going on to solve the crisis, decided to have a bit of a war because it would be good for her, politically – and it was. She turned from being somebody you wouldn't touch with a bargepole to a national heroine in two weeks, at the cost of several thousand lives.

**David Gilmour:** Roger and I had disagreements, but we're from the same side. I was not in favour of Thatcher going in there, but as it was our territory, it was our job to support that territory and there should have been some longer term agreement mapped out before it came to that. It seemed obvious to me at the time that there was a deliberate breakdown of communications between the diplomatic channels of Argentina and the UK in order to create a scrap.

**Willie Christie (*The Final Cut* cover photographer):** Roger's then wife, Carolyne, is my sister. At the time of *The Final Cut*, I had just split up from a relationship and was living over their garage in their chauffeur's quarters. So I was in the house when Roger was making that album in the 'Billiard Room', talking about the songs and explaining what was going through his mind. I knew all about his politics. The jingoists were all for the Falklands war and Roger and co were not. I love Roger, but boy was he tough.

**Andy Bown:** Rick was gone, so I played a bit of Hammond on *The Final Cut*. I know there were all sorts of resentments going on, but I thought it was an interesting album.

We spent so much time with Roger and Carolyne – Christmases together, going on holiday to their house in France – but after their divorce, we lost touch. Roger was an absolute demon snooker player. One time, I thought he was going to come out of the kitchen with a blindfold on – and still win. But I also noticed he'd give me a couple of brandies beforehand, so I'd play even worse.

One of the last times I ever saw him was when I took him to my bowls club as a guest. Roger played a couple of ends all over the shop and then he was on the jack at every end. All these old boys were watching and saying, 'Who *is* this?'

We had a lot of fun together for a while. But *The Final Cut* is very much a 'Roger Waters' thing, isn't it? To me, it feels more like a solo record.

**Roger Waters:** I spent a number of occasions while making this album saying to the others, 'Look, why don't I make this a solo album?' The answer would always be 'No'. Rick had gone by then and Dave wasn't interested.

**David Gilmour:** I'm certainly guilty at times of being lazy, and moments arrived when Roger might say, 'Well, what have you got?' and I'd be like, 'Well, I haven't got anything right now. I need a bit of time to put some ideas on tape.'

There are elements of all this stuff that, years later, you can look back on and say, 'Well, he had a point there.' But he wasn't right about wanting to put duff tracks on *The Final Cut*. I said to Roger, 'If these songs weren't good enough for *The Wall*, why are they good enough now?'

There were three good tracks on it, the rest of it not so good. There was 'The Final Cut', 'The Fletcher Memorial Home'... and, um, I can't remember the other one.

**Roger Waters:** *The Final Cut*'s biggest critic is Gilmour. He didn't like its politics. He didn't like this, he didn't like that. If he'd have had any kind of integrity, he'd have said, 'I don't want to have anything to do with this record.'

**David Gilmour:** Roger has stated that our political positions are radically different, and he has intimated that I was a supporter of this war. I am not a pacifist in the way that Roger claims to be a pacifist, but he is the most aggressive pacifist I have ever met. I am completely against war if it can possibly be avoided. So I do resent Roger stating my political views. The trouble with *The Final Cut* is not its political message. Its worst fault was that there was a lot of music on there I wouldn't have gone for.

**Nick Mason:** *The Final Cut* was originally intended to be the last bits of *The Wall*, with 'the final cut' meaning we still had material that hadn't been used on the record or the film. When we got into the studios, they weren't strong enough and then it was just a case of adding more material, and Roger trying to find another story for it.

**Roger Waters:** The big argument with Dave was whether he'd be getting a production credit and a point off the top for producing the record. He didn't produce the record, but he did insist on getting the production credit.

**David Gilmour:** That period during *The Wall* film through *The Final Cut* was the period where we had lost any ability to work together or communicate. I've always been partial to a drink, and I'm sure things did get a little worse, more out of control at that time.

**Roger Waters:** We were all fighting like cats and dogs. I had to do it more or less single-handed, working with Michael Kamen, my co-producer [alongside James Guthrie]. That's one of the few things the boys and I agreed about.

**Nick Mason:** On one occasion, Roger was attempting to perfect a vocal. Pitch was not coming easily and Michael hadn't said a word for some time. Instead, he scribbled with great focus on a legal pad. Eventually, Roger stormed into the control room and demanded to know what Michael was writing. Michael had decided he must have done something unspeakable in a past life and this was karmic payback. So he had written on his legal pad, line after line, page after page, 'I must not fuck sheep'.

**Roger Waters:** A lot of the aggravation came through in the vocal performance, which, looking back, really was quite tortured. But you can't expect everything to be a fucking masterpiece.

**Willie Christie:** I photographed the medals and the poppies for the album cover. The poppies weren't real as real ones don't last. So a props company made them for us, and they also made a military uniform, with a knife sticking out the back. My assistant, Ian, modelled the uniform and I shot him holding a film canister under his arm. Roger and I came up with this, as the idea was Alan Parker had stabbed Roger in the back over *The Wall* film.

David Gilmour hadn't been consulted about the cover images and I suddenly found myself stuck in the middle. I said, 'Oh, sorry David, I haven't showed you yet....' David looked at the pictures and then said, 'Actually Willie, a knife wouldn't go in like that. It would go in sideways as your rib cage wouldn't allow it to go in straight.' Thankfully, Roger ignored that comment, so we didn't have to re-shoot it.

**Richard Wright:** I didn't like *The Final Cut*, but I knew I could be quite prejudiced about it considering my situation. But I think if you ask Dave or Nick about it, they don't think it's a very good album either.

**Roger Waters:** I was in a greengrocer's shop and this woman of about forty in a fur coat came up to me. She said she thought [*The Final Cut*] was the most moving record she had ever heard. Her father had also been killed in World War II. And I got back into my car with my three pounds of potatoes and drove home and thought, *Good enough.*

✣

*David Gilmour's comment about 'three good songs' on* The Final Cut *is borne out by how his guitar solos suggest a frustrated musician seizing his moment in the spotlight. Gilmour only sang lead vocals on one song, 'Not Now John', a parody of the Little Englander mentality with a British factory worker praising Margaret Thatcher and moaning about foreigners.*

*Its 'Fuck all that' chorus was toned down (Gilmour and the backing singers sang 'Stuff all that' instead) before being issued as a single and scraping into the UK Top 30. There were insightful lyrics throughout (see: 'Southampton Dock', 'Your Possible Pasts'), but the message was diluted by repetition and the songs often felt undercooked.*

*Released in March 1983,* The Final Cut *made number one in seven countries, including the UK but not the US. In the press, Gilmour admitted the recording process had been marred by 'production issues' and what Waters called 'communication problems', while Mason insisted that his recent album,* Nick Mason's Fictitious Sports *(really, a vehicle for jazz musician Carla Bley's songs) didn't mark the start of a budding solo career.*

*Over time, Gilmour revealed just how acrimonious it had become and Waters witheringly recalled how Gilmour preferred playing the new arcade game* Donkey Kong *at London's Mayfair Studios than engaging with the music.*

*Like* Donkey Kong, *these songs about Thatcher, the Argentinian leader General Galtieri and the Soviet premier Leonid Brezhnev were inexorably of their time. It was also the most British-sounding Pink Floyd record since* The Piper at the Gates of Dawn *and must have baffled many Americans.*

*Nobody was going to 'boogie' to this stuff, and the band had no intention of touring anyway.*

*'It would be hard,' said Mason, 'to imagine a show that could follow* The Wall.*' So they all spent 1984 making solo albums instead.*

❀

**David Gilmour:** The whole Pink Floyd thing was falling down, so I thought, *I'd love to just go and have another bash*. But I decided to get some of the top guys in the world to have a bash with. So I got together a fantastic little team of players [including bassist Pino Palladino and drummer Jeff Porcaro] and went off to Paris to make *About Face*.

**Nick Laird-Clowes:** After Alfalpha, I'd gone to New York and seen all these new bands. So I'd say to David Gilmour, 'I'm going to see the Clash tonight.' And he'd say, 'What for?' I'd say, 'You're crazy. They're brilliant.' But that was our relationship. There was always this rough and tumble thing with me saying, 'Listen to this new music – The Police! "Roxanne!"' He didn't like certain things, but he loved others.

When I told him I was starting a new band, The Act, he recommended his younger brother Mark as a guitarist and let us use his home studio while Pink Floyd were making *The Wall* in France. Tony Howard managed us again, O'Rourke was bankrolling us again, but nothing much was happening. Then David started working on another solo album and asked me to go to Paris and write some lyrics. He said, 'I'm not going to give you credits, but I'll give you some money and pay the lawyer's bill.'

**Bob Ezrin:** Gilmour decided he needed some help, so he rang me and I joined them in Paris. I have very fond memories of tooling around in David's Porsche 928 – a right-hand drive in a left-hand country – going around the Champs-Élysées at breakneck speed, thinking I should be driving.

I think David felt liberated and had a good time making that record [*About Face*]. I think when he was on his own, it was a bit too much for one person, so he got me and James Guthrie in there to help and it became easier. He could breathe and create and play and not worry about the production.

**David Gilmour:** I'd met Pete Townshend at Eel Pie [Studios] around the time of *The Final Cut* and he told me he liked my first solo album [1978's *David Gilmour*]. I was a bit dumbstruck by that, but he said we should try working together. He was having difficulty writing music and had loads more words than he knew what to do with. So I sent along three or four tracks of mine and he sent me some words. We did 'All Lovers Are Deranged?' and 'Love on the Air' on my album and 'White City Fighting' for his [1985's *White City*].

**Glen Colson:** I worked on *About Face*. He's a beautiful man, David, very calm – like a Buddhist or something. But obviously he can lose his temper if you wind him up. Steve O'Rourke had record companies jumping all over the place, but I don't think he knew how they worked. He'd say to me, 'Glen, we've got a new record coming out. What do we do?' I'd come up with a few Mickey Mouse ideas. Steve would shout at me and then I'd shout at the guys who ran *The Amazing Pudding* [Pink Floyd] fanzine for information.

**David Gilmour:** I think I made the first solo album too quickly and thought too much about the second one. It was very rocky and, in some ways, I was less true to myself than the first one. 'Out of the Blue' was one of my favourites and I still like 'Until We Sleep', a song about mortality, which I never seem to escape from.

**Roger Waters:** *The Pros and Cons of Hitch-Hiking* was about sexual aspirations in the world of dreams, and about a particular dream I had and remembered upon waking. There was no swapping of songs between this and *The Wall*. They were different marriages. *The Wall* was my first marriage. *The Pros and Cons...* was the second. If I'd not given them a choice and gone to Pink Floyd with *The Pros and Cons...* and said, '*This* is the next album', they'd all have gone, 'Great!'.

***New Musical Express* (review of *The Pros and Cons of Hitch-Hiking*, April 1984):** 'Did Roger actually try hitch-hiking? Wasn't somebody sensible enough to mow the old bore down?'

**Tim Renwick:** I thought I was going to replace 'Snowy' White in the surrogate band for *The Wall* shows, but a Thin Lizzy tour got cancelled and he stayed on longer, to my disappointment. I thought at that point I was never going to do anything with Pink Floyd. Then I got the call from Roger Waters, and did the Hitch-hiking... tour.

**Roger Waters:** The Hitch-hiking... tour sold appallingly in Europe, even in London. I had to use almost all the money in advertising to get people to buy tickets. I cancelled loads of shows – and my budget was based on selling out loads of shows. So, I was about four hundred grand down at the end.

**Dave 'De' Harris (vocalist, Richard Wright's group Zee):** I was in a group called Fashion and we were in New York doing a new music seminar in 1982. A couple of guys there mentioned Rick Wright from Pink Floyd wanted to start a new band. One of them was Raph Ravenscroft, who'd played the sax on [Gerry Rafferty's hit] 'Baker Street'. I was leaving Fashion anyway, so there was me, Raph and a bass player called John McKenzie [ex-Grease Band and Man]. I can't remember who else.

It started with about six of us in a rehearsal room in London and Julian Lennon turned up one day to watch. Then Rick invited us to his studio at the Old Rectory and it became one of those typical band situations – 'Oh, I can't do next Thursday...', 'Oh my mum says no...' In the end, I said to Rick, 'Why don't we just do this together?' He told me he had a solo deal with EMI Harvest and we became a duo, Zee.

Everyone else left, and my wife Sue and I moved into the Old Rectory and lived there for about eighteen months. Rick was tumbling around in the place as he was going through a divorce from Juliette, so there were lots of ups and downs. He had a Fairlight in the studio, never used, covered in dust, and we both thought *This is a great toy* and got stuck on that one thing. But everything we did on it sounded like a fucking robot.

**Richard Wright:** We made the whole record on the Fairlight, which was an amazing machine at the time, but which now seems rather dated.

**Dave 'De' Harris:** Then Rick invited us to his beautiful house in the south of France to write lyrics. I remember being at Heathrow waiting to fly out and two teenage girls came up to us. This wasn't long after Fashion and one of them said to me, 'Can we have your autograph?'.

I thought, *This is so fucked up* and said, 'You do know who this is, stood next to me?' They both said 'No'. 'This is Rick Wright from Pink Floyd.' 'Oh, okay,' they replied. 'Can we have your autograph as well?'

So we went to France for two weeks, but just got pissed the whole time. Rick was away a lot too, flying to Greece or having his boat built, and I was left working on my own. He had a guy who looked after the house called Pink, a wonderful Canadian queen always on the phone to the wives of the other guys in Pink Floyd. I remember spending all night in the studio and he'd turn up in the small hours with some freshly made banana cakes, wearing a pinny. He was brilliant.

Really, I wanted that Pink Floyd keyboard sound with the Hammond. But getting Rick to do it was a nightmare. He just kept saying, 'Oh you do it…'. Eventually, I realised I had no idea what Rick thought of what I was doing because he never told me. I spoke to Juliette – 'I'm concerned he doesn't like this' – so she asked him and he told her, 'Oh I *love* it.'

**Richard Wright:** I always describe the Zee album, *Identity*, as an 'experimental mistake'. But it was made at a time in my life when I was lost.

**Dave 'De' Harris:** It upset me when he said it was a mistake, because it's easy to say that when you've got a body of work like Pink Floyd's. I wouldn't say I'm *not* happy with it, but it was the '80s and Rick was looking for a new thing.

I was still early on in my professional career and I wanted to be producing and writing and earning money. So a production job came up for [Kajagoogoo vocalist] Limahl and Rick got a bit upset, even though I had it going alongside what we were doing. When the Zee album came out and didn't sell, it all fell apart. It was sad, though, because I loved Rick dearly.

**Richard Wright:** After *Identity*, I went off to live in Greece, in an environment that was not very conducive to playing music. I lost touch, if you like. I was happy sailing my yacht around the Greek islands, but perhaps it was a bit of a waste of time.

❀

*All three solo albums arrived one after another in the spring of 1984 and illustrated the challenges their creators faced away from Pink Floyd.* About Face *was big on guitars and lush orchestration, but lighter on lyrics, and included a wonderful song called 'You Know I'm Right', which even then sounded like a dig at Roger Waters.*

*According to* The Pros and Cons of Hitch-Hiking, *Waters' dream involved sex, more sex and sex with Arabs, but the album was frustratingly bereft of tunes. Zee's* Identity *was the bravest of the three albums, but its electro-pop songs were a bit nouveau for Floyd's traditional fanbase.*

*Floyd's carefully nurtured anonymity meant the individuals' names on a record sleeve didn't have the same pull. Gilmour and Waters' efforts hovered around the Top 20; Wright's didn't chart.*

*On the road, Gilmour headlined theatres with a boys' club backing group which included his neighbour, Bad Company guitarist Mick Ralphs, while Waters toured arenas with a cripplingly expensive stage production designed by Mark Fisher and Gerald Scarfe.*

*In early 1985, Bob Geldof approached Pink Floyd to play his Live Aid benefit at Wembley Stadium for African famine relief. Waters offered his solo group instead, but Geldof turned him down. Gilmour appeared at the Wembley show playing in Roxy Music frontman Bryan Ferry's group, where he met 21-year-old keyboard player Jon Carin, who'd later become a co-writer and touring member of Pink Floyd.*

*Gilmour became something of a man about town as his marriage started to fall about. Instead of going home, he stayed up late, performing with Pete Townshend's new ensemble, Deep End, playing sessions for Paul McCartney and producing Nick Laird-Clowes's new group, the Dream Academy, including their charming hit 'Life in a Northern Town'.*

*It was a new beginning for Mason too, who'd split from his first wife, begun a relationship with actress Annette Lynton and formed a TV music company with 10cc's Rick Fenn, which whom he recorded 1985's* Profiles.

*Meanwhile, Waters had been plotting behind the scenes and approached Steve O'Rourke to strike a new deal in which he'd pay the manager a different percentage to his bandmates. Naturally, O'Rourke informed Gilmour and Mason of this, after which Waters attempted to have him fired.*

*The other two, as fellow shareholders in Pink Floyd Music, blocked the move. Waters wanted to pursue a solo career and, in October 1985, took out a high court application to prevent the name 'Pink Floyd' being used after his departure. Gilmour and Mason objected, but it would be twelve months before a legal decision was made.*

*Shortly before Christmas, Waters officially informed EMI and Columbia that he was leaving the group and asked to be released from any further contractual obligations. O'Rourke filed a suit against Waters for breach of management contract and retrospective commissions, although his contract with the band had been a verbal one made almost a decade and a half earlier.*

*Waters composed songs for an animated version of Raymond Briggs' Cold War allegory* When the Wind Blows *and began a second solo album,* Radio K.A.O.S., *inspired by the British miners' strike and the evils of global monetarism. But his battle with his former bandmates would overshadow even those big topics...*

✤

**David Gilmour:** Ever since *The Final Cut*, Roger had been saying, 'Let's call it a day. We've had a jolly good run.' And I'd say, 'I don't want to pack it in. I haven't had enough.' He went on like this getting more and more frustrated. He said, 'You'll never fucking get it together to make a record.' I said, 'We will make a record.' Then he said, 'Well, I'm not leaving. I will sit at the back of the studio and criticise.' But my absolutely consistent response was that I was not prepared to quit.

**Nick Mason:** I think Roger's greatest mistake at this time was to underestimate David's determination and resolve.

**David Gilmour:** Often your worst characteristics are also your best. I am pig-headed and stubborn and determined – it's true. There have been many times when that's been enormously helpful and times when it is destructive too. You could say that it has been destructive to Pink Floyd staying together because of my refusal to kowtow to what was going down. But, at the same time, what would it have become if I had kowtowed?

**Roger Waters:** Quitting the band was a difficult decision because I'd have much preferred that we stopped. I was forced to quit because they were threatening me with all sorts of things. The ensuing debacle was very painful.

**David Gilmour:** He read and understood and signed a recording contract with our record company that provided specifically for this circumstance – that, if he left, Nick and myself could carry on.

**Bob Ezrin:** Roger Waters and I had had a fairly negative relationship after the end of *The Wall*. Then I got a call from him when I was in LA, saying, 'I know I was awful to you, and I apologise, I'm a different guy from who I was back then... and I'd really like to talk to you about working together again.'

I was thrilled. He said, 'Can you come here now to England to talk about this new record [his second solo album, *Radio K.A.O.S.*]?' I said, 'No. Can you come here to LA?' He said, 'I'm not bloody going there.' So I said, 'Okay, I'll meet you in New York City.' We had a good time, laughing and telling stories, and he played me some new material and I heard exactly where I wanted to take it, where I thought it should go.

So we started to work out a deal. He insisted we start work in England in the summer and stay there working for four months through to the fall and not stop until we were finished. The first thing I pointed out to him was that he'd never done anything in four months, so that wasn't a realistic schedule. Also, what was I to do with my wife and kids? He said, 'I'll give you my house down south and we'll get your kids into the American school.'

I was so seduced by the notion of getting back with Roger that I sold my wife hard on it. At first, she refused. Then she slowly came round. I called Roger and said, 'Okay, we'll do it.' Then about ten days later, my wife broke down in tears and said, 'I'm sorry but I just can't do it.' She was more important, so I called Roger's manager Peter Rudge and said I can't do it. Roger went nuclear on me and that was it – Roger was never going to talk to me again.

**David Gilmour:** I had invested a lot in this group and I wasn't prepared to give it up and start all over again. So when Roger sent his letter to the record company in December '85, saying he was out, it was a relief. It meant we could carry on. He could have stopped us doing anything for years simply by saying that he wasn't leaving.

**Bob Ezrin:** Three weeks after Roger, I got a phone call from David. In my conversations with Roger, he'd told me he'd left the band and there was no Pink Floyd, and that the 'muffins', as he referred to them, would never dare carry on without him.

Then David called and said, 'We are thinking of doing another Floyd album. I have some songs and I'd love to come over and play them for you.' And he came over and it was fun. He said, 'You're a family man and I'm a family man. We'll work it out. Half in England, half here, and we'll work out a schedule that allows you to get back to your family.'

David was ready to make a record, but I'm not sure the others were. Everybody else had been off in their own corners. I think there was still the question of whether this legal stuff with Roger was going to get in the way, and for David it was important to get going on Pink Floyd right away. To start with, we worked on David's houseboat studio, *Astoria*, out near Hampton Court.

**David Gilmour:** I had been banned from driving for a year, being silly. So I was being driven rather than driving myself, and as you're being driven, you look out the window. As we were driving along, I saw this metalwork on the top of a wall and I said to the chap driving, 'Can we just pull over here?'... We looked down and saw this incredible boat.

**Bob Ezrin:** The *Astoria* was this Victorian barge that had been [early twentieth-century theatre impresario] Fred Karno's personal knobbing shack. David retained it intact with a studio fitted into what had been the master bedroom. The place was just enchanting, magical.

**David Gilmour:** The first month was just me and Ezrin mucking about with a lot of demos. I had lots of *bits* of songs.

**Nick Laird-Clowes:** After the Act split, I started working with a keyboard player, Gilbert Gabriel, and writing new songs as the Dream Academy. David had a new house [Hook End] and a new studio, and we were there for six months, making demos and getting absolutely nowhere.

Then David heard 'Life in a Northern Town' and said, 'This is the best thing you've ever done' and offered to mix it. Suddenly we were in the middle of a bidding war and signed to Warners. We had a hit single before the album was finished.

Next thing, David told me he was going to make a Pink Floyd album without Roger and asked, 'Do you want to work on the lyrics?'. I said, 'David I'm trying to come up with the second Dream Academy album, I can't.'

**David Gilmour:** I played on a track for Bryan Ferry [on the *Bête Noire* album] on which Pat Leonard was the producer. We got on well. Pat came down to the boat before it was properly kitted out as a studio. He jammed on keyboards and I played a fretless bass and together came up with this piece of music, 'Yet Another Movie', which we later recreated in the studio.

**Bob Ezrin:** I became fascinated with rap in the Afrika Bambaataa days and brought some in, going, 'Boy, I think this stuff with a rock beat would be awesome.' David said 'Oh my God, that would be terrible.' He hated the idea.

**David Gilmour:** At the start of *A Momentary Lapse...*, the phone would be going every five minutes with this lawyer and that lawyer. It was very tricky with Nick Mason, too. There was a period from the end of *The Wall* to *The Final Cut* where he was very dispirited. We were all made to feel like valueless people and that affected Nick and Rick, who wasn't even in it then, to a major degree. They were practically catatonic and unable to take much part in the start of the recording.

**Nick Mason:** I hadn't played seriously for four years and didn't like the sound and feel of my playing, and I struggled to play some of the parts satisfactorily.

**Bob Ezrin:** Nick hadn't been practising and just wasn't sounding like himself. Nobody wanted to make him feel bad. I'm sure quietly he was thinking, *This is a lousy situation*, but he knew he wasn't able to play up to his old standards.

**Richard Wright:** I'd become involved with someone that lived in Greece [his second wife, Franka] and I took the decision to move there to be with her. I didn't do it with the intention of getting away from the music business. But I woke up one day and thought, *God, what have I been doing?* So I phoned Dave up and we met up in Greece and he said he was planning to do another album with the Floyd.

**David Gilmour:** I was in Greece before we started on the album and I had a visit from Rick's wife saying, 'I hear you're starting a new album. Please please please can Rick be part of it?' I left it for a while before I asked him to come down, because I wanted to be sure I knew what I was doing first.

**Richard Wright:** I came back in the middle or towards the end of recording *A Momentary Lapse of Reason*. I remember having a meal with them [Gilmour, Mason, Ezrin] and Steve O'Rourke in Hampstead and I think they wanted to see how I was. I passed the test and I was invited to play on the album and do the tour.

**David Gilmour:** There was a legal issue with Rick rejoining the band as a full member, so he played a little on the album and was paid a salary [supposedly $11,000 per show] for doing the tour. By doing that, he also avoided a lot of the legal shit Nick and I were having to deal with.

**Richard Wright:** I wasn't a member of the band. We hadn't played together for years. I was paid a wage on the sessions. I did get royalties on the album – not as many as Dave and Nick though.

**Bob Ezrin:** Roger was still a presence. They had to leave the studio sometimes to go to meetings and he did actually show up at the houseboat with Carolyne and the children. Michael Kamen was trying to bring him and David together again. It was a nice gesture but I didn't feel entirely comfortable.

**Roger Waters:** They got halfway through [the album] and then scrapped it because the record company said, 'You can't get away with this. You've got to make something that sounds like a Pink Floyd record.' So they started again.

✣

*Waters first made this claim in a 1988 interview with the music critic Timothy White. Waters said Ezrin and Columbia Records' executive Steve Ralbovsky listened to the work so far and told Gilmour over lunch that 'this music doesn't sound a fucking thing like Pink Floyd'.*

*Ezrin told White that Waters' claim was an exaggeration, but that 'the point of the meeting was for me to tell David that what we had thus far was not up to* our *standard of a Pink Floyd project'. Ezrin later back-tracked on this comment.*

*Making what became* A Momentary Lapse of Reason *involved more outside assistance than previous Floyd records. Various outside writers were considered as collaborators but rejected. Finally, Ezrin, Jon Carin, Madonna's musical director Patrick Leonard and Roxy Music's Phil Manzanera became part of the process, with the lion's share of lyrics composed by Gilmour with Anthony Moore, co-founder of the left-field jazz rock group Slapp Happy. A surprise choice then – 'as I'm such a weirdo,' says Moore today.*

✿

**David Gilmour:** I started at the end of September that year and moved gradually forward. I *never* stopped and started again, despite what was said in that Timothy White article. No one ever told me to. If you think any fucking record company person was ever going to tell us what to do... We have a long, long history of just saying, 'Fuck off, you're not coming in.'

Steve Ralbovsky did come down and wanted to hear a few things. He was a mate and it's entirely possible he wasn't impressed with it. We'd only been at it for three weeks. There was a track I'd played him a year before that I'd done at home with [session drummer] Simon Phillips. It was a ripping track, but it wasn't going to fit with anything here. Steve said, 'What happened to that one?'. I said it wasn't going to make it. Whatever his thoughts were, he kept them to himself and wasn't invited to do anything else.

It *was* tough not having Roger there to talk to, to say, 'Shall we do this or do this or that?' It *was* a slow process. But each day you did something that sounded good would build your confidence. We carried on and, by Christmas, we had upped our game and were on our way forward after I wrote 'Sorrow'. I wrote the lyrics first – it's the only song I've ever written the lyrics first for. 'Sorrow' was the turning point.

**Bob Ezrin:** We acknowledged that we'd lost our main lyricist. A lot of people went through my mind and, if you're Pink Floyd, you can go ask for anything. It was great to be able to stretch a little and say, 'Boy, I'd really like to try that one and that one...'

**David Gilmour:** A lot has been made of the different writers I chatted to. There was [10cc's] lovely Eric Stewart, who's too similar to me as we both have melodic, sweet voices. The poet Roger McGough was just before we went to America, but it just didn't quite gel, and Carole Pope was a two-second diversion by Bob Ezrin.

**Carole Pope (Canadian songwriter):** It was January of 1987 and they were looking for somebody to rewrite a batch of David Gilmour's material, so I went over to England for a few weeks. Bob and David also asked me if I had any idea for concept albums in the Pink Floyd style. By the time I left England, they still couldn't decide what to do.

**Phil Manzanera:** I was being managed by Steve O'Rourke and when David started working on *A Momentary Lapse of Reason*, we put a track together [which became 'One Slip']. Months later, Steve took me out for a very nice lunch and explained that Pink Floyd needed the publishing rights to my track, and I had to accept whatever percentage I got. Pink Floyd are very protective about copyrights. But I was thrilled to have contributed to a Pink Floyd album.

**David Gilmour:** Roger's a hard act to follow. I thought I needed help and Bob definitely thought we needed help. Anthony Moore was someone I'd met socially and I got on with him.

**Anthony Moore (songwriter and lyricist):** I think I met David Gilmour in a swimming pool, but I'm not sure. It's a better story, though, so say I met him in a swimming pool. I was at art school in St Albans in 1967 or whenever and remember 'Set the Controls for the Heart of the Sun', though I was more into the Soft Machine.

I'd been working in Germany before coming back to England in 1973 when Slapp Happy signed to Virgin. So I was mingling with Henry Cow and Kevin Coyne and that amazing stable of early Virgin people. *The Dark Side of the Moon* wasn't really on my radar.

**Bob Ezrin:** The guy who was the most pro-active was Anthony Moore. He was fun to write with ... Incidentally, Roger Waters was fun to write with. He was just difficult to live with.

**Anthony Moore:** I didn't know I had any competition, that there were other writers around. But that probably says more about my naivety than anything else. I remember lots of sit-down meetings with Bob, David, Nick and Andy Jackson their engineer, talking about what the album could be, what sort of shape it would have. My recollection of the earliest beginnings was not as a lyricist, but more of a sounding board.

David seemed happy to have me around and so I started going down to the boat for about eighteen months, and that morphed into me writing some lyrics [for 'Learning To Fly', 'Dogs of War' and 'On the Turning Away' with Gilmour]. I think David wanted to concentrate on emotional and personal stuff in the lyrics. He didn't particularly want hardcore socialist propaganda. For 'Learning To Fly', I came up with the couplet 'tongue-tied and twisted', and Bob Ezrin in particular got very excited about that.

**David Gilmour:** Back in 1986, when we were starting *A Momentary Lapse of Reason*, Bob Ezrin did his usual thing of saying, 'Is that everything you've got? I want to hear everything.' I said, 'Well, there's this other thing here by a young synth guy, but I feel it's a bit poppy.' I played it to Ezrin who said, 'No, let's have a go at it' – eventually it became 'Learning To Fly'. Jon Carin got a credit for the groove and the first two chords and Bob and I wrote the rest. Anthony Moore, of course, wrote the words.

**Bob Ezrin:** 'Learning To Fly' was a turning point. It had a literal meaning because David and Nick were learning to fly and were both big aeroplane boys. But it was also about leaving your earthbound tendencies behind and liberating your spirit.

**Nick Mason:** I'd conquered my fear of flying by learning to fly, and David and then Steve O'Rourke also got their pilot's licences.

**David Gilmour:** Obviously there's more to the song than just learning to fly. I'm sure the lovely Anthony Moore would agree that it wasn't 100 per cent literal. That time felt like a new beginning. There was, though, the thing of me not turning up on time occasionally because I was having a flying lesson – so that part is true. That is what sparked it off.

**Anthony Moore:** That houseboat was a wonderful environment to work in. On the lawn beside it was this little hexagonal or octagonal gazebo, and I'd sit in there for hours with a pen and paper. They'd have jam sessions on the boat and bits and pieces would come out to me on cassettes.

I'd play them on a ghetto blaster and out of that came songs and skeletons of songs.

**Bob Ezrin:** The album begins with the sound of the Thames on 'Signs of Life'. I came up with the idea of a rowing sound and we went out at 5 a.m. on a Sunday with [the *Astoria*'s caretaker and designer] Langley Iddins who lived on the boat, both of us freezing our nuts off, because you had to get out there early to beat the church bells.

**Anthony Moore:** I was heavily into sampling too and had brought my sampler down to the boat to show David. I'd done some field recordings and was into the idea of incorporating them into music.

**David Gilmour:** Roger had started legal action against us to stop using the Pink Floyd name, so we were having to deal with phone calls from lawyers, day after day, while we were trying to work on the record.

**Anthony Moore:** David absorbed all this fucking hardcore legal shit and daily hours of crap. He just soaked it all up and it never changed the atmosphere while we were working.

**David Gilmour:** When we got to Los Angeles [in February 1987] to do the drums, it was fantastic because the lawyers couldn't call us in the middle of recording unless they were calling in the middle of the night, and there were loads of great session musicians we could call upon at the drop of a hat.

**Nick Mason:** With time pressure on, I surrendered some of the drum parts to the best session players in LA – Carmine Appice, Jim Keltner. Then, of course, I had to learn the parts anyway before we went on tour.

**Carmine Appice (session drummer):** I came home and there was a message on my machine from Bob Ezrin. He said, 'Hey Carmine, there's a track that's just screaming for some Carmine fills.' I said, 'Where's Nick Mason?' Bob said, 'He's a bit rusty.' So I went down and did it and Nick was there. I said, 'Why aren't you playing?' He said, 'I've been racing my cars and my calluses are a bit soft.'

❦

*In spring 1987, Waters' lawyers sent letters to promoters across the US and Canada threatening to sue if they put tickets on sale for a Pink Floyd concert. The first to ignore it was promoter Michael Cohl who advertised a Floyd date at Toronto's 60,000-seater Exhibition Centre. It sold out in less than a day, so he added two more, eventually grossing $3 million.*

*However, Gilmour and Mason had to cover the cost of these early shows, which required the recently divorced drummer to offer his 1962 GTO Ferrari as collateral before securing his half of the money. So unsure was Steve O'Rourke of their chances that he'd refused to invest in the tour.*

*Other promoters followed and more than fifty Floyd dates were booked for between September and December 1987 in the US and Canada. (The tour would go on to lap the globe and continue off and on until the summer of 1989.) This public demand added even more pressure on the redux Pink Floyd to complete the album, while Waters continued threatening legal action.*

❦

**Nick Mason:** I think *A Momentary Lapse of Reason* is great considering the duress under which it was made. But there was also a feeling we should put everything into it, including the kitchen sink. There's a lot of technology, a lot of machines.

**David Gilmour:** There are some great moments, but like most people at that time, we got trapped in that '80s thing. We were a bit too thrilled with the technology that was being thrown at us – coupled with the fact that Nick and Rick were pretty ineffective at the time. It was a difficult thing to do.

***New Musical Express* (review of *A Momentary Lapse of Reason*, September 1987):** 'Death rattles, no matter how elegantly arranged, are still terrible things to hear...'

**Roger Waters:** They tried to copy the style I'd created when I was in the band as much as they could without me being there. That's why it has that ersatz feeling. Though, having said that, there are a few tracks on *A Momentary Lapse of Reason* I rather like.

**Anthony Moore:** Roger called me an old hack in some article. He said, 'They've hired this old hack'. The funny thing is I come from *so* far over in the left field, it's just not right to describe me as a hack.

**Storm Thorgerson:** I was brought back into the fold for *A Momentary Lapse of Reason*. I don't necessarily think it was to do with my talent – more to do with my historical connection to the Floyd.

**David Gilmour:** Steve and Nick wanted to get other companies to pitch for the cover. So we met up with a couple in Los Angeles, and I thought, *No way, this is not me. These ideas don't fit the ethos. This stuff is shit.* So I said, 'Can't we just go back with Storm?'. Steve and Nick weren't keen at the time because Storm was a lot of aggro to deal with. But then they came round to my way of thinking and Storm flew out and we went from there.

I'd done a drawing of an empty bed with bedside tables and empty picture frames and the bed had been slept in. It was very obviously a thing about absence. Storm went, 'Yes, okay... But how about 500 beds?'

**Storm Thorgerson:** There was a lyric in the song 'Yet Another Movie' that read 'a vision of an empty bed' and I suggested a line of beds stretching as far as the eye could see. So we found as many Victorian wrought-iron hospital beds as we could and shot them on Saunton Sands in Devon [at a cost of £50,000].

**David Gilmour:** If I am completely honest, I think I probably gulped a bit. I remember saying to Storm, 'Can't you just have twenty beds, and draw the rest in?' And he said, 'No, it has to be done for real.'

✣

Thorgerson's high-concept cover screamed 'This is Pink Floyd!'. Inside, A Momentary Lapse of Reason sounded enough like the old Floyd, just with a ritzy '80s production and some heavy lifting from members of Supertramp, Little Feat, Rod Stewart's band and session bassist du jour Tony Levin.

The first voice heard was Nick Mason's. 'When the childlike view of the world went, nothing replaced it,' he murmured, in a nod to Syd Barrett during 'Signs of Life'.

A sample of Mason's speech recorded during his first solo pilot's flight – 'Flaps set, ten degrees ... get ready for departure' was used in the next song, 'Learning To Fly'. The gulf between Pink Floyd's world and Barrett's couldn't have been greater.

'Learning To Fly' was the LP's curtain-raiser, 'One Slip' the pop song and 'Sorrow' its 'Comfortably Numb'. But some of the rest, 'A New Machine, Parts 1 & 2' especially, seemed a bit too beholden to those machines.

The album sounded big, though, and 'big' was on point for September 1987, the era of Def Leppard's Hysteria and U2's The Joshua Tree. A Momentary Lapse... was denied the top spot by Michael Jackson's Bad in both the UK and US album charts, but still became a multi-platinum hit.

What it demonstrated best was that the Pink Floyd brand was stronger than the sum of its parts. Waters' Radio K.A.O.S. beat A Momentary Lapse... to the shops by three months, but failed to reach the Top 20 anywhere.

In 2019, Gilmour oversaw a remixed version of A Momentary Lapse... which dialled back on the '80s technology and added Wright's previously lost Hammond organ parts to create what Gilmour called 'a more timeless feel'.

If the album's success was a Pyrrhic victory, it was still the best validation the duo could have hoped for. With Waters threatening to freeze the group's assets, Gilmour and Mason had paid for the recording themselves (more than $3 million) and only received the record company's advance after they delivered the music.

Meanwhile, set designer Paul Staples and The Wall's lighting and production director Marc Brickman were tasked with bringing the show into the modern age. Those old standbys – the pig, the aeroplane and the circular screen – were joined by an industrial-looking metal-grated stage, red and green lasers, and four moving robotic lighting pods nicknamed 'The Floyd Droids' or 'The Daleks'.

The band scrubbed up, too, with Gilmour trading his usual jeans for a vogueish designer suit. 'But the mid-'80s were pretty disastrous fashion and hair wise,' he said. 'I don't think anything was suiting me particularly.'

Personnel-wise, this was a different sort of Floyd tour too. Peter Gabriel's regular bassist Tony Levin was in the running before the job went to Guy Pratt, who'd previously worked with Icehouse and Bryan Ferry. 'I got the gig because Tony Levin wasn't available,' said Pratt. 'It was as simple as that.'

Pratt, Jon Carin, percussionist Gary Wallis and backing vocalists Margaret Taylor, Durga McBroom and Rachel Fury were all twenty-somethings; the American saxophonist Scott Page was just in his thirties, while the tour's relative veteran was Tim Renwick, a contemporary of Gilmour's from Cambridge.

Wallis and Page were also performers: the former athletically walloping drums and cymbals from inside a percussion cage, while Page (whose resplendent mullet deserved its own postcode) sometimes strapped on a guitar to throw shapes – until asked not to.

Every date sold out and promoters plied them with tickets to the best clubs in town; shows in Washington DC resulted in a tour of the White House. There was a Three – or, rather, Ten – Musketeers spirit of 'all for one and one for all', regardless of seniority or bank balance. Several of the party routinely stayed up too late, aided by the crew's 'ambience co-ordinator', a New Yorker with a seemingly endless supply of cocaine.

In the meantime, Roger Waters had taken Radio K.A.O.S. on the road, with another set designed by Mark Fisher and Jonathan Park. Battle commenced between the two camps, but there was an immediate disparity. While

*Pink Floyd were playing stadiums, Waters and his Bleeding Heart Band sometimes struggled to fill arenas.*

*'If one of us was going to be called "Pink Floyd", it should have been me,' said Waters at the time. 'That's my pig up there, that's my plane crashing... and it's their dry ice.'*

❦

**David Gilmour:** I thought the tour should be big and spectacular – play the new album in the first half, do a greatest hits thing in the second. When the tickets went on sale for Toronto four months before the album was finished and sold out, I thought we really had better be good.

So we ended up with about ten different teams working on all aspects of the show and you only know for real what's going to work in rehearsals. We rehearsed for about a month in Toronto and it was a nightmare trying to juggle everything. You needed a dozen of me.

**Bob Ezrin:** David called me up in August '87 and they were going out in September. He said to me, in his inimitable style, 'I never fail to try to do these things on my own and, as always, I realise I need some help. Can you come out and help me?' I said, 'Of course.'

They were rehearsing in Toronto [in a hangar at Lester B Pearson Airport] and I found the show to be in a little disarray. The problem was, there was no producer or director on stage. David was busy working out which guitar to play and who was going to do what. He couldn't do all the other stuff.

**Tim Renwick:** Bob was quite forceful. You needed someone loud and demonstrative, which he was. He knocked us into shape, because the whole thing was just so *enormous*, with the films and the lights. It wasn't until I watched a live video later I realised everything that was going on behind me. I was completely unaware.

**David Gilmour:** Roger was threatening to stop the shows. The possibility that he might get an injunction was nerve-wracking. We were working like absolute bastards, doing phone interviews with European lawyers from nine in the morning, then going down the hangar and rehearsing until two or three the next morning.

**Guy Pratt:** It's not that David had to become a different person. He had the toolkit, but he hadn't had to use the tools because of the personalities in the band before. There are people who thrive on that responsibility – like Roger Waters. But for others, it must be like you're sitting at home and then one day you become the chairman of Coca-Cola.

**David Gilmour:** We got these extra guys in – a keyboard player to do 'Rick' and another drummer largely to do 'Nick' on tour. They needed that support, but there was a point in the first two months when the real Nick and Rick suddenly started getting back their confidence. So the second drummer could become a percussion player again.

**Bob Ezrin:** The show became more visual. It came with the territory. Gary Wallis and Scott Page were there for that. At the end of the day, a show is a show and people want excitement. There's an 'ooh aah' factor to Pink Floyd. It's all about 'Oh wow, look at that!'

**Guy Pratt:** I think David deserves some credit here because Pink Floyd wrote the book. That then became the thing. They introduced this idea of bands having these multi-generational players and longevity.

But I was amazed when they put me on stage where Roger Waters used to stand. I assumed I would be at the back – though it's not really where you are, it's how much light is on you. But I was put there just for the symmetry during 'Run Like Hell'.

**David Gilmour:** There were things I'd seen done on a small scale and I'd said to Marc Brickman, 'Can we do that and can we up the scale of it?' – like the animated laser wave going over the audience. I'd seen that somewhere and told him, 'I want that.' We were putting on a big, grand show and Marc was absolutely vital.

**Tim Renwick:** At one point, Roger was touring America at the same time as us. In some cases, he was trying to get into certain areas before, and in other places he'd hit a couple of weeks later. A bunch of us got together and went to one of his shows, to see what the competition was like. I thought it was a bit watery, really – if you pardon me, because that's a terrible choice of words.

**Guy Pratt:** A few of us went. I was with Tim Renwick, who'd played before in Roger's band. There was a moment where they shone the spotlight on the crowd and Roger was picking out members of the audience. I was *praying* the spotlight was going to land on Tim.

Our monitor guy was also dispatched, sort of undercover in a Groucho Marx nose, to report back. I remember him giving his report and hearing all these technical terms about pyros and pots and things which were all part of a Floyd show.

**Paul Carrack (vocalist, Roger Waters' Bleeding Heart Band):** The Floyd had more fireworks than we did. But some of the guys in our band knew several of the people in their camp. Having them playing down the road added a bit of spice.

**Roger Waters:** I had a wonderful band, but our concerts were rarely well-attended. Pink Floyd, on the other hand, were on tour and everywhere they played they had huge crowds, often filling up stadiums. And that hurt me very badly. However, the audience that came to my shows were simply great and, at some of the shows, I could even sense the old passion and kinship.

**Guy Pratt:** On the Floyd tour, it felt like we were all in it together. At the first couple of gigs, the local promoter sent a couple of limos and vans for the band. But David would come out of the hotel and get in the van. So you'd have the promoter in a limo with police outriders either side, an empty limo behind it, and everyone in the van behind that, with all the booze for the dressing room.

**David Gilmour:** There would be people who would make their feelings known about Roger not being there, just by shouting very loudly during moments when the rest of the audience was being very quiet. It died away, but there was one or two funny incidents. There was once a whole row of about eight guys with 'Fuck Roger' T-shirts on.

**Paul Carrack:** There was tension. I used to sing 'Money' on the *Radio K.A.O.S.* tour and my live version came out as a B-side [on 'The Tide is Turning']. I actually got death threats for that – people saying I should be shot.

**Tim Renwick:** Pink Floyd had taken the big impressive stage production, multiplied it by twenty and taken it into these enormous stadiums. Some of the ones we did on that tour probably don't exist anymore, probably closed for health and safety reasons. We'd be doing two or three nights in some, like the Cleveland Stadium, playing to about 300,000 people.

**David Fricke (writer, *Rolling Stone*, November 1987):** 'After three full hours of lasers in the face, brain-frying special effects and all those FM radio classics – 'One of These Days', 'Time', 'Us and Them', 'Welcome to the Machine', 'Comfortably Numb' – the 15,000 kids in the Montreal Forum would not budge. For nearly twenty minutes, they stood, screaming themselves hoarse, determined not to move an inch until Pink Floyd came back on stage.'

**David Gilmour:** We agreed to pay Roger $800 a night to clear us in regard to any rights he may or may not have had in various effects, including the pig and bits of animation by Gerald Scarfe and Ian Emes. Roger had gone round these people buying these rights, so he claimed he owned them. However, all of us had commissioned those pieces of work and paid for them. I do not believe he had a leg to stand on.

Someone suggested as a joke that if we altered the design of the pig, Roger couldn't claim it, so someone came up with the idea of adding testicles, as the original version had apparently been a sow. It amused us to put a pair of bollocks on our pig.

**Guy Pratt:** There's so much I would have done differently. I just wish I'd been more present. It's that old saying that 'Youth is wasted on the young'. I was being hired as a professional musician and should have been performing at the top of my game and been aware of all that stuff.

Whereas the way I treated it was I didn't want to be a professional musician. I wanted to be in a band, I wanted to be in a gang – even though these people were much older than me, but that's what I was always looking for. It was a double-edged thing because I felt ludicrously out of my depth, like I was going to get sent home any minute, but also incredibly comfortable with these people.

**David Gilmour:** I was in a marriage that seemed to be breaking up for rather a long time. I had children and didn't want to leave them, but I did want to leave the marriage.

**Tim Renwick:** David was a bit of a party animal and the manager was on a long leash as well. So when the powers that be were into whooping it up, we all joined in. There was a tremendous spirit within the band, a great feeling of liberation, so it all got quite wild.

**Guy Pratt:** At the beginning of the tour, we were doing 'Echoes' and, during 'the wind section', as we call it, you fall apart and then just come back in. Some of the younger players couldn't get their heads around it not being a set number of bars – 'How do you count that?' Well, you don't. You just feel it.

One time, David said to me in exasperation, 'The trouble with modern musicians is they just don't know how to *disintegrate*.' I reminded him of that a couple of years later, and he said, 'Well, you certainly spent the next year proving me wrong, Guy.'

I did hear from someone that, about five months into that tour, David wanted to sack me, but he couldn't because I never played a bum note, even after being up for two or three days.

**David Gilmour:** When we began touring, all we got from Roger was threats but no action. But we still had to have lawyers in every city briefed and ready to go in case it was suddenly put in front of a judge. Eventually, we got to the point where we'd made enough money to keep going even if he did get our assets frozen. As the tour and the album became more successful, all those worries evaporated until it became a minor irritation.

**Roger Waters:** I finally understood that no court in the land is interested in all this airy-fairy nonsense of what is or isn't Pink Floyd. All I'm likely to get out of it is a slice.

**David Gilmour:** I think his lawyers advised him that he hadn't a hope of winning. I met with Roger on the boat on 23 December 1987 to thrash out our divorce, with one accountant, a computer and a printer. It took a while, but we hammered it out over a few hours, printed it out, signed it – and that's the legal document we are bound by today.

**Roger Waters:** Modigliani never sold any pictures. Van Gogh peddled his pictures for a bowl of soup. Some of these geniuses never got any reward at all in their lifetimes – except the reward that comes from doing your work and understanding your connection with the mathematics of life, or God, or whatever you want to call it.

*Two specific events summed up the grand scale of the A Momentary Lapse... jaunt and the Another Lapse follow-up tour. In June 1989, Pink Floyd played five nights at Moscow's Olimpiyskiy Stadium. As Russian roubles were worthless outside the country, the group performed for free as long as their expenses and transport costs were covered. They did it because they wanted to play there and could take the loss.*

*A month later, Floyd staged a free show on the Grand Canal in Venice, opposite Piazza San Marco. The gig was broadcast live in more than twenty countries, seen by an estimated 100 million people, but blighted by disorganisation and civic corruption.*

*The authorities reneged on their promise to keep a pontoon bridge open to allow Floyd's gigantic floating stage to be towed into the canal – until money changed hands. After this, the city's gondoliers threatened to blow* *their whistles for the duration of the show, unless they were paid $10,000. 'That was one bluff we could call,' said Mason.*

*In December 1988, a cassette of the group's new live album,* Delicate Sound Of Thunder, *was taken aboard the* Soyuz TM-Z *by Soviet cosmonauts and became the first album played in outer space. Surely there was no nowhere else left to go.*

✲

**David Gilmour:** We wanted to leave no one in any doubt around the world that we were still in business and we meant business – and no one was going to deviate us from our course.

**Anthony Moore:** Pink Floyd very kindly flew me and my wife out to New York to see the show at Madison Square Garden. And did they play the Palace of Versailles? It's all a blur now, but I remember Versailles.

**Tim Renwick:** That whole tour was a bit overwhelming, because it was such a massive production. We had like 160 people in the crew. You'd finally meet people in the last week, and you'd already been around the world together and not been introduced until now.

I felt like a pretty small cog in it all and slightly disconnected from real life. It took ages to come back down to earth. What? You mean I have to empty the trash? I'd split up with my wife before the tour began. So the end of the tour meant coming back to London and trying to find somewhere to live.

**Nick Mason:** I once worked out that 90 per cent of this particular party had left a trail of broken marriages and partnerships behind them.

**Guy Pratt:** I was aware of it at the time when you start going, 'Where are my *towels*?' Because the point is, that when that all ends, and David, Nick and Rick went home, that is where they lived *all* the time.

I was so addled from all the drinking and drugs, what I should have done is probably have gone to rehab or at least just gone on holiday. But I didn't. I had no concept of holidays. All I could see was work and playing.

I'd split up with my girlfriend during the tour and bought this really shitty little basement flat. I was very messed up, but then I got asked to do the Madonna record and that just led to tons of fantastic work in LA. In a way, that was a perfect bit of running away, because LA was like being on tour. There was no consequences to everything. I guess it was a form of denial.

✲

*Almost twenty years after Venice, Moscow and* Soyuz TM-Z, *David Gilmour is at the Worx studio in Fulham, south-west London, having his photograph taken and talking about 1986. It's a blazing hot, airless day and we've convened to the small shaded courtyard.*

*Gilmour's new album,* On An Island, *recently went to number one and he's about to sell out several nights at London's Royal Albert Hall. So when a District Line tube train pauses on the bridge overhead, you can see a flicker of recognition in some of the passengers' eyes.*

*However, Gilmour seemed more relaxed in front of the photographer's camera a few minutes ago. Back then, he had the Black Strat to hide behind. Now it's just us, and a packet of Haribo sweets that the photographer has left on the table. We both tuck in.*

*Gilmour's also schlepped into London from Sussex for this. 'I had shorts on earlier,' he sighs, easing his trouser-clad backside into a plastic garden chair.*

*If he could go back in time to 1986, what advice would he give himself?*

*'Stop taking cocaine,' Gilmour replies immediately. 'I became too fond of it. I haven't touched it now for thirteen, fourteen years or something like that. But looking back, I can't think of a single redeeming feature it has, whereas I can with everything else. I got divorced and went on the razzle and it all coincided with the Floyd coming back…'*

*Was it a midlife crisis, then?*

*'I don't know whether I had a midlife crisis,' he says, carefully, and I can almost see his guard coming up. Another train pauses overhead. 'But I had... a crisis in the middle of my life.'*

*I look up to see a disbelieving face – inevitably male and fortysomething – peering at us from the train window, wondering if that really is the guitarist from Pink Floyd. And is he really eating sweets?*

## 11

# 'I DIDN'T HAVE THE TIN HELMET ON ANYMORE'

*'I went to sit with the Buddhists', A little critter, 'Have I skimped on the sex?' and 'I got distracted by my opera'...*

✲

'Do you know, I think my brother would have been much happier just playing in the pub,' says Rosemary Breen, in between sips of tea at the Red Lion Hotel in Whittlesford. 'He found "celebrity" impossible to understand and I think it was a relief for him to move on.'

When our conversation reaches the 1980s, Barrett's sister pauses; this was a difficult, often grim time. Syd had long since stopped trying to make music and had been leading a solitary life in London: staying home and watching television (home being two rented flats in Chelsea Cloisters, one of which was filled with instruments and gadgets) or drinking on his own in the nearby Marlborough Arms. He didn't have any close friends or girlfriends.

Roger Waters once saw him carrying a big bag of sweets in Harrods food hall. But none of the group had had any contact with him since his Abbey Road visit.

Winifred Barrett sold the family home in Hills Road in 1973. Sometime in 1981, Barrett walked the fifty-eight or so miles from Chelsea to his mother's new house at 6 St Margaret's Square, in the Cambridgeshire village of Cherry Hinton. He arrived looking distressed and unkempt, and was later diagnosed with a peptic ulcer.

Sadly, his mood swings soon made him a difficult house guest. After smashing the windows and scaring his mother once too often, Barrett was committed for a short stay at Fulbourn Hospital, a mental health facility on the outskirts of Cambridge.

While his ex-bandmates were taking lumps out of each other making *The Final Cut*, social services found a residential place for Barrett at Greenwoods, a therapeutic community in the village of Stock, in Essex.

Barrett remained there for several months, before walking back to St Margaret's Square, after which his mother moved in with Rosemary and her family, until her death in 1991. Barrett lived alone at number 6 for the rest of his life.

Sometime in 1982, a writer and a photographer from the French music magazine *Actuel* turned up on his doorstep, carrying a bag of clothes (velvet trousers, striped pyjamas, socks and a pullover) which Barrett had abandoned at Chelsea Cloisters. The pair took a photo of Syd and later published their brief exchange as an interview.

The more absent Barrett became, the bigger the myth grew. Over the coming years, younger musicians, ranging from the British Syd obsessive Robyn Hitchcock to American indie rockers R.E.M., now cited him as an inspiration. It was easy to see why: Syd was frozen in time, the perennial twentysomething of 'See Emily Play'. He hadn't grown middle-aged and cantankerous.

EMI released another solo Syd compilation, *Opel*, in 1988. Almost on cue, the *News of the World*, already frothing about the perceived threat of rave culture, doorstepped Barrett and published an overheated article under the headline, 'Acid Drove Pink Floyd Rock Star Up The Wall'. By doing nothing, Syd once again became the story.

✲

**Jenny Spires:** Win kept Syd's room at 183 Hills Road for him until he finally left, when she rented it out. She took students in to boost her income. When he did return in 1970 with Gala, he moved into the basement. By 1972, she had decided to sell the house and he had to remove his things and take his paintings out. Some of them he burned.

**Rosemary Breen:** He walked back to Cambridge because he had no money and nobody was paying the rent on Chelsea Cloisters. If Roger

[Syd] wanted money, he used to go to what he called 'The Office', his music publishers, and they'd give him a cheque. But they weren't paying his income tax and Roger never opened brown envelopes from the tax office. He didn't know anything about things like that. He was only a kid when he got involved with the group, so he hadn't grown up and he never did grow up, and nobody was looking after him.

**Anthony Stern:** When we were children, Fulbourn was a place of last resort, like you'd had your 'Vincent van Gogh, Cut Your Ear Off' moment. In those days, if people were incarcerated in asylums, as they were called then, they were usually lost forever. It was terribly sad to hear Syd had ended up there.

**Rosemary Breen:** We used to visit him at Greenwoods on open days. Roger [Syd] was good when he was there. There was a lot of therapy and art, and he made wastepaper baskets. I don't know what happened or what went wrong, I think he fell out with somebody and then he walked all the way home again. After that, we tried to look after him within the family, but it wasn't easy.

***Actuel* magazine (extract from a conversation with Syd Barrett, 1982):** 'What do you do in your London apartment? Do you play guitar? "No... no, I watch television, that's all." Don't you feel like playing anymore? "No. Not really. I don't really have the time to do a lot of things."

'Do you remember Duggie? "Eh... Yes... I never saw him again... I didn't visit anyone in London." All your friends say hello. "Ah... Thanks... That's nice..." Can I take a picture of you? "Yes, of course... Okay, that's enough. This is distressing for me... Thank you."'

**Rosemary Breen:** I'm not sure how genuine the Syd character was. Roger wanted to live a life as Roger. When the people who wanted him – in other words, the press – knocked on the door, he did once say 'Syd doesn't live here.' He wasn't being obtuse. It was just the truth.

**Vivien Brans:** If I saw Syd in the street after he was back in Cambridge, I wouldn't approach him. The family said it was best not to. Once I was almost walking beside him and thought, *This is surreal. I'm walking beside* *this man that I went out with as a boy*. I remember getting off a bus down Cherry Hinton Road as he was getting on and I saw a flicker like he remembered me. I was about to say hello, but then he put his head down. I spoke to him once, though. It was his birthday and I saw him pushing a trolley around Sainsbury's. I said, 'Happy birthday Rog.' He mumbled and then he was gone.

**Roger Waters:** Syd's mother always blamed me for his decline, I guess because she was uncomfortable with the idea that his illness didn't have anything to do with Pink Floyd or rock 'n' roll.

**Rosemary Breen:** I'm pretty certain he didn't have any regrets about leaving the group because I'm sure there was quite a lot he didn't enjoy. He was just playing music with his friends and it took off. He didn't really understand the fame. He just wanted to have fun and it wasn't fun touring and being asked to play when he didn't feel like it.

**Libby Chisman:** I was invited to one of Dave Gilmour's daughter's birthday parties in the early '80s. He and I sat and talked, and I mentioned that Win had told me Syd wasn't getting his royalties. Dave said, 'It's ridiculous. He should have a lot of money. I don't know what's happening.' Then Rosemary rang me and told me he'd sorted it all out.

**Rosemary Breen:** I only remember David Gilmour as a boy in his Perse School uniform cycling up and down Hills Road – that's all. I never really talked to him. But when I was looking after Roger, he was the one who kept in touch.

**Mick Rock:** David used to make sure there were Syd songs on those Pink Floyd compilations, so he was getting some money. Bryan Morrison once said to me, '*Poor* fucking Syd? Poor fucking Syd made two and a half million quid last year, because of [the 2001 Floyd compilation] *Echoes*.' He was still making a couple of hundred grand a year just from those solo albums – and he never spent any of it.

**Roger Waters:** When you go into rock 'n' roll – apart from wanting to get laid and make a lot of money – there is the great joy of being in a band and making all that noise. That's why we do it. We have holes in our psychology and performing in front of large numbers of people is obviously part of the point of doing it and so, when it happens, trust me, it feels fantastic.

*

*'I had to get people to commit themselves and it very nearly killed me,' says Roger Waters. It's not quite lunchtime in August 1992 and I'm experiencing what's known as a 'beer sweat'. Waters has just handed over another bottle of Stella Artois from his mini bar at the Chelsea Harbour Hotel and I haven't had any breakfast.*

*He's talking about the time he plugged another hole in his psychology by performing* The Wall *in Berlin. On 9 November 1989, the city's wall came down, allowing the first free movement between West Germany and the Communist East since 1961. To celebrate, Waters staged his favourite Pink Floyd album at Potzdamer Platz on the former East German side.*

*I'd been warned by a senior music critic that Waters was 'tricky'. In a recent magazine article, the interviewer told him he'd had a near-death experience on the way over when his car was struck by the detached wheel of a passing truck. 'So,' replied Waters deadpan. 'You'd rather* die *than face me?'*

*Today, the forty-nine-year-old looks tanned and expensive, with his feet in leather dress shoes parked on the coffee table. His latest album,* Amused to Death, *about the pernicious power of television, will go on to sell around a million copies. But to do this, he's having to embrace the medium he's vilifying and make a video for MTV.*

*'Cable television is a real de-humanising, deadening experience,' he grumbles. 'I watched MTV a couple of days ago. I thought it was horrible. There was this prat, all mouth and trousers, delivering nasty, cheap, puerile banter...'*

*Waters' latest burst of creativity has been inspired by his third wife-to-be, American actor Pricilla Phillips. 'My divorce [from Carolyne Christie] and falling in love with somebody else has released in me an ability to write in other ways apart from songs,' he says, his tone gentler. 'I've now written four or five short stories based on events in my life going back to 1960.'*

The Wall *in Berlin haunts him, though. Waters partnered with promoter Mick Worwood and veteran RAF Group Captain Leonard Cheshire VC to raise £500 million for Cheshire's charity, the Memorial Fund For Disaster Relief.*

*It was a bells-and-whistles production for which Mark Fisher and Jonathan Park constructed an eighty-foot-high wall. But to raise cash for the charity, they had to sell the show to TV, which required big-name guests. Two months before showtime, Leonard Cheshire went cap in hand to the bank to cover their mounting costs and Waters was still struggling to get Neil Young and Eric Clapton to commit.*

*On 21 July 1990, after much wrangling, Waters was joined on stage by the actors Tim Curry, Albert Finney and Jerry Hall, alongside Joni Mitchell, the Scorpions, Cyndi Lauper, Bryan Adams, Sinéad O'Connor, Van Morrison (whose 'Comfortably Numb' was suitably gnarly) and more, all of whom had agreed to donate royalties from the video and live album to the charity.*

*The show was grand and grandiose, poignant and occasionally comical. US army helicopters buzzed the audience during 'Another Brick in the Wall, Part 2' and a Soviet marching band appeared for the grand finale. Thousands of Berliners chanting 'Tear down the wall!' meant something. Waters dressed as Pink in jackboots and Nazi-like insignia may have been a tough watch for some, though.*

*More than 200,000 saw the show in Berlin with an estimated billion more viewing via satellite TV links around the world. But the big money for Disaster Relief never materialised and the live album failed to reach the US Top 50.*

*'I will never get involved with anything like that again,' sighs Waters, clutching his strong continental lager. 'I'd love to do* The Wall *again in the year 2000, though. I've already got my eye on the Grand Canyon…'*

✿

**Roger Waters:** For Berlin, I had to rely totally on other artists, which put me in a terrible position. Joni Mitchell and Bryan Adams were prepared to say 'yes' from the start, but there were many others who wanted to see who else was involved before they made up their minds.

**Paul Carrack:** Roger rang up, gave me this spiel about how it was going to be the biggest concert of all time and then finally came to the point: 'Do you have Huey Lewis's phone number?'

I said, 'What about me, Roger?' 'You're not famous enough.' There was no attempt to spare my feelings and he probably took great delight in saying it. But I thought it was perfectly reasonable. Nobody did bloody know who the hell I was.

I didn't hear from him again and then, a week before the show, he rang me up. I think they were having problems with the special guests. He said, 'I want you to listen to these six songs, learn them, be aware of them.' And then, two days before it kicked off, I got the call to go over and I covered a few songs.

I knew nothing about the logistics of it, only that it was the biggest gig of that time, and the cameras would have shown my knees knocking. I ended up singing 'Hey You' and had I known I'd have been singing from behind a massive wall, I'd have offered to wear a paper bag over my head.

**Roger Waters:** Everyone was fabulous to work with. Bryan Adams, Van Morrison, Cyndi Lauper – all brilliant. All except Sinéad O'Connor. Oh, God! I have never ever met anybody who is so self-involved and unprofessional and big-headed and unpleasant.

With *The Wall*, she was so worried that there weren't any other young people on the show. I and everybody else were old farts in her opinion, so she was worried that she was doing something that wasn't 'street' enough. And because it wasn't 'street' enough, she came up with this brilliant idea – she said that I should employ Ice-T or one of those people to re-work one of my songs as a rap number.

**Paul Carrack:** I know Roger can be intimidating and demanding, but personally I don't let myself get intimidated and so I wasn't having any of it. Roger is a clever guy thinking on the big scale. I think he sometimes finds it difficult to put over what he wants because his music is very simple and some of the musicians get scared because he doesn't always know how to put over what he's after. His strength is the big concept. He means it and you can't fault his commitment, but sometimes he makes hard work of it.

**Roger Waters:** I loved working with that Russian marching band. It was an extraordinary experience, going to rehearse with them in East Germany. We drove for hours and couldn't find the army base we were supposed to be going to. No one would tell us. We soon discovered it was only a hundred yards down the road, but the East Germans were so bloody terrified that they'd be giving away military secrets.

**Nick Mason:** I was rather entertained by *The Wall* in Berlin. If I had a criticism, it would have been that I'd have liked a different guitarist. Roger also made a point of inviting all our ex-wives to the concert, but not us.

**Roger Waters:** I couldn't write an autobiography without going through all that shit with the band again. Frankly, I don't give a shit about all that anymore. Well, yes, I do give a shit. I probably always will, but I can't face going through it all again.

Dave's done what he's done and that's his problem. It would have been just as wrong if I had carried on using the name. Pink Floyd was four people and as those four people are no longer working together, in my mind that band doesn't exist anymore.

✿

*Pink Floyd played their first show of the '90s, a charity concert for the Nordoff-Robbins Music Therapy Centre, at Knebworth on 30 June 1990. They headlined over Paul McCartney, Elton John and Phil Collins. 'A geriatric afternoon on Mount Olympus,' said Nick Mason.*

*An earlier storm rendered Floyd's circular screen unusable and the band played an abbreviated set in the rain, with Clare Torry singing 'The Great Gig in the Sky'. It was a downbeat ending to a comeback tour that had survived the threats and slanging matches to gross $135 million.*

*Back home, Gilmour played sessions for Kate Bush, Paul McCartney and Grace Jones ('I'm on "Slave to the Rhythm" somewhere'); Mason married Annette Lynton (they'd later have two sons, Guy and Carey); and Richard Wright had begun a relationship with his third wife-to-be, American model Millie Hobbs, with whom he'd have a son, Ben.*

*In 1991, Mason, Gilmour and Steve O'Rourke competed in Mexico's historic Carrera Pan America sports car race and nearly brought Pink Floyd to a sudden end, when Gilmour wrote off the Jaguar he was driving with O'Rourke in the passenger seat. The guitarist escaped relatively unharmed, but his manager sustained a fractured leg.*

*O'Rourke had sold the rights for a movie of the race (1992's* La Carrera Panamericana*), which he hoped would underwrite the costs of the venture. Gilmour enlisted Tim Renwick, Jon Carin, Guy Pratt and Gary Wallis to help record the soundtrack.*

*Inadvertently, then, Pink Floyd were getting back together again – although the release of a retrospective box set,* Shine On*, in '92, gave the estranged partners another chance to snipe at each other.*

*'Roger was never very keen on improving himself as a bass player,' claimed Gilmour in 1992. 'Half the time I would play the bass on the records because I would tend to do it quicker ... At least half the bass on all recorded output is me anyway.'*

*'They took my child and sold her into prostitution,' Waters grumbled. 'And I never forgave them for that.'*

*One night, Gilmour and Waters both attended Paul Carrack's fortieth birthday party. Waters turned round from the bar to be confronted by his nemesis. As much as one wants to imagine saloon doors swinging and a hush falling over the gathering, the reality was more mundane. 'Roger couldn't help but smile,' recalled Gilmour. 'Then he gathered his party and stalked off.'*

✲

**David Gilmour:** Playing the bass on Pink Floyd albums? That may have happened once or twice, because Roger couldn't be bothered. Roger's a good bass player. He does fundamental, solid stuff. He's the best Roger Waters bass player there is. I don't have a thing about his bass playing. There was probably a bit of childish needling forty years ago. The needle was mostly one way. But I sometimes foolishly responded.

There are songs which I did play the bass on because a) I might have had an idea about what to play, and b) I was quicker. Which songs? I can't remember, and it's not a big deal.

**Guy Pratt:** I came down to earth with a bang in 1990. But what was nice was the Floyd family, which had been created on that tour. Durga McBroom had met my mate Youth [musician/producer Martin Glover] when he came out on tour. She went back to London and they became [electronic duo] Blue Pearl, and we all played on the Blue Pearl record. Then I got David to play on the Jimmy Nail record and Kirsty MacColl's album.

**David Gilmour:** I think our first sessions on what became *The Division Bell* were at Britannia Row in January 1993 [before further sessions at Olympic Studios and the *Astoria*]. We did a lot of jamming – me, Rick and Nick for a week or so and then Bob Ezrin turned up. Guy came in and played bass on the second week, until we ended up with lots of pieces of music which I recorded.

**Bob Ezrin:** Steve O'Rourke rang me in his role as the dark side of the band and said, 'Would I do it?' – and then told me how much less he would pay me. He always tried that. When we got to *The Division Bell*, I think David was feeling pleased with himself. Roger had walked and now they'd proved they could it without him, and that tour had brought the boys together and refocused them on being Pink Floyd again.

**Richard Wright:** Saying I was now a full member is partly true, but not in terms of a contract. Dave and Nick didn't want to give away what they've gained and it came very close to the point where I wasn't going to do *The Division Bell* because I didn't feel what we'd agreed was fair.

**Guy Pratt:** *The Division Bell* had an incredibly awkward beginning when they asked me to go and do a week's jamming at Britannia Row. I'd literally just come back from Mexico and my first holiday with Gala Wright [Richard's daughter, whom Pratt would later marry].

I was living in her little house, just around the corner from Rick. So I became Rick's designated driver because he'd lost his licence. I'd only just got my licence back as well, so my insurance was through the roof. I had this shitty little VW Golf that my stepdad had bought me. Rick was cool, though. Rick was only ever adorable, but my relationship with Gala became more of a stick for the others to beat him with.

**Bob Ezrin:** Now we had Rick and Nick fully engaged, and Rick was part of the band again, we said, 'Let's listen to everyone's material and pick some things.' So they all threw their stuff into the pot and we graded everything from one to ten on what we would most like to work on. You could tell a lot from the voting, how secure people felt in the band.

**Nick Mason:** Rick awarded all his pieces ten points and everything else got nul points. So, we had to abandon the points system.

**Richard Wright:** I was part of the creative process because I was writing again, rather than just playing on the material. But I felt that it wasn't going in the right direction all the time. I think we could have gone further towards making a Floyd album as we used to – more thematic, with all the music having a logical link.

**David Gilmour:** Rick always said, 'It wasn't quite the musical direction I thought we should be going in.' He had said that about every record we ever made. That's just Rick.

**Richard Wright:** My influence can be heard on tracks like 'Marooned' and 'Cluster One'. Those were the kind of things I gave the Floyd in the past and it was good that they were now getting used again.

**Anthony Moore:** David said, 'Can we concentrate on a song that Rick can sing?'. I loved the title 'Wearing the Inside Out' – enjoyed the double meaning of wearing one's insides out in the same way that you might wear out a pair of shoes. In other words, you wear your emotional self down to nothing.

**David Gilmour:** It's a very nice, very lovely piece and everyone who listens to it goes, 'Oh God, it's *that* voice, that used to be a part of the Pink Floyd sound and hasn't been so much lately.'

**Bob Ezrin:** There were lots of interesting ideas, but we needed something to unite the spirit of the record. There are concept albums and there are conceptual albums, and then there are sequences of songs. Pink Floyd didn't do sequences of songs. They always had a uniting idea and we were looking for that. But we started off great guns, then lost momentum.

**David Gilmour:** I started going out with [journalist/writer] Polly Samson in 1992 and every night after these jam sessions, I'd go back to where I lived and struggled away working out how to turn these pieces of music into *whole* pieces of music and subsequently into songs.

There were two sides to the process – with Bob, Rick and Nick and [engineer] Andy Jackson during the day, and then Polly and I in the evenings because I started trying to get Polly to help me. Gradually I think I bullied her into taking part properly. She was nervous of the idea at first. I think she was worried about what one might call the 'Yoko Ono factor'.

**Bob Ezrin:** Over the Christmas holidays, David went into the studio by himself and wrote 'High Hopes' – and that's when the album took on its true nature. It was the most emotionally complete and clear song we had. We'd moved back to the *Astoria*, too – on the river in a good grey English winter.

**David Gilmour:** 'High Hopes' just leapt out at me, sitting at the piano in my sitting room in Maida Avenue [in London's Little Venice]. There was obviously a great track in there somewhere – and Polly and I worked on that until we'd really got it nailed.

Polly asked me, 'What is this song about?'. I said, 'Uh, I dunno.' So she jogged my memory and it reminds me of those great days by the River Cam with Storm and all those people. I sat and talked to her about people and places and how all of us left Cambridge to go somewhere where bigger ideas could take place.

**Bob Ezrin:** 'High Hopes' pulled the album together – gave it a different spirit and an idea around which to hang some of the broader concepts. It wasn't easy at first with Polly. It was almost a cliché to have the new woman getting involved in the career. But she inspired David, gave him a sense of confidence and challenged him a lot. Whatever David was thinking at the time, she'd help him find a way of saying it. It did put a strain on the boys' club, though.

**David Gilmour:** Polly came into my life and my work, and she pretty much wrote the words for *The Division Bell*. The press and PR at the time seemed to be saying that David wrote the lyrics and Polly polished them up a bit. That's false, and I'm as much to blame for that as anyone. But perhaps it was also a sign of the very misogynistic culture of '80s pop music and Pink Floyd.

Polly had said she didn't want to be credited and I said, 'You'll regret not having it.' But where Polly has a writing credit for a lyric as well as me, it's usually at least 80 per cent her and a bit of me.

**Nick Laird-Clowes:** The Dream Academy had split up and [writer/producer] Pat Leonard, who was putting a new band together, asked me to go to Los Angeles and write lyrics for them. I did this for months – sitting there with a pencil listening to other people's music.

When I came back, David said, 'I'm making another album. Can I play you what we've been doing?'. He was in a relationship with Polly, she was writing lyrics and the album was almost done. But he just wanted my opinion on his vocals. He said, 'We've worked together before and I trust you if you say something isn't working.' He knew I'd be honest.

Was it George Harrison who said 'I was down to my last 12 million'? Well, I was down to my last thirty grand and I had a tax bill to pay. My accountant was going, 'What are you going to do next year?'. I said, 'I'll do whatever I have to.' 'Yes, but *what*? You haven't got any money.' I said, 'Something will happen.'

**David Gilmour:** For 'Poles Apart', I had been on holiday in Greece where there was an old out-of-tune guitar. I invented a tuning which I, of course, later found out had been invented and widely used for years, and was known as 'DADGAD', but I was pleased with it and created the finger picking body of the music.

Later, in the studio, I came up with a breakdown section, a string melody, which I would describe as having a klezmer flavour. I put that in the middle of the song and took it back home that evening. Polly said, 'This reminds me of fairgrounds'. She had in her collection a vinyl album of fairground barrel organ music which we then used to help create the atmosphere for that middle section.

**Nick Laird-Clowes:** Right near the end, I went over to the house one evening to listen and there were a couple of songs that didn't have lyrics yet. One of them was 'Poles Apart'. I asked David, 'What do you want to write about? How about Syd Barrett because you told me you'd gone to France together when you were teenagers? What are your memories of Syd?' David is very shy and quiet, and then he just said, 'I never thought he'd lose that light in his eyes.' I said, 'That's it. That's a line.'

The three of us started batting it back and forth, and then David asked me what year I was born. I told him 1957. He went down to the wine cellar and came back with a bottle – 'This is a '61, but it'll do. Congratulations, you've contributed to your first Pink Floyd record.'

**Anthony Moore:** I faded out quite early from *The Division Bell*. I got this extraordinary commission from Channel 4 to compose an opera. Polly and David had started to work together on songs and I got distracted by my opera and delusions of grandeur.

**Nick Laird-Clowes:** The other song I worked on was 'Take It Back'. Our writing sessions often went on late into the night. I was driving home at around 4 a.m., when I pulled over to the side of the road with a lyric in my head. 'Now I have seen the warnings, screaming from all sides, it's easy to ignore them, God knows I've tried....'

I didn't think they'd like it, but when I sang it to them, they thought it was brilliant. Then I went off to India and Nepal to sit with the Buddhists for three months and get over the end of the Dream Academy, and Pink Floyd went off and conquered the world.

**Bob Ezrin:** David and I are both headstrong guys. A lot of the time I would say it should be this way and he would say 'No', just gently, and I'd push and push. I was the little critter trying to move the elephant in the cartoons.

But I didn't get a chance to mix *The Division Bell* [Ezrin was replaced by *The Dark Side of the Moon*'s mixing engineer Chris Thomas] and *that* was disappointing. I wasn't thrilled by that. It was the first time it had ever happened to me, but it was their decision.

**Guy Pratt:** I think *The Division Bell* was musically a thousand times better than *A Momentary Lapse*... because there hasn't been a decade since the '80s where music sounded so specific to the time.

**Nick Laird-Clowes:** I suggested calling the album 'Burning Blue Silence'. But David said, 'Fuck off! You can call your album "Burning Blue Silence".'

**Nick Mason:** We couldn't agree on a title. 'Down to Earth' and 'Pow Wow' were two suggestions and, of course, we left it to the last moment. Our friend [*The Hitch-Hiker's Guide to the Galaxy* author] Douglas Adams suggested *The Division Bell*, a phrase taken from the lyrics to 'High Hopes'.

**Storm Thorgerson:** The theme of the album was communication – there was even a song called 'Keep Talking'. So I had the idea of two faces looking at each other, which, if you looked carefully, made a third face in between.

David didn't like it but we convinced him. We had two seven-foot-high stone and metal heads made, which weighed half a ton each. We photographed the stone ones in a field [in Cambridgeshire] with Ely Cathedral in the distance, visible between their mouths.

✿

*Thorgerson's associates, photographers Tony May and Rupert Truman, spent three weeks guarding the heads and waiting for the rain to stop so they could take the cover photo. It was January, the pair slept in a caravan, ate in a nearby Little Chef and cursed Thorgerson for putting art above home comforts.*

*One day, Nick Mason arrived by helicopter to inspect the stone edifices before flying off like a royal dignitary on a whistle-stop tour. The metal versions would later end up on an outside roof at EMI's HQ in west London's Brook Green.*

*Pink Floyd had been late delivering the LP, so Steve O'Rourke offered a seat on Concorde to anyone at Thorgerson's studio who could bring the artwork to Los Angeles the next day. Storm told him it wasn't ready.*

*The album finally appeared in March 1994. Everywhere you looked, there were those heads: on posters, in press ads and on the side of a promotional airship. There was even a curly-haired one in Thorgerson's video for 'High Hopes', which Gilmour complained looked like the Who's Roger Daltrey.*

The Division Bell *went to number one in twelve countries and was a conceptual rather than a concept album. 'What Do You Want From Me?', 'Lost For Words', and 'Keep Talking' (featuring famous physicist Stephen Hawking's synthesised voice) were tenuously linked by the theme of communication.*

*Even Polly Samson's infant son Charlie stuck to the brief by hanging up the phone on Steve O'Rourke.*

*'Hello… Is that Charlie?' asks O'Rourke at the end of 'High Hopes', using that slow, deliberate tone popular when addressing children.*

*'Yes,' the boy gurgles.*

*Click. Dialling tone.*

*O'Rourke: 'Great.'*

*There were leftovers too. Several instrumentals presumably discarded during the points system were later fashioned by Andy Jackson into an hour-long ambient composition, nicknamed 'The Big Spliff', some of which remains unreleased.*

The Division Bell *was also an extended family affair. Dick Parry played sax on his first Floyd record since* Wish You Were Here*; backing vocalist Sam Brown's mother Vicki had sung on the Dark Side of the Moon tour; and Polly Samson said the lyrics to 'Poles Apart' were 'about Syd in the first verse and Roger in the second'.*

*'Marooned' and 'High Hopes' were the standouts, with the latter a contemplative hymn to 'the ragged band' who gathered at Sheep's Green and the Mill Pond in '60s Cambridge. 'It's a later-incarnation Pink Floyd classic,' said Gilmour, 'and* The Division Bell *is a more confident, better record than* A Momentary Lapse of Reason.'

*However, the 'Yoko Ono factor' clouded opinion in a way it wouldn't have if seven of the album's songs had been co-written with another man instead of Gilmour's fiancée.*

*'It's so* Spinal Tap,*' grumbled Waters in 2004. 'And the songs are all fucking awful.* A Momentary Lapse of Reason, *I have to say, had one or two redeeming moments on it, but* The Division Bell – *Jesus Christ!'*

*In the spring of 1994, the band went out for the first of 110 shows, many in stadiums. Fisher and Park's multi-level stage and proscenium arch were both so big that some of the group couldn't see each other. But size mattered in venues like Mexico City's 90,000-capacity Autodromo.*

*On tour, Dick Parry replaced Scott Page, Sam Brown and Claudia Fontaine joined vocalist Durga McBroom, and Bryan Morrison's ex-foot soldier Tony Howard returned as tour manager. Peter Wynne-Willson, now one of the world's foremost lighting designers, oversaw a more sophisticated version of 'the Daleks' and a high-tech version of his original liquid light show.*

*The set was weighted towards the new album, but also exhumed the Barrett-era 'Astronomy Domine' and, later,* The Dark Side of the Moon *in full. But* The Division Bell *had been launched into a marketplace populated by musicians who'd grown up with* Relics *and the myth of Syd Barrett.*

*After a show in Birmingham, Alabama, the party gathered in Gilmour's hotel suite. Blur's* Parklife *went on the stereo, as it had just replaced*

The Division Bell *at number one in Britain. Blur took cues from '60s pop and their vocalist Damon Albarn was the son of artist and UFO club familiar Keith Albarn. Rick Wright listened to a couple of songs before innocently enquiring, 'Why is that bloke singing like Syd?'*

✣

**Peter Wynne-Willson:** After I stopped working with them, I crossed paths again with Pink Floyd in Amsterdam in 1968. The theatrical troupe I was working with fetched up there. David Gilmour very sweetly got the Floyd's management to get me a plane ticket back to the UK as I was living a fairly meagre existence.

Then all those years later came The Division Bell tour, which was a bit spooky. Someone put [Pink Floyd's production manager] Robbie Williams in touch with me because they wanted to do something more with what we called 'the Daleks' [aka the 'Floyd Droids'].

Then I showed Marc Brickman some liquid light things and he got completely carried away and set them up in rehearsals. My business partner wasn't keen on me touring, so I built the equipment, trained the operators and they went off on tour.

It was interesting working with new equipment, seeing how the touring business had shifted – *The Division Bell* was very big business – and reconnecting with the band again. Nick was perfectly cordial, though we'd never been close, David was extremely pleasant, even though we'd never spent much time together, and Rick – who had the most delightful girlfriend – was very pleasant, but a bit of a shell, and I'm not sure he really recognised me at all. There was no reconnection.

**Tim Renwick:** The Division Bell tour was much more staid than the one before. Polly and 'Nettie' Mason had come along by then, so everyone was going to bed earlier. Security was much tighter as well, because they didn't want too many party animals turning up from the last tour. First time around it had been, 'Right, what club are we hitting tonight?' So I think there was a little bit of resentment among the younger band members.

**Nick Mason:** Touring is only as exhausting as you make it. If you stay up all night dealing with your ambience coordinator on a regular basis, you can be finished within three weeks. But in other ways, it's like doing *The Mousetrap*. You fall into the groove and it can be quite relaxing.

**Guy Pratt:** David had Polly and her son Charlie, Nick had Nettie and his kids, and Gala refused to go anywhere near the tour. Having grown up with it, she wasn't into the idea of wives and girlfriends on the road. Her thing was, 'It used to be embarrassing enough when it was my dad.' I was pulling teeth just to get her to come to Earls Court.

**David Gilmour:** As normal, fallible human beings, we fell into the trap of taking sponsorship from Volkswagen for that tour. One has moments of weakness in life and that was one of mine. We gave the money to charity.

**Nick Mason:** Volkswagen produced a Pink Floyd car – an ecologically friendly VW Golf Cabriolet. They knew what they were doing because they'd done a car for Genesis on their last tour.

**Nick Laird-Clowes:** I came home from Nepal to all these messages on my answering machine telling me I should be on the road, and my father telling me Pink Floyd had a number-one record. Then this itinerary dropped through my door – 'Oh my God, they're playing in New Orleans on Saturday and today's Wednesday.'

I called David and asked if I could go to New Orleans, and then I just stayed with the tour, doing what I'd been doing before, making suggestions: 'I really think that number should come here' or 'You weren't quite there in the middle of that song'. Polly was doing it too. I have to say, Steve O'Rourke didn't particularly like me.

**Roger Waters:** David Gilmour invited me to play *The Dark Side of the Moon* with the band at Earls Court. I don't think we would have got through the first half an hour of rehearsal. I knew if I stood on the stage, I'd think, *Oh, I don't like this. I don't want to be here doing this. It does not feel good.* There's too much history.

**David Gilmour:** I thought it would be nice for the fans. It was a genuine offer, but there was also the safety cushion of knowing that he wouldn't do it.

**Guy Pratt:** It was fantastic to do *The Dark Side of the Moon*. We used to do songs from it anyway, but it's weird because they feel like different songs when you play them together as *The Dark Side of the Moon*.

**Tim Renwick:** The tour was enjoyable, but it was a year's touring condensed into eight and a half months, and a lot of people were pissed off it hadn't been made the full year.

**David Gilmour:** There was a certain amount of anti-Polly stuff going on among various people that were part of our production team and our crew, whether it was anti-woman or anti-newcomer. But there was a certain amount of power tripping going on.

**Guy Pratt:** I was still caning it, but not with any great sense of purpose. There was no sense of finality about the tour, though. It all ended on a fantastic note and I didn't know we weren't going to do it again.

**Nick Mason:** I don't think we dealt with the rest of the band as well as we should have. We weren't very good at saying that we wanted to feature ourselves a bit more – as in myself, Rick and David.

When it came to the curtain call on the first tour, there was just the one band, whereas on the second tour it was David, Rick and me. We were trying to be a smaller band and reminding ourselves that there was a nucleus of Pink Floyd, but we didn't work it out properly. Probably a communication issue, as usual.

**David Gilmour:** Pink Floyd is not only me. I am bound by other people's desires and choices and politics and needs – as well as my own. So, the whole thing is a constant compromise of ideals and art all the way through.

⁂

*In the summer of 1996, the first thing I notice about Rick Wright up close at London's Groucho Club is his fabulous plume of silver hair. It makes him look like a sort of handsome prog-rock Michael Heseltine. It's the dying days of Britpop, so there's no sign of the club's hellraisers, actor Keith Allen or Blur's bassist Alex James, snuffling up half of Colombia or asleep on the snooker table.*

*Instead, the door to a private room opens and there's 53-year-old Wright proffering a gentle handshake. Lounging nearby, appropriately, on a chaise longue, is Anthony Moore. 'Don't mind me,' he says, waving a hand in my direction. 'I'm here for moral support.' ('Was I drunk?' Moore asks me years later when I tell him about this meeting.)*

*Moore has co-written and co-produced Wright's latest solo album,* Broken China, *a suite of rather melancholy songs which we later discover are about Rick's wife Millie's depression. It contains a lovely track sung by Sinéad O'Connor called 'Breakthrough', which supports Waters' theory that Wright squirrelled away good ideas for 'his awful solo albums'.*

Broken China *isn't awful at all, but only the most devoted Floyd devotee will end up buying it. Everybody else is probably listening to Blur.*

*Things have changed since The Division Bell tour earned £150 million, making it the highest-grossing of all time. Partway through the trek, Gilmour married Polly Samson (and later adopted her son Charlie. The couple would go on to have three more children, Joe, Gabriel and Romany.)*

*Pink Floyd released a live album,* Pulse *(notable for having a flashing LED light on the spine of the first two million copies), and were inducted into the Rock & Roll Hall of Fame in 1996, where they collected their trophies and acknowledged an absent Barrett and Waters.*

*'People keep asking me when Pink Floyd are going to make another record, but I honestly don't know,' Wright tells me. 'We tend to record in six- and seven-year cycles. So, as the last album was '94, the next one could be in the year 2001.'*

*He looks crestfallen. Really, solo albums are a stopgap for Rick Wright. You sense he really misses Pink Floyd.*

❦

**Richard Wright:** I enjoyed The Division Bell tour, so when I came home, the last thing I wanted to do was sit around and do nothing. I really didn't want to do this album on my own because I don't consider myself a lyricist. I didn't have any music written before Anthony worked with me. We put the whole thing together in my studio in the south of France.

**Anthony Moore:** It's funny. I said I was there for moral support that day, which is true as Rick was very shy. This is a little bit sensitive, so make of it what you will, but that album would never have existed had I not been there. I wrote more than half of it and when Rick wanted Sinéad O'Connor, I was the one despatched to go and talk to her... in her kitchen, if I recall.

I also got my engineer, Laurie Latham, involved, but at the final stages, it was taken out of our hands [and mixed by James Guthrie], which upset me a bit. Our version was spikier. They smoothed everything out and I found that infuriating.

But, by then, I'd started professoring pretty much full time, teaching the history of sound and music in Cologne. I'd gone from being your bog-standard, '60s art school dropout to being shot up to the highest levels of academia and had to reinvent myself pretty damn quick. Brian Eno wrote me a reference – 'I think Anthony would be great for the job, full stop' – like half a line on an A4-sized piece of paper.

**Richard Wright:** Pink Floyd is like a marriage that's on a permanent trial separation. We all respect each other, but we're not close friends. At the beginning, we were friends – we were living with each other twenty-four hours a day. But we were young then and we weren't so serious about our relationships. These days, I think it all comes down to respect. There's a respect between us.

**Roger Waters:** I'm making a rock 'n' roll album. It's about a conversation in a New York bar and one of the characters is a taxi driver from the Balkans and his marriage is falling apart. I've recently got divorced [from Priscilla Phillips] so there's some songs about the breakdown of relationships. I'm not quite sure how it will all turn out but, as you can hear, it's another kind of loony concept thing.

**David Gilmour (speaking in 2000):** 'What do I do all day? I get up at about 7.15. I wake up some children. Make breakfast. Change a nappy. Take a kid to school. Strum a guitar. Doodle in my recording studio some of the time. If the weather's nice, I might fly an aeroplane. It's hard to describe what I do, but I never seem to have enough time to do it.'

✣

*Rick Wright's suggested seven-year cycle didn't happen. The year 2000 came and went without Roger Waters staging* The Wall *at the Grand Canyon, or any new Pink Floyd music.*

*Instead, Waters launched his long-gestating French Revolution opera,* Ça Ira, *co-written with the librettist Étienne Roda-Gil. It had taken six years and many setbacks, for which Waters blamed the French: 'Me being English stuck in the Gallic craw.'*

*His In the Flesh tours, between 1999 and 2002, fared better, with Waters performing as far afield as Bangkok and Beirut, and sometimes billed as 'The Creative Genius of Pink Floyd'. Soon after, he announced a deal with Miramax Films to bring* The Wall *to Broadway. It's still to appear.*

*Meanwhile, David Gilmour sold Intrepid Aviation, the Essex museum housing his aircraft collection, and made headlines after donating £3.6 million from the sale of his house in London's Little Venice to the homeless charity, Crisis. The guitarist received a CBE in the 2004 honours list.*

*As time passed, members of the extended Floyd family fell by the wayside. Tony Howard died in 2001, and Steve O'Rourke and Michael Kamen a month apart in 2003. Gilmour, Mason and Wright played 'Fat Old Sun' at O'Rourke's memorial service in Chichester Cathedral.*

*In the same year, the band's irascible creative director Storm Thorgerson suffered a stroke but returned to work – and to spending the band's money – as soon as he was able to do so.*

*By then, there'd also been a rapprochement between Waters and Nick Mason, after they found themselves staying at the same resort on Mustique. Rather than enduring the holiday from hell, the pair had their first real conversation since the late '80s.*

*'And a large amount of emotional baggage got dumped,' said Mason, who later played 'Set the Controls for the Heart of the Sun' with Waters at London's Wembley Arena.*

*Mason was the closest the group had to an archivist: he'd kept diaries and memorabilia during their early years and had now written a book. His jolly memoir,* Inside Out: A Personal History of Pink Floyd, *was published in 2004.*

❁

**Nick Mason:** I knew Roger was on the island, but we hadn't spoken for many years. I didn't have the tin helmet on anymore, but meeting him again broke the ice and things became better after that.

**Clive Metcalfe (guitarist in Mason and Waters' Regent St Poly group):** About thirty years after I left our group, I spotted Nick Mason at a motor racing meeting. It took a while, but when he realised who I was, he was pleased to see me because he was writing his autobiography and couldn't remember how the band started.

**Nick Mason:** The initial work on the book was completed after The Division Bell tour. Then I ran up against a lot of disapproval, particularly from David, because at one point it was going to be the official history of Pink Floyd.

I think he felt, quite rightly, I would treat the real history with too much levity, but it would also be inaccurate unless I went and pored over hundreds of interviews to try to arrive at the truth, somewhere between mine, David's, Roger's and Rick's.

**David Gilmour:** There was a period of mild deception, as there was a chap taking pictures on The Division Bell tour without me knowing anything about it. I got rather grumpy about the book because I didn't think that what I saw conveyed enough of the artistic process.

**Nick Mason:** Rick faxed his comments from a yacht in the Caribbean. After Roger had read the manuscript, we met up at a hotel to talk through his comments. On one page, Roger had simply written 'Bollocks' across the whole text.

**Roger Waters:** I thought Nick's book was a nice, light read, but, you know, don't take it too seriously. It doesn't tell the truth or the bits of the truth I'd have told. There's a lot of 'We did this' and 'We came up with that', which doesn't seem quite right. With any rock biography, you'd expect there to be some stuff about sex, and he doesn't go near that, which I found quite strange.

**Nick Mason:** Have I skimped on the sex? I think that territory has moved on from rock 'n' roll to football. I dithered and tinkered with it and came round to the idea that it would be more realistic and entertaining to just do my own version of the story. Once I decided to do a book from my perspective alone, then both David and Roger were enormously helpful but on the basis that it was my version. Now, if they care to, they can go and do their own.

**Roger Waters:** We now know – because of all the research that's been done in neurology – that we can't remember very much. So a lot of the arguments about who did or said what are all irrelevant because however much we may think we remember, we now know the brain will invent memories to suit the ego of the person who owns the brain.

**Nick Mason:** Roger and I made friends again, and the long and short of it was that we were proving publicly to our children, if no one else, that you can make friends with your enemies. It was fantastically grown-up and, in some ways, that helped the book because it also gave me a better ending.

**David Gilmour:** I don't like to say that [Pink Floyd] will never do something again, but I suspect that I've done that. One never knows if one's tired old ego might creep up on you and persuade you to give it a go. But the weight of the whole Floyd thing is something I don't feel like lifting these days. I just think I've grown out of it. Finally. Probably...

**Nick Mason:** We wouldn't get back together for an anniversary and I don't think we'd do it for the money. But it would be fantastic if we could do it for something like another Live Aid – a significant event of that nature would justify it. That would be wonderful. But maybe I'm just sentimental... You know what us old drummers are like.

✲

*Nick Mason made his comment about the group reuniting for 'another Live Aid' during a September 2004 interview with the music magazine* Q.

*By then, we'd already discussed his aversion to drum solos ('I never found the time to practise') and that photograph of Syd Barrett in 1975 ('I did wonder whether to publish it') before I asked the inevitable question: 'Will Pink Floyd make another album or play together again?'*

*Months later, Mason's reply was picked up by Bob Geldof, who was launching Live 8, a series of worldwide concerts, including at London's Hyde Park, in aid of Make Poverty History and the Global Call To Action Against Poverty campaigns. Geldof wanted to scare up the heads of industrial nations before they gathered for July 2005's G8 conference in Edinburgh to debate third world poverty and climate change.*

*'I couldn't think of any other business that could force their hands,' said Geldof. 'Sports stars or film stars wouldn't make a difference. Only musicians could get these political leaders of the rich world to bend.'*

❦

**Bob Geldof:** I'd read an interview with Nick that they would never play again unless it was for something like Live Aid. So that triggered a call from me to Nick saying, 'Will you do it?'. He said he would. I then said, 'Would you call Dave?'. He said 'No'.

**Nick Mason:** It was duplicity and diplomacy at its best. Bob asked me if I would ask David and I said, 'No, it won't do any good at all.' The only way it would happen is if Roger said yes and if he suggested it.

**Roger Waters:** I got an email from Nick Mason saying he'd had Bob Geldof on the phone bending his ear about re-forming Pink Floyd to play at Live 8. Nick didn't think he'd have much of a chance of influencing Dave. So I got Bob's number and called him.

**Bob Geldof:** Roger called me and said he'd be up for it, and then I called Dave. And he said, 'I know what you're going to ask. I've read it in the paper and I don't think it's a good idea.' I said, 'Let me come down and talk to you.' And he said, 'No'. I said, 'Why?'. He said, 'Because you'll try and persuade me and it'll be a waste of your time, and I'll just say no.'

**David Gilmour:** I told him I was right in the middle of making an album, but he said, 'I'll come down and see you' and jumped on the train.

**Bob Geldof:** I got to East Croydon when David rang and told me to get off. I said, 'I'm not getting off. Meet me at the station.' So he met me at the station and we drove off to his farm. I laid out my whole pitch – 'You and Roger are too old for this stuff. Just grow up. Rock 'n' roll is the lingua franca...' – and he still said he wouldn't do it. I went home and wrote him a letter and still heard nothing.

Then Roger called me and said 'What did he say?'. I told him and he said, 'Have you got Dave's number?'. So, I gave Roger Waters Dave Gilmour's phone number... which was weird.

**David Gilmour:** Getting that call was surprising. Roger and I had had one phone conversation since our meeting on the *Astoria* in '87. That was a five-way conference call shouting at each other about some argument over a documentary called *The Making of The Dark Side of the Moon*.

Roger and I chatted quite pleasantly for a minute or two and I'd said I'd call him back the next day. Then I thought about it and thought that I'd probably always regret it if I didn't do it and, more importantly, getting over the squabbles with Roger and doing it for this good cause.

**Bob Geldof:** I said to Gilmour, 'You've made an old man very happy ... Not that I can stand you cunts' – 'cos I never liked their music, really.

**Tim Renwick:** I got married that year, and David and Polly came to the reception. David said, 'Oh yes, Live 8's going to be on June 6 or whenever [2 July 2005], so put it in your diary.' I said, 'What? You're doing it?' He said, 'No, we're definitely not doing it. But just to let you know if you wanted to keep that date free.'

Then I got a call about two weeks before it was due to happen from David – he was laughing – and said, 'Oh, we're doing it, and we're doing it with Roger.' I was completely gob-struck. Nothing against Guy – because he's my friend – but it just seemed wrong that Roger should leave, and they should never *ever* get back together again.

**Guy Pratt:** I was playing with Roxy Music now. Gala and I were on holiday with David and Polly in Formentera when the *Daily Telegraph*, I think, said Pink Floyd were likely to perform at Live 8. Roxy's tour manager rang me and asked, 'What's all this about Pink Floyd re-forming?'

My exact words were, 'Look mate, it's going to take a lot more than Bob Geldof's ego to get that lot together.' Then I got home and had a phone call from David saying, 'Are you sitting down?'

David told me Roger wanted to play acoustic guitar on two songs, and they'd need a bass player. But I had a gig that night with Roxy [at the Live 8 concert in Berlin] and I hadn't had a decent gig for eight years. I couldn't believe it. I was pacing up and down, thinking, 'What should I do?' Then the phone rang and it was Phil Manzanera who said, 'You must be *really* pacing up and down...' In the end, I'm glad I didn't do it. Ironically, the last thing you saw on telly before Floyd came on was me with Roxy playing 'Love is the Drug'.

**Roger Waters:** The day they announced the Pink Floyd were to play Live 8, I went out to dinner with a friend and an offer arrived – literally *bang* on the dinner table – for the four of us, the Pink Floyd, to tour again. An offer of $250 million guaranteed.

**David Gilmour:** The first meeting we had [at London's Connaught Hotel] was pretty stilted and cagey. We also talked on the phone about which songs to play and we fell straight into arguing.

**Nick Mason:** We had a shortlist of about six or seven songs and I remember Bob Geldof wanted us to do 'Money'.

**David Gilmour:** The songs that Roger suggested weren't the ones that I thought we should do. 'Another Brick in the Wall' for starving children in Africa? Really?

**Tim Renwick:** David told us it would be a laugh. But we did three days of rehearsal at [London's] Black Island studios and it wasn't a laugh at all. Roger was at least an hour late each day and arrived with this kind of, 'Right, I'm here now, now we can start' attitude.

He also started making wild suggestions like getting people to play different instruments to what they'd originally played and rearranging stuff, because he's done things at different tempos and in different keys with his band.

The thing is, there wasn't a single person in the room who Roger hadn't sort of upset at some point. So there were a lot of people standing around, being tight-lipped and incredibly professional.

In the end, David said, 'Look, we're only doing four numbers and people are expecting to hear the hits exactly the way they sounded in the old days.'

**Roger Waters:** I was willing to roll over, but only this once.

**Bob Geldof:** For Live 8, there were going to be eleven hundred artists playing in nine capital cities around the world, seen by 3.2 billion people.

**David Gilmour:** I made myself a CD of the set on a home computer. I plugged the guitar in and had a microphone coming out of a small speaker and played the whole set four or five times a day, every day for two weeks in the run-up. But there was also a part of me thinking, *I must be fucking mad to be doing this again in front of all of these people.*

✲

*In 1996, I'd asked Rick Wright if he'd had any contact with Syd Barrett in recent times. 'We don't see him,' Wright replied. 'If he's reminded of Pink Floyd, he goes into a depression. His mother asked us to stay away a few years ago. Apparently, most of the time he's quite happy – or was – but our faces can trigger off a lapse.'*

*After the news broke that Pink Floyd would be playing Live 8, the* Cambridge Evening News *contacted Rosemary Breen and asked if her brother was aware of the reunion. 'I saw him this morning and told him, but he did not react,' she said. 'That is another life for him, another world in another time. He is not Syd anymore. He is Roger.'*

*Wherever Roger 'Syd' Barrett was on the evening of 2 July 2005, was he watching Live 8?*

*'No, he didn't watch it,' says Rosemary, sat in the Red Lion Hotel more than a decade later. 'He did have a TV, but he didn't like it very much. It was too much of a distraction from his thoughts. He had so much going on in his head, there wasn't the need for all that outside noise.'*

12

# 'THE BIRDS SEEMED PLEASED'

*'We'll all wind up in the ocean',* The Good Old Days *on acid,*
*'Where do you put a seventy-foot teacher?' and 'Hey ho…'*

✲

The last time Pink Floyd played Hyde Park was July 1970. Nick Mason still had his fedora and Zapata moustache, and the group performed their latest work *Atom Heart Mother*.

The only comparison with Pink Floyd at Live 8 in July 2005, though, is that the show is running behind schedule. The timing has gone awry somewhere between the Who, Madonna, Elton John, Robbie Williams and more, but the culture secretary Tessa Jowell has granted permission to keep Hyde Park open.

Nobody's pulling the plug, then, and Paul McCartney is due to close the show. So, the 200,000-strong audience (and a billion more watching on TV around the world) get to witness a fleeting bit of musical history.

It's just before 11 p.m. when *The Dark Side of the Moon*'s heartbeat announces Pink Floyd's arrival. The quartet are joined by Tim Renwick, Jon Carin, backing vocalist Carol Kenyon and a screen showing images of banknotes, spinning vinyl records, a flying pig and Battersea Power Station.

However, the show belongs to the four band members with their identical faded denim and awkward body language. Mason looks bemused, Wright jittery, Gilmour stern and Waters triumphant. He bares his teeth and mouths the lyrics while Gilmour sings them, as if to say 'These are my songs! This is my band!'. Waters wrote the words, but it's Pink Floyd who spun them into gold, a point driven home repeatedly tonight.

After a balmy, meditative 'Breathe' and a brisk and noisy 'Money' (with old Cambridge buddy Dick Parry playing sax), Roger Waters addresses the audience.

'It's actually quite emotional, standing up here with these three guys after all these years,' he tells them. 'Standing up to be counted with the rest of you ... Anyway, this is for anyone who's not here, particularly for Syd.'

'Wish You Were Here' is sublime, with Waters' cracked vocals adding grit to Pink Floyd's greatest pop song. Then Waters introduces 'Comfortably Numb' with a murmured 'Here we go' and Gerald Scarfe's spartan wall materialises on the screen behind.

'Comfortably Numb' is the perfect distillation of what Pink Floyd did so well: grand, valedictory and coldly emotional. Remove Waters' wounded voice or Gilmour's sweet vocal and it wouldn't work half as well. By the time Gilmour peels off the second guitar solo, an ecstatic-looking Richard Wright is up on his feet. At the end of the show, Waters puts his arm around a reluctant Gilmour before they all take a bow.

The TV cameras pan across Hyde Park to show a multi-generational audience, some of whom weren't born when some of this music came out. Few probably knew what Pink Floyd looked like before this evening. Until now, their image was the prism, the pig and the wall.

Wealthy rock stars parking their differences to raise money for the poor raises many questions, about third world poverty, geopolitics and showbusiness. But Geldof's Live 8 makes an estimated £200 million and nobody's criticising that.

Live 8 is also the best PR campaign for Pink Floyd and its members, past and present. Their photographs appear in the following day's newspapers and all over the internet, and their catalogue sales increase by 1,300 per cent. David Gilmour has a new solo album pending and now everybody knows what he looks like.

✲

**Tim Renwick:** We were supposed to play at 7.30, then 8 p.m. It kept getting put back by an hour, so the hanging about was awful. You're backstage with all these people you haven't seen in ages, and you're not eating or drinking. After we were done, there was no transport laid on and I ended up walking back to my hotel, feeling rather crestfallen.

**Roger Waters:** It was good to transcend all that crap and say, 'Fuck it, let's just get up on stage. We can agree to disagree about all the old stuff and stand up there and play these three or four songs.'

**Nick Mason:** There were still all sorts of undercurrents at Live 8, but I thought it was great that, whatever differences we had, we could put them aside and do something for the greater good.

**David Gilmour:** I had very mixed feelings. Looking back on it, at that time I'd had a mere twenty years of arguments, fights, shit and lies and everything that had not made me fonder of certain people. But Live 8 was okay. I had to keep reminding myself in the run-up that it was Pink Floyd who had been asked to do it. Roger was a guest. Regarding the decision-making process, while I was perfectly happy to listen to what he said, it wasn't up to him.

**Nick Mason:** Would I do it again? My bag is packed and ready to go, but David made the greatest sacrifice doing Live 8. He had a solo project coming out and now everybody's going, 'Oh Dave, great! But when's the band going out again?'

I suspect it was the same with Led Zep when they got back together for that one show [at London's O2 Arena in 2007]. You can't just tour for the money, though. The money is very nice, but as an adjunct. You have to *really* want to do it for the right reasons.

**David Gilmour:** After Live 8, I was offered huge sums of money for Pink Floyd to tour. But the money was the same with or without Roger. To do it again would be fakery and trying to be something that we're not. These days, I'm entirely selfish in that I want to please myself.

**Phil Manzanera:** David had something like 150 little pieces of music recorded before he asked me to co-produce *On An Island*. We managed to get it down to about forty pieces before I scared David by suggesting we make it a triple album, so it ended up as ten songs.

**David Gilmour:** I think there's a warmth, romance and contentment to *On An Island*. But there were reviews criticising the title track, thinking it's about a holiday. The moment that engendered it was during a holiday, but it's a song about the joy and loss by death of some of the participants [including Tony Howard and Michael Kamen].

So, there are moments of dust to dust and ashes to ashes, and this idea that we'll all wind up in the ocean. In many ways, I've achieved some contentment, but that's balanced by resignation – all these joys and sadnesses that go together to make life.

**Rado 'Bob' Klose:** David Gilmour phoned me up and said, 'Are you still playing? Do you want to play on my new record?'. We hadn't played together in forty-odd years. It was a great thing to do. I'd watched with amazement what happened with Pink Floyd, but I'd preferred to watch from a distance.

**David Gilmour:** Rick Wright plays beautifully. My difficulty with him on this record was persuading him to come down and do some work. I managed to get him to play the Hammond organ on one song.

For the tour, we talked about what Pink Floyd songs would be fun to do. It was remarkably unplanned. I've always loved 'Sorrow', but it didn't feel right, so we left it out. We'd played 'Echoes' on the Momentary Lapse... tour and it didn't gel, so we'd dumped it. But it's a different time and a different place, and playing 'Echoes' again felt like a good idea.

**Guy Pratt:** You only have to listen to the final section of 'Echoes' to be reminded of what people loved about Pink Floyd. It was the musical conversation between David and Rick. When Rick and I were playing in David's band on that tour, you'd hear members of the audience in Europe shouting 'Reeeechard!' before he played that first note on 'Echoes'.

✲

*In March 2006,* On An Island *became Gilmour's first UK number-one solo album. Polly Samson dragged it out of him, though. 'She says I'm lazy and she's probably right,' he admitted. 'But, for me, that lyrical muse does require more work.'*

*On tour, he played the new record – lots of string-bending solos and hushed vocals – during the first half, while the second half was wall-to-wall Floyd.*

*The album's backing vocalists, David Crosby and Graham Nash appeared on some dates, while David Bowie sang 'Arnold Layne' and 'Comfortably Numb' at the Albert Hall. The tour ended in Poland's Gdansk Shipyard at the invitation of former president Lech Wałęsa.*

*'We had an enjoyable meeting,' said Gilmour, 'but they gave us a very strong drink – like Schnapps – and afterwards I had to go to a press conference and be asked about Roger Waters.'*

*Meanwhile, Waters' The Dark Side of the Moon Live tour launched in June 2006 and filled the world's arenas off and on for the next two years. Waters wasn't promoting a new album, but staking a claim on his old group's legacy.*

*His band, including 'Snowy' White and Jon Carin, recreated Pink Floyd's most famous album and most of the band's hits and misses. There was also a flying pig daubed with different slogans depending on which country they were playing.*

*'People say "Why do you have to bring politics into it?"' said Waters. 'You have been a Pink Floyd or Roger Waters fan for forty years or whatever and you haven't noticed it's all political?'*

*On 7 July 2006, while Waters and Gilmour were on tour, Syd Barrett died of pancreatic cancer. His health had been declining for some time and he'd lost three fingers to diabetes. 'He was terrible at taking his medication,' explains Rosemary. 'He didn't look after himself and he was still drinking and smoking.' His cancer had only been discovered a few weeks earlier, after he was admitted to Cambridge's Addenbrooke's Hospital.*

*The family announced his death on 11 July and were shocked by the amount of media coverage. But his story was compelling and recyclable.*

*'The* Daily Mail *would re-discover him every three years,' pointed out one Floyd familiar.*

*Over time, details emerged of Barrett's day-to-day life. He still owned a guitar and a handful of jazz CDs; he'd ignored Live 8, but watched* Crazy Diamond, *the BBC's 2001 Syd Barrett documentary, and told Rosemary the music was too loud, but he'd enjoyed seeing Mike Leonard again.*

*Over time, the noises in his head had found an outlet in his singular approach to DIY. At 6 St Margaret's Square, he'd stripped the architrave from the doors, replaced their handles with toy plastic hippos and built a plywood bread bin (which he'd filled with clothes pegs). On one occasion, Rosemary discovered he'd climbed into the attic and tried to rewire the electricity junction box.*

*He also painted every wall a different colour. 'I used to say to him, "Do two walls the same colour,"' recalls Rosemary. '"But why?" he'd say. "They're all different walls."' It may not have made sense to others, but it made sense to him.*

✲

**Roger Waters:** When I heard Syd was ill, I tried and failed to contact his sister. But there was nothing that could be done. It wasn't like he needed any money. Everything that could be done for him was done.

**David Gilmour:** We probably did about as much as we could. But I have a regret or two. One is that I never went to see him, but his family kind of discouraged it. Both Syd and I might have gained something out of one or two people popping around to his house for a cup of tea.

**Rosemary Breen:** Something I was pleased about was that he started painting again in the '80s. Byzantine and Roman were his favourite periods. He loved doing mosaics – the colours and intricacies appealed to him. Modern art not so much. He didn't mind Picasso. He would look at Picasso's paintings and laugh because he thought the big features were funny.

But when he had an idea for a painting, he was really careful crossing the road in Cambridge. He was worried he wouldn't get the idea out in case something happened to him and he'd have to go to hospital. He didn't do art because he wanted to. He *had* to.

When I used to see him not long before he died, I always knew when he'd done a painting or a drawing, because he would be calmer. It really was therapy. But he'd destroy the work afterwards – he'd often burn it or just throw it in the bin. He'd take a photograph of it and then it was gone. That's just how it was – I'm not reading anything into it. It was the same with his music. He never did the same thing twice. Everything had to be original.

**Mick Rock:** I published a book of photographs of Syd [*Psychedelic Renegades*] in 2002 and he signed 320 copies of the first pressing for me. I did it through the family. I didn't go and see him. Later, I asked his nephew Ian why he'd agreed to do that, and he told me – and I'm quoting Ian – 'he liked your pictures'.

**Rosemary Breen:** I was the middle woman and I asked Roger [Syd]. He and Mick had been great friends, and I don't think he'd have done it for anyone else. I'm grateful people respected his privacy, though. I know that a lot of people wanted to speak to him, but the majority were very kind and realised he didn't want to know.

**Vivien Brans:** I was in John Lewis [the department store] once and Syd and Rosemary were in the bedding department. Syd didn't look very well at all. Rosemary said, 'Rog, it's Viv. Do you remember Viv?' He said, 'Mmmm'. 'You know Viv. You used to go round to her house.' 'Yeah, yeah.' Then Rosemary said, 'Actually, he's more interested in getting some towels', and told him, 'Go off and choose what you want.' It was all quite sad.

**Libby Chisman:** I saw him in town once and said, 'Do you know who I am?'. And he replied, 'Of course, you're Libby.' He understood, but he wasn't quite right. My father had suffered a stroke and it hit his brain, and Syd's behaviour reminded me of that.

Later, my daughter was at the university and wearing one of my Biba dresses from the '60s. She saw a man go by on a bicycle and say, 'Hello, little Lib,' as he passed. She didn't know who he was. Then a friend told her it was Syd Barrett.

**Jenny Spires:** In 2006 I was driving along Perne Road on my way to Addenbrooke's Hospital for a check-up, and I overtook a cyclist – and it was Syd. He was cycling along with a huge smile on his face. In my rearview mirror, he looked so well. It was spring, maybe April or May, the trees were blossoming. Then a couple of months later, I turned on the radio and heard he'd died.

**Rosemary Breen:** Not long before he died, Roger [Syd] went to London on the train. He was quite capable of doing the journey and he could be anonymous in London. He was always buying books, right up to the end. He liked atlases and he had a world atlas on his wall. I don't know why. There are a lot of things one doesn't know about him.

He'd visited the Tate [Gallery] and then gone to look at Chelsea Cloisters where he'd once lived. Then, at four o'clock, I had a phone call saying he'd run out of money and couldn't get home. We had to send a gruff old taxi driver from Cambridge to London to bring him back.

So I had to rescue him after he'd spent all of his money. On what? Absolute rubbish. He was like a magpie, anything glittery or colourful. If he wanted something, he had to have it. That was his way. He never grew up, never did a job of work, was never responsible.

He got everything he needed. But I couldn't give him happiness. So what I strived for was to give him contentment. I don't know whether I managed it, but I tried and he knew I was trying. But I would have liked him to have had a friend or two.

**David Gilmour:** I heard that he'd died when we were in Austria, on the On An Island tour. Later, a friend was in Cambridge and asked to have a look around [Syd's] house. Maybe it was on the market or something. He saw one of those plastic tube bird feeders with nuts in it, just took it, brought it back and gave it to me. It amused me. The birds seemed pleased.

✿

*In November 2006, Cheffins of Cambridge put more than seventy items from the house up for auction. These included Barrett's notebooks (filled with inventories of artists, books and fauna), the bread bin, his bicycle, several paintings and an annotated copy of* The Oxford Textbook of Psychiatry, *suggesting he was trying to understand his condition up until the end; all of which helped raise £121,000 for charity.*

*Immediately following his death, Pink Floyd's original producer, Joe Boyd, was approached by the programmer at London's Barbican Theatre to stage a Syd tribute concert. Boyd was about to begin a book tour promoting his memoir,* White Bicycles, *and asked Nick Laird-Clowes to help organise the show. Laird-Clowes pitched his idea to the Barbican as 'The Good Old Days on Acid', a nod to the BBC variety show* The Good Old Days, *which, like '60s psychedelia, took visual motifs from the Edwardian era.*

*The tribute concert, 'Madcap's Last Laugh', included Pink Floyd's final performance and took place on 10 May 2007.*

❊

**Nick Laird-Clowes:** The first thing I said to Joe when he asked me was 'Who have you got?' and he said, 'David Bowie and the Who.' Great! I told [the Pretenders vocalist] Chrissie Hynde's manager that Bowie and the Who were playing. Chrissie didn't really like Pink Floyd, but said she'd consider it.

Then Joe rang and said, 'I've got some bad news. Bowie can't do it.' Oh, never mind, okay. Then Joe called again. 'The Who are out. They need more rehearsal time for their American tour.' So I had to go back to Chrissie and say, 'Actually, we haven't got Bowie and we haven't got the Who.'

Chrissie, being a great person, said, 'Fuck 'em. I'll do it. I used to live with Nick Kent and we listened to Syd's Pink Floyd all the time. I'll do it even if it's just you and me.'

David Gilmour had already said no, and told me, 'I said my goodbyes to Syd when I sang one of his songs in Poland.' But he told us we could use anything we wanted from the Floyd archive.

Then Joe came back to London and, with Chrissie's help, we started to pull something together. She asked Iggy Pop and Steve Jones, but they weren't available, but we did get Captain Sensible from the Damned. I then went to Notting Hill Gate Church where Blur were rehearsing and asked Damon Albarn, who said he'd think about it, and I saw Rick Wright with David and Nick Mason at Abbey Road for Storm Thorgerson's book launch. Rick told me he might be interested.

Then Joe said Roger Waters was going to do it. The night before the show, David rang and asked who was playing. I told him and he said, 'Okay, bye' and then nothing.

**David Gilmour:** I felt uncomfortable about the whole thing. I said, 'I'm not going to do it.' I was literally in a doctor's waiting room in Sussex at 3 p.m. that afternoon, grumbling, when Polly said, 'Just call them up and stop fucking moaning about it.'

**Nick Laird-Clowes:** I was at the Barbican for soundcheck and there was no signal. Joe said, 'Go out and check your phone in case anyone's called.' I did and David had called. I rang him back and he said, 'How would you like Pink Floyd to close the show?'

I said, 'My God, you've left it late.' He said, 'Well if you want it, get a drum kit to the Barbican and we'll just turn up.' Joe asked Roger Waters if he'd do it with Pink Floyd and he said he had to leave early to pick up his girlfriend [actress and future fourth wife Laurie Durning] from the airport. So I asked [Oasis bassist] Andy Bell. 'Do you want to play "Arnold Layne" with Pink Floyd?'

**David Gilmour:** We rehearsed in the dressing room. We had said to Roger, 'Can you do it?' and he said, 'I can't. I have to pick someone up.' People will make a lot of fuss and read something else into that. Once we got up there, it was fine – though we were rusty and under-rehearsed.

**Nick Laird-Clowes:** Joe said when he made the announcement on stage about Pink Floyd, he felt the air in the room go through the top of his hair. It was thrilling and fitting that Pink Floyd closed the show.

**David Gilmour:** That was my tribute to Syd and I suspect that's where I'd rather leave it. I loved the guy, but I can't do anything for him now.

❀

*The show's performers, including Chrissie Hynde, Robyn Hitchcock, Blur's Graham Coxon, Led Zeppelin's John Paul Jones, Captain Sensible and Kevin Ayers, were either contemporaries or acolytes, illustrating Barrett's appeal to several generations.*

*However, Kate McGarrigle's 'See Emily Play', Damon Albarn's 'Word Song' and Nick Laird-Clowes and the Sense of Sound Choir's 'Chapter 24' rose above the rest, and between them touched on three different facets of Syd's writing: pure pop, abstract wordplay and what might best be described as some kind of cosmic church music.*

*A visibly nervous Roger Waters was the only artist to perform one of his own songs ('Flickering Flame'). Then, after Joe Boyd's introduction, Gilmour, Mason, Wright and Andy Bell (Guy Pratt already had a gig with Bryan Ferry) ambled on and launched into 'Arnold Layne'. 'The organ wasn't working properly,' says Laird-Clowes, but the spirit of the occasion carried them over the line.*

*The encore, 'Bike', was a ramshackle knees-up, with all the performers (minus Waters) crowding around Pink Floyd. As the house band's drummer was using the kit, an awkward-looking Nick Mason tapped out the rhythm with drumsticks on the palm of his hand. The show wasn't perfect, but the sentiment was.*

*What none of the performers or audience knew was that Rick Wright would be gone little more than a year later. Wright was still sailing his beloved yacht,* Evrika, *weeks before his death, aged sixty-five, on 15 September 2008. Wright had been diagnosed with lung cancer nine months earlier and had responded well to treatment before a sudden relapse.*

*Waters was absent from Wright's memorial in Notting Hill, but Gilmour, Mason and their supporting musicians performed 'The Great Gig in the Sky' and 'Wish You Were Here' to a backdrop of photographs showing other lost friends, including, inevitably, Syd.*

*Wright's death didn't attract Barrett's level of media coverage, but his contribution to Pink Floyd went far beyond the clichéd 'quiet one' persona. He was part of the group's DNA and intrinsic to 'See Emily Play', 'The Great Gig in the Sky', 'Us and Them', 'Shine On You Crazy Diamond', 'Echoes'… As David Gilmour said, 'Rick had soul'.*

❀

**David Gilmour:** During the '70s and early '80s, it was easy to forget Rick's abilities because he forgot them himself. He went through a difficult time, but he came out of it. He came right back out of his shell. I always liked what Rick did, but I didn't quite believe in him as much as I should have done at times.

**Anthony Moore:** It's how you voice the chords and which parts you give prominence to. Rick had a unique way of playing these keyboard parts, especially in the left hand. That's a simplistic way of putting it, but you could always tell it was him on those records.

**Nick Mason:** Rick wrote songs, he sang, he did a lot of things, but he was eclipsed by everything else going on. He wasn't a natural frontman. He was very droll and very funny, but he suffered from being quieter than the rest of us.

**Jeff Dexter:** I think Rick was gazumped by the energy of the others. After about 1974, he started to retreat into himself and I think he was more badly treated than Syd was.

I went outside with him for a smoke at Storm's book launch at Abbey Road and we had the most fantastic conversation for the first time in years. I said, 'You seem to be having a good time in Dave's band.' And he said, 'Jeff, I'm sorry we haven't spent more time together in all these years.' I said to him, 'Well, you are going to play Syd's show, aren't you?' And he said he wanted to sing 'Arnold Layne', which was just before Joe Boyd came up and asked him.

**Guy Pratt:** I had an idea with Rick of putting a band together for him to play his stuff and some old jazz favourites. But it never happened, probably because neither of us were great organisers.

**Roger Waters (addressing the audience at 'Madcap's Last Laugh'):** 'Of course, I'm terrified. These small occasions are much more frightening than the big ones where you can hide behind all the paraphernalia. But for those of us who suffer from a sense of shame and doom, as I'm sure any of you who know my work will know I have all my life, this is all quite stressful.'

✲

*It's 12 May 2011 and Roger Waters is staging another 'big one': the latest stop on his The Wall Live tour at London's O2 Arena. To gain access to our row, patrons have to squeeze past Gerald Scarfe and his wife Jane Asher, who is currently playing Lady Byrne in the BBC TV medical drama* Holby City. *This manoeuvre takes place several times and involves many predominantly male buttocks hovering far too close to the couple's faces. They never complain.*

The Wall *is now a CGI-fuelled, multimedia extravaganza, using technology that would have been unimaginable when Waters last staged the show in Berlin. This means Scarfe's images are now reproduced via twenty-three projectors on a 240-foot-wide wall.*

*During 'Mother', his ceiling-high marionette of a steely-eyed matriarch rises before us, just as a late arrival arrives bearing a tray of drinks. Waters' plea – 'Mother, do you think they'll try to break my balls?' – is punctuated by whispered apologies as the latecomer inches his cargo down the line.*

*We're only a few rows from the front and, had this been the old days, Waters might have shouted a withering 'For fuck's sake!'. But his attitude towards big gigs has mellowed.* The Wall's *message – about physical, mental and metaphorical walls – remains universal, but this tour is its composer's victory lap.*

*With Gilmour preferring the quieter life as a solo artist, Waters is filling the void. His eleven-piece band are there to 'do' Pink Floyd – and it's paying* *off. By the summer of 2013, The Wall Live will have grossed $450 million, anointing Waters as the third most profitable solo artist in the world, behind Madonna and Bruce Springsteen.*

*The show has proved controversial, though, with images of bombs shaped like American dollar signs, corporate company logos and the Jewish star of David; the last attracting a complaint from the Anti-Defamation League.*

*Waters, a pro-Palestinian rights supporter, later cancels shows in Tel Aviv and announces his support for sanctions against Israel. 'My position is not antisemitic,' he insists. 'This is not an attack of the people of Israel ... But all people deserve basic human rights.'*

*Tonight's show is a really 'big one', though, when a spot-lit David Gilmour makes a surprise appearance on top of the wall for 'Comfortably Numb'. The applause is such that one wonders how it feels to be Waters' regular guitarist Dave Kilminster right now.*

*Nick Mason joins Gilmour for the finale, 'Outside the Wall', and elicits a similar response. Just a glimpse of three-quarters of the golden-years Floyd is enough for people to ask, 'Will they get back together?' – but also, 'Why did Gilmour agree to do this?'*

*A year earlier, Gilmour asked Waters to play at an Oxfordshire fundraiser for the Palestinian refugees charity, Hoping Foundation. 'David said, "If you do [the Teddy Bears' 1958 hit] 'To Know Him Is To Love Him' ... I'll come and do 'C. Numb' at one of your* Wall *shows,"' recalled Waters. Footage of the performance suggests one of them found it easier to hit the song's high notes than the other.*

*Later, film emerges of the two musicians soundchecking 'Comfortably Numb' at the O2.*

*Waters stares up at Gilmour on top of the wall. 'Try not to dive off, 'cos I'll be standing somewhere down there,' he says, in faux theatrical cockney.*

*'I'll try,' replies Gilmour, drier than the Atacama Desert.*

❦

**Gerald Scarfe:** I thought that show was like a really good opera. But everything about it was bigger than the original, including the wall itself. When Roger wrote it, he was talking about his father and the Second World War. But the story fits all walls, from the Great Wall of China to Hadrian's to Israel, walls between people, how we wall ourselves off...

**Roger Waters:** A guy called Hank Steinbrenner, whose father owned the New York Yankees, had an idea to put *The Wall* on in Yankee Stadium. He got in touch and said, 'You ask Gilmour.' I said I didn't mind asking, but that he'd say no. So I got my people to ask his people to ask him and, within about twenty minutes, he got his people to speak to my people and said no – which was totally predictable.

**David Gilmour:** It was okay [playing 'Comfortably Numb' at the O2]. I was strangely more nervous than I thought I might be. I made a mistake with the lyrics. I don't think I've done that before.

**Nick Mason:** There was something so nice about having done the original show – which we didn't do enough of because it cost so much – and seeing it brought up to date. I was amazed how closely Roger had stuck to the original, though. I thought he'd write some extra pieces.

Half the audience wouldn't have known David was appearing. At one point he was doing it in Paris, then he wasn't doing it at all. I was asked two hours before. I'd been in Los Angeles and wanted to be there when they said David was definitely appearing. So I came straight from the airport to the O2 and then the two of them said, 'Do you want to come on at the end?'

**Roger Waters [speaking to the O2 audience, 12 May 2011):** 'Thirty years ago, when David and Nick and I first did this, with Rick, I was a rather grumpy person and disaffected with rock 'n' roll audiences ... as young David will attest. But all that's changed! I could not be happier than to be here with these guys ... and all of you here in this room tonight. Thank you very, very, much indeed!'

**Nick Mason:** I now have a great picture of the three of us laughing. Roger's speech was very odd, though. We can't decide whether he really means it, or thinks it makes him sound like a nicer person and more people will love him.

**Aubrey 'Po' Powell:** Roger never forgave Storm for that situation with *Animals* where he didn't credit Roger's design in Hipgnosis's book. Roger didn't speak to him for something like twenty years.

When Storm was dying of cancer, I flew to LA to see Roger's show. Hipgnosis had broken up years ago, Storm had his own studio designing album covers and I'd been making TV commercials and documentaries with people like Nelson Mandela.

There were all these people backstage, but straight off the bat I said to Roger, 'You need to see Storm. He's dying, and you and he were like brothers when you were young. You need to talk to him and you owe him this.' Roger said, 'All right, Po. Set it up, I'll do it' – and he did.

**David Gilmour:** Storm used to call himself 'the art department'. He would ring me up and say, 'Hi, it's the art department'. After Storm died [in April 2013], Po came and worked for us. I like to have members of, if not my actual genetic family, but my family being part of it.

**Aubrey 'Po' Powell:** Two months before Storm died, he said, 'Listen man, I've spoken to David and I've spoken to Nick. Would you be interested in taking on the mantle of Pink Floyd's creative director?' I didn't know if I was interested, because I was involved in films and other things.

About four weeks after Storm's funeral, I received a call from David and Pink Floyd's manager Paul Loasby saying, 'Look, we need somebody to carry on. Would you be interested?'

I went to see all the managers – Paul, Mark Fenwick, who looks after Roger, and Nick's manager Tony Smith – and I'd prepared a four-page proposal, suggesting we try it for a year and see how it goes. I also asked for a retainer and they burst out laughing. Tony Smith said, 'We don't give out *retainers*, Po.' Did I ever get one? No.

✣

*Among Aubrey Powell's first commissions was conjuring up artwork for a not-quite-new Pink Floyd album.* The Endless River *comprised of four compositions, culled from more than twenty hours of music, initially edited by Phil Manzanera. The end result combined polished* Division Bell-*era outtakes with new contributions from Gilmour, Mason and other Floyd family members.*

*Released in November 2014 (and co-produced by Gilmour, Manzanera, Andy Jackson and Youth), it was also a tribute to Rick Wright. The first voice heard on the record was his, sampled from Adrian Maben's interview in* Pink Floyd at Pompeii.

*'We certainly have an unspoken understanding, but there are a lot of things left unsaid as well,' said Wright, later heard playing the Royal Albert Hall pipe organ during rehearsals for 'The Final Lunacy' in 1969.*

*Gilmour had worked with Youth on the Orb's 2010 album,* Metallic Spheres. *Parts of* The Endless River *('It's What We Do', 'On Noodle Street') explored a similar theme: like Grantchester Meadows meets an Ibiza chill-out bar. Other parts fell back on well-worn tropes and felt a little second-hand.*

*The only vocal track, the single 'Louder Than Words', addressed Pink Floyd's peculiar chemistry. 'If you're in a room, as I was at Live 8, with David, Nick, Rick and Roger Waters, nobody speaks,' said Polly Samson in 2015. 'There is nothing but awkward silences. They have no small talk with each other. They have no big talk with each other. They just do not speak. And then they get on stage and suddenly they're so eloquent, and the way they communicate is beautiful.'*

*The music business had changed significantly since* The Division Bell. *In 2012, Universal Music Group acquired EMI in a £1.2 billion takeover, but not its imprint Parlophone, which later went to Warner Music Group, as part of the EMI divestment.* The Endless River *emerged on Parlophone in the UK and was an anomaly in the age of internet piracy and streaming.*

*'You could say* The Endless River *is not for the iTunes, downloading-individual-tracks generation,' suggested Gilmour, before it replaced boy band One Direction's* Midnight Memories *to become the most pre-ordered*

*album in the history of Amazon UK and reached number one in more than twenty countries.*

❀

**David Gilmour:** What we wanted was for *The Endless River* to be a slightly grander version of 'The Big Spliff' – and a tribute to Rick. 'The Big Spliff' was something Andy Jackson put together for fun and possibilities. I think we filleted it, or most of what was good on it, for *The Endless River*. We thought we'd spend a month or two on it. But, as things do, it got a bit out of hand.

**Phil Manzanera:** Eventually my thoughts developed into a structure with four movements along the lines of a classical composition, with themes and echoes featuring riffs and sequences the three men had produced while jamming. I even drew a storyboard to represent a sort of narrative, which I didn't eventually have the nerve to show to anyone other than my wife, Claire.

**Nick Mason:** It sat around for an awfully long time and was being pushed by Andy Jackson and Phil Manzanera. Various people came and had a poke about with it before eventually we got it to the point where we could get David to go, 'Yeah, I like it' – and enough to want to make a serious go of it.

**David Gilmour:** Polly was fascinated by our interactions during rehearsals for Live 8 and had written notes. Years later, when we were preparing *The Endless River*, we had the piece of music which became 'Louder Than Words'. It was one of those serendipitous things where the music wasn't written for those words and the words weren't written for that music but somehow, they came together.

**Anthony Moore:** I'm on the album and I have to thank Andy Jackson for that. He wrote everything down during *The Division Bell*, every overdub, who did what, every date and time, like a good, classy engineer.

A fragment of keyboard playing came up when they were picking pieces for *The Endless River*. David thought it was Rick. But Andy said,

'Wait a minute, that's Anthony.' The income from it is pretty modest. I should probably be giving Andy half, though it wouldn't buy him more than three pints a year.

**Aubrey 'Po' Powell:** We invited half a dozen designers, including Damien Hirst and Peter Saville, to pitch for that cover. But David and Nick kept coming back to this picture of a man in what looked like an Arab dhow, punting through the clouds. The image came to us from an ad agency, but had actually been taken from the internet and belonged to an eighteen-year-old Egyptian digital artist, Ahmed Emad Eldin. Ahmed spoke very little English and was astonished to discover Pink Floyd wanted one of his pictures on the cover of their new album.

**David Gilmour:** I wanted *The Endless River* to be a smaller thing that just popped out and the record company wanted to sell it as a big album. Understandable. The difficulties are the differences of view between the artist and the people who are involved in its manufacture and sales. I thought of it as something lighter. I didn't want it to be a grand Pink Floyd album to compete with *The Division Bell* or any of the others, but hey ho...

✤

*As with Live 8 and* On An Island, The Endless River *primed listeners for Gilmour's next album, 2015's* Rattle That Lock. *Slightly more upbeat than its predecessor, one track – 'A Boat Lies Waiting' – was another homage to Rick Wright and that rare creature: a Pink Floyd-related song you wished went on for longer.*

*However, Gilmour thought the band had become complacent and fired most of them before the tour's penultimate leg. Guy Pratt, one of the few spared, joined newcomers (including Michael Jackson's former musical director Greg Phillinganes) when Gilmour performed in the US and at Pompeii that summer. The weight of Floyd history was about to bear down on them all – again.*

❀

**Phil Manzanera:** I think David sensed that my time was up with him and that I wasn't particularly happy. I'm hopeless being a sideman. The amount of time I spent in David's kitchen with him trying to teach me how to play 'Wish You Were Here'. I never really played it exactly right… But we're still friends.

**Guy Pratt:** Everyone uses in-ear monitors now, but I hate them. On the first day of rehearsals for our last tour, I had my in-ears in and David said something. I took them out. 'Sorry, what was that again?' And he told me.

Then we played a song and David said something to me and I took my in-ears out *again*, and suddenly realised, actually that's why I'm here. I'm the bloke David can talk to – though I'm sure everyone thinks I know something terrible, that I've got some awful bit of blackmail.

**David Gilmour:** Sometimes you can't be sentimental about it, but you have to do what's best for your art. But there are times when you allow yourself to get stuck in a situation and accept moments of discontent. I'm jealous of those people who seem to chop and change their musicians, as I've always found it difficult, but it's thrilling working with new people.

**Aubrey 'Po' Powell:** Storm had put on a Pink Floyd exhibition in Paris in 2003. The idea had been revived but to make it bigger, grander. The Italian promoter Fran Tomasi, who'd put Pink Floyd on at the Grand Canal in Venice, came on board as a backer.

I started working with an incredible team that included [architects and stage design company] Stufish and Paula Stainton, who'd worked with Nick Mason and Formula 1. At the first meeting I had with Stufish, I brought in a roll of lining paper, laid it out on the table about twelve feet long, took a felt-tip pen and said, 'Here's how I see it. You walk into the Bedford van Pink Floyd drove in 1965' – as I dragged the pen along the roll of paper – 'and then tell the band's story in chronological order.' They looked at me and said, 'That's what we're going to do then.'

Nick was on board and helpful. Then I flew to New York to see Roger who was busy with his *Wall* shows and David who was making *Rattle That Lock*. Neither of them seemed very interested, but gave it their seal of approval.

Fran Tomasi had sold tickets for a space in Milan. Then, six weeks before the exhibition was to be shipped to Italy, he wasn't able to pay his bills – a disaster – and Pink Floyd's management pulled the plug.

I'd spoken to the Victoria & Albert Museum about doing a Hipgnosis exhibition and they'd just put on the Bowie exhibition [2013's 'David Bowie Is']. So I went to see Vicky Broackes, their music and theatre curator, and said, 'Who have you got in mind after David Bowie...?' And she said, 'We were going to call you. We'd like Pink Floyd.'

**Nick Mason:** I'd been to the Bowie exhibition, which I thought was absolutely terrific. Then I had a conversation about Pink Floyd with [V&A director] Martin Roth. But I couldn't see how we would match Bowie because I was thinking in terms of costumes and Pink Floyd didn't have many costumes. We'd kept a few props, but the problem is, 'Where do you put a seventy-foot teacher?'

**Aubrey 'Po' Powell:** A vital component to all this was a book we called 'The Bible', that listed everything our team had sourced from people, warehouses and lock-ups around the world – old pigs and stage props, the Azimuth Co-ordinator, Syd's letters to Jenny Spires, Roger's lyrics for 'Another Brick in the Wall'.

We even found the punishment book from the Cambridgeshire High School for Boys which listed the number of times Storm, Syd and Roger were punished, and how many strokes of the cane they received.

**Roger Waters:** I didn't have to be persuaded to support the exhibition. I embraced it straight away. I think the beatings book is the highlight. Po said he'd been back to the County – it's a sixth-form college now – and they'd still got the book and the cane. I couldn't believe they'd kept it.

✲

Despite Mason's fears, the V&A was large enough to accommodate The Wall's teacher – and much more. Powell's team filled their allocated space with more than 300 relics of varying sizes and rarity.

In February 2017, Mason and Waters took part in a press launch/Q&A session in London's May Fair Hotel. Now in their seventies, they'd become one of classic rock's signature odd couples: Mason's Jack Lemmon to Waters' Walter Matthau.

'If I'm talking on my own, I know I can get away with saying anything,' admitted the drummer. 'But not with Roger.'

'Who has the best memory?' asked the host, BBC radio presenter Matt Everitt.

'How would we know?' Waters growled back.

'Their Mortal Remains: The Pink Floyd Exhibition' was the largest exhibition on one subject ever staged at the V&A. Between May and October 2017, some 300,000 people gazed at The Division Bell's giant heads, a replica of Battersea Power Station and The Dark Side of the Moon's holographic prism, before experiencing 'Comfortably Numb' at Live 8 pumped through twenty-five speakers in 3D audio.

'Their Mortal Remains' moved to Rome before visiting Dortmund, Madrid, Los Angeles, Montreal and Toronto, and closing in Buenos Aires in 2024.

Whatever rifts existed, the exhibition was a reminder of the group's shared history. With that came the constant challenge of how to manage that history, now well-served by expensive box sets, which – as Storm Thorgerson averred – you'd have 'had to lose your marbles to pay for'. But there was also the three individuals' personal relationship with the music to consider.

In 2016, Gilmour turned down an offer for Pink Floyd to play the Desert Trip festival in Indio, California. Waters took the job instead, before releasing Is This the Life We Really Want? (which became his highest-charting UK solo album) and spending most of the next two years on his Us + Them tour.

Most unexpectedly, Nick Mason's in-house tribute, Nick Mason's Saucerful of Secrets, arrived in 2018 and toured Europe and the US with a set-list of *pre-*Dark Side... *songs, a UFO club-style light show and none of Pink Floyd's psychological trauma and enmity. 'At my time of life, I want to be in a band with people I like,' said the drummer.*

⁂

**Aubrey 'Po' Powell:** As creative director, I wasn't guided one way or the other in terms of loyalty. I never felt on the Gilmour side or the Waters side. I just felt that, to get any project done, I had to balance the two. Nick helped me if there was a real problem, but he didn't want to get involved in the issues between those two.

The biggest surprise to me from working on the exhibition was that, despite designing covers and going on tour with them, I don't think I really appreciated how good Pink Floyd were. My respect grew. I knew *The Dark Side of the Moon* was an incredible album when it happened, but now I think it's a bloody masterpiece. That sort of thing only happens once, though – a bit like Hipgnosis's *Dark Side of the Moon* logo. But if you're lucky, you can live off it for the rest of your life.

**Nick Mason:** One of the interesting things about the exhibition is it made us look like we had a masterplan, that we steadily worked our way from *The Piper at the Gates of Dawn* to the present day. Whereas, of course, there were these long periods where we didn't know what to do, or were in constant disagreement about something. It made us seem more organised than we were.

**Aubrey 'Po' Powell:** David Gilmour came along to see it after the opening and after reading these amazing reviews in the newspaper. It absolutely blew him away.

**Roger Waters:** [Festival founder] Paul Tollett at Desert Trip said, 'Would you be interested?' and named the six other acts he was going to ask. When it came to fruition, I had to figure out what to do. I thought, *He's already got the Rolling Stones, Paul McCartney and Bob Dylan, so he's obviously asking me to be Pink Floyd for a day. But if that's what they want, that's what I'll do.*

So, I started looking at songs from *Animals*. I hadn't played 'Dogs' for years and I'd never done 'Pigs [Three Different Ones]'. I thought it was interesting musically and people will misinterpret the lyrics, like they did back in '77.

But there's also a certain amount of nostalgia involved with *Is This the Life We Really Want?* too. My producer Nigel Godrich has a huge attachment to the work I did with Pink Floyd, so there's lots of segueing between songs and hearing the weather forecast for British coastal waters – Cromarty and Humber and all that – like on *The Final Cut*. It's absolutely a concept record.

**Nick Mason:** I enjoyed working with the V&A, but the missing bit for me was playing music again, which was part of the idea behind putting the Saucers together.

Lee Harris [ex-Ian Dury and the Blockheads' guitarist] had the initial idea. He lives in France, saw David play live and thought, *Why isn't Nick doing anything?* He took the idea for a band to Guy Pratt. If Lee had come direct to me, I would have turned it down, as I didn't know him. Instead, Guy said to me, 'I'm sure you *don't* want to do this, but...'.

I thought it was *probably* a good idea. But the concept of us doing versions of 'Comfortably Numb' or 'Time'? No. Roger and David already do it so well, as do the tribute bands, the Australian Pink Floyd and Brit Floyd. So the more we thought about it, the clearer it was to stick with this earlier era.

**Guy Pratt:** The Saucers are Pink Floyd when it was a pop group, before it became that sort of vast faceless obelisk. It feels like another band. It wasn't connecting with the seriousness of Pink Floyd or my dad giving me *The Dark Side of the Moon* and my first bass and all that. This was something else. This was a rock band we used to listen to in the dark at school.

**Nick Mason:** Guy is good friends with [ex-Spandau Ballet guitarist] Gary Kemp and Guy recommended [ex-Orb keyboard player] Dom Beken. I was rather surprised Gary wanted to do it. I thought he might as a special guest, but he was so enthusiastic. One sometimes forgets that we're all musicians, whether it's new romantic or prog or whatever. There's no difference. It's like having Captain Sensible saying he'd like to join us, which he probably would.

We sounded rather amateur at first. We did two days where we just decided whether it was worth carrying on. Then a week, and then another week, before the first gig [in May 2018 at Camden Dingwalls].

I was also keen on the idea of not being too rigorous, not sounding exactly like the recorded versions. There were tracks everyone was up for – 'Arnold Layne', 'See Emily Play', 'Interstellar Overdrive', 'Astronomy Domine', 'Fearless'... Later came the question: Can we do 'Atom Heart Mother'? 'Childhood's End'? 'Obscured By Clouds'?...

**Guy Pratt:** When I introduce 'The Nile Song' on stage, I say, 'this was the first Pink Floyd song I knew because it was on *Relics*, which was the album everybody had because it was half the price of other Pink Floyd albums'.

**Nick Mason:** I was asked, 'Did I need Roger and David's permission?' No more than they needed mine for them to go out again. David sent notes to Guy about his singing and he was definitely monitoring it. Roger was very supportive and got up with us at the Beacon Theatre in New York [in April 2019].

**Guy Pratt:** Roger's always been fine with me. He even said something nice about me in print. But do you know why I'm so glad he got up and did that thing with us? Because Gary Kemp went up to him afterwards and said, 'Thank you so much for doing this for us, and for Nick.' And he said, 'I didn't do it for you, I did it for me.' It's amazing compared to, say, David Bowie getting up with David at the Albert Hall, which was an absolute masterclass in humility and grace.

**Nick Mason:** The whole thing is about enjoyment. I'm not going into it for the experience of being Roger Waters. I think if he were still with us, Rick might have got involved. Rick would have liked the initial concept. Whether he'd have the appetite for what it would become, I'm not sure.

**Guy Pratt:** 'Echoes' was awkward. I absolutely didn't want to do it and I wrote a big letter to everyone saying I didn't want to do it. Nick and the others all did, but I had gone on record saying, 'I'm never playing "Echoes" again' – because David had said he wouldn't play it again after Rick died.

I thought, *I'm obviously never going to play 'Echoes' again because who am I going to play it with apart from David?* So, when this comes along, people weren't happy about it. At the end of the day, though, it's an amazing piece of work. Someone once said 'Echoes' is the song where Pink Floyd invent Radiohead, U2 and ambient music all at the same time.

**Nick Mason:** The fact of the matter is, as most musicians are aware, irrespective of whether they're wildly successful or not, it's still a privilege to be earning your living doing this. Right now, I hope we might do a bit more playing live, but I think, past eighty years, my appetite for mid-priced hotels and tour buses has waned slightly.

✣

*When COVID struck and the UK locked down in March 2020, David Gilmour savoured the tranquillity and the absence of planes over his Sussex farmhouse. 'I don't want to alter the perspective that, for many people, there was a lot of hardship,' he insists. 'But there were things about it that were not a hardship.'*

*Polly Samson was due to promote her new novel,* A Theatre For Dreamers. *Instead, the couple took the promotion online and began livestreaming as the Von Trapped Family. Surrounded by family members and dogs, Gilmour strummed a guitar and Polly read from the book and coaxed her husband into telling stories about Syd Barrett. Gilmour didn't look like he was in any hurry to get back to normal life.*

*However, these cosy familial broadcasts upset Roger Waters who, in May 2020, posted a video on Twitter (now X) complaining that Pink Floyd's official website and social media were promoting the Von Trapped Family at the expense of his solo work.*

*'David Gilmour thinks because I left the band in 1985, he is* Pink Floyd*… and I am irrelevant and should keep my mouth shut,' Waters complained.*

*'This is wrong … We should rise up … or just change the name of the band to Spinal Tap.'*

*While their past grievances had once been aired in the music press, now both parties could reach millions without any editorial filter.*

*In the coming months, Waters shifted his attention from band squabbles to world politics. He voiced his trenchant support for Palestine in the Israel–Palestine conflict and continued mocking Donald Trump during his stage show ('Trump Is A Pig' appeared in huge letters on 39-foot video screens).*

*'We don't seem to grasp the fact that it actually makes us happier to be decent people rather than breaking each other's legs,' he claimed, while supporting the Venezuelan president Nicolás Maduro, who was now being investigated for crimes against humanity.*

*Despite both Gilmour and Waters' solo success, Pink Floyd, the brand, remained a faceless entity, meaning many wondered if Waters spoke on its behalf.*

*In April 2022, Gilmour broke his political silence by reviving the Pink Floyd name for a single, 'Hey, Hey, Rise Up!', recorded with Ukrainian rock star and military reservist Andriy Khlyvnyuk in protest at the Russian invasion of Ukraine. All proceeds went to the Ukraine Humanitarian Relief Fund, an issue especially close to Gilmour's heart as his son Charlie's partner was Ukrainian.*

*In February 2023, Waters described Floyd's charity single as 'content-less … flag waving' during an interview with the German newspaper,* Berliner Zeitung. *'Is Putin a bigger gangster than Joe Biden and all those in charge of American politics since World War II?' he asked. 'I am not so sure. Putin didn't invade Vietnam or Iraq, did he?'*

*In the same month, Russia invited Waters to give a speech at the UN Security Council. 'The invasion of Ukraine by the Russian Federation was illegal. I condemn it in the strongest possible terms,' he said. 'Also, the Russian invasion of Ukraine was not unprovoked, so I also condemn the provocateurs in the strongest possible terms.'*

On 4 February, Polly Samson posted a message on Twitter: 'Sadly @RogerWaters, you are antisemitic to your rotten core. Also a Putin apologist and a lying, thieving, hypocritical, tax-avoiding, lip-synching, misogynistic, sick-with-envy, megalomaniac. Enough of your nonsense.'

'Every word demonstrably true,' stated Gilmour in a separate tweet, posted an hour or two later.

Later that day, Waters tweeted: 'Roger Waters is aware of the incendiary and wildly inaccurate comments made about him on Twitter by Polly Samson, which he refutes entirely. He is currently taking advice as to his position.'

After this, the spat descended further into playground jibes. In June, at London's O2 Arena during his This Is Not A Drill tour, Waters declared his love for 'all my brothers and sisters ... irrespective of their ethnicity, or religion or nationality ... Well, with one possible exception ... All I have to say about Polly Samson is imagining waking up to that every morning.'

Within hours, Gilmour had tweeted a photograph of his wife and the message, 'So lovely to wake up to, this morning as always!'

Later that month, Waters appeared as a guest on journalist Piers Morgan's Talk TV show, where he denied being antisemitic. Soon after, he was the subject of an online documentary by the Campaign Against Anti-Semitism, with Bob Ezrin among those testifying against Waters.

Such was the drama that many forgot 2023 marked the fiftieth anniversary of The Dark Side of the Moon – except for the man who wrote the lyrics and released The Dark Side of the Moon Redux in October. Waters had done away with the guitar solos and used spoken-word vocals to revisit its themes of war, mortality, greed and madness. He recycled the lyrics from Obscured By Cloud's 'Free Four' in 'Speak to Me' and broke the fourth wall in 'Brain Damage'. 'Why don't we re-record Dark Side?' he muttered before cracking up laughing and announcing, 'He's gone mad'. It was a strange, curious record.

Waters performed the work at the London Palladium, but spent an hour at the first show reading from his unpublished autobiography. During a story *about his pet duck Donald, some audience members began heckling and chatting among themselves.*

*'If you want to tell stories, tell them in your own time to your own audience in your own fucking theatre,' he protested. 'By the way, if you can, show constraint and stop shouting again.'*

*Today, David Gilmour refuses to comment on Waters' redux* Dark Side...

*'What did I think of it?' says Alan Parsons, who helped engineer the original. 'Er, no comment.'*

*In October 2024, Pink Floyd followed the likes of Dylan, Springsteen and Neil Young, and finally sold their catalogue. Sony Music officially paid $400 million (some suggest the figure was higher), though the band members retained the rights to their individual song publishing. The sale had been on and off several times since 2022, as the three surviving members and Rick Wright's estate couldn't agree on the details. All parties, including their managers, must have breathed a huge collective sigh of relief.*

✢

**David Gilmour:** It was entirely Polly's tweet, but I obviously knew about it and we discussed it. Many people don't know which band member is which and she was getting a lot of hassle from people thinking that she was married to someone with those views. She wanted to draw a line. I 100 per cent agreed with it.

The whole thing with Roger has moved into another stratosphere. Roger's ignorance shocks me. He says, 'Read, read, read...' I don't think I ever saw him read a book. But I don't want matters of international importance – ie, Ukraine and Israel – to become the subject of a pop-group dispute, which is why, as a rule, I don't like to discuss all this.

**Nick Mason:** I heard the rumour that Roger was working on his own version of *Dark Side*.... There was this suggestion it was going to be a spoiler and Roger was going to go head-to-head with the original version. He actually sent me a copy of what he was working on and I wrote to him and said, 'Annoyingly, it's absolutely brilliant.' It was and is.

**Roger Waters:** The new recording is more reflective, I think, and it's more indicative of what the concept of the record was. It is a reinterpretation and I hope we can gain more from it than we did back in 1973 when it first came out – because it's been part of our lives for fifty years and yet we are still not yet breathing in the air.

**David Gilmour:** Sony bought the catalogue. We have granted them the necessary sync licences, everything apart from the publishing. They didn't get the name. Nick and I still own the name, but they have permanent right of usage. There's a technical difference there.

Obviously, however unlikely, if Nick and I wanted to go and do a Pink Floyd tour, that is a right that we still have. Just as Bruce Springsteen can still be Bruce Springsteen and Bob Dylan can still be Bob Dylan, like all these other people who've sold their catalogues in various ways.

I am enormously pleased to be shot of it. But you have to make a mental adjustment. There will be things that you wouldn't have done, but you have to think, *That's what I have relinquished*. It's a matter of unloading something and saying, 'I am no longer a part of this.'

**Nick Mason:** Did I ever imagine I'd still be talking about all this at my time of life? No, I did not. We made records we knew were good and people liked them, but that didn't mean they were going to be around fifty years later. The future was always a complete fog.

**Roger Waters:** It's like when Van Gogh put that last bit of yellow on his sunflowers or whatever, and the moment when he stands back. I don't know what he was thinking, but this is what happens when I've written a song or recorded a piece of music. There is one fleeting moment when you go, 'That is good.' And then it's gone. And it never comes back. You never hear it again.

✣

# AFTERWORD

It's almost summer 2025, and I'm at south London's BFI IMAX cinema for a screening of the restored *Pink Floyd at Pompeii* film. As the movie starts, I'm reminded of a song on David Gilmour's latest album, *Luck and Strange*, called 'Scattered'. The closing line is: 'It never ends.'

The new film is a work of art, but almost voyeuristic in its detail. Every grimace on Nick Mason's face as he thrashes his kit and every sinew on Roger Waters' sinewy arm are reproduced in vivid colours on a screen 85-feet-wide and 65-feet-high.

Ripples of laughter greet the young band members' interviews in the Abbey Road canteen. 'I still think most people see us as a very drug-oriented group,' purrs Gilmour. 'Of course we're not. You can trust us.'

What's remarkable, though, about watching Pink Floyd hammering pianos and gongs during 'A Saucerful of Secrets' is how they went from *this* to *The Dark Side of the Moon*. Perhaps it's the 'strange magic' Polly Samson wrote about in 'Louder Than Words'.

*Pink Floyd at Pompeii*, the accompanying live album, later goes to number one in the UK – quite a feat for music recorded a lifetime ago by a group whose surviving members have a combined age of 241.

'I thought the film was good and, of course, it brought back memories,' says Gilmour today. 'When you put people and their personalities into a different timeframe, it becomes a different thing.'

Remembering people in different timeframes has become harder, though. On his 2024 tour, Gilmour culled a lot of Waters-era Pink Floyd material from his set.

'There are songs I really wouldn't want to do now,' he admits. '"Run Like Hell"? The words don't do it for me. So I have mixed feelings about one of the songs I wrote 100 per cent of the music for, but don't still enjoy.'

Instead, he played most of *Luck and Strange*, which has his youngest daughter Romany singing a lead vocal. Some of the songs are about growing up in the '60s, others about growing old this century.

'I do have nostalgia,' he once told me. 'I can't imagine there is anyone who doesn't. But I tend to examine my nostalgia and think, *Wow, it really wasn't that great*.'

That aside, Gilmour looked more content, happier almost, on stage than he had done for years. 'I erased a few songs from my thought processes,' he says. 'I have enough post-1985 Pink Floyd stuff and my own solo songs that I can do a very lovely set. Should I still be doing things from over forty years ago? Am I there to create new music or am I there to do what loads of cover bands do perfectly well?'

Pink Floyd did their greatest work when David Gilmour and Roger Waters were together. Today, they resemble a bitterly divorced couple tethered to each other by their offspring. If Pink Floyd were a family wedding, Nick Mason would be the toastmaster and the other two would be sat at opposite ends of the top table, complaining about each other to anyone who'll listen.

'I actually get along with both of them,' said Mason once, 'and I think it's really disappointing that these rather elderly gentlemen are still at loggerheads.'

'I'm now free of hassle and the deliberate spokes in the wheel that have gone on in the many years since Roger left,' says Gilmour. 'It hasn't been easy to try and keep it on an even keel, to keep it honest. There are people who have gripes about various things – but now I no longer have to give a shit.'

Can any of them truly escape, though? *The Dark Side of the Moon*, *Wish You Were Here* and the rest are part of the wider culture, regardless of the musicians' personal rancour. This stuff isn't going away any time soon.

At the time of writing, the Who are about to embark on another farewell tour, and even the Rolling Stones are threatening to return. While there's something noble about Pink Floyd – in any incarnation – not reuniting, the future is out of their control. Under Sony's stewardship, their music is likely to be used in more movies, television adverts and TV shows, meaning another generation will hear that opening four-note guitar figure in 'Shine On You Crazy Diamond' and wonder what it is they're listening to.

Our time is up and David Gilmour has places to go and people to see that don't involve talking about 'our little pop group'. The coach house's front door swings open onto the street as he shouts down a cheery good-bye. The sun is still shining and there's a book still to be finished. But, in the words of the song, 'it never ends'.

# ACKNOWLEDGEMENTS

Thanks to my agent, Matthew Hamilton, and to all at New Modern: Pete Selby, James Lilford, Paul Palmer-Edwards and Nige Tassell.

This book draws on my original interviews with members of Pink Floyd, past and present, and many others conducted between 1992 and 2025. Sadly, some of those sharing memories and telling stories are no longer with us. Thanks to everyone: Paul Bailey, Nick Barraclough, Andy Bown, Vivien Brans, Rosemary Breen, Rob Brimson, Phil Carlo, Paul Carrack, Chris Charlesworth, Libby Chisman, Glen Colson, Alice Cooper, Lindsay Corner, Karl Dallas, Chris Dennis, Jeff Dexter, Peter Dockley, Warren Dosanjh, Bob Ezrin, Mick Farren, Duggie Fields, David Gale, Ron Geesin, David Gilmour, John Gordon, Caroline Greeves, Jeff Griffin, Roy Harper, Dave 'De' Harris, Jeanette Holland, John 'Hoppy' Hopkins, Nicky Horne, Brian Humphries, Sam Hutt, Peter Jenner, Nick Kent, Andrew King, Susan Kingsford, Rado 'Bob' Klose, Nick Laird-Clowes, John Leckie, Michael Leonard, Jenny Lesmoir-Gordon, Nigel Lesmoir-Gordon, Adrian Maben, Phil Manzanera, Nick Mason, Jonathan Meades, Bhaskar Menon, Clive Metcalfe, Peter Mew, Anthony Moore, Iain 'Emo' Moore, Seamus O'Connell, Davy O'List, Alan Parker, Alan Parsons, Gala Pinion, Aubrey 'Po' Powell, Guy Pratt, Stephen Pyle, Andrew Rawlinson, Alun Renshaw, Tim Renwick, Andy Roberts, Mick Rock, Sheila Rock, Evelyn 'Iggy' Rose, Gerald Scarfe, Barbet Schroeder, Matthew Scurfield, Vic Singh, Norman Smith, Jenny Spires, Anthony Stern, Steve Stollman, Storm Thorgerson, Clare Torry, Pete Townshend, Roger Waters, John Watkins, Michael Watts, Clive Welham, Peter Whitehead, Rick Wills, John 'Willie' Wilson, Marc Wolff, Richard Wright, Peter Wynne-Willson, Emily Young and Gary Yudman.

Thanks to Johnny Black, Daryl Easlea, John Edginton, Jerry Ewing, Pat Gilbert, Sylvie Simmons, Phil Sutcliffe, and Peter Watts for kind permission to use additional interview material with Pink Floyd, Bob Ezrin, Roy Harper, Bob Geldof and others; to Jenny Spires and the Syd Barrett Estate for the 1965 letters; Chris Adamson quotes from Roadie Free Radio; additional Bob Geldof quotes from Denny Somach Productions; the late Philippe Constantin, Karl Dallas and Nick Sedgwick for 1974–1976 quotes, the archives of *Classic Rock*, *Disc and Music Echo*, the *Guardian*, *Melody Maker*, *Mojo*, *New Musical Express*, *Prog*, *Q*, *Record Collector*, *Rolling Stone*, *Sounds*, *Uncut*, *The Word*, *Zigzag*; Matt Johns at brain-damage.co.uk, and all at pinkfloydz.com and neptunepinkfloyd.co.uk

Special thanks to David Gilmour, Paul Loasby, Julian Stockton and Storm Studios.

# SELECTED BIBLIOGRAPHY


Appice, Carmine. *Stick It! – My Life of Sex, Drums and Rock 'N' Roll*, Chicago Press, 2016

Bannister, Freddy. *There Must Be a Better Way: The Story of the Bath and Knebworth Rock Festivals 1969–1979*, Bath Books, 1988

Beecher, Russell & Shutes, William. *Barrett: The Definitive Visual Companion to the Life of Syd Barrett*, Essential, 2011

Boyd, Joe. *White Bicycles: Making Music in the 1960s*, Serpent's Tail, 2005

Charlesworth, Chris. *Just Backdated: Melody Maker – Seven Years in the Seventies*, Spenwood Books, 2024

Clark, Ossie. *The Ossie Clark Diaries*, Bloomsbury, 1998

Dallas, Karl. *Pink Floyd: Bricks in the Wall*, Shapolsky, 1987

Furmanovsky, Jill. *The Moment: 25 Years of Rock Photography*, Paper Tiger, 1995

Geesin, Ron. *The Flaming Cow: The Making of Pink Floyd's Atom Heart Mother*, The History Press, 2021

Harris, John. *The Dark Side of the Moon: The Making of the Pink Floyd Masterpiece*, Fourth Estate, 2005

Manzanera, Phil. *Revolución to Roxy*, Wordzworth Publishing, 2024

Maclean, Ingrid. *Behind Open Doors: The Life & Times of Nigel Lesmoir-Gordon, the Acid Messiah of 1960s London*, lulu.com, 2018

Mason, Nick. *Inside Out: A Personal History of Pink Floyd*, Weidenfeld & Nicolson, 2004

Miles, Barry. *London Calling: A Countercultural History of London Since 1945*, Atlantic Books, 2010

Morrison, Bryan. *Have a Cigar! The Memoir of the Man Behind Pink Floyd, T. Rex, The Jam and George Michael*, Quiller Publishing, 2019

Palin, Michael. *Diaries 1969–1979: The Python Years*, Weidenfeld & Nicholson, 2010

Palacios, Julian. *Lost in the Woods: Syd Barrett and the Pink Floyd*, Boxtree, 1998

Broackes, Victoria & Landreth Strong, Anna. *Pink Floyd: Their Mortal Remains*, V&A Publishing, 2017

Povey, Glenn. *Echoes: The Complete History of Pink Floyd*, 3c Publishing, 2007

Powell, Aubrey. *Through the Prism: Untold Rock Stories from the Hipgnosis Archive*, Thames & Hudson, 2022

Scarfe, Gerald. *Long Drawn Out Trip: A Memoir*, Little, Brown, 2019

Sedgwick, Nick. *In the Pink (Not a Hunting Memoir)*, 2004

Thorgerson, Storm. *Mind Over Matter: The Images of Pink Floyd*, Sanctuary, 2000

Watts, Peter. *Up in Smoke: The Failed Dreams of Battersea Power Station*, Paradise Road, 2015

Willis, Tim. *Madcap: The Half-Life of Syd Barrett, Pink Floyd's Lost Genius*, Short Books, 2002

The team at New Modern would like to thank the following individuals:

**Nige Tassell** for copy-editing
**Chris Stone** for proofreading
**Marie Doherty** for typesetting
**Paul Palmer-Edwards** for cover design
**Aubrey 'Po' Powell** for cover image clearance
**Dusty Miller** for publicity
**Charlotte Rose, Andreina Brezzo and the team at Simon & Schuster UK** for sales and distribution